BLOOD IN THE ARGONNE

Campaigns and Commanders

BLOOD IN THE ARGONNE

THE "LOST BATTALION" OF WORLD WAR I

Alan D. Gaff

UNIVERSITY OF OKLAHOMA PRESS : NORMAN

Also by Alan D. Gaff

(ed.) *The Second Wisconsin Infantry* (Dayton, Ohio, 1984)
Brave Men's Tears (Dayton, Ohio, 1988)
If This Is War (Dayton, Ohio, 1991)
(ed., with Maureen Gaff) *Adventures on the Western Frontier*
    (Bloomington, Ind., 1994)
(with Maureen Gaff) *Our Boys: A Civil War Photograph Album*
    (Madison, Wisc., 1996)
On Many a Bloody Field (Bloomington, Ind., 1996)
*Bayonets in the Wilderness: Anthony Wayne's Legion in the Old
    Northwest* (Norman, Okla., 2004)

Blood in the Argonne: The "Lost Battalion" of World War I is Volume
8 in the Campaigns and Commanders series.

Library of Congress Cataloging-in-Publication Data

Gaff, Alan D.
    Blood in the Argonne : the "Lost Batallion" of World War I /
Alan D. Gaff.
        p.   cm. — (Campaigns and commanders ; v. 8)
    Includes bibliographical references and index.
    ISBN 0–8061–3696–0 (alk. paper)
        1. Argonne, Battle of the, France, 1918.   2. United States. Army.
Division, 77th—History.   3. World War, 1914–1918—Regimental
histories—United States.   I. Title.   II. Series.
D545.A63G34   2005
940.4'36—dc22

                                                            2005041791

1   2   3   4   5   6   7   8   9   10

To my buddy, Carl Chalk
An American Soldier

CONTENTS

ILLUSTRATIONS

Maps

PREFACE

All too often, military historians are more hero worshippers than objective chroniclers of events. Such was certainly the case with Thomas M. Johnson and Fletcher Pratt, whose book *The Lost Battalion* has remained the standard reference for that famous exploit since its publication in 1938. The authors unabashedly admit as much in the first sentence of their foreword, which reads, "The siege of the Lost Battalion endures after twenty years as the supreme American hero-story of the World War." These two men, one a former war correspondent and the other a popular military historian, teamed up to "get and tell the full truth." Despite research in American and German official archives and interviews with survivors, they failed to do so.

The best example of Johnson and Pratt turning a blind eye to the truth was in their handling of Lieutenant Maurice Revnes's suggestion that Major Charles W. Whittlesey surrender to the Germans. Although aware of the court-martial of Revnes, the authors barely mentioned his surrender note and subsequent trial, apparently because this aspect of the story did not fit in with their heroic notion of the American defense. The trial transcript contains many dozens of pages of sworn testimony taken just a few months after the Lost Battalion episode, yet Johnson and Pratt ignored this evidence in favor of recollections collected twenty years after the fact. Then the authors turned around and bemoaned inconsistencies in recollections of survivors. In spite of its many flaws, *The Lost Battalion* remains the only source for much information about the affair and has been cited frequently in this work, although the information has been used with extreme caution.

The *History of the 308th Infantry* contains the only published roster of Whittlesey's Lost Battalion, which the author admitted was only "fairly accurate." A new and expanded roster has been included in this work, every attempt having been made to fully identify casualties. This new roster includes soldiers who broke through the German lines on October 2, 1918, including many men from Company E who were left off the original roster, before being killed and captured during the attempted breakout on October 3. A good number of western replacements, who had been overlooked in the confusion of the Argonne fighting, have been added. Only the name of John Gehris has been removed from the original list because he was obviously not with the Lost Battalion.

The current author's intent has been to correct past mistakes, present an accurate account of the Lost Battalion story, including previous and subsequent material to provide context, and give readers an undistorted description of the American military experience in World War I, often in the words of those who lived through these events. This is not a story of generals and headquarters and strategy but of the line officers and enlisted men who did the actual fighting, implementing plans formulated by staff officers who never saw the front lines. Unsettling and gruesome at times, this narrative is about real soldiers, not the armies of politicians and poets and preachers who march into battle singing "Over There" or "The Battle Hymn of the Republic," but exhausted, dirty, often ill-trained troops who preferred bawdy lyrics that would make their mothers blush with shame. The end result, stripped of myth and legend, is not a pretty story, but an accurate portrayal of American combat on the Western Front.

I am indebted to a number of people for their assistance in the research for this book, foremost among them Jeff Krull, director of the Allen County Public Library, and especially Curt Witcher, manager of the Historical Genealogical Department in that institution. Curt's department has long been recognized for its collection of early American sources, but his expansion of the collection to include World War I material happily coincided with my research for this book. Laura Eme and her colleagues at INCOLSA supplied long-forgotten books and articles through interlibrary loan. Ellen Sieber, curator of collections, Mathers Museum of World Cultures; Mel E. Smith, History and Genealogy Unit, Connecticut State Library; Adina Anflick, associate achivist, American Jewish Historical Society; Susan Painter, librarian II, San Diego Library; Dr. John Minton, Indiana-Purdue University at Fort Wayne; and Kristen J. Nyitray, head of Special Collections and University Archives, Stony Brook University, provided important assistance. Mitch Yockelson, National Archives and Records Administration, and Lisa Budreau, doctoral candidate at Oxford University, helped to locate long-ignored records of the American Expeditionary Force. Cathy Arnoldy and my sons, Don and Jeff, read the original manuscript and offered valuable suggestions from the perspective of the casual reader. Don also drew the maps that accompany the text. My wife, Maureen, as always, has conducted research and provided advice and editorial advice at every step of the process. Only Maureen's modesty prevents listing her as co-author.

I have been privileged to receive support from a number of descendants of soldiers of the Seventy-seventh Division and the Lost Battalion. Tom Baldwin, son of Walter J. Baldwin, secretary of the Lost Battalion Association, generously shared correspondence and reunion newsletters from his father's collection. Others who have helped in a variety of ways include Orvin Peterson, Marvin Edwards, Boyd Leuenberger, Tom Bragg, Joe Pagliaro, Joanne and Victor Fritch, John Larney, Julie Girard, Tom Cepaglia, Larry Osborne, Richard Tuite, Bob Esch, Mary Lou Weber, and Mrs. Helga James. Thanks to them all.

CHRONOLOGY

The Seventy-seventh Division in World War I

1917

April 6	United States declares war on the Central Powers
June 5	National Draft Registration Day
June 24	Thompson-Starrett Company contracts for construction of Camp Upton
July 20	Selective Service determines order of precedent for the draft
August 5	War Department authorizes formation of the Seventy-seventh Division
September 1	Newly commissioned officers report at Camp Upton
September 10	First draft contingent arrives at Camp Upton
October 31	Division strength reaches 23,000
December 31	Following thousands of transfers, division strength again reaches 23,000

1918

February 4	308th Infantry parades through New York
February 22	Seventy-seventh Division parades through New York

March 27 to April 16	Infantry units, machine gun battalions, and support troops leave Camp Upton for Europe
April 22 to April 26	Artillery units, ammunition train, and supply train leave Camp Upton for Europe
April 15 to June 5	Division, minus its artillery, trains with British army in Picardy and Artois
May 7 to July 8	Division artillery trains at Camp de Souge
June 21 to August 4	Division occupies the Baccarat sector
July 18	Detached artillery units rejoin the division
August 12 to September 3	Division occupies the Vesle sector
September 4 to September 16	Division participates in the Oise-Aisne campaign
September 26	Division begins Meuse-Argonne campaign
October 2	Major Whittlesey breaks through the German defensive line and his command is isolated from the remainder of the division
October 3 to October 7	Lost Battalion period
October 14 to October 16	Division captures St. Juvin and Grand Pré
October 17 to October 30	Division assigned to corps reserve
October 31 to November 11	Division concludes Meuse-Argonne campaign
November 11	Armistice

1919

April 17	Main units of the division embark for United States
May 6	Last of the division reaches New York City
May 9	Division begins demobilization

BLOOD IN THE ARGONNE

INTRODUCTION

The celebrated Lost Battalion episode was World War 1's most compelling human interest story. It had all the elements of an old-time heroic saga, a thrilling tale of American sacrifice far beyond the traditional call of duty. On October 2, 1918, Major Charles W. Whittlesey led an attack in the Argonne Forest that penetrated German defensive lines and reached his assigned objective, but other units of the Seventy-seventh Division could not keep pace. Enemy forces quickly surrounded Whittlesey, who found himself cut off with a command composed of companies from two battalions of the 308th Infantry, a few dozen runners and scouts from three other companies of that regiment, and a couple depleted platoons from the 306th Machine Gun Battalion. Just prior to the German encirclement on the morning of October 3, a single company from the 307th Infantry managed to link up with Whittlesey, who thus found himself in command of a hybrid group of less than seven hundred soldiers, some of whom had been wounded during the advance. He positioned his men on a steep, heavily wooded slope in the Charlevaux Valley, sheltered from German artillery fire but exposed to enemy machine guns, riflemen, and trench mortars. Trapped about a kilometer in advance of the Seventy-seventh Division's lines, the Americans dug in and waited.

Despite a series of ill-fated attempts, doughboys from the Seventy-seventh Division could not break through the German cordon and reach Whittlesey's isolated command until the evening of October 7. Those trapped in this small pocket behind enemy lines endured five days of sheer hell. Every movement during daylight hours generated a storm of machine-gun and rifle fire that kept the Americans hunkered in their holes. Trench mortars and grenades pounded Whittlesey's position unmercifully. Rations ran out on the second day and men went over four days with nothing to eat except berries, bark, and leaves. Water could be procured only from a small spring and a creek, both of which were closely watched by sharp-eyed German machine gunners. Medical supplies quickly became exhausted and three overworked first-aid men could do little more than remove bandages from the dead and apply them to those just wounded. Allied artillery attempted to protect these besieged doughboys, but their shells often fell on Whittlesey's position, especially during a botched American barrage on October 4 that killed and wounded dozens of soldiers. French and United States aircraft attempted to locate the American position, but failed to do so in the virtually impenetrable forest. Feeble attempts to resupply Whittlesey with food, medicine, and ammunition from the air failed. The German ring of fire remained unbroken.

Successful attacks on another part of the American front finally forced a German withdrawal that allowed advance elements of the Seventy-seventh Division to reunite with Whittlesey's command on the evening of October 7. In reality, Major Whittlesey's isolated force was neither lost nor a battalion, but descriptions such as "beleaguered battalion," "surrounded battalion," and "encircled battalion" had failed to capture the imagination. When one editor first used the catchphrase "lost battalion," that name stuck like glue and, although totally inaccurate, it remains such in American history to this day. General John J. Pershing selected the Lost Battalion of the Seventy-seventh Division as one of three examples that best illustrated "the spirit of the rank and file of our great army" in World War I, but Major Charles Whittlesey's soldiers, typical of most combat veterans, were more restrained in portraying their part in the epic saga.

On December 2, 1918, Private Joseph Henry McElroy (army serial number 3134446) wrote a chatty letter to his wife's parents, Charles and Nellie Biddings of Corvallis, Oregon. Although a patient in the

American Base Hospital at Baune, France, Joe assured his in-laws that he was "still very much alive and feeling fine and dandy." He then admitted, "I don't know just when I will start for home but I do hope it won't be long." For the present, despite being confined in a thirty-thousand-bed hospital, he was feeling sort of lonely, not having received a letter from home since September 15 and having been away from his comrades in Company I, 308th Infantry, since October 8. There was little to do to pass the time and he spent each day in the same routine, "laying around doing nothing only we go for an hrs. walk every morning for exercise."

Joseph McElroy had been born on Christmas Day, 1892, in Chicago, Illinois, to John and Sarah McElroy, natives of Ireland and Scotland, respectively. Sometime after the turn of the century, the McElroy clan packed up and moved from Chicago to Portland, where Joe worked as a stirrup-maker for the firm of Leisure and Van Bebber when the United States declared war on Germany in 1917. Presenting himself for draft registration on June 5 of that year, Joe described himself as Caucasian, single, 5' 8" in height, medium build, dark blue eyes, brown hair, and free of physical defects. Subsequent to his enrollment, Joe married Violet Biddings, but he does not appear to have claimed an exemption from service based on his newly acquired family.

Joe ended up in the Fortieth (Sunshine) Division, then shipped out to France, and was assigned to the 308th Infantry as a replacement just prior to the Argonne Campaign. He told his in-laws, "I was with the first Bunch that started threw the Argonne forest. I guess you read all about it in the paper at home. That had been a quiet sector for about 3 $^1/_2$ yrs. well we sure made a noisy one out of it." Joe then explained, "I now know what it is like to advance threw shot and Shell and threw machine Gun fire." He then told the Biddingses that he had been a member of the famous Lost Battalion, one of only two men from Company I with that command: "I was in with that Battalion of men which got hemmed in for six days without food. She was a rather tough place to be. we were certainly surrounded with Germans and cut off from our back forces. for six days I didn't have a bite to eat and things were looking pretty blue to us when on the morning of Oct. 8th the Boys that had been fighting hard for four days finally got threw to us. well that sure saved us." Joe concluded his brief account of the Lost Battalion with the honest observation, "well I am very thankful that I got out of it and without a scratch. I sure was lucky." After being rescued, McElroy, like many of the survivors, was hospitalized for exhaustion and debility.

In his letter, Joe advised them, "I sure had some experience. some I will never forget. I will tell you all about it better when I see you all." In a subsequent letter, written on March 20, 1919, Joe told the folks, "I will not write much as I will soon be with you all and then I can tell you a whole lot." Joseph McElroy, like so many other World War soldiers, probably never kept that promise. By the time these Argonne veterans returned home, they had silently resolved to shield the American public from the reality of combat conditions in France. Aside from some cursory narratives and a few humorous anecdotes, most men kept their experiences tucked away and shared only enough details with family and friends to satisfy their curiosity. No one would understand anyway. How could a doughboy explain the sheer terror of leaving the relative safety of an earthen trench to advance into a fog-shrouded landscape where concealed German machine gunners waited silently in ambush? How could he recount a high explosive shell vaporizing a buddy into a pink cloud of shredded tissue and bits of uniform right before his eyes? Is it really possible to capture in words the quiet desperation as starving men kept to their posts long after all hope of relief had faded? Certainly not. Even if they had been of a mind to relate their combat experience, the natural process of repressing their terrifying memories had already commenced.

Civilians knew little of what really went on in the United States Army, which was exclusively a man's world, chock full of racism, crude conduct, and profane language. Of course, armies had always been that way, but in previous wars that coarse behavior had been obscured by a public piety more in tune with civilian expectations. Afraid that their sons might be seduced by sinners, Americans wanted them to act as choirboys instead of debased savages. But chivalry no longer had a place in modern warfare and the army was certainly no church meeting. Millions of young men, from the incredibly naïve to the most hardened criminal, found themselves conscripted and swept off to an army camp where back-home morality no longer mattered. They did everything that boys do when first liberated from the folks at home—they smoked and drank and swore and got tattoos and sought out women of ill-repute and then attempted to outdo their mates in all of those endeavors. It was a swaggering, posturing life, almost a religion of virility, where civilians masqueraded as soldiers or, at least, what they thought soldiers should be like. The unique aspect of doughboy life was a willingness to write in their own vernacular to an extent never seen in previous wars.

This narrative contains language that some readers might consider offensive, yet cursing was an essential part of doughboy life. Here are the songs they marched to, the vaudeville routines that made them roar with laughter, and their complaints aimed at the vast army bureaucracy. They were stress relievers as important to American victory as the Springfield rifle, hob-nailed hiking boots, canned "monkey meat," and cigarettes. (The author can testify from personal experience that the same ribald lyrics of "Bang, Bang, Lulu" sung by American soldiers in 1917 were still in vogue fifty years later during the Vietnam era.) Yet popular historians have almost universally ignored this profane aspect of military life in World War I, in essence cleansing the story for their readers and blotting out the very humanity of the soldiers. Paul Fussell, in *The Great War and Modern Memory*, has pointed out that British soldiers, looked upon by Americans as genteel and cultivated, spouted such "unremitting profanity and obscenity" as to attempt "to achieve literary effects." Speaking of their American counterparts, J. Glenn Gray, in *The Warriors: Reflections on Men in Battle*, explained, "The most common word in the mouths of American soldiers has been a vulgar expression for sexual intercourse. This word does duty as adjective, adverb, verb, noun and in any other form it can possibly be used, however inappropriate or ridiculous in application." When coarse and hard-boiled Regular Army noncommissioned officers began to put new recruits through their military training, they did not do so by saying "please" and "thank you," but employed a blistering torrent of monosyllabic synonyms for male and female body parts and functions. The language may have offended civilians, but it served its purpose.

Political correctness has been imposed on those who would have scoffed at the very concept. In addition to being profane, early twentieth-century American society was decidedly xenophobic. Minorities were contemptuously called Chinks, Pollacks, Spicks, Ivans, or Jews, often accompanied by the most loathsome modifiers. These were the racial slurs of peace. Thrust into that melting pot of the training camp, even the most racist simpleton realized that his life depended on the man next to him, no matter what his ethnic background. When bullets started flying and shells began to burst, national heritage and religious affiliation had no meaning. All that counted was a man's ability to do his job. In this respect, the army was the first equal opportunity employer. Of course, soldiers continued to use old epithets, but they now served merely as nicknames without the former derisive intent. Even a college graduate like Major Charles Whittlesey would casually refer to being relieved in the Vesle Sector by a couple of "Wop" battalions and would introduce Irving Liner, one of his headquarters staff, as a "New York Jew." To the soldiers, it was no different from calling Ohio natives Buckeyes or referring to New Jersey residents as Clam Catchers.

Troops from the Seventy-seventh Division would not, at first glance, have seemed destined for immortality. Composed initially of drafted men from the New York City metropolitan area, they came from every imaginable walk of life. New York businessmen left their law offices and stock brokerages, their yacht and tennis clubs, to accept commissions and began new careers commanding Polish street sweepers, Chinese laundrymen, Jewish garment workers, and Dutch and Irish cops. There was no more cosmopolitan division in the entire United States Army, one inquiry discovering more than three dozen nationalities in the ranks. Fully one-fourth of these draftees could not speak English. Turning such a motley mob of civilians into soldiers would take time and a great deal of labor.

The polyglot Seventy-seventh Division received intensive training at Camp Upton, a ten-thousand-acre army camp hacked out of the wilderness on Long Island. Despite a demonstrated proficiency during this training phase, doubts lingered within the army bureaucracy, as well as in the Allied high command, about how well a division of drafted men would perform in combat. These Gotham residents, augmented by later arrivals of conscripts from upstate New York and New England, would be the first division of draftees to reach France and the first sent to the front lines. After a few months of becoming acclimated in a quiet sector, the Seventy-seventh Division joined the war in earnest along the Vesle River, then, strengthened by replacements from the Fortieth Division, plunged into that hell-on-earth known as the Argonne Forest, where it proved equal to troops from the Regular Army and National Guard. But of all the laudable accomplishments of the Seventy-seventh Division, the story of Major Charles Whittlesey and his men of the Lost Battalion stands out as a tale of courage and endurance without parallel in American military history.

1

THE DRAFT

"Two hundred fifty-eight!" Camera shutters clicked, reporters scribbled furiously, and telegraphers deftly tapped out that momentous number, instantly speeding it over crackling wires to every corner of the United States on July 20, 1917. Amid a pressing throng of newsmen, impeccably dressed Secretary of War Newton Baker proudly posed with the slip of paper containing the first number drawn in accordance with the Selective Service Act, thereby setting in motion events that would culminate in one of America's most inspiring war stories. Secretary Baker and his retinue of high-ranking officers disappeared soon after, but subordinates continued the boring task of pulling encapsulated numbers from a huge glass bowl late into the night. This random selection process had far-reaching implications for the 9,500,000 American men, aged twenty-one to thirty, who had registered the preceding month. Within a few weeks, 4,557 local draft boards across the country began sending out "Order of Induction into Military Service of the United States" notices to men whose numbers had appeared high on the list. America would never again be the same.[1]

Although most Americans had descended from European stock, their government had remained aloof from the war that raged on that continent from 1914 to 1917, President Woodrow Wilson insisting that his administration adhere to strict neutrality in both spirit and deed.

Public opinion, however, generally supported the cause of Britain, France, and their allies, although a sizeable minority of United States citizens championed Germany and the other Central Powers. As the war dragged on, Wilson's administration deliberately began to shift its support to the Allies, who provided huge markets for American produce and manufactured goods. When Germany intensified its submarine blockade of Allied ports, Americans were outraged by deaths of fellow citizens aboard torpedoed ships. Although the German government made half-hearted attempts to appease the United States, its announcement of unrestricted submarine warfare in February of 1917 forced President Wilson to sever diplomatic ties. British intelligence agents then intercepted and decoded a message from the German foreign minister in which he broached the possibility of Mexico joining the Central Powers in a war against the United States. The resulting public outcry, combined with the sinking of American vessels by German submarines, resulted in Wilson signing a declaration of war against the Central Powers on April 6, 1917.[2]

After the United States declared war, President Wilson and his administration became embarrassed by the mere trickle of volunteers who stepped forward to fill the ranks of the Regular Army and the National Guard regiments that would be sent to fight overseas. Wilson appointed General John J. Pershing to command the American army and he requested that the president begin immediate preparations to send one million soldiers to Europe. The only way to assemble such a huge army in a timely fashion was to resort to conscription. To avoid a repetition of devastating draft riots that had occurred during the Civil War, Secretary Baker established a system whereby men would be drafted, not by the military but by *civilian* boards. Baker's plan would avoid the appearance of military compulsion by having draftees report to friends and neighbors in their local districts. This illusion was maintained in each "Order of Induction," which, following a cordial greeting from President Wilson, read: "Having submitted yourself to a local board composed of your neighbors for the purpose of determining the place and time in which you can best serve the United States in the present emergency, you are hereby notified that you have now been selected for immediate military service." What could be more democratic and honorable than being chosen to represent your neighborhood in the United States Army! Of course, submission to a local board of neighbors was not exactly voluntary, since there was a one-year prison term awaiting anyone who failed to register. President Wilson kept up the facade of volunteerism with a bit of convoluted logic, claiming that the Selective Service Act was "in no sense a conscription of the unwilling," but rather a "selection from a nation which has volunteered in mass."[3]

Conscripted men were not inducted as reinforcements into existing military units, but would be assigned to what was styled the "National Army," an organization composed entirely of newly created regiments and divisions.

The Kid has gone to the Colors
And we don't know what to say;
The Kid we have loved and cuddled
Stepped out for the Flag to-day.
We thought him a child, a baby
With never a care at all,
But his country called him man-size
And the Kid has heard the call.[4]

Draftees would be assembled and trained at one of sixteen cantonments scattered across the country. The cantonment for the New York City metropolitan area was a ten-thousand-acre tract of sand, scrub oak, and windblown pines in Suffolk County. New Yorkers considered it "one of the most desolate portions of Long Island," the closest settlement being a village with the goofy-sounding name of Yaphank, a nondescript stop on the Long Island Railroad. Named Camp Upton in honor of Emory Upton, a Civil War general and author of *The Military Policy of the United States*, this cantonment lay some sixty miles from New York City and about midway between Long Island Sound and the Atlantic shore.[5]

The Quartermaster Department awarded Camp Upton's construction contract to the Thompson-Starrett Company, which agreed to build thirty miles of roads, over fourteen hundred buildings, a complete water and sewer system, and electric lighting throughout. Thompson-Starrett's stupendous undertaking got off to a rocky start. When the first workers arrived on June 24, many of them promptly turned around and went home. Old tents provided the only shelter from billions of flies and mosquitoes that swarmed about the men and work animals, making any semblance of sustained labor virtually impossible. Workmen who tried to protect themselves with gloves and netting quickly found that clouds of bugs would either bite through the fabric or crawl into the smallest of gaps in search of exposed human flesh. Thompson-Starrett advertised for new employees, offering what were then considered "phenomenal" wages—$3.75 per day for common laborers and $5.00 a day for skilled craftsmen. The work force at Camp Upton swelled first to five thousand, then peaked at ten thousand men by the end of August as workers built barracks capable of holding forty thousand soldiers, making it second only to Brooklyn as the largest city on Long Island.[6]

Axe men began the project by cutting down timber and underbrush, leaving thousands of ragged stumps dotting the landscape. Surveyors and engineers drove stakes to indicate roads and structures. Railroad workers built a series of spur lines from Yaphank, so that construction materials could be shipped directly by rail to Camp Upton. Trucks, supplemented by tractors and mule-drawn wagons, hauled supplies in every direction. Barracks were built in sections, then hoisted into place and nailed together. While the roofers were still nailing on shingles, electricians and plumbers began work on the interior. An entire building, complete with electric lights and running water, could be completed in a few hours. Resemblance to boom towns of the Old West was striking. Everything was hurry, hurry, hurry, for the contract stipulated that the camp should be ready for occupancy in early September. This fevered pace often led to serious accidents. There were also numerous incidents of fraud. The most flagrant involved a supervisor named George Trowger, who approved pay cards for six men who never worked at the site. An investigation revealed that Trowger was actually a Post Office letter carrier, with twenty-nine years of service, then on sick leave from his regular route.[7]

The War Department decided that National Army troops assigned to Camp Upton should be designated the Seventy-seventh Division, whose commander would be Major General James Franklin Bell. A Kentucky native and graduate of West Point, Bell had served on the frontier in the old Seventh Cavalry and was present at the Battle of Wounded Knee, South Dakota, in 1890. While leading the Thirty-sixth United States Volunteers in the Philippines, Colonel Bell won a Medal of Honor for gallantry against a band of insurgents on September 9, 1899. Now at the age of sixty-one and after more than forty years' service, he was a major general in the Regular Army and commander of Camp Upton. His units included:

Infantry – 153rd Brigade – 305th and 306th Regiments
          154th Brigade – 307th and 308th Regiments
Field Artillery – 152nd Brigade – 304th, 305th, 306th
   Regiments
Machine Gun Battalions – 304th, 305th, 306th
Engineers – 302nd Regiment
Trench Mortar – 302nd Battery
Signal Corps – 302nd Field Battalion
Sanitary Train – 302nd
Ammunition Train – 302nd
Military Police Company – 302nd

Other units stationed at Camp Upton, but not a part of the Seventy-seventh Division, were the 152nd Depot Brigade and two "Colored" organizations, the 367th Infantry Regiment and 351st Machine Gun Battalion.[8]

The first officers assigned to the Seventy-seventh Division, all graduates of the Plattsburg Military Camp, arrived on September 1 and were dismayed by conditions at Camp Upton. One of them recalled: "It wore an air of having just been begun and of never wishing to be finished. A few white pine barracks stretched gaunt frames from the mud against a mournful sky. Towards the railroad two huge tents had an appearance of captive balloons, half-inflated. For the rest there were heaps of lumber of odd shapes and sizes, and countless acres of mud, blackened by recent fires—half-cleared land across which was scattered a multitude of grotesque and tattered figures." A second officer described wandering about amid "a myriad of sweating workmen, teams, wagons, motor trucks, jitneys, lumber piles, stables, shanties; over fresh-broken roads, felled trees, stumps, brush and sticky mud." A third remarked that "the civilian workmen swarmed like so many ants, and often with as little apparent aim." Accommodations were rudimentary and many officers purchased iron cots from laborers eager to sell stolen equipment. Messes were formed and gentlemen who had previously hosted formal dinner parties now found themselves cooking their own meals. This situation was intolerable to genteel folks, so officers pooled their resources and hired chefs from New York City hotels.[9]

The first noncoms reached Camp Upton in early September and, Good God!, what a bunch of misfits and outcasts they were! Officers in Regular Army regiments had been ordered to send their best noncoms to train draftees at Camp Upton. While a few did send good soldiers, many commanders saw this as an opportunity to banish deadbeats and malingerers from their own ranks. Service records of these newly arrived sergeants and corporals told of innumerable courts-martial and summary punishments and hinted at countless scrapes with civilian authorities. A close examination of promotion dates disclosed that many of these noncoms had, in the strangest of coincidences, been given their chevrons only days, sometimes just hours, before being transferred to the Seventy-seventh Division. In carefully chosen words dripping with sarcasm, an officer in the 305th Field Artillery noted that "few commanding officers had parted with their jewels."[10]

With two thousand drafted men scheduled to arrive on September 10, impatient young officers were "as excited as a young girl preparing for her debut." These conscripts had been ordered to report at their local boards by 8 A.M., dressed in old clothing and carrying a minimum of baggage. There they were given identification cards and placed under the temporary command of a "district leader," who carried the all-important paperwork for his detachment. After receiving some trinkets, listening to important, yet soon-forgotten speeches, and enjoying some rousing band music, men marched to the trains that would carry them to Camp Upton. Along the way, they vigorously waved signs, boldly painted messages that proudly proclaimed "From Harlem to France," "Harlem's Hun Hunters," "Kaiser Kanners," "To Hell with the Kaiser, "We'll Kick the Kaiser's Ass," and other slightly more vulgar slogans.[11]

A Toast to the Kaiser
Now, here's to the Kaiser, the Limburger cheese—
May the swell in his head go 'way down to his knees—
May he break his neck over the Hindenberg line
And go to Hell croaking "The Watch on the Rhine."[12]

Crowds at the train stations were immense, family members and friends jostling one another as they attempted to say good-by. Mothers, sisters, wives, and girlfriends brushed away tears, hugging and kissing embarrassed young men one last time. Fathers and older brothers tried to appear calm and dignified as they stoically shook hands. Younger brothers wanted to go along and pretended that they, too, were soldiers in the Great Adventure. Finally the trains bound for Yaphank pulled away and those thousands of waving handkerchiefs faded into the distance. Draftees quickly divided into two groups. One

Brooklyn draftees en route to Camp Upton. From Moore's *U.S. Official Pictures of the World War.*

bunch hung out the windows or clung precariously to platforms, waving flags and yelling at bystanders. Civilians along the route waved back and cheered lustily for the boys. As the trains left Brooklyn and chugged into Long Island farmland, even the cows stopped grazing, looked up, and seemed to smile approvingly. Unfazed by those rowdies at the windows, another gang lit up cigarettes, cigars, and pipes, filling the cars with thick, pungent smoke that hung like a cloud over intense games of poker, pinochle, euchre, and whist. Total strangers were soon chatting like old chums, introductions often taking place over a proffered flask of whiskey. One conscript recalled, "Our feelings ranged from drunken hilarity to sober, quiet pondering." There were thousands of questions asked and answered on that glorious train ride—"Where's the conductor?" "What's your name?" "What's trump?" "What business are you in?" "Where do we take a piss?" "You married?" "Did she kiss you?" and on and on and on.[13]

Young officers, dashing in crisp uniforms with shiny gold and silver bars on their collars, were appalled by the sight that greeted them on these first trains. The draft had acted like a giant vacuum cleaner, sucking up men from every walk of life, and one commander was dismayed to discover that his draftees included "the gunman and the gangster, the student and the clerk, the laborer and the loafer, the daily plodder, the lawyer." Some conscripts could not wait to brownnose and vigorously shook hands with the lieutenants and captains, telling them how dapper they looked and how wonderful it was to meet them. Others adopted a wise-ass attitude, pretending the officers were actually conductors and loudly refusing to pay their fares. Two recruits, John Barleycorn and Al K. Hall, could be found on every train. Chaplain James Howard watched one batch of new arrivals: "Fifth Avenue and the lower East Side, men who had lived on inherited incomes and men who toiled as day laborers, university graduates and illiterates, those whose ancestors had fought under Washington and those whose parents were still living in Italy and Russia walked side by side in a column of twos through the dust and confusion of the camp."[14]

"Hay, Tony! Finish off that bottle before these officer guys can grab it." "Grabba da hell. My gal, she givva me a charm against da evil eye of officers."[15]

Upon reaching Camp Upton, draftees were assigned to temporary quarters, or casual barracks, as they were called. What a sight these rookie soldiers presented! There were men wearing Panamas, smashed derbies, and top hats that looked as if they had been stolen from corpses. Despite an admonition to come attired in old clothes, some arrived dressed in dinner jackets, Palm Beach suits, starched collars, silk stockings, and Sunday-go-to-meeting outfits. Vito Catarino, a Harlem barber, came directly from an all-night wedding reception, garishly attired in a red silk shirt, pink bow tie, borrowed patent leather shoes, and a "stunning green Alpine hat." Some draftees proudly sported remnants of uniforms from bygone days in the National Guard

An early Camp Upton street scene. From Moore's *U.S. Official Pictures of the World War.*

or at military school. One former Marine wore his old dress uniform, complete with an Expert Rifleman Medal on his chest. Everyone carried valises, grips, suitcases, or hastily folded bundles of necessaries, but some of the more naïve appeared destined for some sort of elegant spa. These rubes could be identified by their umbrellas, tennis rackets, bathrobes, pajamas, and bathing suits. Crusty old sergeants could only look at such sights and shake their heads. No amount of swearing could do justice to that human crazy quilt.[16]

Lists of draftees forwarded by the local boards never, ever matched up with the squads of men who actually reached camp. Roll calls commenced in a vain effort to sort out the discrepancies, but there were just too many men who could not speak English. One Long Island boy complained that the foreign accents and strange languages sounded like a modern-day Tower of Babel. A man named Valli, son of Italian immigrants, knew only three words of English—two were "Merry Christmas" and the other was "fuck." Those first roll calls were simply amazing. One officer called out, "Morra, T." "Here." "Morra, R." "Here," from the same individual. "Does your first name begin with a T or an R?" "Yes, sir." "Is your first name Rocco?" "Yes, sir." "What is your first name?" "Tony." At another roll call, the following colloquy occurred: "Tomaso." "Here." "Tortoni." "Here," from the same individual. "Who are you, Tomaso or Tortoni?" "No spigh Ingleesh." By one count, men from forty-three different nationalities would serve in the ranks of the Seventy-seventh Division.[17]

No linguist could correctly pronounce a roster filled with names of men from Transylvania and Morrocco, Venezuela and Bulgaria, Sweden and Mexico, Lithuania and Greece, and dozens of other countries. One officer was heard to call out, "Krag–a–co–poul–o–wicz, G." When no one answered, he tried again. This time there was a muttered response from the ranks, "Do yuh mean me? That ain't the way tuh say my name. Me own mother wouldn't recernize it." "Quiet. Say 'here.'" A bolder retort burst from the ranks: "Then I ain't here. That's all. I ain't here." Appreciative snickers greeted this insubordination, but the officer simply gritted his teeth and went on to mangle yet another name. In one company, a draftee had mysteriously answered "Here" at every roll call for the entire first week before officials belatedly discovered that he had never even reached camp. For several days, officers were confounded by another conscript, whose language no one in camp could understand. This puzzle was solved only when his English-speaking brother arrived in a later detachment and could act as translator.[18]

According to the odd segregationist logic of that period, black men were assigned to what were styled "Colored Regiments," a discriminatory system first instituted during the Civil War. Men from every other race, however, were treated as equals to Caucasians under the draft laws. One prominent draftee from the mysterious Orient was Robert Yap, the only native from the Hawaiian Islands at Camp Upton. Twenty-seven-year-old Yap, son of a Congregational minister of Chinese descent, taught his bunkmates to play the ukulele and regaled them with stories of how he had played on the first Hawaiian baseball team to tour America. On the other hand, there were hundreds of Chinese in the ranks of the Seventy-seventh Division. Chin Wah had owned the Oriental Hand Laundry on East 155th Street until he received his draft notice. Wah sold his business for $300 and set out for Camp Upton. Sing Ing, Wah's pal, wanted to go along. Ing's draft number was too high, so he traded places with a neighbor who had been drafted and went off to join Chin Wah, who greeted him with the comment, "Me likee almee vely much. Evly lettle ting vely fine."

These inseparable Chinese friends had but one question, "Say, when we go this here damma Germainee?" No doubt the oddest character in Camp Upton was a short, bushy-haired Igorot, a native of the Island of Luzon in the Philippines. Prior to joining the army, he had been billed as "Amok, the Headhunter" in Colonel Jim Edwards's Coney Island sideshow, where his job consisted of hanging from a pole and shrieking "synthetically bloodthirsty cries" at gullible sightseers. Now J. R. Amok confessed to a newspaperman that he had never really hunted heads, but claimed that his brother was serving time in prison for doing so.[19]

The first stop for all new arrivals was the bath-house. Some objected, but the gruffly shouted response was always the same, "I don't care what you did last year. You're in the army now!"

> *Oh, the army, the army, the democratic army,*
> *They clothe you and they feed you*
> *Because the army needs you. Hash for breakfast,*
> *Beans for dinner, stew for supper-time.*
> *Thirty dollars every month, deducting twenty-nine.*
> *Oh, the army, the army, the democratic army,*
> *All the Jews and Wops, the Dutch and Irish cops,*
> *They're all in the army now.*[20]

Rookies quickly discovered there were no baths to be found in the bathhouse, just cold-water showers. After a thorough scrubbing, draftees were herded into their new barracks, where they received mess gear and bedding (straw mattress pad, three blankets, but no pillow), and then got bunk assignments. After marching to the mess hall, newcomers became introduced to the hurry-up-and-wait routine, standing in long lines like human derelicts destined to spend their days waiting in breadlines for a free handout. Food was surprisingly good, although not quite so delicious as Mom and Grandma used to cook. This high quality was due to cooks from the Hotel Men's Association, who had volunteered to feed the Seventy-seventh Division while its commissary department was being assembled.[21]

After draftees returned to their barracks, officers interviewed them individually, asking about next of kin, previous occupations that might correspond to army jobs, and any preference for branch of military service. One ambitious man replied to the latter question, "I wanta be a Lootenant!" A second draftee, a bit more apathetic, responded matter-of-factly, "Oh, Hell! I don't care, just so I lick the Choimans." Following these interviews, men stood around large bonfires built from scrap lumber, trading observations with total strangers and filling the

Waiting to be mustered in at Camp Upton. From the author's collection.

air with songs and other "nasal agonies" until sergeants sent them scrambling indoors with the shouted warning, "Lights Out!" Men obediently went inside, but the novelty of their situation kept sleep at bay. One draftee was appalled to find himself "in the midst of an awful crowd who continually cursed and urinated out the windows of the barracks." Each darkened building soon witnessed a cacophony of belches, animal sounds, real and mock farts, conversation, shouts, and just plain odd noises. Practical jokers pounced upon those who nodded off early and either folded them inside collapsible cots or encased them in their mattress and threw the entire bundle down flights of stairs at breakneck speed. But gradually, even the most rowdy dozed off to sleep.[22]

Sergeants and corporals, swaggering through the barracks and shouting at the top of their lungs, jolted sleeping men awake in the morning. Every man made up his own bed (a novelty since that had always been considered woman's work), downed a hurried breakfast, then marched to the hospital, the first stop of a process that saw draftees shoved "like meat through a sausage mill." More than two dozen doctors poked and prodded and questioned each man. They were told to read the top and bottom lines on an eye chart, one veteran recalling, "whether you did it correctly or not you were told your eyes were alright, or twenty-twenty and you were shoved ahead for the ear test." After that exam, they were told to strip and doctors carefully inspected each individual's heart, lungs, feet, throat, and teeth. Those hoping for medical discharges helpfully pointed out defects to the doctors, recounting real or imagined ailments in great detail. Except for about three percent who were obviously too seriously deformed for military service, the response to these complaints was always the same, "You'll do."[23]

Soon after these exams, men were introduced to "The Needle." Word spread rapidly that everyone would be inoculated against smallpox, diphtheria, typhoid, and paratyphoid. Some men fainted before the needles even touched their arms, while others pretended to be weak in the knees in hopes of avoiding the trauma, but no excuses were accepted. A nervous rookie exclaimed that "it felt more like someone carving a piece of flesh from the arm than the jab of a needle!" Someone else whined that the medical personnel were nothing more than butchers and claimed that, in his case, "The Needle" was plunged at least three inches into his tender flesh. Sore-armed and ill-tempered men concluded the day by having their fingerprints taken, rumors circulating that officers would hereafter treat them all like criminals. They swaggered back to barracks, cocky and proud of having survived their contest with "The Needle." But Regular Army noncoms deflated their pride with the comments, "Wait till you get your second shot!" "And third!" Next morning, men's arms "assumed gigantic proport-ions," accompanied by headaches and nausea. Officers showed no pity, passing out axes and rakes and sending the boys out to clear brush from the parade grounds. It was little wonder that one American of Italian descent simply announced, "Boss, me no lika dis job. Give me my money. I'm goin' home."[24]

Commanders of the temporary companies took their men on short hikes to begin the process of physical training, but on these first excur-sions many simply ambled along while smoking and talking among themselves. Within days that relaxed attitude had changed dramatically and officers marched their troops about camp at the cadence of 120 steps per minute, heads held straight and arms swinging in unison at their sides. Simple gymnastic calisthenics, called "setting up exercises," were instituted on the West Point system. Classes began in boxing and jiu-jitsu, the latter being described by a participant as "peculiar methods

Poking fun at "The Needle" and the vaccination process. From *Trench and Camp.*

of choking and resuscitation." Amateur athletics were encouraged and eventually leagues were formed for football, basketball, baseball, handball, volleyball, cross-country running, wrestling, and boxing. Famous American sportsmen, now serving as officers in the Seventy-seventh Division, took charge of the athletic programs. Among them were Edward "Eddie" Grant, a retired utility infielder for the New York Giants baseball squad; All-American Douglas Bomeisler, an end on Yale's 1912 football team; Clarence Griffin, who had represented the United States in Davis Cup tennis matches; and Crawford Blagden, formerly coach of the Harvard football team. Tom Owens had played baseball for a time with Babe Ruth, now a popular pitching sensation for the Boston

Red Sox. These leaders had learned the importance of teamwork in competition and now began teaching military teamwork to thousands of eager, if somewhat less physically gifted, conscripts.[25]

After a few days in the temporary barracks, recruits were assigned to companies and moved to regular quarters, making room for the next bunch of draftees. Barracks were two stories high, the upper floor being used for sleeping quarters. The first floor contained a mess hall, kitchen, and storeroom, along with orderly and supply rooms. Fresh air came through dozens of double-hung windows kept open at all hours, the evening chill being fended off by large stoves that burned twenty-four hours a day. Behind each barracks was a latrine that contained modern toilets, a washroom with a series of faucets, and a shower room with eight large nozzles. Chaplain James Howard explained the transformation that ensued: "Men who had been in the habit of never changing their clothes from one end of winter to the other found themselves compelled, by good husky sergeants, to bathe regularly and change their clothes frequently, and to keep themselves clean-shaven and neat in appearance."[26]

U. S. Government sign posted in Camp Upton: "Please Do Not Shit In Fence Corners."[27]

According to a War Department directive, officers could no longer use terms like "drafted men" or "draftees" or "conscripts" when referring to men at Camp Upton. Henceforth the soldiers would be called "recruits" or "enlisted men." This important change was highlighted by the swapping of civilian clothes for army uniforms. Supply sergeants, many of them pants cutters, merchants, or dry goods clerks just a few weeks earlier, found themselves in the impossible situation of handing out "made-by-the-million" uniforms to men who did not even know what size clothing they wore. When someone with a size 32 chest complained that his olive drab blouse was a 36, the reply would be, "You're in luck. That's a wonderful fit." When a hat dropped over a man's ears, the supplier would remark, "That hat isn't too big for you. Gives your hair a chance to grow." Long, lean uniforms were handed out to short, fat men and vice versa, so that each company looked like some sort of bizarre masquerade party. One soldier remembered that the new clothes "were all tight where they should have been loose, loose where they should have been tight, and too long or too short." Recruits had the appearance of "mis-pulled taffy." After taking one look at these outrageously fitting uniforms, practical officers instructed their men to go into the barracks and trade clothing among themselves. That helped and the first rain shrank the material to fit the "notches and crotches," so that "viewed from a distance through a bad set of binoculars, it wasn't a half-badly dressed army."[28]

New shipments of draftees continued to pour into Camp Upton. The quota that arrived on September 20 was more picturesque than most, coming as it did from the Gas House District and Hell's Kitchen. Gas House boys carried placards boasting their familiarity with "gas warfare." Not to be outdone, a gang of ruffians from lower Tenth Avenue came into camp behind a sign that read: "Hell's Kitchen, That Is Us! We're Going To Cook The Kaiser's Goose!!" The draft apparatus continued to pull in a cross-section of New York society, a veritable melting pot of humanity, although, according to one observer, most army pots did not present "such diverse and interesting ingredients for their brews, such highly seasoned condiments to dash in here and there." That giant vacuum cleaner sucked up thousands of New Yorkers, then gradually expanded its circle to include those from the surrounding counties, upstate New York (particularly from the Buffalo, Rochester, and Olean areas), followed by men from Connecticut, New Jersey, and Massachusetts. One Buffalo resident offered an observation: "Boys from the docks mingled with boys from Delaware Avenue and vigorous youngsters from the far East Side; Sunday school teachers and prize-fighters and boys from the farms became bunkies. It was a typical haul of the draft law magnet and it missed no element of the white race in Buffalo or the towns." After a few days, these new men also became full-fledged "veterans" of what was now being called the Melting Pot Division.[29]

Various bigwigs dropped by to inspect the progress at Camp Upton, but the heartiest reception was given to Theodore Roosevelt, former president and fellow New Yorker, who was still immensely popular with the troops. He had been invited to give an address by his old secretary of war, Henry Stimson, now serving as lieutenant colonel of the 305th Field Artillery. Roosevelt's words had special meaning for thousands of foreigners in the melting pot, when he proclaimed, "Universal suffrage, to justify itself, must be based on universal service. It is only you and your kind who have the absolutely clear title to the management of this Republic. It is only the man willing, when the need arises, to fight for the nation and to die for the nation—it is only these who are really entitled to have a voice in the halls of the nation."[30]

With no disrespect to distinguished visitors, the most popular arrival in Camp Upton was a shipment of rifles that arrived on September 28. Although these weapons proved to be old Spanish-American War Krag-Jorgensens rather than the regulation Springfield, Model 1917 that would appear later, soldiers liked drilling with them much better than with wooden sticks. These "ancient and honorable" rifles came packed in large shipping crates, each weapon smeared with a thick coating of heavy grease to prevent rust. Soldiers began to clean them with gasoline, in the process transferring most of the grease to pant legs and shirt sleeves. This was a big step for many of the New Yorkers. One lieutenant said that of the fifty-eight men in his platoon only three had ever fired a rifle. Company officers and noncoms, after four weeks of training, marched to the firing range, where they each shot 150 rounds of live ammunition at both bullseye and silhouette targets, at ranges of 100, 200, and 300 yards. After posting high marks, successful marksmen became qualified instructors for the remainder of the division. Artillerymen openly expressed their jealousy of the infantry and its rifles, since they had no cannon or horses for their batteries, gunners going through their drill with sawhorses and wooden guns.[31]

Advent of rifles brought an increase in guard duty. Ignorance of all things military then became apparent on the guard posts. When some guy named Joe came back to camp after a night on the town, he was stopped by a guard, who commanded, "Advance and be recognized!" Joe obliged and was again told to halt. The guard followed instructions and asked, "What's your name?" Joe replied with a laugh, "Ah, you no guess it in a thousand years." On another evening, a major was stopped by a shouted command, "Halt!" He did so, but the sentry cried, "Halt!" again. Somewhat irritated, the major yelled, "Well, what do you want?" Again the guard cried, "Halt!" and added, "Now I think about time you run—I shoot!" Taken aback, the officer called out for help. A brief inquiry revealed that the foreign-born sentry had misunderstood his orders to shoot only if a man refused to identify himself after being challenged three times.[32]

The most hated duty was stump pulling, or "forest dentistry" as it was commonly called. While Thompson-Starrett workers concentrated on construction work, the 302nd Engineers supervised clearing the parade grounds, drill fields, and firing ranges. Soldiers spent days on end hacking away at the scrubby growth with picks, axes, poles, and brush cutters. At first, entire squads were detailed in rotation for "the cheerful game of stump pulling," but soon that detail was reserved exclusively for those earmarked for punishment by their sergeants. Small stumps were literally pulled out by dozens of men tugging on ropes, but larger stumps were removed either by powerful steam-powered stump pullers or blown to pieces with dynamite. This rugged duty brought out the best in men's vocabulary skills and it was claimed that, if a soldier could not apply at least five hundred adjectives to the noun "stump," he "was frowned upon as mentally deficient or as one affecting an ultra religious pose."[33]

Kitchen Police, or KP, was hated only slightly less than stump pulling. KPs worked for His Majesty the Cook, who reigned supreme in the kitchen. Those detailed to this "Cinderella duty" got up before daylight and hauled in firewood to start fires for breakfast. Under the cook's direction, they prepared food, served it to the tables, refilled empty dishes, washed utensils, cleaned tables, mopped floors, and began preparations for the noon meal. This routine continued all day. Irving Crump recalled his stint on KP: "Shovelled nine tons (almost) of coal into the coal bin, as a starter. Then peeled a sack of potatoes, scrubbed an acre of floor and a half-acre of table tops and benches, washed twenty ash cans, and other kitchen utensils." One self-titled "kitchen slave" spoke for them all when he complained about having to take orders from "a pie faced, frog eyed, long eared, narrow chested, bow legged, long tongued, empty headed shrimp who thinks he is a cook." Most descriptions were laced with considerably more profanity.[34]

Soupy, soupy, soupy,
  Without a single bean;
Porky, porky, porky,
  Without a streak of lean;
Coffee, coffee, coffee,
  The weakest ever seen.[35]

Although unable to discourage the universal habit of cursing, General Bell made great strides in providing a safe, moral environment at Camp Upton. The historian of the Seventy-seventh Division would later boast that "camp-followers of yore, the harlot, the beggar, the thief, had disappeared. In their stead rose those praiseworthy institutions which have played such a great part in alleviating the hardships of the soldier—the Red

Cross, the Salvation Army, the Knights of Columbus, the Y. M. C. A., and other organizations." This was a noble assertion, but rather naive. County officials had quickly imposed a ban on the sale of alcohol within five miles of the army base, but soon felt compelled to stamp out those "evil conditions that are slowly but surely creeping up around Camp Upton." Sheriff Biggs reported that whiskey was readily available in the prohibited zone, theft was a constant problem, numerous pickpockets plied their trade, and "women whose presence is not desired parade in the villages where the soldiers from the camp go when off duty." The sheriff, district attorney, and local judges urged county supervisors to beef up law enforcement dramatically and ask for assistance from the New York State Police. Detectives from New York City came out to identify career criminals.[36]

In reality, New York soldiers generally were well-behaved, thanks in part to those social organizations that offered a variety of diversions to fill off-duty hours. Foremost among them was the Young Men's Christian Association, which operated a headquarters building, a three-thousand-seat auditorium, and eight "huts" scattered throughout camp. At one end of each hut was a stage, on which were presented boxing matches, movies, and theatrical productions, as well as Sunday religious programs. "Red Triangle workers," so-called from the YMCA's insignia, stood ready to hand out stamps and writing paper, check out books or pamphlets, or simply answer questions. The main auditorium was reserved for important speakers or talent from the Broadway stage or movies, superstars such as Mary Pickford, Douglas Fairbanks, and George M. Cohan. The Knights of Columbus operated three huts in Camp Upton, their layout being similar to the YMCA buildings except the halls could be converted into basketball courts. To counter rumors that only Catholics or Knights of Columbus members could use these facilities, workers erected large signs that proclaimed "Everybody Welcome." Bibles were valued gifts, but often for the wrong reason. One recruit confessed, "The

> **Sign over the Door of a Camp Upton YMCA Hut:**
>
> *SWEAR, if you can't think of anything else to say, but do it softly— very, very softly, so no one else but yourself will hear you.*[37]

Bible is printed on nice, thin paper, and is excellent for rolling the makings of a cigarette. In fact, I have smoked through the New

Testament as far as 'Second Corinthians.'" One man who actually read the Bible did not care for many of his new associates, complaining that they gambled and cursed, then declaring, "Men here are like animals."[38]

Despite camp amusements, most soldiers would have done anything for a weekend pass in New York City. When it was rumored that Jewish soldiers would be allowed to go home to celebrate Yom Kippur, one man promptly asked for a pass. "You want to go in for Yom Kippur?" "Yiss, sorr." "What's your name?" "Patrick Shea." It was a bold appeal, but there would be no pass for the earnest Irishman. At first, passes were given freely for family emergencies, but officers soon noticed that these crises increased in both number and severity as Saturday approached, so more scrutiny was employed. Those lucky enough to receive a weekend pass had the option of traveling either by automobile or by train. Soldiers employing the former method lost valuable time as vehicles shook apart on rutted country roads or suspicious police officers flagged them down to check their paperwork. A trip by rail was preferable, but there was no schedule at first and trains departed as soon as cars could be crammed full of men. Although passenger cars were intended for only forty occupants, observers saw that "men standing in the aisles overflowed onto platform and steps, and even to the coal piles of the engine tenders."[39]

Tragedy struck the railroad depot on October 28 when a passenger train backed into a line of freight cars, pushing a boxcar into a milling crowd. One soldier died after being run over by the wheels, the mangled corpse finally being identified as Joseph Messina of Battery F, 306th Field Artillery. Frank J. McFarland, an Amherst College graduate now serving as a private in Battery A, 305th Field Artillery, was finally pulled free after an hour, only to die of his injuries a few days later. Over a dozen soldiers were hospitalized, the first significant losses suffered by the Seventy-seventh Division in the Great War.[40]

Soldiers would never forget those initial casualties, just as they would always remember their first heroes at Camp Upton. One of the first to gain prominence was a Corporal Carney of the 306th Infantry, who owned a new glow-in-the-dark radiolite wristwatch. Excited comrades would awaken Carney at all hours of the night just to see him tilt his arm, check his watch, and sound off with the correct time. Jimmy Flaherty became the idol of Company F, 306th Infantry, when he drove his personal car to Patchague on a mission to repair Jean

Francaise's broken dentures. The company's civilian cook had announced that, without teeth, he had no choice but to return home, but Flaherty's wild race across the Long Island backcountry saved the day. Jimmy returned triumphantly to camp with a set of newly patched store teeth, Francaise agreed to continue cooking for the boys, and he planted kisses on both cheeks of the embarrassed youngster. In addition to these selfless acts of heroism, new recruits also paid homage to wonderful feats of strength and endurance. Foremost among these new Olympian athletes was a fellow named Rocco from Company B, 308th Infantry, who one day sat down and, to the delight and amazement of cheering spectators, proceeded to eat three dozen frankfurters.[41]

A few men of the Seventy-seventh Division had already served in the European War. Foremost among them was Harry Booten, a Cockney from Whitechapel, who had been wounded four times while fighting at Mons with the London Fusiliers. After his recovery, Booten was promoted sergeant and detailed as a bomb dropper in the Royal Flying Corps. While raiding a German naval base, the pilot of his plane was killed by anti-aircraft fire. Although wounded, Booten switched seats in midair, took over the controls, and flew three hundred miles back to England where he managed to land safely. Then, in his own words, "I fointed loike a bloomin' loidy." Summoned to Buckingham Palace, Harry Booten was given a Distinguished Conduct Medal by King George. Invalided out of the British service, Booten stowed away on the Swedish steamer *Arendale*, bound for America, but that ship was torpedoed and the plucky veteran had to be rescued from a watery grave. After arriving in New York, Booten found work at the A-Z Motion Picture Supply Company. When America entered the war, this irrepressible young Cockney convinced his local draft board to accept him for service in the American artillery.[42]

William J. Atkins had enlisted in February of 1915, signing on with the Eaton Machine Gun Battalion, which left Toronto with twenty-seven officers and eleven hundred enlisted men. A few months later Atkins was in the Battle of Ypres and gave this account of the fighting: "Four days we fought without relief. Wave after wave of Germans in solid mass formation rolled on us—and the old Colts drove 'em back. The whole earth was rocking from the big shells and we was fighting day and night. Time and again they took our first and second line trenches, but we always got 'em." By the time these Canadians and their Colt machine guns were withdrawn, they numbered but ten officers and thirty-three men. As for Atkins, naturally dubbed "Tommy" by the New Yorkers, he had been struck by shrapnel and awoke in an English hospital. Atkins said of himself, "I was nothin' but a jelly fish. I could not talk; I couldn't see and I was 90 per cent dead." Although he had been discharged from the Canadian Army as an invalid, "Tommy" convinced American doctors that he was able-bodied enough to fight with the Seventy-seventh Division.[43]

Milan Steffanovich had graduated from a Belgrade military academy before joining the Serbian Army to fight against the Bulgarians. Lieutenant Steffanovich told of how he had killed three Austrians before being captured in December of 1915: "We fight hand to hand—I kill one and another he goes down. But he grabs my foot and a third attack me from behind. He pull my head back, strike down with his bayonet—look, here is the scar on my chin where the bayonet go, and I grab the sharp bayonet with my bare hand. Look— see the scar in my hand. But he tear his gun loose and stab me here in the side and then I get him down and kill him so." After escaping from captivity, Steffanovich came to America and found employment playing villains in New York films. Now he wanted nothing more than to avenge the deaths of two brothers, both of whom died as Serbian soldiers, and his sister, a Red Cross nurse who had been hung by the Bulgarians.[44]

Although not veterans themselves, other men in the Seventy-seventh Division had equally compelling reasons for joining the war in Europe, none more than James Kelly, a native of Glasgow. An older brother had been killed while serving with the Scottish Highlanders and a younger brother had joined the Black Watch, been captured, and tortured to death by the Germans. Following the death of his second brother, James Kelly left New York for Scotland to enlist, but was rejected because he had bad teeth and "a tobacco heart." A similar attempt to join the United States Army was also rebuffed. Kelly was painting U-boat hunters in an American shipyard when he drew a low number in the draft and figured this would be his last chance to join the war. The young Scot quit smoking and spent fifty dollars to get his teeth fixed, then persuaded his local board to accept him. While in training at Camp Upton, Kelly received a letter from his mother, who told him that a sister, serving as a Red Cross nurse, had been killed by an artillery shell while tending wounded soldiers near the front. In closing her melancholy message, Mrs. Kelly wrote: "You're the last boy I have, Jamie, but I thank God every night of my life that they're allowing you to go now. Two boys and a girl is a lot to pay, Jamie, but I'll pay all rather than have the sacrifice be in vain. Oh, thank God for America."[45]

2

CAMP UPTON

Although each soldier at Camp Upton had his own unique story, the American army had no use for individuals. What the army wanted was a machine composed of interchangeable parts, where troops could be added or removed at random without interfering with its smooth operation. Soldiers must be trained to follow orders without hesitation, a habit of subordination devoid of personal aspirations or thoughts of consequence. Officers had started to instill that obedience as soon as the first draftees arrived at Camp Upton, attempting to kill the spirit of individualism that has always been a symbol of American character. Men accustomed to absolute freedom of thought and deed must now submit to what many considered dictatorial treatment at the hands of officers who, just a few months earlier, had been their social equals or inferiors. Seemingly trivial activity took on added importance for the captains and lieutenants, who sometimes naively told recruits that "the fate of the Nation, together with the balance of power in Europe, hung on our ability to render a correct salute."[1]

In fairness to these new officers, it was a tough job to teach even the basics of close-order drill and guard duty when they had yet to master the rudiments of their own jobs. Oftentimes, company officers could be seen drilling their men while reading directly from the manual. Many lieutenants, fresh from college classrooms, had far less life experience than their enlisted men, who contemptuously referred to them as "ninety-day wonders" or "Sears and Roebuck lieutenants," the insinuation being one could replace them in three months or order a new set from a mail-order catalog. But at times it seemed that an officer's problems were almost insurmountable. One lieutenant spent three hours teaching his company the important details relating to patrolling, posting guards, establishing outposts, and instructing pickets. To ensure that everyone understood, he asked the company barber, "What is a picket?" To his dismay, the man responded, "A picket iss a board mit sticks tacked on it."[2]

After the war, one soldier identified three problems associated with training at Camp Upton—"first, our own colossal ignorance of all military matters; second, the lack of ordnance and other field material commensurate with our requirements; and third, the inexperience of the officers." There was also a fourth difficulty that would only later become apparent, the fact that American training "proved of little use in camp and of no use on the battle line." The Allied Powers tried to remedy this last situation by sending instructors to National Army camps, where they shared their wartime experiences, led training classes, and told soldiers what to expect when they headed overseas. But this effort to educate American soldiers failed simply because the nature of war on the Western Front had completely changed by the time the Seventy-seventh Division saw its first serious action. After the war, one soldier made the astute observation, "Looking back now at our special training at Camp Upton, one is struck with the great difference between the war as it had been up to that time, and the war that the Regiment actually experienced."[3]

Ranks of the Melting Pot Division continued to swell as additional graduates of officers' training camps arrived to lead thousands of new draftees who filled the camp's barracks. Hard-bitten Regular Army noncoms were augmented by the promotion of draftees who had demonstrated an aptitude for military life and an ability to enforce discipline. Local draft boards kept conscripting men and funneling them out to Long Island, where it soon became obvious that some civilians were being overzealous in their procurement of new soldiers. Many men, unable to speak the English language and therefore misunderstanding questions asked of them, had stated that they were single, when, in fact, they were married with dependent children and therefore eligible for exemption. One draftee, certified as single by his local board, turned out to have a wife and five children living in New York. To one observant officer, it appeared that local board members were often "more concerned over the safety of its native sons than over the rights of its foreign-born residents." Military authorities had no authority to correct mistakes made by civilians on the local boards, so most foreigners entitled to exemptions found themselves stuck in the ranks.[4]

The draft continued to dredge up men with what was then called "a past." Captain William Harrigan was startled one day by a private from his company, who suddenly blurted out, "Say, Captain, I've had a little trouble up in New York. I was mixed up in a manslaughter case." Taken aback by this sudden admission, Harrigan asked, "Are you a gunman?" The private responded, "Naw, I'm a knife worker." As any good officer would do in this situation, he made the man an instructor in the use of the boot knife. Harrigan later recalled, "He made a great soldier."[5]

They put my Lulu into jail
And a sad thing came to hap,
The sheriff and the warden both
came down with a dose of clap!
Bang, bang Lulu.
Bang her good and strong.
What'll we do for banging
When Lulu's dead and gone?[6]

Michael Telesco was a city kid, formerly a professional boxer and a wagon driver for the New York Street Cleaning Department when called into service. He confessed, "I've been a good boy and a bad boy. I've been all sorts." Telesco's draft notice dramatically changed his carefree lifestyle, which heretofore had consisted of "knocking about the city, drinking, dancing, boxing, keeping all sorts of hours, no discipline." He thought himself pretty tough since he could box and street fight, but admitted that army life had made him even tougher. Although standing but five feet two inches, Private Telesco had gained nineteen pounds while in camp and claimed, "I'm just all muscle now," boasting, "Just bring on your Germans, I'm ready for 'em all!"[7]

The biggest obstacle to making soldiers out of the various nationalities in camp was not characters of questionable backgrounds, but the staggering number who could not understand English. Census reports had been misleading about literacy in the United States, a country that boasted of having the greatest free school system in the world. After all, when a census taker asked if a man could read and write, it was easy enough to simply answer in the affirmative and avoid the stigma of being branded illiterate. It quickly became apparent that *fully one-fourth* of the soldiers who had reached Camp Upton were "unable to read the Constitution of the United States or an American newspaper, or to write a letter in English to the folks at home." An 1889 law had stipulated that a man could not be enlisted into the army "unless he could speak, read and write the English language." The damning fact was that there were not enough of those men to fill the draft quotas, so Congress soon passed an emergency bill to eliminate that outdated requirement.[8]

A concerned General Staff quickly established Development Battalions in the National Army training camps, these units evolving into what were eventually styled Recruit Education Centers, whose purpose was to teach the English language so every man could "receive, understand, execute and transmit verbal or written orders, and to read and understand drill regulations as printed in soldiers' handbooks." Company officers could not afford to wait for their illiterate men to graduate from three-month courses of instruction and forced them to learn on the job. One frustrated infantry commander took the unusual step of posting a notice that read, "If you can't speak English, you can't eat." Another announced at roll call, "When you get into the trenches the order to duck your head will be given in English, and if you don't understand it your head will be blown off." When this last statement was translated for thirty-two men in the company who could not understand it, attendance at language class increased significantly.[9]

After a few months, calisthenics, close-order drill, overland hikes, trench training, and healthy meals had changed the appearance of most New Yorkers. Generally smaller of stature than soldiers from the Middle West or western states, these city boys gradually began the transformation from pale, sickly-looking draftees into sun-browned, hardened soldiers.[10]

To keep the men healthy, medical officers conducted sanitary inspections "which for minuteness made a company officer inspecting a rifle appear a

The Infantry have hairy ears.
They piss through leather britches.
They wipe their ass on broken glass,
Those hardy sons-of-bitches.[11]

mere novice." Shelter-halves were hung between bunks to cut down on the transmission of disease and doctors scrutinized the kitchens, looking for anything that might contaminate the chow. Sick call was held twice each day and those who became seriously ill were whisked away to isolation wards. There were small epidemics of mumps and measles. Venereal disease became "a serious menace." Pneumonia was the most feared illness because of its high mortality and "many promising careers were cut short by this dread disease." To indemnify family members in case of a soldier's death, the government offered $10,000 of War Risk Insurance. Only when regiments were pitted against one another, as if in some sort of patriotic competition, did soldiers swarm the allotment officers and many units ultimately headed into battle with one hundred percent participation in the insurance program. For some soldiers, naming a beneficiary posed a problem. A chap named Pietro had to choose between his brother, who had once lent him a dollar, and his father, who had beaten him every week of his life. Pietro, who was remembered for having a strange craving for raw pork chops, finally decided in favor of his brother.[12]

Competition was also employed during the Liberty Loan Drive. The 306th Infantry allotted $100,000 more than any other regiment in the division, not because Liberty Bonds were such a good investment but primarily "because they refused to be outdone in anything." There was great pressure from division headquarters to sign up every man in camp for this bond drive, but some officers refused to participate, claiming that family and insurance allotments already took too much of a soldier's pay. Foremost among those objecting was Captain Charles W. Whittlesey, formerly a lawyer but now commanding Headquarters Company, 308th Infantry. Whittlesey was described as "one of those half-frozen New Englanders, and you couldn't tell what went on behind his round spectacles and poker face. He was always fretting about regulations and checking up. If it was in the regulations, it had to be done." When an order came from regimental headquarters that everyone had to subscribe to the Liberty Bond program, Whittlesey checked the regulations, discovered that men could not be forced to do so, and allowed his men to make up their own minds.[13]

The U. S. pays us thirty per,
Or so the papers say;
But if you get a dollar ten,
It's a helluva big pay day![14]

Everyone looked forward to Christmas, but the big question was who would spend the holiday with family and friends. General Bell employed the wisdom of Solomon and sliced his division in two, one-half the men receiving forty-eight hours' leave for Christmas and the other half going home the following week for New Year's. Captain W. Kerr Rainsford

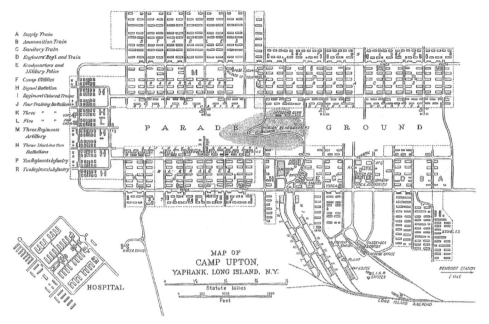

A *Supply Train*
B *Ammunition Train*
C *Sanitary Train*
D *Engineers Regt. and Train*
E *Headquarters and Military Police*
F *Camp Utilities*
H *Signal Battalion*
I *Regiment Colored Troops*
J *Four Training Battalions*
K *Three   "   "   yards*
L *Five   "   "*
M *Three Regiments Artillery*
N *Three Machine Gun Battalions*
P *Two Regiments Infantry*
R *Two Regiments Infantry*

MAP OF
CAMP UPTON,
YAPHANK, LONG ISLAND, N.Y.

Diagram of Camp Upton. From *National Geographic Magazine.*

remained in camp for Christmas and saw how depressed soldiers gathered "disconsolate in the empty barracks, wishing they too were at home, or looking apathetically out on the fine rain that gathered in icicles along the eaves." To alleviate this gloomy depression, a thirty-foot pine tree at division headquarters was decorated with colored lights and Christmas ornaments. Volunteers scoured the woodlands for pine boughs and vines to decorate mess halls and Red Cross workers distributed holiday packages to everyone who remained behind. Rainsford remembered these gift boxes came "prettily tied with ribbons, enclosing things to eat or smoke, and things to play with or use, and a card of Christmas greeting from some girl, unknown and therefore lovely." Cheered by these decorations and gifts, and with comrades sharing the loneliness, soldiers at Camp Upton found "a cozy seclusion, and Christmas found its way again into the heart."[15]

That winter saw men cooped up in barracks for days on end. Coal for the stoves had to be hauled in regimental wagons, which often got stuck before reaching the barracks, their loads being carted the rest of the way in wheelbarrows. Alternating periods of snow, thaw, and freezing temperatures kept the ground a solid sheet of ice. Drill often took place in the mess halls with wind whipping through chinks in the walls, but on mild days, ashes from the stoves were scattered about the drill fields to provide traction. Soldiers swore that thermometers plunged to twenty below zero and it was common to see icicles hanging from the showers. Michael Shallin of the 308th Infantry froze his nose one subzero night and, sixty years later, at the age of eighty-two, confessed that "the damn thing still bothers me."[16]

During these bleak and unsettled winter months, the most dependable source of amusement was the phonograph. Most companies took up a collection of one dollar per man, accumulating funds for purchase of a phonograph and an assortment of popular recordings. Determined record spinners had selections that harmonized with the daily bugle calls. Reveille was followed immediately by the strains of "It's Nice to Get Up in the Morning, But It's Nicer to Lie in Bed." Retreat at sunset was echoed by "The Darktown Strutter's Ball," while the notes of "Taps" brought forth a final selection, "Give Me the Moonlight, Give Me the Girl."[17]

The rich girl's watch is made of gold,
The poor girl's is of brass,
My Lulu needs no watch at all
There's movement in her ass!
  Bang, bang, Lulu.
  Bang her good and strong.
  What'll we do for banging
  When Lulu's dead and gone?[18]

For months the residents of New York City had seen thousands of their young men disappear into the Long Island wilderness, returning only as disorganized mobs on leave. An attempt to update New Yorkers on the soldiers' progress occurred in late January, when a cameraman received permission to film the Machine Gun Company of the 307th Infantry. Gun teams assembled on the bank of Gold Fish Creek, dragged their weapons up the slope, and opened fire at paper targets posted just twenty-five yards away. This newsreel ran in New York movie houses, and photos from the exercise appeared in various pictorial supplements of metropolitan newspapers. One of the machine gunners captured on film admitted that everything looked "very realistic," especially since the cameraman "considerably omitted to look at our objective."[19]

In order to present an even more impressive show, Colonel Nathan K. Averill led the 308th Infantry in a parade up Eighth Avenue and down Fifth Avenue on February 4. Averill was a no-nonsense officer from the old school—veteran of the Seventh Cavalry, winner of a Silver Star at Santiago in the Cuban War, military attaché in Russia, and faculty member at West Point. Following their new regimental colors, the first presented to any National Army regiment, the 308th Infantry dazzled a huge crowd that gathered despite bitter cold temperatures. Among the witnesses was Governor Charles Whitman, who confessed two days later that "the glow of enthusiasm . . . is still with me." Offering his congratulations to General Evan Johnson (temporarily commanding the division while General Bell was off on an inspection trip in France), Whitman continued, "It seems to me impossible that men could have undergone such magnificent physical improvement as was yesterday so noticeable, without having at the same time experienced a marked uplift and advance in mentality." Word of the successful showing by the 308th quickly reached Washington, where Secretary Baker immediately ordered all divisions across the country to hold themselves "available for parades or reviews in towns or cities near their training centres." To show their appreciation for Colonel Averill's regiment, editors began to refer to the 308th as "New York's Own," an appellation quickly extended to the entire division.[20]

In obedience to Secretary Baker's order, ten thousand men from the Seventy-seventh Division paraded through Gotham streets in observance of Washington's Birthday. This time the route stretched up First Avenue to Fifty-ninth Street, then down Fifth Avenue to Madison Square, soldiers marching through a driving snowstorm, the pure white flakes accenting olive drab uniforms and newly issued winter caps. Despite occasional spills on slippery pavements, this parade was also proclaimed a great triumph. Although there was sloppy slush underfoot, one officer declared that the soldiers "marched with a swing and a snap and a precision truly remarkable." The Washington Birthday affair was almost exclusively an infantry show, only Battery A, 305th Field Artillery crunching through the fallen snow with their four three-inch rifles. Glancing to the right and left, soldiers witnessed an inspiring sight. "From sidewalk to skyline the Avenue was banked with faces as the repeating ranks passed in review. There were radiant faces, curious faces, admiring faces, tear-stained faces, and smiling faces that hid weeping hearts." The only blot on the Seventy-seventh Division's inspiring parade was a large number of men who got drunk, became lost in the city streets and took several days to find their way back to

Long Island. These stragglers were promptly court-martialed upon their belated appearance at roll call.[21]

Less than six months earlier, the Seventy-seventh Division had been nothing more than a name on a piece of paper. The draft plucked men from "their clubs and their kitchens, their offices and their Chinese laundries, their limousines and their taxi-driver seats" and plopped them all down into the melting pot at Camp Upton. Then an amazing thing happened. Army training, often scornfully looked down upon by progressive civilians as rote work fit only for dolts and dullards, began to fuse the entire polyglot mass into one vast machine with thousands of interchangeable parts. "Alla right, Boss" gradually became "Very good, Sir." Army uniforms and impartial discipline made all men equal. *The Literary Digest* would later explain, "We talk of Americanization. Never has it been so strikingly and yet so unconsciously developed as in this war—and perhaps, in this war, never so strikingly as in the Seventy-Seventh." None put it better than Charles Minder, 306th Machine Gun Battalion, who confessed to his mother, "We have about every nationality you can think of in my company. There sure is some mixture, and I think it is about the finest thing in the world for anyone, who like myself, has always suffered with race-prejudice, to be mixed up in an outfit like this. The last six months of my life in the army, living and suffering with these fellows, has done more for me to get rid of race-prejudice than anything else could have done." Soldiers not only found themselves making friends with those from other ethnic backgrounds but also from different religious faiths. A religious census of the troops at Camp Upton disclosed that thirty-five percent were Roman Catholic, thirty percent were from some variety of Protestant faith, and twenty-five percent were Jewish. Tolerance became an accepted part of army life.[22]

When ordered by the War Department to designate an official symbol to represent the Seventy-seventh Division, General Bell's staff made a logical choice. Major Lloyd Griscom, division adjutant, suggested a reproduction of the Statue of Liberty with the numeral "7" on each side of the base, a design that was created by Captain J. S. S. Richardson, division intelligence officer. Painters stenciled this design onto every large piece of portable equipment in the division, while mechanics hammered numbers, names, and unit names onto leather and metal gear. Rumors swirled about Camp Upton that the division would soon ship out for France, this gossip bolstered by arrival of supplies "in unprecedented quantities." Overnight, neat and tidy barracks became warehouses piled high with "clothing assorted into sizes, revolvers, tents, saddles, harness, canteens, belts, and the thousand and one accoutrements which are necessary adjuncts to the fighting man." Crates, boxes, and barrels all bore the same markings—a blue stripe, a Statue of Liberty insignia, and the vague, but ominous, address of "American Expeditionary Force." This ubiquitous symbol gave the Seventy-seventh Division its fourth nickname. Now in addition to The Melting Pot Division, The Metropolitan Division, and New York's Own, New Yorkers would also be known as "The Statue of Liberty Division," soon shortened to simply "Liberty Division."[23]

Training intensified in March when scuttlebutt claimed that the day of departure was rapidly approaching. Technical manuals were issued that bore the sinister warning, "Not to be Carried in the Front Line Trenches." Battalions began a series of night marches. Noncoms brushed up on the old drill regulations, map reading, map making, and principles of firing. Squads tramped into the woods on tactical assignments, but these forays quickly "degenerated into nothing more than wild games of hare and hound, pursued without the slightest regard for military regulations." Bayonet training was again emphasized, fierce-looking men charging across open fields yelling at the top of their lungs "like Cherokee Indians." More and more time was spent firing live ammunition on the rifle range, each man learning how to set his sights correctly and regulate the windage, so that he could "bring down a German at five hundred yards." Gas officers drilled their men until they could put on their masks in a matter of seconds. This drill was especially disgusting since there was only a limited number of masks for each company. One artilleryman complained, "We were compelled to put in our mouths the mouthpieces which had been used by others, an unsanitary and most unpleasant feature which we vainly attempted to mitigate by washing the mouthpieces in a nauseating solution of creosote." Although the training might be repugnant, it was essential because anyone who could not get his mask on and properly adjusted in twelve seconds was considered a dead man.[24]

A simulated battle resulted in simulated casualties, which provided training for ambulance and hospital companies of the 302nd Sanitary Train. Delbert Davis recalled how the "battlefield" looked to the 307th

Ambulance Company: "Wounded men lay scattered everywhere; some with gun shot wounds, others with shrapnel; some with broken legs—on the whole it presented a pitiable sight. Medical aid was being given as rapidly as possible." Severely injured soldiers were evacuated by motor ambulance, while those less seriously wounded were carried from the field on stretchers to a temporary dressing station. Attendants took good care of their patients, at least until they reached the division hospital. Assuming that the simulation ended here, litter bearers unceremoniously dumped casualties from their stretchers and celebrated their role in the mock battle by drinking up all the hot chocolate intended for victims.[25]

Doctors began a round of physical examinations designed to weed out those not fit for service overseas and among those found to be in poor health was Major General Bell, who had recently returned from France. Medical officers determined that the old Indian fighter, then sixty-two years of age, was not up to the task of leading the Seventy-seventh Division in action. Bell remained in New York during the war and died on January 8, 1919, while the Liberty Division was still in France. Very few soldiers were found unfit for service during these spring inspections. Most of those either mentally or physically deficient had already been weeded out by discharge or transfer to Camp Gordon in Georgia.[26]

Throughout their stay at Camp Upton, company officers were constantly besieged by paperwork requesting "every possible kind of enlisted man, whether auto-mechanic, landscape gardener, or 'left-handed Presbyterian.'" This constant drain of manpower, combined with new arrivals of conscripts, kept company rosters "in a state of continual change and disruption." Taking their cue from Regular Army counterparts who had culled out their noncoms for duty at Camp Upton, exasperated captains tried to keep their best men and passed along soldiers whom they "desired enormously to get rid of." Men high on the list for transfer included conscientious objectors, those with histories of AWOL or venereal disease, and soldiers who had fallen into disfavor with superiors. Captain W. Kerr Rainsford reported, "Camp Gordon, strangely in need of men, offered a certain safety-valve, and the man whose face seemed irreconcilable with a steel helmet, whose name on the roll call consisted only of consonants, or who had cast his rice pudding in the mess sergeant's face often completed his training there." Those who remained behind quietly said good-by to their friends headed for Georgia, one commenting philosophically on the latest exodus, "What's the use of grouching? That's what war is—saying good-by. Just saying good-by, fellows. Might's well get used to it now."[27]

As a date for embarkation loomed, it was found that these transfers had left the Seventy-seventh Division short of men. To bring the Liberty Division up to its war complement, large detachments of New England and upstate New York soldiers were shifted from Camp Devens in Massachusetts to Camp Upton. Among the group that arrived on March 17 was a coal shoveler named George E. Blowers, from Ledyard in Cayuga County, New York. Blowers had been in the army less than three weeks and his recollections of life at Camp Devens were limited. Among the highlights were eating oatmeal that "would hold up wallpaper on the ceiling," exercising in the bitter cold with no covering for his ears, and being quarantined for almost two weeks with chicken pox. Although he had never handled a rifle before, during his first morning at Camp Upton Blowers took a Springfield rifle and, along with other Massachusetts newcomers, joined in company drill. The novice later confided, "Of course, I did not know what it was all about." Veterans from earlier draft quotas derisively referred to these recent arrivals as "upstate farmers" and "hicks," under a misapprehension that everything outside of New York City was farmland. On the other hand, upstate boys thought their Gotham comrades were pretty damned stupid because they couldn't tell the difference between straw and hay.[28]

Rumors swirled through camp that the division would leave on March 10 or March 16 or not at all or at any moment. So many anticipated dates of departure came and went that soldiers started to refer to themselves as a depot division, one that would never see combat but would only provide replacement troops for other divisions. All this dejection ended in the early morning hours of March 27, when the 305th Machine Gun Battalion marched past the infantry barracks just as sleepy men tumbled out for reveille. Gunners from the "Suicide Club," a common nickname since machine gunners supposedly had a life span of only seven minutes after reaching the trenches, smiled broadly at the shouted question, "Where are you birds going?" These "Seven-Minute Men" just kept smiling, but the bulging packs and barracks bags provided a silent answer. The movement to France had begun.[29]

These were days of "meagre tonnage and myriad submarines," so the vast ethnological collection of the Seventy-seventh Division would have to be ferried across the Atlantic aboard whatever ships were available, but generally in those of British registry. Officials estimated that it would take a full month to transport twenty-seven thousand men and their equipment. Boarding cars of the New York, New Haven and Hartford Railroad, the machine gunners rode along to Long Island City, but instead of taking ferries for the Hoboken docks, they stayed in the train as it chugged across the Hell Gate Bridge and headed for Connecticut. The troop train reached Portland, Maine, later that morning and halted almost under the prow of the White Star liner *Magentic*, now sporting wartime camouflage to confuse the aim of German submariners. Afraid that any light at sea might jeopardize the ship, officers told the gunners to turn in all of their matches. After being assigned sleeping quarters (those toward the bow noted an abundance of rats!) and stowing their gear, soldiers wandered back topside for a smoke. Although forced to give up their own matches, passengers quickly discovered that a British sailor had them for sale in the ship's canteen. Amid much murmuring over this fine state of affairs, the *Magentic* slipped its anchor and steamed north to Halifax, Nova Scotia, bearing not only the Suicide Club but also division headquarters and the military police.[30]

At daylight on March 29, the 302nd Engineers and 302nd Field Signal Battalion boarded trains bound for Astoria, where they transferred to ferries that deposited these units at the Cunard Line dock on the Hudson River. Waiting for them at the dock was the *Carmania*, formerly a British cruiser that earlier in the war had sunk the German raider *Cap Trafalgar* and still bore scars from that engagement. The *Carmania* left port that afternoon, engineers and signal men welcoming aboard a small group of women telephone operators working for the Signal Corps. After joining the *Magentic* inside the submarine net at Halifax, both ships lay at anchor until after Easter. No one was allowed ashore and the only distraction was the first in a series of lifeboat drills, which everyone participated in except Captain Frederick S. Greene. The captain had recently purchased a complicated life preserver apparatus that was guaranteed to be safer than any lifeboat. Greene gave a demonstration of that wonderful invention during the first drill, but something failed to work properly and the captain had to be saved from drowning in his fabulous life preserver.[31]

On April 2 the *Magentic*, the *Carmania*, a ship carrying Chinese coolies, and another loaded with horses and mules left Halifax for England, the convoy's lone escort being the British cruiser *King Alfred*. The voyage was generally uneventful. There was not much to do of a military nature beyond boat drills, physical training, and submarine watch. Diet required getting used to the taste of oleomargarine. Although oleo was a part of the British navy's ration, most of the American soldiers used it to grease their hiking boots. There was also the problem of communicating with the British crew, who, according to one of the Yanks, "didn't speak our language." At daybreak on April 11, the convoy was joined by British destroyers as it entered the Irish Sea. About 8:30 A.M., the bubbling wake of a torpedo passed just fifty feet ahead of the *Carmania*'s bow, followed almost immediately by an explosion at the stern of the *King Alfred*. Destroyers put on speed and began to drop depth bombs. *King Alfred* took on water, but was able to limp into port at Londonderry, Ireland. Now on a constant state of alert after that close call, the advance guard of the Seventy-seventh Division steamed on and reached Liverpool on the morning of April 12. The first order of business for tired doughboys was to write home, advising wives and girlfriends of a safe arrival in England.[32]

A second convoy departed on April 6, the first anniversary of America's declaration of war. Units were brought up to full strength by transfers from the artillery regiments and two companies from the Depot Brigade stood by to furnish replacements for those who might desert at the last moment. There were no desertions, the historian of the 308th Infantry proudly noting that "the Regiment left without the loss of one man." Louis Ranlett described the last day in Camp Upton: "Squads were detailed to destroy everything not the property of the Government, then remaining in the buildings. Pictures were ruthlessly torn from the walls, books, civilian clothes, boxes, and

Advice given by Miss Information, a popular army columnist:
"Be careful what you put on post-cards you send her, and be extra careful in selecting the post-cards. If you send her one of a cathedral, and then write on it, "Having a fine time, wish you was here," she'll know you're lying. Send her something neutral with a flag on it or something; she'll think its fine. They all do."[33]

packages, valuable or worthless, were all seized and burned, though many a hard word was spoken as the cherished but non-portable stuff perished." Floors were carefully swept, earthen yards raked one last time, and windows nailed shut.[34]

That last night in camp was bitterly cold and soldiers slept on the floor or the bare spring mattresses after having turned in their bedding. Corporal Ranlett remembered that sleep was "impossible" and the hours passed with "frigid slowness." Captain Rainsford found a few of his men drunk, but everyone present. Reveille on April 6 was at 4 A.M. and one of the tired soldiers recalled that "we dug our hip bones out of the hard wood" and assembled in the mess halls to wait. There was nothing to do but talk, sing, or play cards as the hours passed, although some noticed that "the sun never rose more beautiful" than it did that morning. Finally the long-awaited order to march arrived. Suddenly "solemn and serious," men grabbed their packs and marched toward the sunrise and the railroad station. Not yet six weeks in the army, Private George Blowers remembered that each man was allowed seventy-five pounds of baggage, but to him the load "felt like 175 pounds." Captain Rainsford said of those last few hectic hours, "All squads reported full, all material shipped or turned in and credited, and all paper work complete—rather incredible."[35]

Colonel Averill's 308th Infantry boarded three British transports that lay at the North River docks, the First, Second, and Third Battalions going on the *Lapland*, *Cretic*, and *Justicia*, respectively. One soldier wrote that he and his comrades marched "like a file of ants entering its hole, to terminate in a small opening in the

> A sob clings choking in the throat, as file on file sweep by,
>   Between those cheering multitudes, to where the great
>   ships lie;
> The batteries halt, the columns wheel, to clear-toned
>   bugle-call,
>   With shoulders squared and faces front they stand a
>   khaki wall.
> Tears shine on every watcher's cheek, love speaks in every
>   glance;
>   For your dear lad, and my dear lad, are on their way to
>   France.[36]

rivet-pimpled side of the Red Star liner *Lapland*." Major Kenneth Budd, ranking officer on the *Cretic*, found that 2,032 soldiers had been crammed into accommodations designed to hold but 1,500. Over 5,000 crowded aboard the *Justicia*, one of the largest ships then afloat. Everything was a jumble. One officer related that units had been "hopelessly mingled," noting that men from one platoon had been tucked into four different parts of the ship. Immediately upon boarding, each man was given a postcard on which was printed the message, "I have arrived safely overseas." These cards were signed and addressed to family members, then deposited in a box for delivery after the convoy safely reached Europe. By midmorning everyone was stowed aboard and the transports slipped their anchors and began the journey north to Halifax.[37]

As the Coney Island Ferris wheel receded in the distance, soldiers settled down to a routine aboard ship. No lights were permitted and smoking on deck was forbidden after dark, although men could always enjoy fresh air topside during daylight hours. Despite claims that there was "ample accommodation for all in case of accident," a quick survey of the lifeboats on the *Justicia* disclosed that "accommodation" would have to include "swimmers holding to the edge of the rafts," a serious miscalculation indeed. At sunset on April 9, seven ships swung into line behind the United States cruiser *St. Louis* and steamed out of the Halifax harbor. The ships from New York were joined by the *Queen Victoria*, carrying tanned, hardy Australian troops; a ship full of Canadians; and another carrying Chinese coolies. The convoy also included a British auxiliary cruiser. On shore, women and children gathered to wave the Stars and Stripes, while British and American sailors lined the rails of their ships to cheer and wave their hats at the departing troops. Musicians aboard a British battleship tooted out "Over There," then ran up the American flag and played "The Star Spangled Banner." New Yorkers on the *Justicia* responded with "God Save the King." Other bands chimed in with "The Marseillaise" and "The Girl I Left Behind Me," this impromptu concert ending with a Marine band's rendition of "There'll Be a Hot Time in the Old Town Tonight." An officer said of the raucous sendoff, "It was everything we had wanted and missed at New York."[38]

Ship captains offered a reward of one hundred pounds sterling to any man who might spot an enemy submarine. Sharp-eyed sentinels never collected the prize, but they did keep sailors hopping around to check out sightings of floating barrels, boxes, and other flotsam. At one point, the *St. Louis* sprang into action and steamed off to investigate a partially submerged submarine that appeared to be stalking the convoy. Word soon came that the warship had been chasing a whale. Many of the troops became so nauseated by seasickness that they took no interest in the submarine hunt. Men stood for hours along the rails puking their guts out—"feeding the fishes" was their quaint term—until there was nothing left in their stomachs. George Blowers confessed, "I just heaved but could not get anything up," then added, "I had lots of company." Part of the problem was British rations. Michael Shallin complained that "all they kept feeding us was rabbit stew, and, I swear, it still had the fur on it." Shallin was certainly no Anglophile. He would later recall how a British sailor would walk through the ship every morning at 5 A.M., shouting the traditional wakeup call, "Arise, arise, ye sons of the King." The response from seasick New Yorkers was always, "Lie down, lie down, ye son-of-a-bitch!"[39]

Before entering the Irish Sea, seven British destroyers came to provide protection on the last leg of the voyage. Landlubbers who had become used to the lumbering cruiser were amazed by these smaller warships. Captain Rainsford described them as "ducking and dodging through the spume like a school of porpoises," while Captain Miles watched them bobbing up and down "like bits of cork" and "quartering back and forth like bird dogs." One of the upstate New Yorkers remarked, "Boy, could they jump around like hoptoads." Under this vigilant screen of destroyers, the convoy skirted the south coast of Ireland and "many a son and descendant of Erin raised his hat in silent reverence." Although a French merchantman had been torpedoed just fifty miles away, no submarines were sighted. On the evening of April 19, weary men of the Seventy-seventh Division watched with interest as their convoy steamed up the Mersey River and anchored in the harbor at Liverpool, the city itself lying enshrouded by mist. Corporal Ranlett recounted the arrival of the *Lapland*: "Crowded ferries dashed by and we cheered them just as we had cheered the New York ferries two weeks before; we cheered the other ships of our convoy as we passed them; the band played furiously; we cheered every tug and row boat, every floating log or orange peel."[40]

There was no secrecy surrounding the departure of the 153rd Brigade from Camp Upton. The frenzied activity was captured by Delbert Davis, who said, "Every train was crowded beyond capacity; every road brought autos of every description, from the Flivver to the Stutz and its kind. Though it was absolutely forbidden to give out the news that we were about to set sail, it seems as if everyone had confidential information about it, and were there to say the last good-bye. The camp took on the appearance of a great carnival—wives and sweethearts looked their prettiest; mothers and fathers, though serious within, outwardly showed their simple gaiety; and sisters and brothers all joined to make this day a lively and pleasant one for the departing soldiers." As the day wound down, the mood changed from one of carefree happiness to somber reality, when "fathers stoically embraced their boys for the last time; mothers bravely endeavored to withhold their emotion as they clasped them to their bosoms; and wives and sweethearts clinging as they never did before in this their last good-bye."[41]

Except for the artillery regiments, the remainder of the Seventy-seventh Division left camp on April 15 and 16. Disaster struck almost immediately. In the early hours of April 15, a train carrying the Second Battalion of the 305th Infantry derailed. Jolted from a sleepy haze, one rider described the accident: "There was a terrible rumble and a crash and a grinding—and darkness; terrible moaning as someone crawled out from under the pile of seats, packs, rifles, glass and dirt, to strike a match. We were lying on the ceiling of the cars, gazing through the debris up toward the floor. Somebody chopped a hole through the floor, through which we clambered only to find the whole train in the same topsy-turvy condition." Dazed soldiers stumbled out and built bonfires to light the wreckage, discovering that three men had been killed outright and some sixty others injured so badly that they could never rejoin the regiment. That afternoon shaken members of the battalion climbed aboard ship, "looking as if just returning from France, instead of going."[42]

As doughboys marched up gangplanks, every building in lower New York seemed to be filled with yelling spectators waving handkerchiefs, while ships in port boomed out a raucous greeting of whistles, bells, and horns. Despite this public demonstration of support, soldiers were ordered below decks so that German agents would not suspect a troop movement was underway. An officer in the 305th Infantry grumbled about this insane attempt at secrecy, "Oh, well, let's try to get a thrill out of fooling ourselves even though we fool nobody else." The worst part of being confined below deck was a missed opportunity to say good-by to the "Old Girl," whose image adorned their equipment. Since her dedication on October 28, 1886, Lady Liberty had welcomed thousands of these soldiers, as well as the parents of thousands

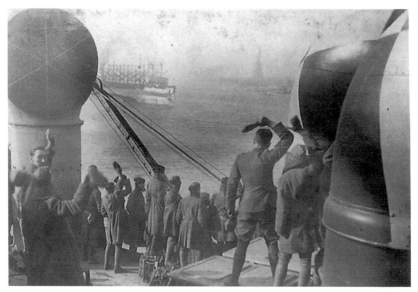

A last glimpse of New York and the Statute of Liberty. From the author's collection.

more, upon their arrival in America. They had come as Lithuanians, Germans, Greeks, Jews, Italians, Slovaks, Moslems, Russians, and any number of other ethnic and religious backgrounds. Now these men were off to fight in France for the freedom that Lady Liberty personified. Ancestry meant nothing. Religious tolerance was the rule. Backgrounds were ignored. Every man was an American soldier, nothing more, nothing less. Men would be judged simply on how they, as individuals, performed at the front. They all shared the same feeling, "wanting so much to prove their courage, hoping that they could face fire unflinchingly, but not knowing. Afraid of being afraid."[43]

Conditions aboard ship on this third convoy of the Seventy-seventh Division were the same as on those preceding—"crowded, rushed, confused, smelly and disagreeable." The *Cedric* crammed four thousand troops into quarters previously used to transport eighteen hundred. The *Karoa* carried over two thousand men in a situation called "worse than the cattle-pens." As before, the Liberty Division ships rendezvoused with a convoy at Halifax, this one escorted by the American cruiser *Philadelphia*. A soldier on the *Kashmir* left his impressions of the voyage: "Everybody turn in their matches. Got 'em in the commissary, though.

Lines waiting for mess. Couldn't eat it when they got it. Fish, more fish. Still more fish. Inspections. Abandon-ship drills. Wish we could abandon ship. No place to go, though. Companies, platoons, squads even, scattered fore and aft. Hammocks to sleep in. No room to turn over. Deck harder, but more comfortable. British sailors. Fresh busboys. Seasickness." There were few diversions, so one colonel innocently ordered a series of games and physical training. His well-intentioned program quickly fell apart since "there was scarcely room enough to take a deep breath, much less fling arms and legs about in the gyrations" of playing and exercising.[44]

Charles Minder best described conditions aboard the *Karoa*. There had been an inauspicious beginning in New York Harbor when one man, "a nut on keeping track of things," reminded his comrades that it had been exactly six years since the *Titanic* sank on her maiden voyage with the loss of over fifteen hundred lives. Nervous soldiers bombarded him with shoes, mess plates and other equipment, threatening to toss him overboard if he didn't shut up. Food was terrible. Beef that should have been roasted was boiled and made into some sort of "a rotten stew," referred to by the charming name of "slum."[45]

Coffee served from large garbage cans turned the stomach, but when "rotten English tea" was substituted, the boys begged for garbage-can coffee. After choking down food that "wasn't fit for dogs," many soldiers ran to the railings and shared it with "Neptune's Minions," despite orders that nothing was to be thrown overboard. Zig-zagging to avoid "Hun undersea craft" compounded the problem. When informed that this was the *Kashmir*'s first trip across the Atlantic, one queasy soldier joked, "Yeah, I could tell she didn't know the way."[47]

> *Everyone knows that there are at least three different kinds of slum—the watered kind, the more solid variety and the occasional special sort that wears a pie-crust. The Marines describe these three types in sea-lingo: "Slum with the tide in," "slum with the tide out," and "slum with an overcoat."*[46]

The most common diversions aboard ship were smoking and card playing. Minder watched the proceedings and told his mother, "The gamblers are still playing poker, black-jack, and banker and broker. This boat is another Yukon gambling dive. The smoke is thick from the fellows smoking and the gamblers wager recklessly." Card players stopped only long enough to eat and sleep. Men unaccountably arose

sleepier than normal each morning, a condition finally explained by
experienced seamen who told the soldiers that their eastward progress
caused the clocks to be moved forward from thirty to forty-five minutes
each day. Despite passing by the watery grave of the *Lusitania* and a
great deal of floating wreckage, there was no real submarine threat to
this third convoy. When land was sighted on April 27, men raced on
deck. Everybody began to shout and PFC Minder admitted, "Surely the
joy of Columbus, when he saw land, had nothing on us." The first
thing they noticed about the port at Liverpool was an immense black
and white sign that read "Spratt's Dog Biscuit." There was much banter
about the strange name and why dog food would warrant such a huge
sign, but these Yanks would soon learn that British hardtack rations
came packed in boxes bearing that very logo.[48]

Five days earlier, in the wee hours of April 22, the artillery had left
Camp Upton. These high-spirited gunners left behind signs nailed to
the barracks that proclaimed, "Summer Home to Let—Owners Gone
to Europe for the Summer," "To Let—Inquire Uncle Sam," and "Good-
by Upton—Will Return in the Spring." They reached the Hoboken
docks and, "amid a flurry of hot coffee and crullers from the Red
Cross," strode up the gangplanks of the *Leviathan*, a monstrous ship
that had formerly been the German *Vaterland*. Like all troop transports, the *Leviathan* used "The Sardine System," leaving soldiers from
Headquarters Company of the 306th Field Artillery "feeling a bit like
a circus on an excursion, with a surplus of monkeys." One disgruntled
passenger described the lodging arrangement as "almost suitable for
tenth-class passengers, though on the whole it would have made a first-
class opium den." Witty men assured their more gullible pals that the
overcrowding was actually for their protection, "the idea being that if
the boat was captured we could be safe because the Germans couldn't
get thru the aisles of our bunks." When one man, possibly one of those
rubes from upstate, first saw the *Leviathan*, he balked at boarding her,
saying that a boat made with so much steel could not possibly stay
afloat. A well-educated buddy calmed his fears by assuring him that
the ship was actually constructed of iron.[49]

The *Leviathan* began its voyage on April 24 and one soldier admitted
"there seemed to be nothing to do on board but eat, sleep, and pray the
Almighty to guide us past submarines." There were about five hundred
nurses on board and, for once, guard duty had its rewards. Privates liked

nothing better than to halt any wayward officer "who sought gallantly to click his spurs before some azure-footed Venus" on the nurse's deck. In honor of the women, band members assembled each night and "ripped out rags and jounced out jazz so that divers nice officers might twitter and flitter and fritter with divers nice nurses on the upper deck." As for the enlisted men, they quickly made friends with a miscellaneous band of Regular Army, National Guard, and drafted replacements. New Yorkers loved them dearly because "they were always willing to swap three cans of smoking tobacco for one can of chewing. Ours was a smoking outfit—theirs was a chewing." After a fairly routine journey of eight days, the *Leviathan*, escorted by a plane and four destroyers, anchored in the harbor at Brest, France. When a small tug came alongside and "a French dignitary with a gold-plated uniform shouted a gallon of unintelligible conversation at the ship through a four-quart megaphone," the Americans stopped throwing cigarettes at French crewmen. Their responses showed the typical enlisted man's respect for authority: "Sure, come on up!" "Where's the war?" "Get an American megaphone, so we can savvy you!" and "Are you French?" With this impertinent flourish, the last of those arrogant Yanks from the Seventy-seventh Division had reached European shores.[50]

3

OVER THERE

Whatever their day of arrival, infantrymen from the Seventy-seventh Division shared the same basic experiences. As brogans clomped onto Liverpool docks (a size 11 ¹/₂ EE "of unfinished leather with half-inch soles filled with hobs, and steel plated heels" weighed seven and one-half pounds!), all shared the same thought, "What a relief to stamp upon old terra firma again!" Falling into ranks, New Yorkers, spearhead of hundreds of thousands of National Army troops who would soon follow, shouldered their packs and barracks bags and headed for the railway trains that would convey them to God only knew where. One soldier quickly learned that "hob nails and cobble stone pavements are rather incompatible," although a bystander was heard to say in admiration, "Gawd blimme but these bloomin' Yanks can march." A hike through the city finally offered sea-weary Americans "something to look at besides one wave after another in an interminable expanse of water," but Liverpool was described by the succinct comment, "Strange clothes. Strange streets. Strange signs." Gotham boys did spot one reminder of America, a Woolworth's 3 & 6 Pence Store, some sort of strange relative of the five-and-dime back home. At the station, ladies from the Women's Auxiliary Army Corps sold ginger buns and hot coffee to hungry and tired soldiers. When informed that the cost would be "tuppence, ha' penny," dumbfounded Yanks just stared stupidly. The ladies had no idea how much money that would be in American currency, but they soon settled on an exchange rate of one nickel being equal to the strange-sounding tuppence, ha' penny. Michael Shallin heard one old lady ask, "Did ye come over to die?" The proud young warrior responded, "Well, lady, I hope not, not if I can help it." Shallin's friends erupted in laughter, as the old lady quickly said, "No, no, what I mean is, did ye just arrive."[1]

Trains waiting for the Seventy-seventh Division prompted a torrent of ridicule. One American said they "resembled toys at Coney Island more than means of transportation," another laughed at "the absurd little freight cars," while a third described how "the brightly painted green engines about the size of a Ford runabout certainly looked queer to men who had ridden in man size trains all their lives." Passenger cars were divided into five compartments, each holding eight men, with doors on the sides, "not at the end, like the American trains are." Troop trains took a variety of routes as they ferried the Americans toward embarkation ports on the English Channel, and the countryside boasted picturesque stone houses, each one surrounded by hedges and luxurious meadows. The Yanks had left Camp Upton at the tail end of winter, with everything brown and depressing. Two weeks later, they landed in England among "the luxuriant evidences of spring." Flowers bloomed everywhere. Apple, cherry, and pear trees filled the air with scented blossoms. Well-tended hedges lined both sides of railroad tracks that were kept "scrupulously clean." One machine gunner, used to the gritty rail yards in America, said in wonderment, "There is no junk alongside the tracks in this country."[2]

Trains headed southeast, stopping occasionally for water and coal. At one stop in Rugby, Charles Minder received a cup of hot coffee from a British Red Cross woman and said simply, "It was a life-saver." Captain Rainsford remembered that the journey was "bitterly cold," the only bright spots being "an unusually pretty girl" handing out coffee and a bright sunrise that revealed a landscape "white with hoar-forst and cherry-blossoms." Captain Miles wrote that at Rugby each man was given "a cup of weak, sugarless tea and a fish sandwich," a poor meal by any standard. As one train pulled into the Leicester station, a soldier threw a penny toward a young boy standing on the platform, starting "one of the biggest scrambles in modern times." Sensing an opportunity for some fun, men amused themselves by tossing pennies

and nickels into a tangled mob of shouting children until ordered out
of the cars for their first cup of English "war coffee," some sort of weak
and terrible-tasting liquid that was coffee in name only.[3]

Trains generally passed through the London suburbs, but a few
followed a route directly through the city, where thousands of women
and girls, many dressed in black, watched silently from tenement
windows. Other women, strangely dressed in overalls and bloomers,
left their places in munitions factories to watch the Yanks, who waved
small American flags from the car windows. Children cheered from
backyards. Southeast of London, the troop trains began to meet hospital
trains, carload after carload filled with wounded soldiers whose
bandages covered gruesome wounds. Upon reaching the towns of
Dover and Folkestone, soldiers marched to camps on the famous cliffs
overlooking the English Channel. One well-read officer admitted, "From
the appearance of the low rambling houses silhouetted against the sky
and the narrow crooked streets, one almost expected to see Oliver
Twist saunter out of a doorway and bid the Division welcome." After
a good night's sleep, they awoke next morning to the sight of seagulls
skimming over the glistening water, the feel of a salt-tinged wind, and
the sound of British soldiers marching to band music. There were more
troops than transports, so some of the luckier Americans were cut
loose and allowed to sightsee in the city. Residents seemed genuinely
pleased to meet the "the Sammies," those tough-talking nephews of
Old Uncle Sam.[4]

After baths, a few meals of tea, jam, and cheese, and some much-
needed sleep, New Yorkers marched down to the docks for transport
to the continent. French authorities had learned of the imminent
arrival of the Liberty Boys and naturally assumed that, since this was
the first sizeable force of United States troops bound for Calais, General
Pershing would be with them. A gala reception had been planned,
complete with a band that tried its damnedest to play "The National
Anthem," but a greeting from some British Tommies at the French
docks was less cordial. They took one look at men green with seasickness from the Channel crossing and asked, "I sye, are you going to the
war? Why, you're half dead now!" Trains of ambulances rolled down
with their loads to fill the now empty steamers. Greetings and cigarettes
were exchanged by veterans and rookies. One of the 306th Infantry
recalled the scene: "A salute—with the left hand from necessity. A

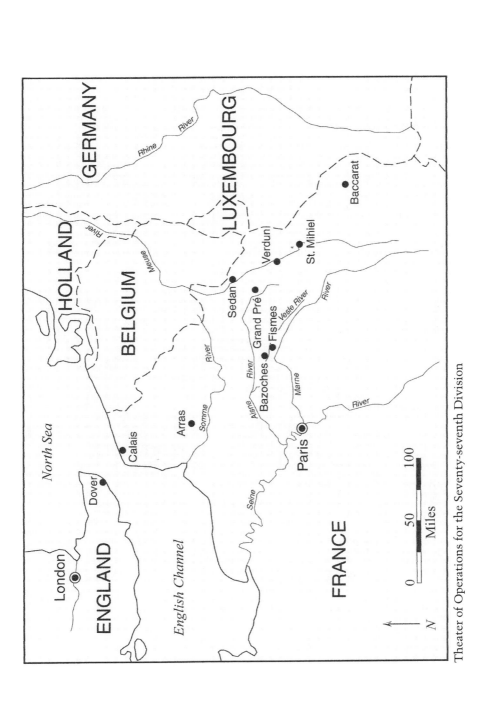

Theater of Operations for the Seventy-seventh Division

British Tommy, with both arms gone and blanket sagging suggestively where one leg should have bulged, laughed at his own joke. They were going home. What did anything else matter."[5]

One of the most urgent problems facing the newly arrived Americans was to figure out just what to call everyone. At first, the British greeted the New Yorkers as either "Sammies," close relatives of Uncle Sam, or "Teddies," in honor of former President Roosevelt. Americans preferred the term "doughboys," an expression for United States infantry that had gained popularity either during the Mexican War or the Civil War, depending upon which story one believed. The Allies soon began to use that word exclusively. A British soldier was a "Tommy" or a "Tommy Atkins," a name taken many years before from sample enlistment forms. As for the French, they called themselves *poilu*, from the word for hair, a sort of macho slap on the back. The Tommies, and Americans too, disparagingly called them "Frogs."[6]

German troops had a multitude of nicknames. Early in the war they were often called "Fritz" because so many men had that first name. Some called them "Squareheads" because the typical Teutonic skull was of that shape. "Hun" was used to express disgust, especially after the world press began to document alleged atrocities against civilians in occupied territories. Canadians and Americans often used "Heine" or "Hiney" to describe their enemy, apparently because the former was a common German surname. "Jerry" became popular late in the war, although there is only speculation over its origin. French soldiers referred to the Germans as "Boche" or "Boches," the name coming from a slang word for "chump." Since the Seventy-seventh Division spent so much time in French sectors, Americans picked up this latter term and used it extensively.[7]

Buildings along the waterfront at Calais had been bombed so often by Boche airmen that they stood mute and empty, windowless relics of the war. George Blowers said that, at first glance, the city appeared to be some sort of ghost town, the only inhabitants being "old people and small children." Swarms of "tenacious urchins" followed the Americans everywhere, offering to sell candy or cakes and constantly crying out, "Penny, penn–ee!" Soldiers from America gaped at the rainbow of uniforms worn in the streets by soldiers from France, Scotland, Belgium, England, Morocco, Canada, Algeria, Australia, Italy, Serbia, and New Zealand. German prisoners carried stretchers and worked on the roads, smiling at the new arrivals from America. Charles Chavelle grumbled, "They're the happiest-looking guys I've seen since I left New York. Never saw a better-fed looking bunch of fellows before. Nothing for them to worry about." Chinamen, whose filthy dress "would have made Gunga Din look like Beau Brummel," sat "chattering, gibbering, howling, grinning" at the Americans. Some sauntered right up to the Yanks and, in their strange lingo, shouted "Melicans très bon," their impassioned greeting always being rewarded by a cigarette. There were so many coolies hanging about town that doughboys joked they must be close to a chop suey factory. Men who had never gone more than a few miles from Broadway and 42nd Street now found themselves plunked down in a strange land thousands of miles from home. In typical American fashion, New Yorkers collectively struck a pose and remarked, "Say, where the Hell is all this trouble, anyway?"[8]

American troops had reached France just in time. A tremendous German spring offensive had rocked the British Army to its very foundation, pushing it backwards toward the vital channel ports. Artillery fire from the front could be plainly heard at Calais and to some the Kaiser's army "seemed to be almost within speaking distance." The ports must be held so that men and munitions could continue to flow unimpeded from England. America had almost 1,500,000 soldiers in training, but it would take too long for them to be shipped overseas. Britain had agreed to transport American troops to Europe, but in return had demanded that American divisions be assigned to the British Army for training and possible deployment in case of emergency. Such a critical emergency now existed and the Allies desperately needed the Seventy-seventh Division. One author summed up the urgent situation with little exaggeration when he said, "The destiny of the Anglo-Saxon nations rested upon the strength of the National Army of the United States—man-power superabundant but of quality yet unknown." How would these subway guards, clerks, sign painters, plumbers, poets, waiters, and garment workers perform in "The Vital Untried Experiment" of throwing a division of drafted men into battle? In the false bravado of Frederick Palmer, at least "they ought not to be alarmed by shell fire after having survived New York traffic."[9]

General Pershing approved a temporary transfer of the Seventy-seventh Division to British control and its units, minus the artillery regiments that had been assigned to a French artillery school, marched to Rest Camp No. 6 on the outskirts of Calais. Delbert Davis wrote

**American definition of A. E. F.—
After England Failed.**[10]

that the camp "consisted mainly of tents, sand, mud and stew and English soldiers who had passed through terrible experiences at the front and wanted to tell us about them." Here the Americans had another steady British diet of jam, tea, bread, meat, and cheese, all sprinkled liberally with sand that blew into and onto everything from nearby dunes. When the 305th Machine Gun Battalion sat down for its first chow in camp, a British officer entered the mess hall, proudly announced that after the meal there would be dessert, then directed the men to "Carry on!" Henry Smith explained what happened next: "From one quarter it was 'After this there will be beer, Carry on!' From another quarter, 'After this there will be Champagne, Carry on!' and numerous others." Amid the uproar, the embarrassed officer quietly retreated out the back door.[11]

Within hours of reaching Rest Camp No. 6, regiments of the Seventy-seventh Division marched back to Calais, where they exchanged their Springfield rifles for British Enfields. When puzzled doughboys asked why, they were told simply, "The Boche has broken through, and the Seventy-seventh is to fill the gap." A march back to the rest camp was followed by another hike to a supply depot where gas masks were issued. Henry Smith approvingly described the process: "Entering a large tent, an English soldier, who seemed to be somewhat of an expert at judging the faces, shouted out the mask sizes. It was number four, number two, number three as fast as the men filed in and, with few exceptions, he seemed to hit it right off." They were then herded into a large building with sealed windows and gas was released so the men could get used to breathing through the mouthpiece under battle conditions. After emerging from the gas building, soldiers were given a small whiff of phosgene and mustard gas, the most lethal in the German gas arsenal. A British sergeant ended one exercise with the words: "These are all good masks. Every one of 'em's seen service. The fellows who 'ad 'em all went west some wye or t'other, and now they've been fixed up for you uns." It was sobering for a soldier to realize that his newly issued gas mask had formerly been used by a dead man.[12]

Troops then marched to the "hat shop," where they each exchanged a wool cap for a steel helmet, one of the most versatile pieces of equipment imaginable. It shed water like a roof, acted as a chair in the mud, and could be instantly turned into a candlestick in the dark. A helmet could even turn aside the occasional piece of shrapnel. After an eight-kilometer hike back to camp, soldiers dozed off under recycled blankets, stained by blood and stinking with delousing solution.[13]

There was little sleep at night. Sirens would jolt men from slumber, warning them that a German air raid had begun and everyone must take shelter. Americans responded in their typical reckless manner, crawling out from under blankets and wandering outside to watch the show. One of them re-

Me and my two thin blankets
  As thin as my last thin dime.
As thin, I guess, as a chorus girl's dress,
  Well, I had a dandy time.
I'd pull 'em up from the bottom,
  Whenever I started to sneeze,
A couple of yanks to cover my shanks,
  And then how my "dogs" did freeze.[14]

called, "Numerous searchlights played about the moonlit skies. Soon they discovered a Jerry plane and, Wow! it seemed that a veritable hell broke loose. 'Archies' [anti-aircraft guns] and machine guns opened up until the din was terrible." High above could be heard the "characteristic fluctuating drone" of German bombers, the warplanes sounding to one observer like "the drowsy hum of swarming bees." Eluding flashing searchlights and bursting Archie shells, aviators dropped their explosives on Calais and turned for home. By now most of the Americans had taken shelter, not from fear of falling bombs, but to avoid pieces of shrapnel and stray bullets that came raining down after missing their mark. Considering the loss of sleep, long marches to receive new equipment, and lousy British rations at Rest Camp 6, it was little wonder that soldiers complained, "All we rested at that camp were our stomachs."[15]

After a couple of days at Calais, units were ordered on into the countryside of Pas-de-Calais where division headquarters had been established at Eperlecques, regiments and battalions being assigned to neighboring villages. There was a short march to the rail station, moving columns shadowed by crowds of children clambering for coins thrown by grinning doughboys. Small girls came forward with tiny bouquets of spring flowers, but the boys wanted cigarettes. "Mais tu es bien trop petit (You are much too little)," said an officer to one pestering youngster. The kid simply grinned and replied, "C'est pour mon pere (It's for my father)!" Soldiers finally eluded the swarms of children and entrained on quaint little boxcars that bore the markings

"*Hommes 40, Chevaux 8*," meaning they were meant to carry either forty men or eight horses. Americans were new to this war thing and scrupulously followed the rules, diligently loading exactly forty men into each car. Following a few such trips, transportation officers learned to ask for more boxcars so that only thirty men would be assigned to each. But for now, a machine gunner grumbled, "Unfortunately we were 'hommes,' so we were crowded." Charles Minder said he "felt like a hobo" riding in a boxcar, but many New Yorkers seemed right at home "standing in a real subway jam."[16]

A hard winter and late spring at Camp Upton, followed by the voyage overseas, had softened muscles and the march to assigned billets was hard on everyone. Charles Minder remembered it as "a terrible hike" along a never-ending road lined with stately poplar trees, although the otherwise delightful view now held no fascination. He explained, "I was suffering too much to enjoy any trees or scenery. The perspiration just streamed from me. My legs and back pained terribly, especially my shoulders where the straps of the pack were. Everybody suffered and the heat made us more miserable."[17]

Soldiers had looked forward to their billets, some of which had been "so vividly pictured in some recent magazine articles, attractive little French cottages, with *Monsieur* and *Madame* welcoming us with open arms." To their dismay, billets usually turned out to be "old barns with dirt floors, daylight streaming in through the roofs, and holes in the walls for windows." Chickens, rats, the ever-present manure piles, and limited washing facilities added to the depressing scene. All the soldiers had rat stories. One doughboy awoke to find a rat sitting on his foot. After

Doughboy from 305th Infantry on his first night in French billets:
"'For the love o' Mike.' I said, 'get over on your own side and let me sleep.' I struck a match and found, to my great surprise, that my partner was a two hundred pound porker. Sleeping with hogs was no game for me, so I grabbed my blankets and straggled into another part of the barn."[18]

they exchanged stares, the soldier suddenly kicked his foot, sending the rat flying through the air. But the rodent landed squarely on the man's chest, setting off a mad rush as that brave New York hero scrambled to get out of the building. In another barn, a large member of the genus *Rattus* fell from a wire directly onto the face of a man who was closely watching the rodent's circus performance. He instinctively screamed, grabbed its tail, and flung the animal onto a sleeping comrade, who jumped up and pitched the rat at yet a third man who took a swipe at the rat with his bayonet, but missed. The rat escaped. There was a Jewish fellow in Company G, 308th Infantry who was deathly afraid of rats. Whenever he dozed off, some buddy would invariably reach over and run the tip of a bayonet up the sleeper's leg. Awakening to the sensation of a rat crawling on his pants, the frightened man would always bolt up screaming and race for the doorway, as friends snickered their approval of the joke.[19]

Training for the Seventy-seventh Division would initially be conducted by officers and noncoms of the Thirty-ninth British Division, Brigadier General Wyeth commanding, which had been frightfully cut up while blunting the German offensive only a few weeks earlier. After a short period with Wyeth's survivors, the division would be split up and assigned for advanced training to either the Second or Forty-second British Divisions in what was called "a very reserve position." Americans quickly learned to hate British food even more than they hated the Germans. Rations aboard ship and at Rest Camp No. 6 had been but a precursor of the nastiness of British cuisine. Hardtack, a slice of bacon, and cold tea was a typical meal, with cheese added for "a real spread." Dessert was jam (either apple or plum, no exceptions!) on a soda cracker. Corned willy, also known as monkey meat, and gold fish (canned corned beef and salmon) made their first appearance here, their taste being acceptable at first due to the sheer novelty of the fare. But an overfamiliarity with these rations would soon breed contempt for them.[20]

Gas training was intensified. Phosgene and mustard gas were again whiffed, along with lachrymatory (tear) gas, the latter smelling a little like new-mown hay. At one point, British officers took a battalion out to experience a "cloud gas attack." Gas was released upwind, but, much to the chagrin of the instructors, the Yanks simply walked out of the way and allowed the gas cloud to drift by harmlessly. On another occasion, General Wyeth stopped to see how General Johnson's Yanks were doing with their gas training. When assured by Johnson that the men had been thoroughly instructed, Wyeth tried a practical demonstration. He screamed out "Gas!" at a passing doughboy from the Liberty Division. The soldier stopped and stared. General Wyeth yelled "Gas!" again in an even louder tone. The soldier made no move to put on his mask and continued to stare. Wyeth cried out, "Don't you know enough to put on your mask when you hear that warning?" The irritated general was then treated to an old Camp Upton dodge, when the man responded, "Me no speak-a da Eenglis."

The King's English was beyond the grasp of most Americans. George Blowers complained that "you could hardly understand their brogue," while an ambulance man said it was "a fallacy" that men from the two countries shared a common language. He explained that "the fellows had just as much difficulty understanding the English as they did the French, and in many cases it was much easier to make one's desires known to the Frenchman."[21]

Hungry soldiers sought to supplement their monotonous rations by contacting local farmers, language difficulties being overcome by a liberal use of pocket dictionaries and exaggerated gestures. *Oeufs, pommes de terre, vin blanc* and *vin rouge* were often intoned and in great demand, prices rising as Frenchmen learned that Yanks earned the fabulous sum of $1.10 a day. George Blowers found that he could buy a glass of beer (some said the beverage tasted more like rain) for three cents, but "they sold out right away and when they got some more, up went the price." After a brief exposure to the tuppence, ha' penny monetary scale in England, soldiers now had to learn the exchange rate for francs and centimes. One pair of pals, who had ordered two bottles of wine and two meals, was astounded to find that the tab totaled only fifty cents. Many men discovered that white wine, red wine, and champagne were cheaper than food and drank supper, returning to their billets, where they "drove out the chickens and pigs, and slept soundly."[22]

The Seventy-seventh Division spent about six weeks in the British sector. Captain Rainsford looked back on that time as "probably the pleasantest in the army experience of any, theretofore or thereafter." He said that "the country was beautiful, the weather immaculate, the training systematic" and confessed that "there was little to mar the tranquillity of the summer days." Of course, being an officer, Rainsford had a different perspective than the enlisted men. British and American officers bonded quite nicely, the former hosting elegant banquets, complete with gourmet food, vintage wines, and musical entertainment. Captain Miles recalled the thrill of hearing bagpipes from the Highland Light Infantry whenever Scottish officers sat down for a glass of port wine. There were even baseball games and, when General Sully-Flood actually hit a home run, everyone declared that the mighty blow "was almost as good as an Allied victory." Above all else, Captain Rainsford remembered the "painstakingly kindliness of the British officers."[23]

Officers and noncoms took short trips to the front south of Arras, where they inspected trenches and dodged an occasional sniper's bullet or shell from a *minenwerfer* (trench mortar). There the observers got their first glimpse of The Front, "an area pitted with shell holes, scarred by rotting tangles of wire, broken gun carriages, cannon, broken down tanks, bewildering mazes of disused and new trenches, battered chateau, wrecked roads and villages, forests then nothing more than a flock of stark, withered skeletons." It was a sobering sight. Sergeant Harold Kaplan of Company E, 308th Infantry, liked this taste of danger so much that he went AWOL for several days so he could remain under fire with the Tommies. Lieutenant Paul Knight received a slight wound on one such visit. Everyone seemed to be amazed by the constant shelling and "the tremendous amount of noise and metal required to kill a man." However, it was the British attitude that made the greatest impression. Whether officer or enlisted man, the British always appeared to treat the war "as a huge sport and went to it like big game hunters." But above all else, Americans noticed that the British Army observed its daily tea ritual precisely at four each afternoon, no matter how hot the shelling.[25]

One enlisted man recalled his time with the British as being devoted "to grub away in the earth, learning how to ply the festive pick and shovel on a trench system; how to throw live grenades, how to shoot, how to play games for which the British are very strong, and how to wield the bayonet." During bayonet drill, an overly enthusiastic soldier lunged at an imaginary foe, but lost his footing and fell into the target. A patient Tommy sergeant observed, "Fine spirit, but go slaow, there,

Popular refrain shared by British and American officers:
Now I, friend, drink to thee, friend,
As my friend drank to me,
And as my friend charged me, friend,
So I, friend, charge thee.

That thou, friend, drink to thy friend,
As my friend drank to me,
And the more we drink together
The merrier we'll be.[24]

British bayonet instructor:
"In the crotch, in the crotch. If you come at 'im from underneath, you'll stop 'im for sure. And I'll tell yah bloody Yanks another thing, if the Boche comes out with 'is 'ands up yelling 'Komerad,' give 'im the bayonet in 'is bloody balls."[26]

go slaow. Ye'll win the Victoria Cross that wy, hal-right, but yer mother'll wear it."[27]

While engaged in training near the heavily traveled Arras road, Private Stanley Belen was killed by a shell from long-range German artillery and Private George Schiesser was seriously wounded; both belonged to Company I, 308th Infantry. Colonel Averill noted the event in general orders, a nicety that would be ignored once casualties became more common. Being the target for enemy artillery fire was a new experience and Captain Miles admitted that "no one forgot that first crashing detonation, at once so sharp and loud, and the great geyser of earth and debris which spouted up into a gigantic mushroom of smoke and then drifted slowly off." Other men in the 308th Infantry lost their lives in less glamorous ways. Private Alfred Ferguson died from anthrax, one of many dozens of soldiers in the AEF to succumb to that dread disease. An investigation would later disclose that nearly all of this mortality resulted from infected bristles on shaving brushes.[28]

Even though the Liberty Division had not yet been to the front, casualties continued to mount. Tragedy struck Company B, 305th Infantry on June 3. This company was out drilling when a French soldier salvaging unexploded shells happened to drop one. He was blown to bits and fragments from the missile tore into the ranks of Company B, killing fifteen and wounding almost forty more. When this long list of casualties reached New York, home folks assumed that the Liberty Boys were already in combat. German bombers also continued their midnight raids. After one failed attack on a nearby ammunition dump, George Blowers commented dryly, "I heard one of his bombs killed a cow." Other air raids were more productive. Corporal James Hamilton became the first man wounded in Company E, 308th Infantry when he was struck by a scrap of bomb. On another occasion, eight men were killed and wounded when another bomb struck near division headquarters at Eperlecques.[29]

Doughboys saw constant streams of ambulances heading to the rear with their loads of human woe. Charles Minder began to lose his enthusiasm for war in the face of such sights. He confessed to his mother, "I have no desire to harm anyone, I don't want to kill. I am being forced to do something against my will, that's what bothers me. They may be our enemies but I know that many of them are being forced to kill, just as I am." Minder then pointed the finger of blame at those in the military establishment who ran the show, "It's the blooming militaristic crowd that they ought to make fight if they are so bloodthirsty. They never come near the battle fronts, they force the civilians to kill each other." He likened his own sense of horror to that of livestock he used to see lined up at the slaughterhouses at First Avenue and Forty-fifth Street, where "they saw the other animals hanging up around the place being cut open and skinned." In one letter, a despondent Minder asked, "Is this evil force, War, more powerful than God?"[30]

On May 10, General Johnson resumed his permanent post as commander of the 154th Brigade and Major General George B. Duncan took over command of the Liberty Division. A Kentuckian and West Point graduate, Duncan had served in Cuba, Puerto Rico, and the Philippines during the Spanish-American War, the only American officer to fight on all three fronts. A graduate of the Army War College and former member of the General Staff, Duncan had commanded the Twenty-sixth Infantry when the First Division reached France in June of 1917. He participated in the 1917 Verdun offensive and was the first American officer to receive a Croix de Guerre from the French government after the United States entered the war. General Duncan was still getting acquainted with his new command when, on June 4, it appeared that he might be out of a job. Orders arrived announcing that the Seventy-seventh Division would be broken up and assigned to British brigades. Only platoons would remain intact when the Americans were consolidated into British units. But General Pershing came to the rescue, arguing that American troops should fight only under American commanders. Pershing won his point with the Allied high command only twenty-four hours before the division was to be absorbed into the British ranks. Two days later, freed from British domination, Yanks traded in their Enfields for their own beloved Springfields, exchanged their other equipment, and marched away from the British sector, bidding the Tommies a final "Cheerio!"[31]

The Yanks took with them a constant reminder of their time spent in billets behind the British front. Lice. Cooties. Seam squirrels. Shirt rabbits. Squads had gradually taken on the appearance of apes grooming themselves in a zoo. At times it seemed that hundreds of men were sitting around and reading their shirts. Bathing became popular. Boiling the uniforms failed to get rid of the pests and a current joke was that next time soldiers were to be boiled as well. Medical officers issued little sacks of repellent to suspend from the neck, but sufferers soon discovered that "the little gray fellows seemed to grow fat on it."[32]

Wrap both your elbows up around your neck
And scratch, scratch, scratch!
Don't stop a second—if you do, by heck,
Your troubles start to hatch.

What's the use of sulphur salve?
It never was worth much;
So wrap both your elbows around your neck
And scratch, scratch, scratch![33]

There were also impressions of the French people. It seemed to rain three-fourths of the time behind the Arras front, so Liberty Boys naturally assumed that was why French soldiers were called "Frogs." In their off-duty time, soldiers scoured village shops for funny postcards to send home, being sure to avoid those with names and pictures that would give information to German spies. George Blowers told how shoppers often found more than they expected: "While we were looking, the madam would bring out cards from under the counter with pictures of naked women and all sexy pictures and asked us if they were '*bon*' (good) and we would say '*oui*' (yes). Some of the fellows would buy them and carry them around in their pockets. Before we left France to go home, we were searched to make certain we were not carrying anything like that to the United States as it was a criminal offense in the States at that time." Youngsters were fascinated by the *soldats Americana* and followed them everywhere. When doughboys marched into new territory and wondered if other Americans had been there before them, they simply asked the kids. They would immediately start talking about "American sons of bitches this" and "American son of bitches that," leaving nothing to the imagination. It was obvious that the youth of France had picked up more than American pennies.[34]

The Liberty Boys laughed and joked as they marched away from their reserve positions behind Arras. No more monotonous apple and plum jam! No more British tea! No more stinking cheese! No more "Cheerio, carry on, Yanks!" No more British cigarettes with their silly names—Ruby Queens, Bee's Wings, Gold Flakes, Woodbines, Red Hussars, Wild Rose, and Three Castles! Good-by to hideous mutton stew! Hello to good old American beef, bacon, potatoes, Chesterfields, Lucky Strikes, and Camels! All relations with the British Army were to be forever severed and life was again glorious for soldiers of the

National Army. Tommies rejoiced at the Yanks' departure, as well. Whenever the Americans moved, they left behind treasure beyond comprehension to European soldiers—toilet sets, fancy razors, sweaters, socks, underwear, and sewing gear. Britishers rummaged to their heart's content through the surplus that Yanks pitched out.[35]

There were long marches from the rat-infested billets along roads cleverly concealed by canvas and burlap camouflage. Everything started well, with each unit occupying its proper interval and fresh men lustily singing marching tunes, such as this old favorite:

> Lulu took the farmer's horse and team
> To drive to the country store,
> But she eloped with the old studhorse
> And won't come back no more!
>> Bang, bang Lulu.
>> Bang her good and strong.
>> What'll we do for banging
>> When Lulu's dead and gone?[36]

Fifty minutes of marching, ten minutes for rest every hour, left men wobbling along on blistered feet, asking the unanswerable question, "Gawd, how much further have we got to go?" Joking had long since ceased and one soldier admitted that "what the boys thought about the army at that time was unfit for publication." Everyone agreed with the wisdom of a doughboy who observed, "One feature of the French kilometer is that you not only kill a meter, but also kill yourself, particularly when you've got this pack on your back." There was nothing to do but grind out the kilometers, "eyes becoming fixed on the rhythmic rise and fall of the hob-nailed shoes of the man ahead."[37]

After reaching the nearest railroad stations, weary men climbed aboard the 40/8 Pullman cars and cuddled together in pretzel shapes with stinking comrades for a pleasant journey to yet another unknown destination. Those lucky enough to embark at Longpre discovered a genuine YMCA canteen stocked with American cigarettes, tobacco, biscuits, and chocolate. Samuel Shookhoff remembered, "We bought as much as the law allowed and then hit the line for seconds." Trains headed west and south, passing through the cities of Amiens and Forges-les-Eaoux, then turning southeast on a broad sweep past Paris and through Versailles, Toul, and Nancy. Passing through one tiny village, a soldier with a map announced that it must be Sens. Another naïve doughboy, probably one of those hicks from upstate, said no, the sign on the depot read "Hommes." A third spoke up, "Hommes, you nut! That's the toilet sign. There's one on every station. Where have you been all these years?" Gradually, news leaked out that the division had been ordered to the Lorraine front. It was a miserable, cramped train ride of three days and three nights. Hungry soldiers went foraging at Neuvelle St. George during one extended halt and returned with fresh bread, sardines, liverwurst, and bologna. Hot water from the engine's boiler allowed men to wash and shave before sitting down to a picnic lunch. There were pretty women to be seen (by now most women were starting to look especially beautiful) and, occasionally, kissed if they were willing.[38]

Here's to the girls who will,
And here's to the girls who won't
And here's to the girls who say they will
And then you find they won't.
But of all the girls I've met
I'm sure you'll say I'm right
The girls I like the very best
Are those who say they won't
And look as though they might.[39]

On the down side, soldiers discovered that French farmers were more than willing to fill canteens with cold water, but only for a price. Michael Shallin complained that "all these jerkwater towns would up their prices when we'd pass through," then admitted, "There's nothing a New Yorker hates any more than having a rube take him for a ride."[40]

Unknown to men on the trains, New York's Own had been ordered into the front lines, the first National Army division to take up such a position. It would be a great test to determine whether this motley throng of draftees had indeed been transformed into soldiers capable of holding their own against the iron will of a mighty German war machine. Officers would now lead soldiers in combat. Mistakes would get men killed. But first there were a few days of rest, the Liberty Boys being billeted in and around the town of Rambervillers, which acted as division headquarters. Over the period from June 16 to 26, General Duncan's Camp Upton boys relieved the Forty-second "Rainbow" Division, so-called because it was made up of National Guard units from all across the country.[41]

Division headquarters moved to Baccarat, a pleasant city on the Meurthe River that was famous for its fine crystal and lacework. Front lines in the Baccarat Sector were only a few miles from the Alsatian border and had been relatively stable for almost four years. The city had been overrun by the Germans in 1914, but they had been thrown out almost immediately and the French retained control, although about one-third of the buildings had been destroyed. Villages closer to the front, such as Badonviller, Montigny, and Herbeviller, had been quite demolished by artillery fire. Badonviller, in the regimental sector assigned to the 308th Infantry, had once been as famous for its pottery as Baccarat had been for its crystal. Now it was a hollow shell of a town, only some half-dozen houses still standing and the streets littered with barricades of brush and cement.[42]

Even though roads and trenches had been camouflaged by strips of canvas and burlap, all military movements were conducted under the cloak of darkness to conceal them from observation. Colonel Averill led the 308th Infantry up to the front in an inky blackness on the night of June 18–19. Shadowy columns of soldiers shuffled by one another along the strangely dusty roads, some heading for the front and others marching to the rear. Suddenly the Liberty Boys met up with hundreds of other New Yorkers, men from the old Sixty-ninth Regiment, now the 165th Infantry, serving in the Rainbow Division. Completely contrary to orders that absolute silence be maintained, soldiers began to yell at one another. Some veteran would shout, "Look out for the Heinies or you'll be eating sauerkraut in a prison camp!" A Liberty Boy would quickly retort, "We're going up to finish the job that you fellows couldn't do!" Rookies would exclaim, "The Germans will find out what American soldiers are like when we get a crack at them!" Someone from the Sixty-ninth would counter, "What are you givin' us, we was over here killin' Dutchmen before they pulled your names out of the hat!" A Camp Upton veteran would then yell, "At least we didn't have to get drunk to join the army!" This verbal sparring, often good-natured but occasionally with a sharp edge, continued to escalate.[43]

As moonlight dimly outlined these two moving columns, questions were thrown back and forth. "Anybody there from Greenwich Village?" "How are things in New York?" "Any of you guys from Tremont?" "Is Fat O'Dea there?" "Lower East Side?" "Brooklyn?" Men called out for friends and relatives. When somebody asked, "Is John Kelly there?" dozens of doughboys asked with a laugh, "Which one?" One young man from the Liberty Division somehow managed to locate a brother among the shuffling multitude in the Rainbow column. Although burdened by their packs and field gear, the two hugged one another awkwardly. Apparently overcome by this unexpected encounter, the siblings exchanged brotherly punches and a few thoughtful curses until ordered back to the ranks. No one ever knew who first started up the refrain, but, almost instantly, miles of roadway erupted into song. Father Francis P. Duffy, chaplain of the old Sixty-ninth, listened to this impromptu midnight serenade as thousands upon thousands of New York soldiers, sharing a chance reunion far from home, burst out with their favorite tune:

> East side, West side, all around the town,
> The tots sang "ring-around-rosie, London Bridge is falling down."
> Boys and girls together, me and Mamie O'Rourke,
> We tripped the light fantastic on the sidewalks of New York!

As Father Duffy passed around a bend and lost sight of the Liberty Division, he could still hear them, off-key but lustily enthusiastic, bellowing out, *"Herald Square, Anywhere, New York Town, Take me there!!"* The two divisions marched on their separate ways toward future battlefields, leaving the padre to murmur a silent prayer for the newcomers: "Good lads, God bless them, I hope their wish comes true."[44]

4

BACCARAT AND THE VESLE

Captain W. Kerr Rainsford detailed the sights that greeted New Yorkers upon their arrival at the Baccarat front: "In places the woods had been blown to pieces with artillery fire, and in places the meadows were pitted with craters of sun-cracked clay. One particular stretch of open marsh, near some abandoned artillery emplacements on the Line of Resistance, had been churned up into something like the surface of a sponge, and still, on misty nights, reeked with the sickish acid smell of gas. The white dusty roads were lined with dilapidated festoons of burlap, or screens of wilted and dust-covered rushes—to shelter from observation such traffic as must pass." Rainsford further observed that "little half-ruined villages of roofless walls and tumbled masonry, like empty sea shells upon some desolate coast, lined the high-water mark of early invasion—and in the center of each rose the skeleton of some beautiful old church, its tower pierced with shell-holes and its entrance blocked by the fallen chimes."[1]

Since these Americans were new to the war, the Allied high command decided that the Liberty Boys would hold their positions jointly with the Sixty-first and Sixty-second French Divisions so veterans could show the new men how to defend a section of front, a plan that had apparently been conceived by some bozo at regimental headquarters with scrambled eggs for brains. In reality, few officers and almost none

of the enlisted men could speak French, leaving those "whispered consultations in No Man's Land somewhat unfruitful of result." Machine
gunners had an additional problem. Having switched to the air-cooled
Hotchkiss machine gun after leaving the British sector, gunners found
that all manuals had been written in French and were thus completely
useless. Guns were disassembled "to find out what made the wheels
go round and what made it tick," individual parts being given American
names that seemed to identify their size, shape, and purpose. For his
part, the average French soldier appeared content to occupy his quiet
corner of the front and was "terror-stricken" that impulsive Americans
would initiate some sort of ruckus that might get him killed. That same
laid-back attitude was also shared by civilians. A watchful sentinel at
an outpost closest to the Germans remembered his first night on guard:
"I was very cautious and worried all night lest the enemy advance and
annihilate our gallant little band. But with the dawn's early light I
beheld in the middle of our No Man's Land a French peasant cutting
hay with a horse-drawn mower."[2]

Germans had learned of the relief of the Rainbow Division by
thousands of boys from Gotham shouting out the lyrics to "The
Sidewalks of New York" in the middle of an otherwise quiet night.
Rumors spread that German observation balloons displayed banners
that read "Good-bye, 42nd Division—Hello, 77th Division," while
some men produced leaflets bearing the same message that German
aircraft had dropped over the American lines. In addition to these
public welcomes, the enemy had a special reception in store for the
new arrivals. Additional German artillery had been deployed, gas shells
had been stockpiled, a battalion of storm troops had been detached to
the Baccarat front, some companies of flamethrowers had been brought
into the line, and bombers and fighter planes had been assigned to hit
the American trenches. Completely unaware of this powerful force
being assembled opposite them, Liberty Boys congratulated themselves
on their successful relief of the Rainbow Division and remarked that
war at the front did not seem so bad after all.[3]

All hell broke loose at 3 A.M. on June 24. High explosive shells,
alternating with phosgene and mustard gas shells, tore into the 154th
Brigade and over the next two hours some three thousand rounds
slammed into positions occupied by the 307th and 308th Regiments.
Captain Miles said that this intense barrage sounded like "the whistles

and explosions at midnight of New Year's Eve, a background of steady roar supplied by the discharges of far off guns, punctuated with the sharp and broken reports of shells exploding near at hand." Commanders had no idea what was happening in their front. This first barrage, with shells raining down like hailstones, caught everyone off-guard and Charles Minder remembered, "My heart was in my mouth." Corporal Ranlett recalled that first gas barrage as his masked squad stood helplessly in a dugout lighted by a single candle: "Just at the edge of the little circle of light ranged a row of huge staring eyes in black, pointed faces from the snouts of which a shaking pipe led down into the darkness. The mud-colored helmets hid the men's foreheads. Only their ears, white and large, projected out on either side of the weird mask faces. Conversation was reduced to a mere series of gurgles." Ranlett said the scene reminded him of "Captain Nemo and his faithful followers gathered about some treasure chest on the sea bottom."[4]

Shelling at the front stopped abruptly and the Germans swarmed forward, firing machine guns and throwing grenades, while overhead aircraft either strafed American trenches or dropped bombs on them. Liquid fire from flamethrowers shot through the gray, smoke-filled dawn. This attack smashed into Lieutenant John Flood's platoon of Company C, 308th Infantry, which was "about the most cosmopolitan platoon of the most cosmopolitan company that came out of the melting-pot of New York." As soon as the barrage shifted to rear echelons, Flood ordered his platoon out of the dugouts and into the firing trench, where they opened up with rifles and French light machine guns, or Chauchats. For a few minutes there was a confused whirl of German hand grenades and American bayonets. Flood described the ensuing brawl as "a hand-to-hand fight—kicking, biting, stabbing, scratching, anything to get the other fellow first." He personally shot two attackers before falling with a wound that would cost him a leg. After inflicting casualties of well over fifty percent, including seventeen dead, enemy raiders gathered up about twenty dazed and slightly wounded prisoners and withdrew.[5]

There had been no thought of surrender by Lieutenant Flood's men, who had proved that soldiers of the National Army really would fight. This spirit had been exemplified by the death of two enlisted men. Corporal J. J. Sullivan, one of the prisoners who had been carried back almost to the German trench line, refused to go any farther and, fighting his captors with only bare hands, went down with nine bayonet wounds in his body. Private Racco Rocco, a little Italian who could barely speak English, had tried to rescue Flood, taking on four Germans with his bayonet in the confined trench. Before losing consciousness, Flood saw him "with his bayonet first at 'high port,' then at 'on guard,' just as he had learned it at Camp Upton." Rocco's by-the-numbers charge was stopped only by a grenade that exploded at his feet. One of the Company C boys confessed, "Most of us were new at this war business and we certainly got our baptism of fire."[6]

This German raid also struck the 307th Infantry at the village of Neuviller, held by one French and two American platoons. There was a decided difference in combat tactics, wherein the Yanks had been taught to hold their ground, while the French generally preferred to withdraw and counterattack. When the barrage lifted, German raiders rose out of a swamp and swarmed into the smoking village. French troops, with but few exceptions, fell back at once, while Americans, broken into isolated squads, fought back among the maze of streets. Those trapped in buildings and basements were killed by grenades or incinerated by flamethrowers. Outnumbered doughboys grudgingly abandoned the town, leaving "a few charred rifle-barrels from which the stocks had been burned away" as mute evidence of Jerry flame-throwers. Casualties among the American and French defenders in this attack were relatively heavy, well over 100 killed, wounded, and missing. Another 180 Americans had been gassed, although it was later learned that most of these casualties had resulted from removing gas masks too soon, rather than failing to get them on promptly. The extent of enemy casualties was unknown, but these well-trained German raiders had obviously won this first encounter with the Seventy-seventh Division.[7]

I want to go home! I want to go home!
  The whizzbangs they whistle, the cannons they roar;
  I don't want to stay here any more!
Oh, take me over the sea
  Where the Germans can't get at me.
  Oh, my! I'm too young to die!
I want to go H–O–M–E!!![8]

Following this shocking initiation to trench warfare in a supposedly quiet sector, life settled into a repetitive pattern of rotation from the front to reserve positions. Bored soldiers on guard amused themselves by throwing grenades at rats that crawled around in No Man's Land. "Kill or capture" combat patrols nightly went out into No Man's Land in search of prisoners and information, but they seldom encountered Germans and often got lost in the tortured maze of trenches and tangles of wire. These first patrols were mixed Franco-American affairs composed of as many as fifty soldiers, often carrying shotguns for trench fighting, but the number sent on each patrol was soon cut back dramatically. Despite diligent searching and many cunningly crafted ambushes, no prisoners were ever taken. The only information gained on this part of the front came from three deserters, who startled sentries by abruptly walking into the American lines one night.[9]

The biggest problem in the front lines was a scarcity of water. Usually one canteen of precious liquid was a day's supply and would have to be rationed for drinking, washing, and cleaning mess kits. To conserve water, mess kits were often scoured with mud and wiped clean with paper. One corporal explained how he managed to cope: "There was hardly any water for toilet purposes; I shaved once during the week, using as a shaving mug my canteen cup from which I ordinarily drank my coffee or ate my rice pudding, and washed my face and hands from the same cup full. Many of the men used coffee for shaving, both because it was hot and because it was more abundant than plain water."[10]

Highlights of the next few weeks included twin celebrations to honor the Fourth of July and Bastille Day. Both events called for feasts, good smokes, and a multitude of toasts. Americans drank a great deal—"a Polish wedding had nothing on some of those parties" is how one soldier explained it—but mostly beer and light wine since hard liquor had been banned. Chlorinated water issued to the troops tasted terrible, hence the increased thirst for alcoholic beverages. But worried folks at home were assured, "There was no more temptation to become a wine drunkard there than to become a castor oil drunkard in America." The two national holidays also saw numerous sporting contests, although participation was limited almost exclusively to the Americans. One baseball game was held while enemy shells exploded only a quarter of a mile away, each player keeping one eye on the ball and one on the shell bursts. French soldiers excelled in less physical contests, such as an international "making faces" competition, which, incidentally, was won by one ugly Liberty Boy.[11]

Companies in the reserve battalions had perhaps a worse time than those at the front or in support. There was certainly no rest for these soldiers, what with reveille at 4:45 A.M., followed by a day of physical training, police duty, drill sessions (heavy on bayonet and gas tactics), field maneuvers, and fatigue details. At least there were baths and delousing in reserve areas. Men stripped off all clothing and any equipment not made of leather and placed everything inside large mesh bags that were tossed into large boilers that forced steam through every fiber. Naked soldiers bathed while their gear was steam cleaned. Efforts to remove furrows in the pants and shirts were futile since not even a hot iron could remove those wrinkles installed at a delousing plant. Once clean, soldiers felt better and could attend a band concert, watch the latest silent film, or catch performances of a few burlesque troupes that toured the rear areas. One of the most popular was the Seventy-seventh Division Players, which offered female impersonators and classical music, such as "She Took Away My Identification Tags Because She Thought They Were Francs."[12]

While on the Lorraine front, promotions came for graduates from the last officer class held at Camp Upton, and these valuable leaders were transferred to other divisions. This loss was exacerbated by orders removing one officer and one noncom from each company to serve as instructors in training camps back in the United States. Those selected were at first overjoyed at their good fortune, but soon bemoaned having to leave comrades and friends who had become closer than their own families. In addition to these losses, the 308th Infantry was stunned by the death of Captain Philip Mills. A son of General Samuel Mills, the popular captain had served as a volunteer ambulance driver in France before the United States entered the war. As the only officer familiar with the newly issued French rifle grenade, Mills was instructing a class in how to properly fire this weapon when a defective bomb blew up, killing him and wounding two others. George Blowers had served in Captain Mills's company and considered him "a good scout."[13]

The last great German offensive of 1918 began near Rheims on July 15 and elements of the enemy actually gained a foothold on the western shore of the Marne River, before being thrown back. To counter this new threat, all available manpower headed for support positions in the Soissons–Chateau Thierry area. The Allied high command ordered French divisions to pull out and leave the Americans completely in control of the Baccarat sector. New Yorkers had grown to love and respect the French *poilus*, dressed unpretentiously in faded blue uniforms and so unlike the snappy British Tommies. Captain Miles said of their French comrades, "There was no excitement, no long series of detailed orders with instructions and memoranda so familiar to ourselves. Four years of realistic war had worn off all non-essentials (if they had previously existed) and only the fundamental was left, namely common sense." This sense of simplicity extended even to the high command, where an absence of typewriters meant all paperwork had to be completed in longhand, thereby cutting down on both haste and unnecessary red tape.[14]

One result of the French pullout was a reunification with the division's artillery brigade, which had been assigned to the French artillery school at Camp de Souge, a delightful spot about eleven miles from Bordeaux. Here the confident and seemingly well-trained Yanks had a rude shock. Sergeant Milton Goodman explained: "It seemed that our artillery methods of old Upton were most excellent for fighting Mexicans but painfully inadequate against Germans. Officers and men were told to forget everything they knew and begin all over again." Guns had not yet arrived, so there would be weeks of physical training, repetitive drill, lectures, and practice with compass, goniometer, scissors instrument, plotting board, and signal flags. City boys began to learn the proper techniques for grooming, feeding, harnessing, and riding thousands of half-broken animals. Sergeant Goodman admitted that "consternation and curses" flowed among the Liberty Boys, "for these horses were not your amiable milk wagon nags, nor the knowing cabby's plugs of an older day, but great, raw, burly, snorting, untamed monsters for the guns, and scraggly, mean, vicious mounts for the officers and special detail men." Goodman concluded, "If there is a Camorra, a Black Hand, and an I. W. W. among horses, our horses belonged. They were desperate characters."[15]

Guns came in early June, 75mm howitzers for the 304th and 305th Regiments and 155mm howitzers for the 306th Regiment, all French ordnance to be used with French manuals and tactics. The light French 75mm guns, generally employed against enemy troops, fired projectiles (shrapnel, high explosive, or gas) three inches in diameter and weighing about fifteen pounds. The heavy 155mm Schneider howitzers, used primarily against villages, trenches, and machine gun nests, fired projectiles (almost always high explosive) about six inches in diameter and weighing ninety-six pounds. Ammunition was exclusively of French manufacture. Detachments began firing on the range after just one day of familiarization with their guns and the 306th had only eleven days of live firing practice before leaving Camp de Souge. Artillerymen boasted that the 152nd Field Artillery Brigade was ordered to the front in almost record time, while "many divisions were never supported by their own artillery because the latter could not graduate from training camps in time to join them at the front."[16]

After a long train ride, the gunners reached Baccarat on the evening of July 18. Units approaching their assigned positions, confused by darkness and unfamiliar territory, usually took the wrong turn wherever the road forked amid dense woods. Being lost and apprehensive about their destination was compounded by the fact that pistols were not at hand, having been packed into the saddlebags because there were no holsters. The 306th Artillery finally reassembled in the morning and, according to one eager doughboy, "sat down and waited for the war to start." What they saw shortly after dawn startled them: "Out of a neighboring house came an old man and an old woman, each with a scythe across the shoulder. They trudged to the wheatfield by the woodside and began cutting in measured swathes. Then, along the road, came another old man trundling a barrow. We began to wonder where all this war business was being transacted." It was then that the gunners began to realize that Baccarat offered "a sort of summer vacation," despite wild lies told by the infantry about bloody German raids, daring patrols in No Man's Land, and blinding clouds of killer gas. Newcomers got one more surprise when they received billet assignments. Instead of being quartered in some count's medieval castle or a glistening palace, "they found themselves in a hayloft, approached by a rickety ladder and requiring caution in its use, lest while sleeping peacefully, you should roll through a hole in its floor and disturb the night's rest of the antique cow which bunked below you."[17]

The division artillery got into action too late to give supporting fire on July 21 for an ill-fated raid led by Captain F. Blanton Barrett, formerly a reporter for the *New York Tribune* but now commanding Company B, 307th Infantry. Supposing the German trenches to be thinly held, some simple-minded officer at headquarters had devised a simple plan whereby Barrett's detachment (himself, a lieutenant, and fifty-two men) would advance across No Man's Land, cut through the German wire, angle to the right, and take a few prisoners before withdrawing, all this to be conducted in broad daylight and without artillery support. Surprise would obviously be critical to the plan's success, but the Germans, who had watched Barrett's advance the entire way, opened up from "a hasty yet elaborate ambuscade." All at once, machine guns chattered from three sides, grenades and rifle fire being added to the murderous attack. Barrett ordered his lieutenant to take a third of the men and get back to their own lines, while he deployed the remainder and provided covering fire. Both parties were cut to pieces. Although wounded by the first volley, Barrett staggered forward to his death, while all of his main body were either killed or captured. Lieutenant Arthur McKeogh said of the affair, "The raiders had walked into an empty stretch of trench sown at every foot with death." Battle-hardened Germans had beaten the Liberty Boys again.[18]

Relative quiet reigned over the Seventy-seventh Division's front for the next ten days, but events unfolding elsewhere would impact the New Yorkers. German forces had been driven back from the Marne salient as a series of hammer blows by Allied divisions pushed them back to and beyond the Ourcq River. Casualties were heavy and the Liberty Division was withdrawn from Baccarat to join in this offensive, being replaced by the Thirty-seventh Division of Ohio National Guard men. This withdrawal began during the last days of July and continued until August 10. Marching over muddy roads, riding in packed 40/8 Pullmans and trucks, the division slowly but surely headed northwest toward the Rheims-Soisson front. It was a massive movement, transportation officers stating that it took fifty trains of fifty railroad cars each to move this one American division and its equipment. Of course, enlisted men again had no clue as to their ultimate destination. Some privates claimed that men prominent in the social, political, and civic circles of New York were "all anxious to make names for themselves and to get tons of glory," so the division must be en route to where the action

Oh, I'm going to a better land,
  They stay up every night;
The cocktails grow on the bushes,
  So everyone stays tight.
They've torn up all the calendars,
  They've busted all the clocks,
And little drops of whiskey
  Come trickling through the rocks.[19]

was hottest. Others disagreed and asserted that "those great men would be needed after the war, and should not be permitted to get within reach of German guns that could blast them into very inconsequential little bits."[20]

In a village northeast of Paris, somewhere between Chateau Thierry and Fere-en-Tardenois, Lieutenant McKeogh glimpsed an ancient French woman, "old beyond telling," standing amid the ruins of her home and waving a blue handkerchief at the Yanks as they poured down the road by truckloads. He remembered: "Only two walls of the house were standing. Through the gaping windows—eyes poked out, they seemed—could be seen the pitiable remnants of her possessions, a jumbled, tortured heap of furniture and masonry from which projected, like some ironic burial marker, a stovepipe. As the little old woman waved, her face went into a network of wrinkles that was a smile." McKeogh continued: "At her shoulder on the wall was yet nailed a frowning sign in German script—'Kommandantur.' But topping the sign and caught tenaciously in a sagging shutter, was a little patch of faded cloth that waved faintly—as she did—with the breeze. It was the only flag I saw at the front—the tricolor."[21]

While the Liberty Division was on the road, German forces had made a stand on the north bank of the Vesle River, a tributary of the Aisne River in northern France. The division history described the Vesle as "a narrow, muddy, snake-like, sluggish-flowing stream winding through a partly wooded valley with more or less steeply inclining ridges on both sides." Although not much to look at, the Vesle "proved more valuable to the Germans than a hundred dozen tons of barbed wire." All bridges had been destroyed and the river filled with barbed wire and other obstructions that made it difficult either to swim or ford. Here and there, bodies caught on the wire bobbed slowly in the current. Liberty Boys began to relieve exhausted doughboys from the American Fourth Division and *poilus* from the Sixty-second French Division on August 10. It was here that the New Yorkers had their first whiff of a real battlefield, a gagging combination of excrement, powder, stale gas, blood, decaying flesh, and sheer rot. This was war in earnest. Nothing could be truer than an officer's observation, "Lorraine was only a boxing match, but the Vesle, that was a real fist-fight." By the time New Yorkers could fight their way across the valley, it would forever be known as "The Hell Hole of the Vesle."[22]

Upon their arrival at the staging area for the advance across the Vesle, many troops camped in a woods north of the Nesles Chateau.

Tired doughboys bivouacked in the darkness, seeking whatever shelter and comfort they could find. Upon arising next morning, some discovered that the logs that had sheltered them overnight were actually the bodies of Germans who had been dead for several days.[23]

Lieutenant Arthur McKeogh, 308th Infantry: "In the Nesles Wood an officer of the 77th, standing under a tree, heard a drip drip drip on the leaves near his feet. The weather, remarkably enough, had been dry. He looked aloft. Sprawled across a fork of the branches was what had been a Boche sniper."[24]

The whole woods reeked of death and one soldier recalled the "infernal stench" that "got into the nostrils, there to remain, and those hot, dry days of August only served to intensify the odor." One story made the rounds of a gas guard pacing up and down through the pitch-dark forest, when suddenly he stopped and sniffed. Detecting an odor different from the ubiquitous human corruption, the guard instantly screamed out "GAS!!" and hundreds of his comrades hurried to get their masks on. But it was all a false alarm; an investigation soon disclosed that the guard had stepped on a dead cat, the resulting emission being mistaken for German gas.[25]

New Yorkers entered the Vesle front "on the fly" and had virtually no preparation for what they found there. Trench warfare was a thing of the past. Battles would now be fought in open country with tactics to match. Unfortunately, the Seventy-seventh Division had had time for only one day of training in "open order formations." New combat tactics would now be learned on the job. Such was the emergency that the first infantry regiment to arrive, the 305th, took over the entire front of the Fourth Division. A message sent back to the advancing column caught everyone's attention: "The dugouts are mere holes in the ground. You will be shelled morning, noon and night with shrapnel and high explosive, and during the intervals between shelling, they will throw gas at you." Soldiers pressed forward, each carrying two extra bandoleers of rifle cartridges or a musette bag crammed with Chauchat ammunition. German and Austrian shells from a huge concentration of artillery on the Aisne Plateau began to drop onto the ridge south of the river. One agitated private in the 305th ran over to his corporal, crying, "What shall I do? What shall I do?" The squad leader just looked up from his hole in the ground and replied, "Do the same as I'm doing, you damn fool. Say your prayers!" Regulars from the Fourth Division, happy as hell to be relieved, scrambled out of their holes and disappeared into the night, leaving behind truckloads of equipment and their unburied dead.[26]

Officer of the 304th Field Artillery on the relief of the Fourth Division:
"I don't know what ailed them, but I never heard such a lot of growlers. We all remarked it. Doubtless they were tired out. One man stopped right alongside my horse, at a halt, leaned over and vomited. Then, in a matter-of-fact, disgusted way, he exclaimed, 'God damned gas!' and went on his way."[27]

Everyone either found a funkhole or learned how to dig one in record time. Funkholes were the "trenches" of open warfare. Although newspaper correspondents would refer to them as "foxholes," such a term was seldom used by combat soldiers at the front. Holding either one or two soldiers, funk-holes generally measured some five feet long and perhaps three feet deep. Lieutenant McKeogh related that the holes were "scooped out by the pack carrier shovel, the cover of a mess kit, a Boche helmet, bleeding finger tips—anything that will lower the doughboy and his buddy a few inches under the streams of machine gun bullets that graze the grass." Veterans threw away their American shovels and grabbed the cast-off German variety, which had a wider blade and could move more dirt when seconds meant the difference between life and death. Exploding shells would throw fragments upward and outward for several hundred feet and a soldier in a funkhole would often survive nearby bursts that would kill a man above ground level. After digging in, a platoon had "the appearance of a magnified warren of prairie dogs." Lieutenant Edward Graham described the Vesle front to his mother, "This is a cowering war—pigmy man huddles in little holes and caves, praying to escape the blows of the giant who pounds the earth with blind hammers."[28]

Artillery fire was called "stuff" and, no matter what variety, it was "undeniably mean stuff." The "Minnie Werfer" or "Iron Mermaid" shell was fired from large trench mortars. The "Whizzbang," fired by 77mm howitzers, came so fast that there was no time to put a hyphen between the "whizz" and the "bang." Shells from larger howitzers, which plowed craters ten feet deep and nearly twenty feet across, were called "Tons-of-Coal," "Whimpering Willies," "G. I. Cans," or "Jack Johnsons," so named because they packed a knockout punch like the first black heavyweight boxing champion. In describing artillery fire on the Vesle, one soldier reported that "the smaller guns were sending over quart cans of dynamite, and the larger ones cook stoves."[29]

The Second Battalion of the 308th Infantry received an order on August 15 to advance along the road and "hold the bridge head" across the Vesle. There were just a couple of problems with that order. First, there was no road leading to the bridge and, second, there was no bridge. After discovering there were only two companies beyond the impassable river and literally no bridgehead to hold, Colonel Averill ordered his men to assume a defensive position and reported the situation to division headquarters. General Duncan, erroneously informed as to affairs at the front, relieved Averill from command for this supposed impertinence and shipped him off to the Third Division. Partly as a result of muddled thinking at division headquarters, the Second Battalion of the 308th lost heavily, first in support of the 305th and then during this relief. Company H had almost two hundred men on its rolls at the beginning of the month, but by midnight of August 15 it numbered but six men.[30]

Funkholes and dugouts in which doughboys spent most of their days and nights were

Doughboy's Definition of War: Take General William Tecumseh Sherman's definition and multiply it by six.[31]

"indescribably filthy with the refuse of former occupation, and haunted by incalculable flies." Captain Rainsford remembered, "At night they hung in black masses over the walls and roof, noisily propagating their species through the hours of darkness, and every crashing discharge of the 155's overhead would bring down an avalanche of chalk and flies." Another officer said, "The worst little railroad restaurant in America is a paradise of cleanliness, so far as flies are concerned, compared with mess time in those woods." The most disgusting thing was to pick dead bugs carefully from a spoonful of soup, then "discover that a fly had been picked up in transit from plate to mouth." Yellow jackets were especially troublesome whenever jam or other sweets were issued, when "it was practically impossible to separate the two long enough to eat one without the other." One soldier complained, "Every bit of syrup, grain of sugar, can of jam, or anything else had its share of yellow jackets sticking to it dead, or buzzing around to get inside, or humming their last in an effort to get away from the sticky mass." Machine gunner Henry Smith complained that "the place was alive with flies that sailed from the dead men onto our food and back again and when

the Karo syrup cans were opened, around swarmed the yellow jackets."
Private Clifford Brown, one of the upstate New Yorkers, remarked,
"We had to get our drinking water out of the river, which was filled
with the dead bodies of horses and men. The water was about the color
of milk and also tasted strongly of mustard gas." It was little wonder
that dysentery became epidemic.[32]

Henry W. Smith,
305th Machine Gun Battalion:
"There was a number of dead German
soldiers lying between the rails while at the
top of the opposite embankment one
fellow was propped up in a sitting position
against a tree and he was watched with a
certain morbid curiosity as day after day he
gave way and slumped nearer the earth."[33]

Those wounded or gassed
at the front were taken to temporary aid stations where they
received first aid and started to
the rear by stretcher or ambulance, those most seriously hurt
having priority. Dressing stations in the reserve lines ran
three shifts round the clock,
received casualties (usually "by ambulance loads") and sorted them
into wound or gas categories. The former were given anti-tetanus
serum and their wounds were redressed if necessary. Morphine inject-
ions were given to critical cases; those exhibiting symptoms of shock
went into a special room where they were warmed and circulation was
restored. Men with slighter injuries received a hot drink, chocolate,
and a cigarette before being evacuated to field hospitals to the rear.
Each dressing station had a temporary morgue that held bodies until
they could be interred in nearby cemeteries. After patients had been
cleaned up, medical officers could assess the damage. Delbert Davis
saw hundreds of men "burned to blisters over every exposed part
of their bodies with the mustard gas; others wheezing and gasping
for breath from the effects of Phosgene; and still others, their eyes
great swollen masses, their faces burned and lips parched and moaning
with pain." Davis then confessed with a bit of pride, "To bathe and
treat these men, and see them at first wild with pain, gradually
become quiet and easy under your treatment is the greatest pleasure a medical man can find in all of his work among wounded and
sick men."[34]

Battalions continued to rotate up to the front, but there was never
enough time for soldiers to recoup their physical and mental vigor.
Men had no inclination to shave, and one dirty, bearded veteran said,
"It seemed ages since we had seen anything of a hot meal and so far as

a bath was concerned we had commenced to think that that was something we read about in books." Men completely lost track of the day of the week and, if they should ask a watch-toting buddy what time it was, the response was invariably, "What do you care, you're not going any place." Rations consisted of an unending parade of cans containing corned willie and goldfish. Famished soldiers violated standing orders and opened their cans of reserve rations, preparing relatively sumptuous meals of hardtack fried in bacon grease and coffee boiled over tiny fires built from wood splinters. A deep depression settled over the once cocky Liberty Boys, who now realized that death could come to anyone at any time. Reminders were everywhere. Landmarks bore names such as Dead Man's Curve and Dead Man's Corner. A despondent Charles Minder confessed, "There is no glory for us up here. We never know when a shell is going to drop on us and snuff us out. We all feel like it's coming, and makes us uneasy, just like a doomed prisoner feels in the death-house, knowing he is going to be electrocuted. The torture of waiting for it is the real punishment."[35]

On August 22, German shells swept the entire division front with high explosives and gas in preparation for an attack on two 308th companies holding the north bank of the Vesle. Four companies of Germans, reinforced by flame-throwers, assaulted Company I.

Was there ever a life behind us,
A life that we knew before,
With never a shell to find us,
Crouching in mud and gore;
With never a pal to bury
As part of the bitter test,
With never the cry of a last good-by
From a mate who is starting West?[36]

A lieutenant commanding the fourth platoon reported that fire came from the front, flank, and rear simultaneously, but pointed with pride to the conduct of his enlisted men: "Private Bologna, a New York bootblack, covered the retirement of Sergeant Riley's post, turning and firing his chauchat from his shoulder, mowing down a file of Germans pursuing his detail along a narrow pathway. Private Comparelli, a day laborer, insisted on keeping up fire from the path over my dugout, although four little red spots on his buttocks showed that a machine gun bullet had threaded its way in and out of him four times." On the left of I, Company K fought off a determined assault, then retired to the riverbank under heavy pressure. Only one German survived the attack there and he was knocked down by the butt of Private Spinella's Chauchat, then killed with his

American infantry weapons (a Chauchat team in the foreground). From *History of Company D, 308th U.S. Infantry.*

own bayonet. By the time the line had been stabilized, thirty of Company K's seventy-nine effectives had been shot down.[37]

When General Evan Johnson initiated a plan to relieve Companies I and K with the First Battalion, Captain Lucien Breckenridge pointed out that heavy casualties, disease, and a myriad of details had reduced his four companies to only four hundred men. Half the officers were gone and grenades for infantry fighting were nonexistent. Confusion was widespread as platoons were hastily dispatched across the Vesle as soon as they arrived from widely dispersed positions. Captain L. Wardlaw Miles, commanding Company B, said the resulting situation was "the sort of thing that taught the innocent novice that war was a business no less messy than murderous." When Miles's advance platoon crossed the river, it ran right into a superior force of Germans. Only six men out of forty-five returned. Lieutenant Richard Sheridan took two platoons across, after commenting, "Well, I expect this is going to be a real Irish wake," but he was quickly cut down by machine gun bullets. Company D attacked two hours after the artillery barrage and in broad daylight, but managed to regain the original line of outposts.[38]

When the Liberty Division first reached the Vesle River, communication with troops on the north bank was accomplished by means of a single wide timber and one partially damaged footbridge. On August 21, after several abortive attempts, the Engineers finally succeeded in dynamiting a couple of trees that fell so as to create a couple more rude bridges. On the night of August 23–24, an Engineer Corps captain and twenty-five men advanced with a portable footbridge under heavy fire. After assembling the bridge, these Engineers discovered that it was ten feet too short. Starting to work with axes and ropes, they quickly lengthened the span. A second detachment of Engineers constructed another footbridge nearby despite being under fire for three hours. These new bridges, after being suitably camouflaged, greatly facilitated the passage of troops and allowed the division to increase pressure on the Germans.[39]

Doughboys with the big guns had a bad time of it as well. Living in shallow dugouts covered with tree branches, canvas tents, and dirt to protect themselves from flying splinters, they would emerge to fire when-

When the storm troops wait at the river banks,
And each stone bridge is blown,
And the stream's too deep for the fat old tanks,
And the pontoons must be thrown
Where the water boils with the shell and shot,
It's "Engineers, 'toot sweet,'"
They will lose one-half of the men they've got,
But build that bridge, complete![40]

ever commanded to do so. Any other activity was curtailed by gas and high explosive shells that pounded the artillery emplacements. All at once the air would be "filled with the whistle and explosion of shell and with the whine of flying fragments as they flicked the dirt outside our shallow splinter-pits, or pattered through the branches of the trees." After each barrage, soldiers would peek out of their holes to see branches hanging from shattered tree trunks or littering the ground, surrounded by every imaginable piece of smashed and torn equipment. There were so many shell craters that it was difficult to tell the old from the new and there were always casualties, men's bodies either torn and punctured by jagged metal fragments or their eyes and skin blistered by gas.[41]

Part of the German success for holding the Vesle River was due to air superiority. American pilots were as yet too sparse to provide adequate cover to all their country's divisions, while the British and French had very few aircraft to loan out. On the morning of August 17, two American planes returning from a patrol had just crossed back into Allied lines when three German pilots suddenly attacked from above. In a frenzied effort to elude the attackers, the Americans collided. One plane sheared off a wing and breathless spectators on the ground watched it begin to fall, slowly at first, "then with appalling speed, gathering impetus with every fathom, nose first, in one plummeting chute, the sunshine gleaming on its painted sides and the whirr of its motor growing to a deafening roar, sliding like a lost soul through thousands of feet of air, a glistening, living thing headed for utter destruction." It crashed a few moments later, followed by the second plane, which spiraled downward into a grove of cottonwood trees before overturning on the ground. Doughboys raced to the scene to attempt a rescue, but both Lieutenants Smythe and Wallace had died on impact.[42]

German artillery had deflated one of two observation balloons that floated just beyond the Nesles Woods on August 12. A few hours later, a German pilot began a long dive on the remaining balloon. Crewmen on the ground tried to winch it to safety, but the daring pilot, amid some intense anti-aircraft fire, succeeded in destroying his big sausage-shaped target with a phosphorus bomb. As the attacker fled back to his own lines, three planes from the Allied balloon patrol belatedly reached the scene. One disgusted doughboy was overheard to remark, "Here they come, like the cops after a fight, taking the names!" Shooting down American pilots and busting Allied observation balloons made for exciting patrols, but German pilots played a more significant role when engaged in aerial surveillance at the front. They would send back the coordinates of any carelessly exposed troops or gun positions, "even one lone man crossing an exposed field," prompting a small barrage from so-called "sniper batteries."[43]

Just before dawn on August 27, Captain Charles Bull led Company G of the 306th Infantry into the village of Bazoches after it had been subjected to a punishing barrage of high explosives. Germans responded with their own artillery and streams of machine gun bullets from the smoking ruins. Moving carefully from one jumbled pile of masonry to

the next, two of Bull's platoons managed to reach the northern outskirts of the village, but there were overwhelmed. Lieutenant McKeogh
said that they "disappeared completely" and speculated that they may
have been annihilated by flamethrowers. Unaccustomed to the process
of securing a village where defenders could hide in cellars and dugouts,
some New Yorkers fell after being shot in the back. A later assessment
of the attack would conclude that, given the American lack of training
and stout German defense, at least a full regiment would have been
needed to take and hold the objective.[44]

While Captain Bull's company assaulted Bazoches on the left flank
of the division, the Second Battalion of the 307th Infantry attacked a
strongpoint named Chateau du Diable on the right. This assault was
simply murder. Two companies of the 307th started for their objective,
but were cut down by as many as fifty machine guns which dominated
that sector. To dazed doughboys, "the woods seemed alive with them."
Company E's advance platoon worked its way into a woods and not
one man was ever seen again. Meadows and woodlots became an
"inferno of noise" where the attack quickly faltered, then receded,
leaving the enemy in possession of the battlefield. In the twin attacks
on Bazoches and Chateau du Diable, the Liberty Boys had been given
impossible assignments. Scores of corpses littering those battlefields
were a testament to their cour-
age, as well as a condemna-
tion of the incapacity of their
commanders.[45]

These failures by New
York's Own apparently cost
General George Duncan his
job and he was sent off to
lead the Eighty-second Division. The Seventy-seventh
Division's new commanding
general, Robert Alexander,

Oh, the bugs crawl in and the bugs crawl out,
They do right dress and they turn about,
Then each one takes a bite or two,
Out of what the War Office used to call you.

Oh, your eyes drop out and your teeth fall in,
And the worms crawl over your mouth and
chin,
They invite their friends and their friends's
friends too,
And you're all chewed to Hell when they're
through with you.[46]

had been born in Baltimore on October 17, 1863. He read law and was
admitted to the bar, but had a burning desire to be a soldier and enlisted
as a private in Company G, Fourth Infantry on April 7, 1886. Within a
year he was first sergeant of his company. Advanced to second lieutenant, Alexander served with the Seventh Infantry against the Sioux

Nation during the winter of 1890–91. A series of promotions followed, along with service during the Pullman Strike of 1894, in Puerto Rico during the Spanish-American War, and on occupation duty in the Philippines, where he was one of the few American officers ever to be wounded by a bolo. After graduating from the Army School of the Line and the Army War College, Major Alexander commanded the Seventeenth Infantry during General Pershing's Punitive Expedition into Mexico in 1916. He was ordered to France in November of 1917 with the rank of colonel, but soon became a brigadier general in command of a depot division. On August 3, 1918, General Alexander assumed command of the Sixty-third Infantry Brigade, his first combat command in the war. Twenty-three days later, after leading his brigade in the Second Battle of the Marne, Alexander was elevated to major general and given command of the Seventy-seventh Division. He was a dynamic leader with an innate knack for directing men in battle and would bring the battle-weary New Yorkers back to a peak of efficiency.[47]

General Alexander took over a totally different division than the one that had arrived in France. Soldiers had undergone their baptism of fire in the warren of funkholes and dugouts that lined the Vesle River. One veteran portrayed the Baccarat Sector in Lorraine as "a sleepy old lion, who only rarely awoke to stretch his claws." The Vesle front, however, he considered "some sort of monster hell-cat which scarcely for a moment ceased to spit and scratch, and whose very breath was death." War correspondent Frederick Palmer had followed the Liberty Boys from Camp Upton to France and now said of them, "The melting-pot was put to the test of the fire that crucibles require— the old, old test of facing sudden death, of suffering pain from wounds and of submitting self to superior orders and to the will of destiny." Palmer continued, "The stories about the comradeship formed between men who knew their morning baths and the clubs with men from the tenements were true. It was 'Buddy' back and forth between bunkies, whatever their origin; they had learned to appreciate the man-quality in each other." Captain Miles explained how things stood in his own regiment: "Conditions on the Vesle were bad, but not bad enough to break the spirit of officers and men of the 308th."[48]

New Yorkers had belonged to a recruit division when they reached the Vesle, but now they were experienced veterans who could take anything the Germans threw at them and come back for more. They soon understood what British instructors had meant when they said it would take "guts" to fight the Germans. Officers realized the immense responsibility that came with leading men in combat, when the slightest miscalculation could cost lives. They began to understand the concept of "leadership" and lead they did, often into the hottest fire imaginable and with the expected consequence. By the end of August, there were only eleven line officers to command the twelve companies of the 308th Infantry. Sergeants and corporals accepted the burden of command and often led platoons and, occasionally, even entire companies. One writer said of that regiment, "It lost one third of its strength. Many of the Camp Upton officers gave out. Morale was not so good, but one thing had happened: the men were veterans now and passed on what they had so dearly learned to green replacements filling gaps in the ranks." Germans had won all the encounters thus far, but the Liberty Boys had developed into one damned powerful American war machine. All they wanted was another chance.[49]

5

Aisne and Argonne

Nothing of note happened under General Alexander's leadership until the afternoon of September 2, when large clouds of smoke began to rise from behind enemy lines. Following a heavy barrage next day, American observation balloons confirmed an apparent withdrawal, so Engineers advanced on the night of September 3–4 to commence building bridges for both foot and motorized traffic. On the right of the division, the 307th Infantry advanced past its August battlegrounds and crossed the Vesle at Fismette. About dark German artillery opened fire, one shell demolishing the bridge and another killing fourteen and wounding ten others, including nearly every member of Second Battalion headquarters. Despite heavy losses from machine gun fire, the 307th advanced to the village of Merval while trying to keep some sort of liaison with the Twenty-eighth Division on its right. Pinned down there, the division objective on the north bank of the Aisne River seemed as far away as America and would remain so for ten days "without notable event beyond a slow but steady drain of casualties from artillery and machine gun fire, and a constant drenching of gas."[1]

The Third Battalion of the 308th crossed the Vesle and reached the heights beyond without encountering much opposition. But when advancing into the next valley, its first wave of two companies was hit hard by withering machine gun fire and, in the simple words of one attacker, "the first line began to fade." Men ran for the crest behind them, carrying along the two companies supporting this abortive advance and leaving wounded and disoriented comrades behind to be scooped up as prisoners. After two hours of throwing whizzbangs at the attackers, German defenders withdrew and the Third Battalion was again off in pursuit. One of the Americans remembered, "The men were so tired that when we had to halt for a few minutes to reconnoiter the road, more than half would fall asleep and had to be kicked to awaken them." They stopped at dawn and dug in around the wooded slopes of Butte de Bourmont, about eight kilometers beyond the Vesle, the only unit in the division to reach its objective. These exhausted soldiers, without food, drinking water from puddles, and all suffering from diarrhea, would hold that position for "ten memorable and trying days."[2]

Charles Minder had been among those watching the infantry begin its advance on September 4, many units passing by at the double-quick. He remembered, "They were all out of breath, and I felt sorry for them. Many of them will be killed off, and they even have to run to their deaths. It's funny! They seemed like dumb animals, afraid, but not knowing what danger they were running into." Minder continued, "They were going into battle, but nothing at all like what we used to read about in our histories, where they told us how the soldiers went into battle with flags flying and with music playing. There wasn't a sign of anything patriotic about the way they were going up. It was grim murder and nothing more. You go to your death here in filth and mud, and you suffer to the end sometimes, alone." Minder and his comrades had learned firsthand that patriotism was for civilians and politicians, not for soldiers at the front. Flags and inspirational music meant nothing to those who did the actual fighting and wanted nothing more than to live long enough to go home. Death had become a constant companion, taking victims seemingly at random, although most soldiers would have argued that the best men were always the first to die. War was a life and death lottery. The more you played, the better your odds of being cut down by machine gun bullets or an exploding whizzbang. But everyone had to play and play often.[3]

General Alexander's entire division was on the move, the Vesle Valley filled with moving columns of men, motor transports, artillery, sanitary trains, ammunition trains, pioneers, engineers, and military cops, all bottlenecked behind the bridges. Even a horde of oddly out-of-place French cavalry crossed the river and galloped after the retreating foe. Those in advance found themselves far beyond the rations they so desperately needed. Cooked food had ceased to exist. One detachment of fifteen machine gunners carefully shared two cans of monkey meat and seven packages of hardtack for lunch, "not leaving a crumb behind." The strain was beginning

> **Charles Minder,**
> **306th Machine Gun Battalion:**
> *"There is no glory in this bloody business, not for these poor devils at the battle front, anyhow. They'll build statues of the Generals, who are always back in headquarters. Their names will go down in history."*[4]

to tell on everyone. A soldier from Company D, 307th Infantry described the situation, "They were exhausted, dirty, hungry, and ragged. They were vermin infested and miserable, but they pushed forward." Few officers remained and "most of the platoon sergeants were in hospitals; corporals were doing the work of holding the men together; and the privates were hanging on grimly." To ease the constant tension, Charles Minder confided, "I smoke two and three packs of Bull Durham a day." One diary entry from that period said honestly, "I do wish this thing was over. I can't stand it any longer."[5]

The country between the Vesle and Aisne was honeycombed with caves and old chalk and limestone quarries. Before being used by the Americans as dugouts, these natural hideaways had to be cleared of booby traps. In one cave near Fismes, an alert officer discovered a 105mm shell hidden under a table festooned with flowers, a trip wire running to a nearby sofa. Two cooks for the 302nd Engineers were killed by a concealed mine in a dugout. Company E of that regiment was ordered to inspect a large cave that General Evan Johnson wanted to use as headquarters for the 154th Brigade. The cave was full of mustard gas that had settled onto bunks and other debris inside. Engineers had to work without gas masks as they looked for pitfalls, finding one mustard gas shell timed to explode that night. After a few hours, the cave had been cleared, but more than seventy men had been gassed so badly they required hospitalization. The headquarters staff moved in its equipment, then carried the German bunks back inside. Lieutenant McKeogh said of the affair, "Jerry was ever a crafty sort. He knew that a mattress, to a man who had been wallowing in muddy funkholes for weeks, would prove to be a nocturnal bit of fleece-lined heaven beyond his resisting." So they proved to be, but body heat soon activated the gas-saturated mattresses and almost the entire brigade staff—General Johnson, aides, and runners, some fifty men in all—became casualties.[6]

Coordination during the advance was almost nonexistent, especially on the right flank with the Twenty-eighth Division, which continued to lag so far behind that a gap of about one thousand yards developed. Patrols managed to keep intermittent contact, but about noon on September 6, the Germans overran an outpost and launched an attack on the 307th. Americans responded with rifle and Chauchat fire, repulsing the attackers and killing the enemy commander. When German soldiers fled in disorder, New Yorkers shot them in the back. Enemy artillery on the Aisne Plateau unfailingly supported these brief German attacks and Henry W. Smith described how one shell exploded in a dugout occupied by four men from the 305th Machine Gun Battalion: "Corporal Kelly was on his knees handing in rations at the time and, strange as it seems, it left him with only a slight case of shell shock. Almost at his fingers' ends the lives of the other four were snuffed out."[7]

On the evening of September 8, advance battalions of the 307th and 308th Regiments received orders to attack the village of Revillon behind a barrage set to begin at 6:45. Precisely on time, the Second Battalion of the 307th, supported by two companies from the First Battalion, set out across open meadowland "through a veil of glistening rain and spanned by a rainbow arch." There were no leprechauns with golden treasure at the end of this rainbow, only steely-eyed German machine gunners. There was also no protective rolling barrage. Captain Rainsford said two companies on the left "were met by a hurricane of shells and machine gun fire" that sent men staggering back to the woods from which they had started. In his opinion, "The losses were bravely taken, but there was never a chance of success." The Second Battalion withdrew to its original position with an effective strength of 247 men, one-fourth of its authorized strength. After this bloody repulse, a message arrived that the artillery barrage could not commence until 7:30, yet another example of poor intraservice communication.[8]

The 308th had made limited gains during this attack, one patrol silencing a machine gun nest, but the disaster on the right made the newly captured ground untenable. For the next few days desperate fighting swirled around the right flank of the Seventy-seventh Division as doughboys fought in and through the villages of Merval, La Petite

Montagne, Glennes, Ravin Marion, and Revillon. The Germans still retained their air superiority (one bugler recalled that in a single day he blew sixty-two airplane alerts), so any daytime movement brought down a rain of German 77mm or Austrian 88mm shells. Companies with paper strength of six officers and 250 enlisted men had left the Vesle averaging about two officers and less than 150 men. This pursuit toward the Aisne had further depleted the ranks. When Company A of the 308th was told to advance on Revillon after a series of failed assaults, the one remaining officer sent back this succinct note: "Send me more men. Only 27 of company left."[9]

> **Charles Minder,**
> **306th Machine Gun Battalion:**
> *"While we were advancing last night, going up one hill and not looking where I was walking, I stepped on something and it gave way and caved in. I looked down and found that my foot had crushed the chest of a dead German."*[10]

Affairs at the front were fluid, at best. Fighting often degenerated into isolated squads, platoons, or companies blundering into similarly disjointed enemy units. Platoons from Companies I and M of the 307th were sent forward in broad daylight to occupy some wooded slopes that, according to the maps, would provide cover. The maps proved to be wrong. Caught in the open, doughboys hugged the ground, exposed to "the swift rush of sound, the instantaneous crash of the explosion, and then the scream of some disemboweled comrade—again and again, and nowhere on earth to turn for help." Company K of that regiment mistakenly tried to attack a German entrenchment some nine hours behind schedule, moved into open fields, lost over fifty men, and came reeling back. According to Captain Rainsford, "Few even reached the wire; none crossed it."[11]

Company L of the 307th had the misfortune to be repeatedly shelled by American artillery. A field message book of the company commander furnished details. At 2:45 on September 9, the lieutenant wrote, "Our artillery is firing within 25 yards of Company Headquarters." An hour later came this observation, "Our artillery just dropped a shell 100 yards east of Company Headquarters, in woods where we have a platoon." Fifty minutes later, he wrote, "Our artillery barraged Serval in our rear," then added, "It is beginning to tell on the men." A final message, composed five hours after the first dispatch, read, "Our artillery just fired some low trajectory shells from our left in woods 75 yards in front of Company Headquarters." This was followed by the plaintive appeal, "Do try to stop them." Although division staff officers would claim that German artillery had actually been the culprit here, those who huddled in funkholes during the shelling had no doubt that it was friendly fire.[12]

Captain L. Wardlaw Miles, who would one day chronicle the history of the 308th Infantry, was a unique character even in the Melting Pot Division. Miles had graduated from Johns Hopkins University and the University of Maryland Medical School, then received a doctorate in philosophy from the former institution in 1903. He was assistant professor of English at Princeton University when the United States entered the war. Leaving a wife and three children, he began his military service as a lieutenant in Company B, 308th Infantry. Promoted to captain on the Vesle front, Miles took command of Company M on September 11 and led it in yet another ill-fated attack near Revillon three days later. While engaged in cutting the German wire, he was hit by machine gun bullets that fractured an arm and both legs. In the words of Lieutenant McKeogh, "He ordered himself placed upon a stretcher and with the bearers carrying him up and down the field, directed the attack reclining, until the trench objective had been taken." Miles refused to leave the field until ordered to do so by his commanding officer. He would later receive a Medal of Honor. Commenting on the courage of his men in their last advance, Captain Miles remarked, "To have had the opportunity to lead men who, after such a long and trying experience at the front, were ready to advance so gallantly across wire and under fire into an entirely coverless open, was indeed a privilege for which any man might be grateful as long as he lived."[13]

The 305th and 306th regiments kept pace with the 307th and 308th on the Liberty Division's left flank. Men from the Second Battalion, 305th Infantry had just reached a rest area where they planned "to pick cooties from [their] clothes by the hundreds, to splash in the River Ourcq, a dinky stream hardly big enough to hold a fish, and to lie around naked in the grass." Shortly thereafter, the battalion, loaded down with extra rations, ammunition, and grenades, marched northward to join the general advance over the Vesle. Passing through the devastated village of St. Thibaut, New Yorkers saw "columns of troops in single file, motor trucks, limbers, fourgons, ammunition trains boldly occupying avenues down which had poured streams of machine gun bullets, waist-high and whistling." After crossing the river, the battalion column passed through Bazoches, now a smoking ruin that was "as calm and quiet as the seventh inning of a world series game at the Polo Grounds." Every highway and country road was jammed with traffic heading north toward the Aisne River.[14]

Captain Frank B. Tiebout, 305th Infantry: "Full in the road lay the body of a German soldier over which the trucks were passing, to and fro. 'Ah,' said the boys, 'there's a good German!'"[15]

The First Battalion of the 305th reached the high ground overlooking the Aisne River and dug in, beginning "another period of semi-stabilized warfare, such as had been experienced on the Vesle." Enemy shell fire "was at times of the most furious density," with hundreds of guns concentrating on the doughboys. Gradually, American artillery caught up with the infantry advance and responded to the Germans shell for shell. One Liberty Boy caught in the middle of this massive artillery duel figured that Heiny and American gunners had made a secret pact that read, "I'll blow your infantry to bits while you try to bust mine." There were fumbled attempts to advance to the canal that bordered the Aisne, but all failed due to lack of coordination. An order to attack on September 7 was countermanded, but Company A failed to receive this message and advanced alone and unsupported. According to Captain Tiebout, "The company commander was killed, the only other company officer wounded, and many more grievous casualties sustained."[16]

On the front occupied by the 306th Infantry, Lieutenant Charles O'Brien led Company C in an attack on a rectangular wood called Les Cendrieres. While this point had been described as "woods" by Intelligence officers, the trees had, in fact, been cut down. O'Brien led his men forward and, after being struck in the leg by a shell fragment, shouted, "They can't stop us now!" The next shell that burst killed him. Lieutenant Cleveland, although twice wounded, led Company A forward and it finally captured the "woods," actually reaching the bank of the Aisne Canal. But headquarters now decided that holding Les Cendrieres would cost more than the position was worth. After spilling a great deal of blood in taking the "woods," the 306th was ordered to abandon it, a movement judged to be "equally as dangerous." This ill-fated advance allowed General Alexander to claim that "his division was the only one in the American Army that actually reached the

Aisne Canal." Alexander's boast would be little consolation for the families of those slain and mutilated in this senseless attack on a treeless forest.[17]

Few men had bathed over the last month and everyone dreamed of hot water, cootie-free barracks, and a release from the perils of front line service. Everything that had been taken for granted back home in New York now seemed so very far away. A soldier in the 306th Artillery explained the situation: "We wanted to get away to some place, any place, where towns were not in ruins, where whistling shell did not make us hunch our shoulders, and where stores could offer a few of those non-essentials so prized by soldiers at the front. Perhaps, who could tell, we might actually sit down at a table and order a meal. There was also the primitive desire to be among women and children." Another homesick doughboy had a recurring fantasy of actually seeing a door, "a real, honest-to-goodness door with a knob on it and panes of glass."[18]

There's a long, long trail a-winding,
Into the land of my dreams,
Where the nightingales are singing,
And the white moon beams;
There's a long, long night of waiting,
Until my dreams all come true,
Till the day when I'll be going down,
That long, long trail with you.[19]

The Eighth Italian Division, commanded by a grandson of Giuseppe Garibaldi, began to relieve the Liberty Division in mid-September, first exchanging places with the 153rd Brigade, then the 154th. A few veterans of the 306th Infantry had seen the Italians training in the rear, laughing out loud as they would "charge imaginary trenches with bayonetted rifle and with murderous-looking knives in their teeth." Soldiers from the 305th watched in amazement as the newcomers bunched up in the roads, stupidly offering themselves as targets for German guns. Luckily, German aviators did not spot these relief columns. One American observed, "If Jerry had ever gotten a line on them and planted a few shells in their midst, Marc Antony would have had to write up another burial oration." But all went well and one doughboy could write that they had been successfully "relieved by the Roman Army." As New Yorkers began to depart, they noticed that the Italians "put six or seven men into a hole where two of us had felt crowded before, and left cabbage leaves, cheese rinds, and all sorts of garbage lying around." What rookies![20]

Rear echelons of the 307th Infantry were still in a cellar in Fismes, a village now described as "a dreary place of dust and debris and sun-scorched carrion," when two battalions of Italians came marching up after dark. Americans stared as these relief battalions ran smack into a column of French *poilus* on the bridge over the Vesle between Fismes and Fismette. To make matters worse, a truck had broken down on the road and the American MPs could not make either the French or Italians understand their orders. Horrified veterans of the previous month's shelling watched helplessly as the Europeans sat down and lit cigarettes until "the place looked like a hay-field filled with fire-flies." For some inexplicable reason, only one shell exploded among the logjam of humanity gathered about the bridge. Captain Rainsford, "adrift in a world of loneliness and foreigners," recalled that, on September 16, Roman officers would "demand explanation of things that no one knew about in a language which no one understood; and meantime there were being sent hither and thither messengers who seldom found the proper recipient of their message, more seldom returned with a reply, and almost never solved the difficulty referred to." When the last two American companies withdrew that night, they were overjoyed to see the Italians "live long enough to effect the relief."[21]

When some of Garibaldi's regiments marched past the 306th Field Artillery, happy gunners greeted them with the salutation, "Hey Wop! Shine?" Thinking this to be a genuine greeting, Italians replied with cordial and long-winded comments of their own. A few with connections to America would hurl back, "Oh, you subway!" or brag "Me worka Grand Central!" Captain Charles Whittlesey commanded the First Battalion of the 308th Infantry when Italian officers from the Brescia Brigade came forward to make arrangements to relieve the Americans. When these officers began to bicker among themselves, Whittlesey found himself in a quandary since regimental headquarters had already left. He sought advice from the commanding officer of the 307th and appeared to have everything smoothed out. But then, Whittlesey recalled, "To my horror, when it came night up pops both of the Wop battalions—and such a milling around in the dark! So finally I sent off my battalion and kept a dozen men (runners, etc.) with me— stuck one Italian battalion in place, and spent the rest of the night trying to lodge the other. It was a pretty discouraged Wop commander, when we finally had to go away."[22]

General Alexander settled his soldiers into temporary camps in the Coulonges-Villers-Agron-Aquizy area, where they lined up for pay, mail, "oodles of cigarettes," baths and shaves in cold streams, wine from the locals, and food in abundance. A guy in Company D of the 308th wrote with obvious delight, "We were given underwear!" Everyone ate until almost sick, one hungry doughboy admitting, "Had a young meal of beefsteak, potatoes, onions, coffee, bread, rice, crullers, jam and four cartons of cigarettes." He then confessed, "I et till I near bust." The Liberty Division recrossed the Vesle as a dependable veteran division, but that status came at a terrible price. Company D of the 307th, having lost 115 of its roster in the last six weeks, "came out of the lines without an officer and with only a handful of tired, sleepless, ragged men, who above all wanted rest." This company was no exception, for every infantry unit in the division had suffered just as badly and all "were rather discouraged, very ragged and utterly tired." Rest and replacements were critical to replenishing the Liberty Division to fighting trim.[23]

Although thrown back from the Marne and the Vesle, Germans still tenaciously held the Meuse and

> *We started with fifty-odd non-coms and men,*
> *We started with fifty and now we are ten!*
> *And if this bloody war doesn't end pretty soon*
> *There'll be nobody left in the ruddy platoon![24]*

Aisne valleys north of Verdun. This region was vitally important to the Boche war effort because it guarded the Carignan–Sedan–Mezieres Railroad, one of only two such routes used to supply the Kaiser's army in France and Belgium. If the Allies got possession of this critical railway, they could cut off German troops west and north of Sedan by depriving them of supplies and reinforcements. General Pershing finally had almost one million American soldiers at his disposal, many of them in National Army divisions. He planned to assemble his American First Army behind the French lines that stretched from the Meuse River to the Argonne Forest, concentrate all his available artillery, then launch a surprise offensive. Sledgehammer blows by this vast concentration of American manpower would be followed by a series of Allied attacks farther north. Already on the defensive on virtually every front, the Germans would be hard pressed to counter all of these offensives with limited reserves on hand.[25]

As staff officers worked out details of this grand scheme to end the war, doughboys put their hobnails on the highways again. This time they marched to transportation centers where they boarded camions, French motor trucks, instead of 40/8 Pullmans. Captain Rainsford remembered, "The journey by motor trucks was unqualifiedly awful. They were desperately crowded and quite innocent of springs, so that he who found room to sit felt as though perched upon a cocktail shaker; and it lasted for sixteen hours." Another Liberty Boy related how exhausted French drivers careened along the roadways: "Without illumination of any kind, the trucks tore through the night. At dawn their speed in the direction of Verdun increased to the point of recklessness. Drivers dozed at the wheel and trucks collided, crushing the careless feet which hung over a tailboard; they ran into the ditch; they interviewed unyielding trees; one truck overturned, sending a couple of men with broken ribs to the hospital." There were occasional halts in the Champagne District, where men jumped out and stole grapes and apples from vineyards and orchards along the roadway. After reaching their destination at some strange, French-sounding place, soldiers climbed out to rest their weary and bruised bones.[26]

Privates inquired as to their destination. Corporals promptly asked sergeants where they were bound. Sergeants, not knowing, asked the same of their lieutenants. Officers, not wanting to appear uninformed, asked the privates who ran the telephone exchanges and loitered about headquarters. Those in the know whispered something about St. Menehould. Next day they marched about thirty-five kilometers to near Florent, where division headquarters had been established. One marcher described the experience of an average doughboy: "His hair is matted, his hands unbearably moist, his clothes cling to him, and at every crunch of his muddy shoes cold water oozes up between his toes. His legs are drenched and numb, except for the twinge of shooting pain from the tightness of his rolled leggings; and now and then his knees give way a trifle, as if unable to support the unnatural weight above him." A march in the rain quickly devolved into a repetitive rhythm of "tramp, tramp, scrape, splash, scuffle, scuffle, tramp, tramp, tramp."

Hiked last night,
Hiked the night before.
We're going to be hiked to-night
As we never hiked before.
When we hike it always rains or snows,
Where we're hiking to God only knows.[28]

Each unit reached its destination in two distinct factions, "the superhuman half of the Regiment, and the human half in charge of the provost guards."[27]

Allied commanders gave the Seventy-seventh Division the unenviable assignment of attacking enemy defenses in the Argonne

Forest, although they never really believed that New Yorkers could actually fight their way through that tangled mass of real estate. If the Americans should by some chance gain ground in their initial attack, the Kriemhild Stellung Line, a sector of the formidable Hindenburg Line, awaited them. German troops had occupied that region for four years and had constructed distinct lines of resistance, each carefully engineered to take advantage of terrain admirably suited for defensive tactics. General Pershing explained the situation on his front: "These natural defenses were strengthened by every artificial means imaginable, such as fortified strongpoints, dugouts, successive lines of trenches, and an unlimited number of concrete machine gun emplacements. A dense network of wire entanglements covered every position." Pershing would begin his offensive with nine divisions of the American First Army, committing almost as many more later as reinforcements.[29]

There was much to do in the next few days. Battalions and regiments marched toward the front, trading places with French troops who strolled to the rear "lazying along in groups of three or four in their sensible way." Hundreds of thousands of Americans were supposed to hide from keen-eyed observers in German aircraft, so no one could be about during daylight hours. According to Captain Charles Whittlesey, enlisted men "were packed in barns like sardines, and had to pay Frenchmen to bring them water and soup and cigarettes." Whittlesey described the crowding as "pretty ugly" and told how battalion commanders had to go to improvised stockades each night to retrieve soldiers who had been caught wandering around in the open. As commander of the First Battalion of the 308th Infantry, which would be in the first wave over the top, Whittlesey took his company commanders, dressed in French overcoats and helmets to conceal their identity, to reconnoiter the trenches where his men would start off. They found a thin line of French outposts protecting the small town of La Harazee, which "looked as though it had been destroyed in the middle ages." The region was also criss-crossed by "whole systems of mossy caved-in trenches," complete with wonderfully spacious dugouts. After this brief glimpse of their jumping-off point and their objective—

Darling, I am coming back,
  Silver threads among the black;
Now that peace in Europe nears,
  I'll be home in seven years.
I'll drop in on you some night
  With my whiskers long and white;
Home again with you once more,
  Say by nineteen-twenty-four![30]

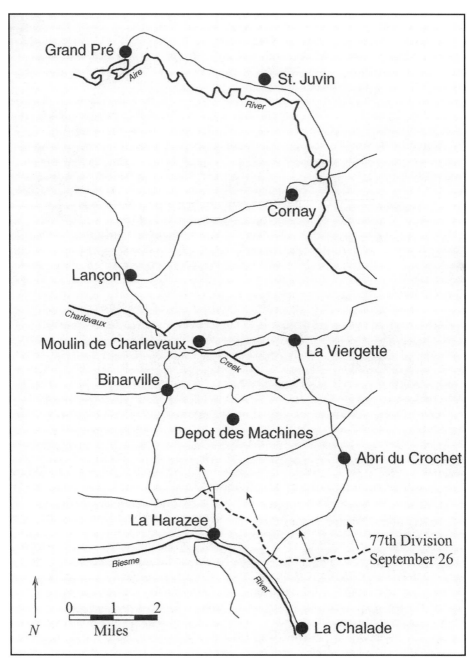

Grand Pré

St. Juvin

Aire

River

Cornay

Lançon

Charlevaux

Moulin de Charlevaux

Creek

La Viergette

Binarville

Depot des Machines

Abri du Crochet

La Harazee

77th Division
September 26

Biesme

River

0 1 2
Miles

N

La Chalade

Seventy-seventh Division in the Meuse-Argonne Campaign

the "black, gloomy, forbidding" forest—Whittlesey and the others, troubled by what they had seen, rejoined their commands.[31]

Replacements had finally arrived to make good the terrible losses sustained on the Baccarat and Vesle fronts. On September 20, some four thousand soldiers had been transferred from the Fortieth "Sunshine" Division to reinforce New York's Own. These were western men, originally National Guard troops from Arizona, California, Colorado, Nevada, New Mexico, and Utah, "of unsurpassed physique, hardy and enduring." As the Liberty Division had represented the New York melting pot, these new arrivals embodied "the bone and sinew of the great west, full of its boldness, replete with its spirit of initiative and practicality." Troops from the Fortieth Division "came from the ranches and the mines, from the forests and the factory, from the vineyards and the marts of commerce. Every practical handicraft, every business, every learned profession, was represented." On September 16, 1917, National Guard troops from these six states, many of them veterans of the Mexican border affair of 1916, were assigned to the Fortieth Division and rendezvoused at Camp Kearny, California. Before its departure for France, the division was reinforced by thousands of draftees from National Army cantonments at Camp Lewis, Washington, and Camp Funston, Kansas. Sidney Smith, one of the draftees from Camp Lewis, said, "We were all sheepherders, cowpunchers, bricklayers, and the like. They threw us together to make an army."[32]

By the time the Fortieth Division left Camp Kearny on July 26, 1918, about fourteen thousand of its men were raw recruits. Their trip across the Atlantic had been uneventful, the highlight on one ship occurring when an unpopular lieutenant became seasick and began puking his guts out while standing at the deck railing. Just as he let loose, another seasick soldier on a deck above vomited the contents of his stomach all over the sick officer below, his men approving with an outpouring of "hearty guffaws." Upon reaching France, the division was sent to La Guerche, where it was broken up and its troops sent forward to fill depleted ranks of veteran divisions. Many of these new officers from western states outranked veteran New Yorkers who now commanded companies. Such a situation existed in Company C, 308th Infantry, where Second Lieutenant Gordon L. Schenck had assumed command as senior officer on August 23. A graduate of Adelphi and Yale Universities, Schenck had been a Manhattan banker before he

Second Lieutenant Gordon L. Schenck, killed by a trench mortar shell on October 7 while leading Company C, 308th Infantry. From *Brooklyn and Long Island in the War.*

graduated from the Plattsburg Training Camp on August 15, 1917. Schenck had served with Company C during its entire tour of duty in France and officers and enlisted men alike were "proud to have known and been associated with him." The lieutenant was a splendid combat officer and Captain Whittlesey had recommended him for promotion. But now command of the company would pass to "an utter stranger," Captain Leo A. Stromee. He had come up through the ranks of Company K, Seventh Infantry, California National Guard, having first enlisted as a corporal on April 8, 1908. A resident of San Bernadino, Stromee had been a captain for over a year. Although Stromee had never been under fire, by virtue of seniority he outranked Schenck, a respected old hand from the Baccarat and Vesle.[33]

Private Ralph E. John was a sample of the western men who joined the Liberty Division just prior to its latest campaign. Born on January 19, 1890, John was a farmer near Marmarth, North Dakota, when he registered for the draft on June 5, 1917. A native of Kansas, John was tall, medium weight, blue-eyed, and had dark brown hair. His only disability was a weak knee. John was inducted into the army at McIntosh,

South Dakota, on May 24, 1918, and set out for Camp Lewis, Washington. Admitting to being single and "used to a care-free life on the range and farm," Ralph John confessed that "my parents were the only care I left behind." He remained at Camp Lewis for about five weeks, learning a little drill and turning down a promotion to corporal, then entrained for Camp Kearny, where he joined the Sunshine Division. Although he had received only a scant four days of rifle practice, the young man did not mind, saying, "I had carried a pistol or rifle with me all the time while riding the range back in South Dakota, and I could shoot." After leaving California in late July, Private John described his seven-day train trip to the East Coast succinctly: "Across mountains, onto the plains, into cities bulging with factories all booming with industry and the final stop at Camp Mills in New Jersey." This was just "a brief stop to get our ground legs again and a breathing spell, and onto a big boat for the hop across the pond."[34]

The 308th Infantry had received some 1,250 men from the American West, most of them wild as range cattle and "entirely unbroke to the matter of war." They appeared to be "fine material," but

He was just a long, lean country gink
From 'way out west, where the hoptoads wink;
He was six feet two in his stockin' feet,
An' kept gittin' thinner th' more he'd eat.
But he was as brave as he was thin,
When th' war broke out he got right in;
Unhitched his plow, put th' mule away,
Then th' old folks heard him say:
Good-by, Ma! Good-by, Pa!
Good-by, mule, with yer old hee-haw!
I may not know what th' war's about,
But you bet, by gosh, I'll soon find out.[35]

"their lack of training was as unquestioned as their valor." Without a doubt, some soldiers in the 308th "took the jump-off into the Argonne battle who did not know how to use a hand grenade or to work the magazines of their rifles." Colonel Cromwell Stacey said of them: "They were brave and loyal, and willing to do anything they could. The only trouble was that they didn't know how to do anything." One New Yorker actually charged a rookie five francs for showing him how to insert a clip! In the 307th Infantry, replacements numbered about nine hundred, the "largely untrained and wholly inexperienced" westerners being divided up equally between the companies. Captain Rainsford said of them, "Though none had apparently ever seen a grenade, and many seemed never to have fired a rifle, yet they were healthy-looking, untired, and well-clothed, which was true of not many of the others. These men had in fact been inducted into the service only three months before, and had spent two of those three months in travel." Companies had to be reorganized and rookies assimilated into existing squads, then provisional promotions to sergeant and corporal were made to handle the private-heavy rosters, since the Fortieth Division had retained most of its noncoms for training purposes. One veteran officer noted that newcomers "were quick to absorb the pointers handed out by the older men" and "had the proper spirit, which was the only real equipment necessary."[36]

Lieutenant Weston Jenkins of the 307th gave a scathing critique of the scanty preparation that replacements had received. He noted that most of their training had consisted of close order drill, but "not half enough of this to inculcate habits of obedience and discipline." Then Jenkins gave specific examples. Many westerners "did not seem to understand the use of a rifle as a weapon, and seemed to be absolutely ignorant of the bayonet and its use." Additionally, "not one of them had seen a hand grenade or a rifle grenade," and, in fact, "they had never heard of them." Jenkins pointed out that they had never seen a Chauchat automatic rifle and had "no idea of target designation or fire control." Duties relating to guard and outposts were a mystery to them, as were skills related to scouting and patrolling. In Lieutenant Jenkins's opinion, written after the Seventy-seventh Division had gone over the top, replacements "were excellent material individually, but they lack the training and discipline which made the majority of them uncontrollable in battle."[37]

This unique East-meets-West blend of soldiers in the Liberty Division would conduct operations in the Argonne Forest under a new set of combat instructions issued by General Headquarters of the AEF on September 5. It had become clear that the machine gun would be the primary German defensive weapon and new tactics would now be employed for attacking enemy positions. Small detachments of scouts would lead any advance, deployed "at wide and irregular intervals, 10 to 50 paces, to present a poor target to hostile machine guns." The job of scouts was simply "to compel the enemy machine guns to open fire and so disclose their location," or, in plain English, to be human targets. Once the enemy opened fire, the advance platoon came forward "individually or in small groups," adding rifle and Chauchat fire to that of the scouts and pinning down the Germans. Those on the right and left were to wrap around the German flanks and close in on the machine gun crew, being careful not to expose their own flanks while doing so. According to these new instructions, a platoon leader with the ability to size up a situation and formulate a plan of attack could pin the Germans "by frontal and flanking fire, under cover of which some portions of the platoon, usually those sent against the hostile flanks, can close by short rushes with the enemy." Staff officers felt that one infantry platoon could thereby "capture one or even a pair, of hostile machine guns."[38]

In addition to giving platoon leaders much wider latitude in dealing with enemy machine guns, these new combat instructions placed more responsibility on battalion commanders. To give them more firepower, each front line battalion would be reinforced by a machine gun company, whose captain would report to the infantry major, but place the guns himself. Two one-pounder guns, "the most effective single weapon in the infantry regiment for use against machine guns," and two light Stokes Mortars were also assigned to each advance battalion. Officers from supporting batteries would accompany each advance to provide "close and direct liaison between the artillery and the infantry," allowing battalion commanders to add fire from 75mm guns to their already formidable arsenal. This new directive then concluded, "Where strong resistance is encountered, reinforcements must not be thrown in to make a frontal attack at this point, but must be pushed through gaps created by successful units, to attack these strong points in the flank or rear."[39]

Of course, these new combat instructions merely codified what infantry companies had already learned the hard way. German tactics dictated that machine guns fire short bursts and never more than one hundred rounds at a time, the better to keep positions concealed from American eyes. But each New Yorker had become more and more proficient at locating machine guns, which were often protected by sheet iron or logs and masked by rocks or branches that would suddenly send "those bullets chirping like the quick sweet notes of the meadow lark (for it is thus they sound) just above his helmet." Trained eyes would watch for "a thin bluish haze" of expended smokeless powder or matted grass and leaves forced flat by muzzle blasts. Leaves with their undersides turned up could indicate an unnatural arrangement of tree branches. Bits of vines or bark or leaves floating to earth would indicate the path bullets had taken.[40]

Once an enemy machine gun had been located, gangs of infantrymen went after it. These New York soldiers, some of them once members of street gangs, now ganged up in a novel tactic adapted for the modern battlefield. Each gang numbered between eight and twelve specialists trained to cooperate as a team, with a platoon typically divided into four gangs. Rifle fire was generally ineffective against a well-positioned machine gun, so the riflemen and a Chauchat team would keep the German crew pinned down while grenadiers would carefully work toward the objective. If grenades could be used effectively (tree branches and heavy brush had a tendency to stop a grenade's flight prematurely), the bayonet men would spring forward and finish off any dazed survivors. In an ideal situation, two gangs would work together, one cautiously moving toward the right flank and the second toward the left before closing in for the kill.[41]

Unfortunately, there were few officers and men familiar with these tactics remaining with the Seventy-seventh Division in late September. Veteran status had come at a frightful cost. In speaking of the First Battalion, 308th Infantry, Lieutenant Arthur McKeogh stated that there were only ten officers instead of the twenty-nine authorized by regulations "and that instead of the paper strength of one thousand men, we had less than seven hundred, and more than half of them, new from the States, *had never before been under any kind of fire!*" McKeogh then remarked sadly, "Of our original Camp Upton battalion, just two hundred and seventy-five 'old-timers' remained." As far as possible, replacements would be relegated to carry rations and ammunition or to cook or to guard duty or to any other post that would free up veterans for deployment in the firing line. Unfortunately, companies were still so short-staffed that officers found it imperative to shove many of these rookies into the maelstrom that lay ahead.[42]

Last Letter of Private Joseph B. Dyrdal, Company B, 308th Infantry: "Whatever you do, don't worry. I am getting along fine. Don't expect letters too often, because it sometimes is pretty hard to get a chance to write, as we do a lot of moving around, but will write whenever I get a chance. From your soldier boy, Joseph."[43]

Officers received orders and studied maps, veterans bitched about cramped quarters in French barns, replacements tried to learn the names of their corporals and sergeants, all marking time as plans were laid for the massive undertaking scheduled to commence on

September 26. Behind a thin screen of French outposts, nighttime hours saw feverish activity. Picked details from the 302nd Engineers, reinforced by the Fifty-third Pioneer Infantry, crept forward to construct bridges over unused trenches and to cut lanes through the tangles of barbed wire that protected French outposts. Men assigned to these wire-cutting parties discovered "a chaos of trench, *chevauz de frise*, and the most amazing barricades of wire" they had ever encountered. No Man's Land was filled with "jungles of barbed wire" that probably could not be cut before the attack began, so Engineers resorted to a couple of novel plans. First, they would carry forward torpedoes, two-inch pipes filled with TNT. Once placed under a section of wire, their explosions would obliterate wire and posts alike, leaving gaping paths for the infantry. The disadvantage of this scheme was "to transport these dainty weapons in safety and to explode them where needed." A second plan called for the manufacture of large chicken-wire nets that could be thrown over the barbed wire, but again the transport of such bulky netting presented a daunting difficulty.[44]

Once the attacking infantry got across No Man's Land, it would run into the labyrinth of German wire. Cutting lanes through this obstacle would be the responsibility of the division artillery. Every available cannon had been placed in position for the greatest barrage ever fired by an American army, some two hundred guns behind the Seventy-seventh Division alone. There were 75mm guns of the 304th and 305th Artillery, 155mm pieces of the 306th, 8-inch howitzers from the corps artillery, and 6-inch rifles on loan from the French Army. The Liberty Division's "Boche Battery" was there too. Organized at Camp Upton and trained at Camp de Souge, the 302nd Trench Mortar Battery had never fired its 6-inch Newton-Stokes Trench Mortars in combat. During the Vesle campaign, Captain Samuel Reid used his men to staff a battery of captured 77mm German guns and remained continually in action using Hun ammunition against its former owners. The "Boche Battery" had now been equipped with 105mm German howitzers captured on the advance to the Aisne River. Captain Reid remembered, "The boys of the 302nd could not understand the German marks on the shells, but they soon managed to load the howitzers and use them to advantage against the Fritzes."[45]

This vast array of cannon lay concealed in dense forests bordering those few roads that transected the division front. Secrecy was paramount and nothing was done to alert the enemy. No new observation posts were built and no American guns were allowed to fire in response to stray German shells. Maps and gun coordinates were aligned by the stars. A complete telephone system had been constructed between the batteries, but Captain George Dyke explained they "were under orders not to talk or even ring up, for fear of Germans listening in and discovering our preparations." Dyke did comment that finally, on September 25, "all lines were to be tested by noon by ringing and saying '*Oui*' or some other French word." The artillery would begin its barrage at 2:30 A.M. on September 26 and continue for three hours. After cutting lanes through the German wire and pounding reserve positions, the 75mm guns would start to drop shells on the German front line trenches at 5:30, while the bigger guns kept hitting the back areas. Precisely at 5:30, infantry would go over the top. They would follow behind a rolling barrage that would begin five hundred meters to their front, advancing in one hundred-meter increments every five minutes. General Alexander told his infantry commanders to stay close to the barrage and advised them, "If you lag behind and it passes on, before you get there, the enemy is up and using his weapons. Keep as close to it as you can."[46]

Happily for the doughboys, enough American aircraft and crews had arrived to establish some sort of parity in the air. The Fiftieth Aero Squadron, just three weeks in existence and its airmen still "green as gourds," had been assigned to the Liberty Division's front. They flew two-seater biplanes, DeHavilland DH-4s, nicknamed "Flying Coffins" and sporting the Dutch Girl trademark of Old Dutch Cleanser, an emblem indicating American determination to "clean up" the Germans. Floyd Pickerell remembered that prospective pilots reached training camp only to be told, "There is your airplane—go fly it." Demand for American pilots and aircraft at the front was so critical that those who could not solo in six hours were booted out of the program. Pickerell would later admit that he had no more than three hours of flight time in a DeHavilland and had never fired a machine gun from an aircraft before being sent up to fight the experienced German airmen. What they lacked in experience, American pilots made up in numbers and General Alexander hoped that they could at least keep German observers from sending targeting information to their batteries on the ground.[47]

Unaware of all these preparations, infantrymen finally learned that they would jump off at 5:30 A.M. on September 26. All four regiments of the Seventy-seventh Division would be in line, from right to left, the 305th, 306th, 307th, and 308th, this latter regiment occupying the left not only of the division, but also the First Army Corps, and the American First Army. Ground between the Liberty Boys and the Fourth French Army would be assigned to Groupement Durand, a mixed force consisting of the 368th Infantry, Ninety-second Division from the American Army and the French Eleventh Cuirassiers a Pied.[48]

Soldiers of the Liberty Division huddled in soaking wet woodlots, waiting for the word to form for the attack. Lee McCollum, one of the replacements, noticed, "Gone were the merry-making and quips of bravado." When a bugler blew the alarm call as a German airplane flew overhead in the dark, anti-aircraft batteries opened fire. Seeing fear on a newcomer's face, one old hand said quietly, "Dat's nuttin' buddy. Wait 'til yuz gets a load dumped on yuh!"[49]

During the night of September 25–26, Americans received the long-awaited order to move forward to their jump-off positions. In addition to battle packs, they also toted extra iron rations, bandoleers crammed with ammunition, sacks of hand grenades, boxes of rifle grenades, signal rockets, and wire cutters. To make room for all this extra baggage, division headquarters ordered all tents, blankets, extra boots, overcoats, and raincoats left behind. Men would travel light and fast. All that mattered was food and ammunition. Finally, officers clutched their orders, maps, and aerial photographs and started their commands to the assigned trenches, but problems began to crop up immediately. Military Police directed the marching columns, but French guides, who thought the whole idea of attacking in the Argonne was insane anyway, made only half-hearted efforts to lead the Americans. Runners disappeared into the muddy blackness and never returned. Orders passed back from the head of a column never reached the rear since, as Captain Rainsford observed, "a Polack or some limited intellect would invariably intervene as a non-conductor." Some units were still stumbling blindly forward when the guns began to roar.[51]

6

OVER THE TOP

"Hell broke loose in scores of thundering voices," in the words of one officer, who then added, "Mount Vesuvius, the San Francisco earthquake and Niagara Falls, rolled into one and multiplied by ten, blazed, crashed and roared through the Argonne that night." Captain Bradford Ellis exclaimed in wonderment, "Lordy! How the big guns did roar!" A gunner from the 306th Field Artillery described how the big 155mm guns fired off round after round: "'Bang' goes a howitzer and the hot barrel recoils smoothly up the cradle. The breech is opened on the way up and is quickly washed with a wet cloth. The loading tray is placed on the runners. A shell, cleaned, greased, and fused, is immediately lifted on it, and, with a hollow clank, is rammed into the bore. Up comes the powder bag, away goes the tray, slam goes the breech, in goes a primer, 'Ready,' calls the gunner, and the crew stand clear and hold their ears. 'Fire,' calls the sergeant; 'Bang,' roars the howitzer."[1]

Gunners standing beside the 304th Field Artillery's 75mm guns listened as battery after battery began to rock the forest. After what seemed like an eternity, their orders arrived: "Then, at a nod from the section leader, each number two picked up a shell and shoved it into the breech of his gun. Number one closed the breech with a bang and took hold of the lanyard. There was a tense moment of waiting. Then,

'Fire!' In an instant every gun in the regiment leaped on its carriage and sent its shells hurtling over the tops of the trees in the valley below. Now the whole mass of artillery was crashing forth its storm of destruction into the trenches and dugouts and ravines on the other side of No Man's Land. The roar of the guns, the tinkling of the empty shell cases as they were tossed aside, the voices of the officers and section chiefs as they gave the commands, the whizz of the departing shells all mingled in one vast racket and confusion of noise that no pen can describe." So it went, round after round after round for hours on end, men standing to their work amid a storm of man-made thunder and lightning.[2]

Precisely at 5:30 A.M., the artillery switched to a creeping barrage. Men from the sidewalks of New York and the California beaches and most places in between climbed out of the old French trenches and started forward into No Man's Land. Rookies had been paired with veterans wherever possible. Now the western men followed the old-timers, who moved forward "cautiously in a half crouched position" with bayonets fixed. When the first rounds of German fire came buzzing past, doughboys responded by shooting blindly into the underbrush. Lee McCollum, under fire for the first time, observed, "It is strange how quickly you learn all of war's sounds and what they mean. The chatter of the machine guns and the sharp whining zing of bullets were within a few hours as familiar a sound as street cars to city dwellers."[3]

Hey! You know Tony the barber,
* Who shaves and cuts-a the hair?*
He said skabooch to his Mariooch,
* He's gonna fight over there.*
When Tony goes over the top,
* He no think of the barber shop;*
He grab-a da gun and chase-a da Hun
* And make 'em all run like a son-of-a-gun![4]*

Soldiers could see only a few yards through the shroud of dense mist hanging so thick that platoons and companies quickly lost all connection with one another. Californians said it was "as thick as a San Francisco fog." Flickers of light up ahead marked the pace of the Allied barrage, but cautious doughboys moved slowly, because "everything was confusion and everybody seemed to be lost." An officer in the 307th recalled, "One literally could not see two yards, and everywhere the ground rose into bare pinnacles and ridges, or descended into bottomless chasms, half filled with rusted tangles of wire. Deep, half-ruined trenches appeared without system or sequence, usually impossible of crossing, bare splintered trees, occasional derelict skeletons of men, thickets of gorse, and everywhere the piles of rusted wire."[5]

Captain Rainsford gave the classic description of No Man's Land through which the Seventy-seventh Division advanced on September 26: "It was a bleak, cruel country of white clay and rock and blasted skeletons of trees, gashed into innumerable trenches, and seared with rusted acres of wire, rising steeply into clawlike ridges and descending into haunted ravines, white as leprosy in the midst of that green forest, a country that had died long ago, and in pain." Captain Tiebout described ground "so barren, churned, pitted and snarled as to defy description," all choked with "billows of rusty, clinging wire" that grabbed at both cloth and flesh. William Harrigan said it reminded him of a scene from Dante's *Inferno*.[6]

Lieutenant Arthur McKeogh accompanied the advance of Major Whittlesey's First Battalion of the 308th Infantry: "We went through such rank growth that there was always danger of losing the man ahead, although he was almost within arm's length. Vines clasped your neck and roots entwined your feet till you were prisoner of untamed Nature. And with it all the fog hung persistently over the valley." Seeking to emphasize the difficulty of advancing through this loathsome woodland, McKeogh declared that fighting in the Argonne made it seem that, by comparison, General U. S. Grant's Wilderness Campaign had been fought on a polo field. Fortunately for the attackers, this initial barrage had sent most Germans scampering for the rear, leaving behind bodies of those either too slow or too stupid to evacuate their trenches immediately. Private Sidney Smith jumped into an abandoned trench, where he found "some old man in his 60s" who had been hit between the eyes. A few dazed survivors from the Second Landwehr Division, "pitiably middle aged, with stringy hair and shallow cheeks," were easily made prisoners. A soldier from the 308th looked at these forlorn creatures and muttered, "This is a hell of a battle so far! Like fighting your grandfather!"[7]

It had all seemed so cut and dried during operational meetings when regimental, division, and corps objectives had been carefully traced on the maps by staff officers who lived in the rear echelons. Out in the forest, officers tried dutifully to guide their commands by compass readings, but promptly got lost in the first swamp, tortuous ravine, or tangle of underbrush they encountered. Befuddled squads and platoons wandered in circles, bumping into similarly confused units from other regiments. It reminded one man of the old story of a lost Indian, who saved face by declaring, "Indian not lost. Indian here. Wigwam lost." The Liberty Boy then added that "now it seemed probable that both the wigwam and the Indian were lost, together with most of the tribe!" There were brief bursts of rifle fire, but German defenses were surprisingly quiet now that the rolling barrage had far outstripped the infantry advance. Whenever gunfire would erupt, men appeared suddenly out of the fog as they charged forward to get in on the fight. As German resistance stiffened and the fog began to lift, the American advance began bushwhacking on a massive scale and Captain Tiebout said, "We continued to stalk our prey from tree to tree." German snipers and machine gunners began to take a toll on the doughboys. James Larney watched the casualties come back from the advance: "One man walked by with his eye bandaged and his face covered with blood. Another wounded in the stomach. Others in sides and legs, ankles, knees, etc."[8]

Among those officers trying to sort out that jumble in the jungle, was Major Charles Whittlesey, commanding the First Battalion, 308th Infantry. Born on January 20, 1884, in Florence, Wisconsin, young Charles

I've got my wind up, honey,
A-laying' way out here in No Man's Land.
Where the shells are fallin' fast,
And I think I'm smelling' gas.
For machine gun bullets are whistlin' 'round me,
The old tin hat's a-feelin' mighty small;
Inside it I'd like to crawl and hug the ground
Just like a porous plaster.[9]

moved with his family to Pittsfield, Massachusetts, and graduated from the local high school. Nicknamed "Chick" by his schoolmates, Whittlesey graduated from Williams College in 1905 and earned a degree from Harvard Law School in 1908. He joined a New York City law firm, but in 1911 formed a partnership with his friend, J. Bayard Pruyn, and opened an office at 2 Rector Street in New York. Whittlesey served as a private in Company L, Seventh Training Regiment at Plattsburg in July 1916 and again in the Officers' Training Camp during the period May 14–August 20, 1917. Commissioned a captain of infantry at the conclusion of training, Whittlesey left his law firm on August 8, 1917, and reported to Camp Upton, where he was assigned to command Headquarters Company, 308th Infantry.[10]

Major Charles W. Whittlesey, commander of the Lost Battalion. From *Williams College in the World War.*

Arthur McKeogh recalled that his first impression of Whittlesey "left me thinking of him as an affable, extremely reticent and somewhat professorial sort." Only later did McKeogh learn that the seemingly aloof Harvard lawyer actually had a sense of humor "keen as a safety blade" and was really a "regular guy." L. Wardlaw Miles, a fellow officer at Camp Upton, recalled, "He would recount the absurd happenings of that period with so keen an eye for the ridiculous and such dry humor as to cause the lieutenants to collapse hopelessly in merriment." After a week of military duty at Yaphank, Whittlesey would head into New York City and unwind at the Williams Club on Saturday night, where, as Miles recalled, "he would get telling some of his fool stories and half the club would end up sitting at that table." His dry wit would occasionally creep into official communications, as on September 12, 1918, when friendly artillery began clipping off tree branches overhead. Whittlesey sent this message to the offending battery: "Twice within the last fifteen minutes your shells have cut down some of the smaller branches in the trees over our heads here, at approximately 205.4–269.45. If your range contemplates a still flatter projectory will you advise us so we can keep cover when the heavier branches come down?"[11]

McKeogh described his superior as "slender to the point of being thin, and his six feet two inches of height did nothing to detract from his appearance of tenuous elongation." Once when the two officers, "crowded as twin peanuts," shared a funkhole near the Aisne River, while shells burst around them, the captain abruptly exclaimed, "Oh, why didn't God standardize me!" Whittlesey never learned that the regulation stride for a quick-time march was only thirty inches and he would constantly set a furious pace "almost Prussian in its rigors," earning him the nickname of "Galloping Charlie."[12]

Whittlesey's adherence to duty was obsessive in the extreme. On one occasion, he refused to furnish runners to his own colonel because his command had been assigned to brigade reserve and was thus subject only to the brigade commander's order. Another time he closed the company kitchens, even though men were still in line for breakfast, because he had orders to advance at a specified time. But Whittlesey could also be seen in the Argonne "handing out uncut bread and cold, greasy bacon to the men, like any delinquent doughboy punished by assignment to 'kitchen police.'" Minutes later, someone spotted him calmly directing troops against a German machine gun "with a piece of bacon between his fingers as a baton." McKeogh said he was "absolutely indifferent" under fire, "not wantonly courageous, but seemingly oblivious of the danger." Although promoted to major just before the Argonne offensive, he steadfastly refused to replace his captain's bars with gold oak leaves. When Adjutant McKeogh offered to do the honors one night, Whittlesey simply stuck his fork into a can of beans and remarked softly, "I suppose it would be wise to wear them. I suppose a major gets better treatment than a captain in the hospital. But it's so dark you'd get them on crooked, Mac. Guess we'll wait."[13]

Major Whittlesey led the advance of the 308th Infantry into the Argonne Forest despite a lingering case of dysentery, as well as a severe cold that had left him unable to speak above a whisper. Galloping Charlie attacked German trenches at the head of battalion headquarters—a hodge-podge of about seventy runners, scouts, cooks, telephone linemen, and medical men—at his typical pace, going through the Argonne Forest as if it were nothing more than papier-mâché, at least according to Lieutenant McKeogh. Whittlesey could often be spotted in the lead, clearing pathways through Boche obstructions with a long-handled pair of wire cutters. It was no surprise to anyone that First Battalion headquarters, essentially a noncombatant group, was the first organized unit to reach the corps objective on that first day. His fighting companies came up a few minutes later.[14]

Overall, American casualties had been slight on September 26 and they had taken several prisoners. Battalion headquarters were established for the night at Karlsruhe, a village of German huts constructed of iron and concrete, carefully whitewashed and tastefully appointed with cots, chairs, and tables. Bottles of mineral water belonging to the previous occupants were passed around to thirsty doughboys, who held the front either in captured trenches or water-filled funkholes along a swamp.[15]

Orders arrived too late for the infantry to follow the morning barrage, so there was no serious advance on September 27 until almost 2 P.M., the morning being taken up with consolidating the previous day's gains, transmission of orders, improvising defenses, and much premature congratulation. Now well within the Argonne, the Americans had a chance to examine their oppressive surroundings. Lieutenant McKeogh offered a description: "Huge trees tower protectingly above their brood of close-grown saplings, branches interlacing branches overhead until no patch of sky is visible and the light is the sickly half-light of early dawn. The ground hides under a maze of trailing vines, prickly bushes, rheumatic tree branches, imbedded in soggy leaves, with here and there a clump of rank fern. The undergrowth is so tangled as to give the impression that nature had gone on a debauch and later, viewing the havoc, in a moment of self-spite had added to her riotous handiwork. No birds sing. No living thing moves. Like the sear leaves, like the rotting tree trunks, it is a place of death." Edwin Lewis saw "a maze of thick wire grass, interspersed with chocolate pools of mud and sterile stumps of trees that had died in the artillery barrages of the first

PFC Charles Minder, 306th Machine Gun Battalion: "There is one fellow in our platoon, his name is Hamilton, who doesn't believe in God at all. When he sees the fellows down on their knees, he ridicules them, and says, "What the hell good is all that praying going to do you? If your name is on one of those shells, you are going to get it no matter how much you pray. Don't you think that the men who have been killed already in this war for the past four years prayed? Don't you think their wives and mothers prayed for them? What the hell good did it do them?"[16]

months of the war." Lewis concluded with the comment, "In shell holes on this heath of hell the witches of war could have cooked a horrible brew."[17]

Because the enemy had been given time to reestablish machine gun nests hastily abandoned during the initial American barrage, when the attack belatedly continued on the afternoon of September 27, progress was much slower. Advancing in squad columns, Whittlesey's companies found themselves arrested time and again, so that "Stokes Mortars, chauchats, bombs, and rifles were all employed to dislodge the enemy machine gun nests." Company A fought a series of engagements, Corporal Joseph Demaree recalling that hand-to-hand confrontations were avoided "only by the precipitous flight of the bewildered Germans." Company D found "dense woods and barbwire in abundance," compounded by their Chauchat's ammunition jamming repeatedly, forcing the men to rely solely on rifles and grenades. Abraham Krotoshinsky, an immigrant Polish barber before joining Company K, 307th Infantry, said the Argonne was "a regular jungle full of swamps, vines and heavy underbrush." Used to dodging New York City traffic and pedestrians, Krotoshinsky now discovered that "everywhere you went were barbed wire and machine gun nests. You never could tell how near you were to the Germans, as you could not see ahead of you, the woods were so thick."

Martin Lokken wrote of the Argonne advance, "I never thought that it could get as bad as it did and then have humans in it."[18]

Rations came up on the morning of September 28, a welcome sight since the veterans had shared their reserve rations with newcomers and everything edible

Captain Bradford Ellis, Operations Officers, 306th Infantry: "I shall never go into woods again or into underbrush without having my heart come up into my throat. The only way to discover a machine-gun nest was by the sudden dropping of yourself or your neighbor."[19]

had been consumed. Company E feasted on "cold cabbage, beef, and bread," while Company B enjoyed "bacon, butter, bread, and a one pound cannon barrage from the Germans." Whittlesey's battalion, now merged with Major Kenneth Budd's Second Battalion, started off at 7 A.M. and after two hours reached a German cemetery four hundred yards south of Depot de Machines. Heavy resistance from the area around Moulin de l'Homme Mort was countered by an American artillery barrage. The attack then continued in two columns.[20]

Companies B, D, E, and G advanced north along the eastern edge of a large ravine, ran into a storm of fire near Depot de Machines, and fell back to the cemetery. Edwin Lewis, fighting with this column, recalled, "A line of skirmishers in that tangled brush and swamp land would become disorganized into a line of stragglers in half an hour, no matter how hard the officers and N.C.O.s tried to keep in touch with their men." Before Company B had gone far, it completely lost touch with troops on both flanks, was raked by German fire from the right and rear, and retreated after losing twenty men, including eight noncoms. Company D attacked "after spending a long, cold sleepless night in trenches partially filled with water," men cramming captured German potato-masher grenades into their belts in anticipation of the day's work. Sidney Smith would always remember one particularly wicked potato masher that "hit this fella right in the chest and the explosion shot his heart right out his back, I believe for 20 feet. His gun was at port arms, and that grenade made a fish hook out of his rifle."[21]

New combat instructions issued to battalion commanders just before the initial advance had proven to be virtually worthless. One-pounder guns and Stokes Mortars could scarcely be lugged through the wilderness, and firing them was actually more dangerous to their crews than to the Germans, since shells would hit branches and burst almost immediately. Rifle grenades were similarly useless. Machine gunners, those "heroes of the Hotchkiss," never acquired targets and simply blasted blindly in the direction of supposed enemy positions.[22]

Nothing could be expected from the artillery, all liaison between it and the infantry having fallen victim to the forest. Observers had nothing to observe and there was absolutely no method to determine accuracy of fire. Innumerable gullies and ravines and jagged ridges "complicated the calculation of all data." Opposing forces became so closely intertwined that often American shells fell on American soldiers. Captain Rainsford confessed that American artillery support "had frankly become a thing to dread." He explained that "infantry and artillery officers were actually taught quite dissimilar methods of representing a given point on the map by coordinates," a discrepancy compounded by "an almost criminal inexactness on the part of very many officers in map reading." Infantrymen became afraid to call for artillery support. Held up by machine gun fire, one company commander in the 307th Infantry sent the following message: "Can't locate guns close enough to get them with Stokes and think artillery had better be put on them. But if so let us know in time to withdraw, as it has a habit of hitting us."[23]

All things considered, fighting in the Argonne was an infantry slugfest. German officers would gradually withdraw their own infantry, leaving behind camouflaged machine guns to contest the American advance. After gunners disclosed their locations by mowing down a few Americans, doughboys would literally crawl under cover to within a few yards of concealed nests before attacking with hand grenades, rifles, bayonets, and fists. One soldier said, "Stalking through the woods, like walking automatons, we seemed to be without blood, or flesh, or heart, or soul." Death walked alongside them. According to the division history, "East-siders and West-siders of New York, the soldiers from Third Avenue, and from Central Park West," along with those western-state reinforcements, "were becoming adept woodsmen and learning the craft of the forest hunter." It was Darwinian survival at its most brutal—those able to master the art of fighting in the Argonne could live for a few more hours, those who failed would soon die.[24]

A view in the Argonne Forest with a dead German soldier in the foreground. From Miles's *History of the 308th Infantry.*

Private Ralph John, the young man from Marmarth, North Dakota, wrote out his experiences in the Argonne drive and remembered starting off with a peculiar sensation, not fear or dread so much as "a feeling of wonderment at what we might see or learn." Before long, John could confess, "I didn't think anything of stepping over dead bodies of men with whom I had started out or wading through a pool of blood." He explained that the Argonne drive had settled into a dangerous but monotonous routine of "hiking, crawling, searching for machine gun nests and routing them out." On one occasion, Private John crept forward and threw a grenade toward an enemy position, but it either hit a branch or exploded prematurely, or he simply could not throw it far enough. As dirt and stones pelted the Americans, his sergeant yelled out, "Good God, man, can't you throw any farther than that?" It was worth a laugh and John explained that without telling a little joke or repeating a popular vaudeville routine now and then "many fellows would have gone raving mad."[25]

It was Christmas Day in the harem
  And the eunuchs were standing around.
In strode the bold, bad Sultan
  And gazed on his marble halls.
"What would you like for Christmas, boys?"
  And the eunuchs answered, "Balls!"[26]

On the afternoon of September 28, while Companies B, D, E, and G were encountering heavy opposition on the eastern side of the ravine, Majors Whittlesey and Budd led Companies A, C, F, and H along the western edge and made considerable headway, but were finally checked by German forces. Lieutenant McKeogh described this advance as "machine gun Indian warfare," where "bayonet and pistol clashes were common." McKeogh also saw that "every abandoned trench, every innocent-looking clump of bushes might conceal nests that would wait for the invaders to pass and then drop them from the rear." Corporal Demaree reported, "With stealth and cunning, crawling sometimes from tree to tree, caught often in the hidden wire and finding protection in the sunken ground, we reached our objective, captured a number of machine guns, and, as we had expected, found the Germans had withdrawn." Near dark Whittlesey and Budd consulted their maps and decided they were only one hundred yards south of l'Homme Mort, the corps objective. They deployed their four companies in a square and the men dug funkholes in a heavy rain that left everyone feeling that "his whole body was wrapped in iced towels." Lying in funkholes half-filled with mud—"a night of utter wretchedness," according to James Larney—doughboys gladly filled their canteens with rain that dripped from leaves and helmets, the first clean drinking water they had found since the captured German mineral water. Before dozing off, Adjutant McKeogh sent two messages to regimental headquarters, requesting food, ammunition, and flares to signal Allied aircraft. The first dispatch went by carrier pigeon, although when last seen the bird was flying northward over German lines, while the second was sent by messenger back along a series of runner posts, "two or three men at intervals of a few hundred yards," which was supposed to expedite communication. Neither message reached its destination.[27]

Early on September 29, officers both near l'Homme Mort and at regimental headquarters realized that the line of runner posts had been broken. Colonel Cromwell Stacey ordered Lieutenant Colonel Frederick Smith to reestablish communication with Majors Whittlesey and Budd from the south. Smith set out just after daylight, leading a party composed of two officers, a guide, and several enlisted men to act as runners, everyone carrying ammunition for the cut-off troops. They followed a path up to within a quarter-mile of Whittlesey's position when a machine gun suddenly opened fire on them. Everyone dove for cover, then pulled out pistols and began shooting wildly at the Germans. Smith fell wounded in the side, but struggled to his feet and continued to fire. He staggered back to get a few grenades from the enlisted men, refused to accept first aid, and was killed while attempting to gain a position to bomb the concealed nest. After the patrol withdrew, the Germans carried Smith's body about a hundred yards into the forest and searched it for documents. In a letter to his widow, Major Whittlesey would write, "There was no one in the regiment whose death has been so keenly felt. Officers and enlisted men alike were heartbroken at the news."[28]

On the northern end of the chain of runner posts, Majors Whittlesey and Budd decided to send Lieutenant McKeogh, in charge of five three-man Chauchat teams and a bunch of new runners, to reopen the line that had been cut at the cemetery. McKeogh's small party had not gone far before the men began shooting Germans at both ends of his column, mortally wounding an officer who admitted there were large numbers of enemy troops in the immediate vicinity. Upon reaching the cemetery, McKeogh spotted three Germans behind a bush and ordered a

German-speaking Jew to tell them to surrender. After considerable shouting back and forth between the interpreter and the Germans, McKeogh demanded, "Damn it, what's he saying?" "Why, lieutenant, he expects us to surrender—to do a Kamerad to them!" This bizarre conference continued over a cemetery wall until McKeogh "cut short this little international debating society" and ordered an attack. German rifles answered American pistols and wounded McKeogh's only noncom.[29]

Now additional German machine guns opened fire and later McKeogh remembered that the thick woods sounded "like a riveters' competition," a few rifle grenades being lobbed at the Americans for good measure. Two Chauchats jammed, leaving the doughboys seriously outgunned as they faced at least six machine guns. McKeogh's party began to take casualties: "One poor chap who lay at my right, within reaching, raised his head a few incautious inches just as a stream of bullets clipped off fern leaves above our helmets. He slumped forward without a sound and lay still. I wriggled over to his side. But there was nothing to be done for him. Indeed, it was he who served us—even in death; for he had a full pannier of ammunition." As the Americans grimly hung on, John J. Monson came dodging through the woods, carrying a message from Whittlesey instructing the adjutant to take two enlisted men and somehow get back to regimental headquarters. McKeogh sent Private George W. Quinn back with an acknowledgement, then selected Monson and Jack Herschowitz to accompany him. Quinn disappeared and his fate remained unknown until January of 1919.[30]

They didn't give Quinn the D.S.C., for they didn't know how he died,
But three still forms around him sprawled, they could have testified:
They could have told before he was cold—if he hadn't plugged their hide.

No one was there when the thing was done, deep in the Argonne glade,
No one but Quinn and the three in gray, and there the four have stayed,
Where the night winds' hush through the soughing brush is a psalm for the Unafraid.[31]

As the rest of the patrol left to rejoin Whittlesey's main force, McKeogh, Monson, and Herschowitz drew their pistols and began to crawl slowly around the machine guns. After about forty-five minutes of creeping under bushes and around trees, the three messengers discovered a wide path that led due south toward the American lines.

Private George W. Quinn, killed on
September 29 while acting as a runner
for Major Whittlesey. From Foreman's
*World War Service Record of Rochester
and Monroe County, New York.*

They began to make good time, when suddenly two German officers
emerged from a side trail. Everyone began firing pistols. One German
fell with a bullet through his brain and the other one scampered off.
McKeogh, who was wounded in the arm during this spur-of-the-
moment gunfight, commanded, "Herschowitz, go over and see if he's
dead." Jack did not care for McKeogh, who had once contemptuously
referred to him as a "buttonhole maker," and he had no desire to see
a dead man, but he went as ordered. Herschowitz and Monson rifled
through the German's pockets, looking for anything that might help
the intelligence division, then took a photograph of the body. Afraid
that their brief skirmish would bring more Germans, the Americans
crawled back into the jungle, where they all reloaded and Monson
hurriedly dressed McKeogh's wound.

After napping until sunset, the three again began "the eternal
crawl," a sort of "crawfish stroke" where "the elbows are pushed out
ahead and upon them as anchors the rest of the body is then drawn
up." Eventually, they found themselves apparently surrounded by
enemy funkholes. When McKeogh heard the snap of the safety on a
German rifle, he sprang up and shouted out the decidedly unmilitary
command, "Spread out and beat it!" The Americans scattered into the

darkness, making no effort to hide, just running "hell bent through the brush." McKeogh saw some cover and jumped into it feet first. He recalled, "I landed on something soft and opened my eyes to find that my legs were straddling the neck and shoulders of a Hun. Standing right in front of me, within touching distance, was another German soldier, and all three of us, the Germans and myself, for a second were too surprised to speak." For perhaps fifteen seconds there was stunned silence as the German under McKeogh struggled to get free. The lieutenant continued, "Then I guess my brain functioned an instant quicker than the brain of the Heinie staring at me, for I got out my automatic and plunked him twice through the face. He dropped with a grunt, and then I shot downward between my legs into the back of the German I was straddling and killed him."

Surrounded by "an uproar of shouts and shots and flashes," McKeogh ran for his life. Tripping over a root, he slid down a hill and landed in a pile of leaves that provided a hiding place as enemy soldiers searched for the intruder. While thus concealed, he heard pistol shots in the distance where Monson killed another German. Taking advantage of a driving rainstorm, all three men eventually staggered into regimental headquarters with news of Whittlesey's plight. After describing his adventures to Colonel Stacey, McKeogh concluded by stating "that Herschowitz and Monson were a couple of damn fine kids and ought to be recommended for the D.S.C. or something." In fact, all three men would receive a Distinguished Service Cross for their perilous journey that night, Herschowitz and Monson also being awarded the French Medaille Militaire and Croix de Guerre.[32]

Back at the four-sided pocket, Whittlesey sent off a series of carrier pigeons with messages to the 308th PC (Post of Command). He informed headquarters that patrols sent out to establish a connection with the four companies east of the ravine had failed to return. Although badly in need of ammunition and food, no carrying parties had been able to get by those Germans who had occupied the cemetery. Major Whittlesey understood his mission was to "advance and to maintain our strength here," but admitted, "it is very slow trying to clean up this rear area from here by small details when this pricking sack of machine guns can be used by the enemy." He then asked, "Can line of communication not be kept open by units from the rear?" Sergeant Herman Anderson of Company A had led a patrol about two miles to the southwest in search of Groupement Durand, but found only a few pieces of discarded American equipment and a whole lot of Germans. Sergeant Major Ben Gaedeke had taken another patrol to the north, killed a German lieutenant and sergeant, and returned with a map showing a hitherto unknown trench system. Unable to establish a connection across the ravine to the east and with Germans in strength to the north, west, and south, Whittlesey's four companies were completely isolated.[33]

This situation had developed because of a combination of German tactics, "aided by our unfamiliarity with the region and the natural confusion of American forces." There was also a complete absence of roads on the front occupied by the 154th Brigade. Every scrap of food and every round of ammunition had to be carried forward by hand and, as the Americans gained ground, more and more men were required to carry supplies over greater and greater distances. Front-line battalions would thus be reduced in numbers, while ever more tenuous supply lines were liable to be cut at any time. Whittlesey's situation was not unique, so he consolidated his position, set out small observation posts, and waited for relief. Now it was the Americans' turn to get even: "A snapping of twigs in the bushes, the noise of a stealthy approach brushing aside the branches would fall on the ear. Not a sound from our line. Suddenly the air would be torn to shreds by the racket of a hundred rifles and Chauchats going off at once. A dozen men would shout 'I got him' and someone would run out and drag in a limp form of a Boche machine gunner, caught in the attempt to steal forward under cover and get our men by surprise. Often there were at least fifty bullet holes in the body."[34]

Help arrived in the late after-noon hours of September 30, when Company K found McKeogh's

Captain Charles M. Bull, 306th Infantry: "The best way to take a prisoner is to shoot him first."[35]

north-south path and followed it to Whittlesey's pocket. A lieutenant with the relief column found the four rescued companies worn out, starving, and insatiably thirsty. Immediately upon being relieved from this pocket, Major Budd reported to the General Staff College and Captain George G. McMurtry, Company E, assumed command of the Second Battalion. Born November 6, 1876, McMurtry was a student at Harvard University when the Spanish-American War began, but left school to join Troop D, First United States Volunteer Cavalry, Teddy Roosevelt's famous "Rough Riders." Returning to New York after the

Captain George G. McMurtry, Major Whittlesey's reliable second in command, who was wounded in the knee and shoulder. From Hussey's *History of Company E, 308th Infantry (1917–1919)*.

war, he became a successful stockbroker before heading off to the Plattsburg Training Camp, where he graduated as a first lieutenant. Promoted to captain in December of 1917, McMurtry proved to be dedicated, solid, and dependable. A brother officer called him "as cheery and cool as he was conscientious and capable." Another contemporary said, "I don't believe that a braver or more heroic soldier ever trod a battlefield. He was stern and determined but kind, and had a keen sense of humor. No sacrifice was too great for him to make for the comfort of his men. They all loved and honored him."[36]

Attention of the 307th and 308th Regiments now centered on Depot de Machines, a vast German supply dump and terminus for a narrow-gauge railroad that snaked through the Argonne. Captain Rainsford remembered, "The whole slope of timber south and southwest from the Depot de Machines seemed to be filled with machine-guns, and the long east and west ridge to the north of it was lined with them." General Alexander ordered his artillery to blast the enemy from their entrenchments. Infantry huddled in funkholes under persistent shelling, when suddenly the American gunners opened fire, seemingly "trying to outdo the Germans in the amount of shells thrown over." Someone in Company D of the 308th recalled that "in the afternoon our barrage fell short and it seemed for a bit as though our own artillery were going to drop a couple in on us, it being necessary for us to signal the artillery the facts of the case." Pushing forward behind the American shelling, the 154th Brigade overran Depot de Machines, dug holes and rested that night. Private Krotoshinsky remembered that the Boches "drew back to the next row of hills that crossed the woods, leaving us in the jungle valley to breathe their gas and eat their Minnewerfers and Seventy-sevens."[37]

Some food finally caught up with the advance battalions. John Nell remembered, "Just before night a ration detail came up with American made white bread and white Karo syrup and bacon, but hardly enough bacon to go around. The bacon ran out just before it got to me. It was then two slices of bread and two spoons full of syrup for each man." Despite being ravenously hungry, Nell admitted, "I was getting pretty damn weak, but all of this shelling and machine gun fire kept me under such constant strain and fear that food was not a priority. All I could think of was to be on guard at all times, and do what I could to survive." On the brighter side, part of Nell's battalion had at one point occupied an old trench on the edge of "the first open space that had been encountered in the drive to date."[38]

The capture of Depot de Machines cannot be overrated. Details from the 302nd Engineers quickly connected the French narrow-gauge railroad at La Harazee with its German counterpart, simplifying the shipment of food and ammunition and evacuation of casualties. Some sixty freight cars had been abandoned, although every locomotive had been run off or destroyed. Appeals by General Alexander for replacement engines went unanswered, so "traction was supplied by the U. S. Army mule." These mules performed admirably for the Seventy-seventh Division, hauling 850 tons of supplies into the forest and 500 wounded men back to hospitals. Without this rail system, Alexander admitted that "a continued advance in the forest—on our left at least—would have been found entirely impracticable." But the booty included so much more than just the railroad. Millions of dollars' worth of construction equipment proved "a God-send to the engineers," one of whom explained,

"From this time until the Armistice, the Regiment relied almost exclusively on the material abandoned by the enemy."[39]

Promptly at 6 A.M. on October 1, Major Whittlesey ordered the First Battalion from its bivouac on the slope north of l'Homme Mort and followed a friendly barrage deeper into the Argonne. Captain McMurtry's Second Battalion trailed at a distance of about three hundred yards. Captain Leo Stromee wrote with a touch of optimism in his diary, "On our way to beat Fritz. men in good spirits & growing strong." Some lucky men had been refreshed by their overnight stay in captured German dugouts "made of concrete with mission furniture and fancy upholstery, electric lights, and all the conveniences of a well-regulated home." One of the men grumbled that "it was hell to take us out of perfectly good dugouts to make us sleep on the bare ground." Despite an irrepressible spirit, men's bodies were beginning to break down and nearly everyone suffered from diarrhea. Uniforms were constantly wet, either from rain or sweat, and cootie bites had turned into large infected sores.[40]

John Brown's baby's got a pimple on his—shush!
John Brown's baby's got a pimple on his—shush!
John Brown's baby's got a pimple on his—shush!
The poor kid can't sit down.[41]

Everyone was just plain damned tired. One of Whittlesey's men admitted, "It wasn't any easy go by a long shot, and at nights the whole outfit were moving so slowly, from a distance they hardly looked as if they were moving at all." A Montana replacement added, "I was near all in. I took the bayonet off my rifle because I had to catch myself from falling two or three times, and I was afraid I would fall down on my bayonet."[42]

Lieutenant William Scott's Company A, "exhausted, and without food and water" according to Corporal Demaree, led off on the left flank where the underbrush was much less dense than that encountered previously. In one clearing they stumbled upon a German headquarters building that had been smashed by an artillery round. Splintered logs and dead Germans littered the ground. "For three hours they climbed and trudged, fighting their way through the wire and brush," until brought to a halt under machine gun and trench mortar fire near an apple orchard. After being checked here for an hour while Stokes Mortars tried to blast the enemy's line, the battalion launched an attack as its own machine gun detachment finally got into action. McMurtry's support battalion came up with Whittlesey's line and the combined command advanced together. Ralph John described the scene: "Pop! Pop! Pop! started a machine gun. All of us dropped as close to the ground as we could. There were a lot of them who didn't get close enough to the ground. As soon as Jerry stopped shooting, we crawled around until we found the door leading to the machine gun nest. I threw a hand grenade in and just as it hit the door, it exploded. Here they came out and really acted as if they were tickled to death to get out alive. There were six of them. Three looked as if they were around seventy years of age and had great long whiskers. But the other three looked very young." Doughboys then examined this dugout according to their prioritized checklist: live Germans, food (usually nothing but "old dank black bread"), ammunition, and souvenirs. As for the latter, there was always a vast array, so they took only "the best and smallest," weight of an object always being an important consideration for those who had to tote it around.[43]

Lieutenant Karl Wilhelm, commanding Company E since McMurtry's elevation to battalion command, had recently returned after being seriously gassed on August 15 on the Vesle front. Now he heard his two advance platoons become heavily engaged and rushed forward, accompanied by his orderly, "a little Italian from New York." Wilhelm told what happened next: "The orderly was preceding me by 15 or 20 yards when I suddenly heard him shout and lunge with his bayonet behind a group of bushes. Much to my amazement a six-foot German was partially hidden there and in a moment the German and the orderly were hot at it with their bayonets." Confessing to his surprise, Wilhelm stared at the deadly contest for perhaps thirty seconds, then came to his senses, ran forward, and shot the German. Expecting to receive at least a "thank you" for saving the man's life, he was shocked when the disgusted orderly turned around and blurted out, "Oh, hell, Lieutenant, what did you want to do that for? I'd have had him in a minute myself!"[44]

Company A got beyond the orchard, but only after losing Lieutenant Scott, who had assumed command that morning, and First Sergeant Herman Bergasse. Private Lee McCollum said that "men were being wounded faster than they could be handled" by the medical detachment. Sergeant Herman Anderson took over and, after losing over ninety men, ordered Company A to fall back and make connection with the rest of Whittlesey's command. There was not much of Company A left. It had started on September 26 with 205 men, but now casualties and large details for runners and stretcher bearers had reduced that number to less than forty rifles. Lieutenant Wilhelm's Company E began with over two hundred soldiers and now totaled two officers leading just over fifty men. Lieutenant Harry Rogers counted less than one-half of his original strength in Company B. One of Rogers' doughboys said simply, "Grit was carrying them forward." Despite such horrific losses, rear echelon staff officers thought that not enough was being done at the front.[45]

All attempts to advance farther along the steep western slope of this large north-south ravine had been thwarted by automatic weapons, so Whittlesey halted his men for the night about three hundred yards north of the Moulin de 'l Homme Mort—Binarville Road. He would later report that "this day showed considerable losses and very little progress." His force became further depleted when an order arrived to detach thirty men from Company G to establish runner posts back to regimental headquarters along the narrow-gauge railroad. This command separated two buddies from Griggs County, North Dakota, Carl Michaelson and Sigurd Lima, who had left Cooperstown together in the same draft contingent on May 24, 1918. They first went to Camp Lewis, Washington, then were transferred to Camp Kearny, where the pair got split up and lost track of one another. Both men somehow ended up as replacements in the same squad of Company G, 308th Infantry. Now Michaelson, a native-born North Dakotan, and Lima, a foreign national from Stavenger, Norway, waved good-by to each other as Michaelson marched off with the runner detachment. They would never see one another again.[47]

Notes on Recent Operations, No. 3, General Headquarters, A.E.F., October 12, 1918:
The divisions participating during the first few days of the Meuse-Argonne offensive, as a rule, did not display the markedly aggressive spirit which is required by the American mission in this war. Advances were generally too slow and too cautious. The fruits of victory were, therefore, not what they might have been. The infantry sometimes seemed more concerned with the avoidance of loss than with a desire to close with the enemy. . . . Troops have been taught not to make frontal attacks against machine guns. It may be that such instructions have over-emphasized the conservation of men until timidity has been produced.[46]

After posting the other runners, a sergeant returned to the Second Battalion with his last pair of men and announced, "You two boys will be battalion headquarters runners for the night." John Nell, one of the duo, remembered that the ravine was crowded with "old log sheds, a few larger log buildings, a little railroad, and some dead Germans." One doughboy described it as "a regular village," with dugouts, a mess hall, bathhouses, latrines, and a place for religious service. Captain McMurtry had taken over a three-room log cabin near the German railroad, while regimental headquarters had been established in a concrete dugout about two hundred yards away. Nell recalled, "There was a little car sitting on the track with board sides and both ends open. A dead German with his head and feet sticking out over both ends of the car was stinking terribly. I recall he had a sandy red mustache. I gave the car a shove with my foot, and the car ran about a hundred feet then left the rail. This got the terrible odor away from us." Over at First Battalion headquarters, James Larney did what he could for his mortally wounded boyhood friend, Edward B. Smith of Company A, who lay in the night air, "groaning and vomiting" and occasionally murmuring softly, "O, Lord!"[48]

Lieutenants Eager, Heitman, and Harrington, who had just been reassigned from the 366th Infantry, a Negro regiment of the Ninety-second Division, reached this German village about 11 P.M. on October 1. They had just finished a four-week stint of front line duty in the St. Die Sector and had now been transferred to the Seventy-seventh Division, which was still desperately short of officers. After reaching division headquarters at Florent, they trudged forward to the rear echelon of the 308th Infantry, where their paperwork was examined, then walked another three miles to Colonel Stacey's headquarters. Lieutenant Sherman Eager recalled their chilly reception: "We were taken inside where we were introduced to Major White, the Adjutant, who in turn introduced us to Col. Stacey, Commander of the Regiment. Col. Stacey seemed to be very nervous and excited and his nervousness seemed to be reflected in his whole headquarters staff. Our reception was very cold and short. In fact, we seemed to be looked on as intruders on his eminent domain. We did not stay in that charged atmosphere very long but soon wandered outside." After about five minutes, Adjutant White emerged and told the three to "move farther away as the Colonel was afraid the dugout might be shelled if German observers should notice us hanging around." A little later, Colonel Stacey came out and told a cook to give them a meal from whatever food he had left. While the lieutenants dined on a supper of prunes and bread, Stacey assigned Heitman to the One Pounder Squad, Eager to Company G, and Victor Harrington to Company E.[49]

7

BREAKTHROUGH

On the morning of October 2, Whittlesey attempted another advance west of the ravine, but found the Germans could not be budged and admitted that his "chief difficulty was in trying to manage both sides of the ravine at the same time." Companies D and F, supported by A, G, and H, held the line west of the ravine where the Germans seemed most numerous. Companies B and C, supported by E, operated east of the ravine. About 10:00 A.M., Colonel Stacey sent Whittlesey instructions to leave D and F, under Lieutenant Paul Knight, as "a containing force" (although it was the Germans that actually contained them), then advance vigorously along the eastern edge with his other six companies, accompanied by nine teams from Companies C and D, 306th Machine Gun Battalion. Once this command had reached its objective, the La Viergettes–Moulin de Charlevaux–Binarville Road, one company would be detached for an attack on the rear of the Germans to the west. Tired soldiers from Companies A, G, and H slid down the steep slopes to the ravine floor and climbed the opposite side to join the attacking force.[1]

At 11:35 A.M., Major Whittlesey received the following order from Colonel Stacey:

The advance of the infantry will commence at 12:30. The infantry action will be pushed forward until it reaches the line of the road and the railroad generally along 276.5 where the command will halt, re-organize, establish liaison to the left and right and be ready for orders for a further advance. This does not change the plan as given you by Detroit 1 [Colonel Stacey's code name]. You still leave two companies on your left as a containing force, that is the remainder of the 1st and 2nd Battalions. The general says you are to advance behind the barrage regardless of losses. He states that there will be a general advance all along the line.

To carry out his orders, Whittlesey placed the companies in this approximate arrangement:

```
        c    o    u    t    s    s    c    o    u    t
s                                                           s
                         1st Bn HQ
    C C C C                   mg                   B B B B
    C C C C          mg               mg           B B B B
    C C C C
                         2nd Bn HQ
    E E E E          mg    mg    mg                 H H H H
    E E E E          mg    mg    mg                 H H H H
                                                   H H H H
                    G G G G
                    G G G G
                    A A
```

Although McMurtry recalled there was "no regular set formation," each company would generally advance by platoons in single file. Patrols operated on each flank, but when it became imperative "to have a group here and there, that group moved forward and they would string out in zig zag formation just as the situation demanded it." No one could be spared for even a minute, so officers issued commands that "no man leave the column to urinate or defecate, he was to do it right where he stood." During this advance, Whittlesey's front would cover somewhere between three hundred and four hundred yards as the column either expanded or contracted to avoid obstacles in the terrain or enemy fire.[2]

Prior to jump off, details brought up quantities of doughnuts, syrup, jam, and bread, along with a one-day supply of hardtack and corned beef, but several companies did not receive their rations prior to the advance. Even Captain McMurtry failed to get something to eat because he was absorbed in the process of consolidating Company A, now numbering less than thirty men, into Company G, which had been greatly reduced by the previous day's runner detail. Each rifleman carried 220 rounds for his Springfield, but details sent back for machine gun ammunition failed to return and those teams would go forward with only about five boxes per gun. The gunners would have a tough time lugging their equipment over the rugged terrain that lay ahead, since each machine gun weighed sixty-eight pounds, the tripod another sixty-seven, and each box of ammunition about thirty-two pounds. This was the real war, not the abstract game played at regimental, brigade, division, corps, and army headquarters where advances and reverses were traced by brightly colored pins stuck into a map. Officers would congratulate themselves whenever the pins would move forward and look concerned if the markers had to inch backward, but, as Lee McCollum noted, they never saw the mud or blood or "weary, war-worn men *who died that pins might move.*"[3]

As the Allied barrage commenced, Lieutenant Wilhelm went in search of a Chauchat outpost that he had posted beyond the edge of the ravine the previous night, but now could not be found. Since he had placed the men himself, Wilhelm figured he could find them. Instead, he ran into trouble: "I came upon a group of five figures who were looking at right angles to me and who, of course, could not hear of my approach because of the noise of the barrage. Never doubting but what they were my post I advanced to within some 15 or 20 yards of them when suddenly one of the figures saw me approaching and without getting up, fired at me with a revolver over his shoulder. Luckily the bullets merely struck the little finger of my left hand and as a matter of fact I did not know for some time that he had wounded me, being too much plain scared." As the Germans lobbed a few grenades in his direction, Wilhelm, now thoroughly frightened, raced back to his company. Assembling a squad, the lieutenant returned to give battle, but found that the foe "had left for parts unknown."[4]

Once Wilhelm returned, Major Whittlesey gathered his company commanders together, discussed their orders and objective, and gave the command, "Leaders, get your men up!" Promptly at 12:30, with 75mm shells screaming overhead, the major saw that everything was in order and gave the command, "Let's go! Forward!" They started north in the ravine bottom, following the narrow-gauge railroad that paralleled a small stream. Lieutenant William J. Cullen, a red-headed New York lawyer, remembered that they had only advanced about two hundred yards before being hit by fire from trench mortars and concealed machine gun nests. Cullen noted, "Snipers were all over the damn place and it was getting pretty warm." Germans fired from the high ground on both the left and right, but the scouts had a hard time locating them in the heavy underbrush. Whittlesey pressed his men on down the ravine, which happened to be an undefended gap between the flanks of two German corps, neither of which had officers with enough forethought to construct defenses or pile up barbed wire in the gully itself. Soon the scouts had penetrated beyond the enemy trench line. Lieutenant Rogers sent Company B's flank patrol farther to the right, where it captured two officers and twenty-eight enlisted men from the Third Company, 254th Regiment, Seventy-sixth Reserve Division. Men from Company H discovered and destroyed several abandoned machine guns.[6]

From: The Allies.
To: W. Hohenzollern, Germany.
Subject: Travel Order.
1. Proceed plumb to hell.
2. The travel directed is necessary in the military service.
By direction of
General Good.[5]

John Nell said that "bullets popped and cracked as they passed through the air and hit the brush, taking their human toll as usual." At one point, he "could feel hot puffs of air and hear the hissing of bullets going by" within a few inches of his face. Nell fell to the ground and watched as the stream of projectiles nearly cut an eight-inch tree in half. A couple of minutes later, Nell saw one soldier strike a match to light a buddy's cigarette. Suddenly, a shell hit the man with the cigarette square in the chest, "blowing his insides out on the ground, and knocking the boy holding the match unconscious for a while." Some heavy gunfire from the west struck Richard Hyde in the hand and knocked him back against Emil Peterson, who helped his buddy staunch the blood gushing from the wound. Ralph John thought that to continue north would be "sure suicide" and was relieved when Whittlesey diverted his column to the right up a tributary of the large ravine and onto the slopes of Ridge 198. Nell recalled the forest was so

German prisoners captured by a squad from Company B, 308th Infantry, when Whittlesey's command broke through enemy lines on October 2, 1918. From Moore's *U.S. Official Pictures of the World War.*

dense that "our vision was only in and around where we were standing or walking." Snipers fired constantly and Lieutenant Eager remarked, "The bullets seemed to come from all directions. Even if you wanted to get behind a tree you couldn't tell which side of the tree to get on for safety." Whittlesey described his progress as "necessarily slow"; often the only way through the thickets would be to follow some of the small paths worn through the brush during four years of German occupation. Clifford Brown remembered, "We kept moving on in the face of heavy fire." Occasionally, one of the scouts would yell, "Everybody that's gone ahead has been killed!" Each time this happened, the advance would slow down. Exasperated by these delays, Major Whittlesey finally shouted out, "Advance until the last man drops!"[7]

Shortly after 5 P.M., tired doughboys reached the crest of Ridge 198 that overlooked the Charlevaux Valley. Across a sluggish stream and more than midway up the opposite slope could be seen a gray streak that delineated that day's objective, the La Viergettes–Moulin de Charlevaux Road, at this point running generally east and west. Whittlesey and McMurtry examined the terrain with field glasses and spotted several small groups of German soldiers walking along the roadway well off to the left. After a short consultation, they decided to occupy a position just south of the road, the steep reverse slope making it impossible for German artillery to reach them there. Lieutenant Cullen's Company H, the largest, would hold the left flank, partially sheltered by a small ridge that jutted south from the road. Strung out to the right of Cullen would come Lieutenant Rogers's B and Captain Stromee's C. Whittlesey and McMurtry, surrounded by the runners and scouts (including a scattering of men from Companies D, F, and I), would set up their headquarters in the center of the line. To their right would be posted Lieutenant Fred Buhler's hybrid company of G and A, with Lieutenant Wilhelm's Company E occupying the right flank. After deciding where to locate his riflemen, Whittlesey conferred briefly with Second Lieutenant Marshall Peabody, Company D, 306th Machine Gun Battalion, about placement of the nine automatic weapons.[8]

Slipping and sliding down the slope, Whittlesey's scouts entered the bottom of an east-west ravine that farther west formed a "T" with the large ravine they had followed north from l'Homme Mort. Fed by springs off to the east, a small stream flowed westward between marshy banks on its path to the Charlevaux Mill, some five hundred yards west of the defensive position chosen by Whittlesey. The valley itself was from sixty to a hundred yards wide, while the brook and its muddy banks had been spanned by German engineers with a wooden footbridge about five feet wide. Although choked with weeds and clumps of bushes, the valley offered an open view to both east and west, one of the few instances during the last week when soldiers could see farther than fifteen or twenty yards. There was also a patch of open ground that appeared to have been used as a drill field and a dirt road along the stream. But the Germans could see in this opening as well. Because Germans had been spotted to the left of his position, the major built his line from the left, Cullen's company crossing the stream first, the rest of the men following in a long single-file, snake-like formation. Lieutenant Eager said, "We crossed the bridge one at a time and as fast as we could run," amid a scattering of sniper shots and machine gun bursts that wounded a few men. While crossing the low ground, someone stumbled upon a young German soldier, who, finding himself suddenly surrounded by a bunch of Americans, raised his hands and yelled, "Kamerads! Kamerads!" Herbert Tiederman, one of the headquarters men, remembered that Whittlesey took the youngster along and kept him nearby during the next few days. Charley Meyers, a German-speaking Minnesotan, asked the captive how he liked the war and received the response, "Not very well."[9]

McMurtry said that the companies "were gradually filtered to their positions," where soldiers began to dig funkholes in the stony, root-clogged soil of the steep hillside. By 6 p.m., taking advantage of exposed tree roots, stumps, and fallen timber, the doughboys had gotten under cover in what Whittlesey described as "an oblong formation," some three hundred yards long and sixty yards deep. Within the space allotted to each company, men dug their holes wherever they liked. Edward Kennedy, one of Peabody's machine gunners, recalled that the funkholes had simply been dug "in zig zag shapes all over." Men scooped out earth with sticks or whatever tools they had. Julius Langer, one of Lieutenant Cullen's men, explained, "I had only a messkit spoon and the bayonet to dig with, but it is wonderful how fast one can dig when bullets are whistling around. There was dirt flying in all directions for a few minutes, and it was everybody for themselves." John Nell recalled, "I was still carrying an old broken hoe I had picked up. We would break the dirt and rocks loose with the hoe, then dig it out with our hands." Soldiers joked grimly about digging their own graves.

Privates Leonard N. Glenn and Raymond E. Hammond, two replacements from Idaho who shared a funkhole during the five-day ordeal. From Peterson's *Lost Battalion Survivors from Minnesota and the Northwest.*

Raymond Hammond and Leonard Glenn, a couple of pals from Idaho in Company B, dug in at the foot of a big tree but were never satisfied with their shelter, the latter explaining, "Every day we dug a little deeper."[10]

A friend of Herman Ratonda became one of the first casualties: "On Oct. 2nd, I dug in a short distance to the side of a tree, and I told my buddy that we ought to dig in behind the tree for better protection. He was sitting up and I told him he better get down, and just then a shell came over and he was killed. The piece that hit him looked like an old plow lay." Clyde Hintz came close to sharing that fate. Cut off by machine gun fire while crossing the swamp, he was forced to hide in the chilly water until it was safe to emerge. Hintz finally rejoined his comrades and dug a hole, completing his shelter just moments before a shell burst a few feet away. There were wounded men lying in the swampy ground along the creek, including Adlare LeMay and two others who could see Germans walking around and hear them conversing. One of the three Americans could speak German and he would occasionally call out an offer to surrender. After two days, all three were taken captive, but LeMay, who had been slipping in and out of consciousness, awoke to discover his captors had stolen "about $50 I had, as afterwards I could only find ten cents."[11]

Concerned about those Germans who had been spotted earlier, McMurtry selected a two-man patrol from his old company, George "Hully" Newcom and John Hott, and sent them off to the west in search of the French, who had not been seen since the jump off on

September 26. Newcom and Hott followed McMurtry's advice to "keep under cover of the road." They crawled through the dense brush that lined the highway, careful to stay at least five yards apart, and had gotten almost within sight of Charlevaux Mill when the pair heard voices above them on the road. Newcom ducked into a thicket, but a rather naive Hott asked, "What outfit is that up there?" A response came in the form of a German corporal pointing a Luger at the American's chest, while nine other Germans emerged from the underbrush with rifles and a machine gun. When the corporal ordered Hott up to the road, Newcom silently took aim at the enemy squad leader. But the German rifles were pointed directly at Hott, so Newcom figured to spare his buddy's life and held his fire. The Kansan sank to the ground, watching as the captors took away Hott's rifle and began to search his pockets before slipping away in the shadows. Waiting until dark, Newcom crawled back to Whittlesey's position and reported that, yes, indeed, there were a lot of Germans off to the west.[12]

The road that the patrol had followed, apparently one of those old Roman highways constructed of stone blocks rather than concrete, had been cut into the ridge and sloped gently from east to west. This road-way would be their firing line to the north, although the steep slope above it was heavily wooded and thick with underbrush all the way to the crest, so that Germans could get in close by dodging from tree to tree. To the south, soldiers could see across the valley before their vision became blocked by foliage on Ridge 198. Whittlesey dispatched a mes-sage along the string of runner posts, stating his present location to Colonel Stacey. He then sent a patrol over the crest of the ridge, placed guards on each flank, selected sites for latrines, and ordered his men to have supper. Those who had received rations that morning shared with those who had not. Four men from the medical detachment—James Bragg, Irving Sirota, George Walker, and Saul Marshallcowitz—tended to dozens of wounded soldiers who had been carried along with the column. Although Whittlesey's command had suffered about ninety casualties, many of those hit early in the advance had been carried back to first-aid shelters north of l'Homme Mort. The dead, out of necessity, had been left behind. Although most of the line remained undisturbed that night, Germans probed the defenses of Company H. Lieutenant Cullen remembered, "We heard them coming up, although we could not see them." The attack began with a few bursts of machine gun fire, then "they came in close and bombed us with potato mashers." A few nervous men shot at the sounds of men moving about in the brush, but the lieutenant cautioned them to be patient. As the Germans drew closer, Cullen yelled, "Commence firing!" He said later, "The crack of those rifles was certainly music to me and after about ten minutes the Boche were gone and came no closer that night." Whittlesey's command rested safely, although the blankets, overcoats, and slickers that had been left behind on September 26 would have provided comfort against the cold. William J. Powers had a bad feeling about this new position: "I was leery of the place. The air had that quietness about it that seemed to say, 'All is not well.' I could hear voices speaking German back where we just came from."[13]

Did you ever lay out in the cold all night,
When the frost just creeps thru the ground;
With an empty gut and a parched tongue,
In a place not fit for a hound?

If you have, perhaps you can sense,
Of the things I'm a tryin' to tell,
And why every man who came out alive,
Could say that he'd lived thru Hell.[14]

At 6 A.M. on October 3, Whittlesey gave instructions to Lieutenant Wilhelm on how to implement the last portion of Colonel Stacey's attack order of October 2. He was to take all of Company E, numbering only about fifty rifles, across Charlevaux Valley, work them around the north and west slopes of Ridge 198, and attack the rear of that stubborn German force holding up Lieutenant Knight's two companies. A messenger had already been sent to Knight, alerting him to watch for Wilhelm's arrival and urging Companies D and F to push forward and rejoin their battalions. Whittlesey had considered using Company H to reinforce Wilhelm's attack, but decided that Cullen's men would stay put and instead sent along a small ration party and Marshallcowitz from the medical detachment.[15]

Company E got started just after daylight and was slowly working its way around the base of a western slope that overlooked the north-south ravine, which had at this point narrowed to about fifty yards, when a voice from somewhere uphill shouted, "Americans?" Someone answered, "Yes," as they all dove for cover. Then the concealed questioner inquired, "What company is that?" Several helpful doughboys responded, "E!" Wilhelm was instantly suspicious and sent a scout climbing through the tangled underbrush to investigate. When the scout failed to return, Wilhelm crawled up far enough to hear German

Second Lieutenant Karl E. Wilhelm, Commander of Company E, 308th Infantry, who managed to escape the German encirclement on October 3. From Hussey's *History of Company E, 308th Infantry (1917–1919)*.

voices. Creeping back to the company, Wilhelm signaled his men to resume their advance quietly. Just as they started forward, "a shower of hand-grenades greeted them," followed by a fusillade of rifle and machine gun fire from both sides of the ravine. Private Henry I. Miller, formerly a maker of musical instruments in Brooklyn, crawled forward for a shot at one particularly annoying rifleman. Someone heard Miller's rifle crack and heard him shout, "I got him!" Seconds later a machine gun raked the spot and killed the American.

Doughboys fired back, while Wilhelm took ten men and crept forward in search of a way out of the crossfire. After five of his party had been shot before they had gone one hundred yards, the lieutenant correctly decided that escape in that direction "was not feasible" and started to retrace his steps. But a small group of Germans had closed in and cut Wilhelm off from his company. Unable to advance, retreat, or cross the ravine, the only option was to move toward the German position on

Private First Class
Nathaniel N. Rochester.
There would be a plaque
erected to commemorate
his death in the Episcopal
Church of the Messiah in
Santa Ana, California.
From Foreman's *World
War Service Record of
Rochester and Monroe
County, New York.*

the hill above. After creeping only a few yards in that direction, Wilhelm discovered "there were Germans all around us," so he, Sergeant William Callahan, and two privates "crawled into thick underbrush and lay there all during that day." The historians of Company E wrote matter-of-factly, "It was only natural that there was some confusion among the men" at this time. One group followed First Sergeant Harold Kaplan around the northern edge of Ridge 198, but most of them were soon killed or captured. Lieutenants James Leak and Victor Harrington fought their way out of the trap with less than twenty men and managed to rejoin Whittlesey's command. In the middle of the night, Wilhelm and Callahan ever so cautiously managed to crawl through the German position and rejoin the Americans north of l'Homme Mort, carrying word of Whittlesey's location and plight to regimental headquarters.[16]

Among those killed in Wilhelm's abortive attack was PFC Nathaniel N. Rochester, who had left the Santa Ana Polytechnic High School to join Company L, Seventh Regiment of the California National Guard for service on the Mexican border in 1916. A great-great-grandson of Colonel Nathaniel Rochester, one of George Washington's officers and the founder of Rochester, New York, Nathaniel mustered out, returned to school, and resumed his plans to become an architect. When America entered the war in 1917, he rejoined Company L, which soon was mobilized as part of the 160th Infantry. After explaining his motives to his family, Nathaniel said, "Mother, even if I should be killed you must remember I shall always be somewhere." When she objected to the very thought of him dying so young, the soldier sought to reassure her by saying, "But Mother, that would be just like skipping a grade at school." Now PFC Rochester lay dead, killed by shrapnel a month short of his twenty-first birthday.[17]

Informed of Whittlesey's breakthrough by a runner on the night of October 2, General Johnson ordered the Third Battalion, 307th Infantry, to follow his route and exploit that gap in the German defenses. By now Johnson had learned that whenever his advance faltered, the enemy had time to regroup, cut new fields of fire for their deadly machine guns, and string more defensive wire. It was best to keep the Germans moving backward and off balance. Company K, under the command of Captain Nelson Miles Holderman, led the column of reinforcements. Holderman had joined the California National Guard in 1904 and served as an enlisted man until 1915, when he was commissioned second lieutenant of Company L, Seventh Regiment, which came from the Los Angeles area. He served at Nogales, Arizona during the Mexican affair of 1916 and was captain of his company when it mustered into Federal service on August 5, 1917. Assigned to Camp Kearny, Holderman's unit was redesignated Company L, 160th Infantry of the Fortieth Division. Nearly his entire company was transferred to Company K of the 307th Infantry just before the Argonne drive, Holderman joining his new command on September 25. A fellow officer from the Liberty Division said that Captain Holderman "took to soldiering like a kitten to catnip." But Holderman was sick on October 1, although he refused evacuation, telling his lieutenant that "he would rather die on the field than to have the men believe he was trying to avoid the heavy fighting." Thomas Pool, a Texan who had previously worked as a lawyer at Camp Funston, commanded Company K while Holderman was incapacitated.[18]

Captain Nelson M. Holderman, Commander of Company K, 307th Infantry, wounded eight times by German rifle fire and shell fragments. From McCollum's *History and Rhymes of the Lost Battalion.*

About 11 P.M., Pool led Company K northward up the large ravine along the railroad tracks, found the first of Whittlesey's runner posts, and followed those guides through an almost pitch-black night that compelled a soldier to keep in line by grabbing the belt of the man ahead of him. Captain Holderman brought up the rear and tried to maintain connection with Companies M and I, which were supposed to be following behind him. At one point in the inky blackness Pool heard German voices and whispered the command, "No talking, boys, keep quiet and follow the lead man." Their herky-jerky progress, as men bunched up, then strung out, consumed most of the night, but about 4 A.M. Holderman's column had followed those runner posts to the ridge overlooking Charlevaux Valley. Instead of blundering ahead into the 308th, he halted the column and told everyone to get a few hours of sleep. Company K had enjoyed a good supper before starting off, but carried no additional food. Holderman had prudently sent a detail of eight men for rations, including Peter Koshiol, a newcomer from Minnesota. Koshiol recalled that his ration party loaded up and started after the company in an eerie darkness, "so quiet we thought the war was over." They found the railroad and followed it northward, but ran into a force of Germans, whose fire forced them to retreat precipitously with the precious food. Companies M and I, supposedly following Holderman, wandered about in the dark, failed to locate the railroad line, split up, and never passed beyond the German defenses.[19]

After alerting Whittlesey of his arrival, Holderman left his bivouac after sunup, crossed the bridge, and placed his seventy-nine men in the funkholes just abandoned by Company E. Private Krotoshinsky tried to enlarge his newly acquired hole, but soon gave up because "the soil was too rocky." Everyone spent the next few hours digging in "with vigor," enlarging the shallow holes scooped out the night before, digging a large command post to replace the individual funkholes occupied by Whittlesey and McMurtry, and excavating some deeper dugouts for the wounded. Lieutenant Peabody selected permanent positions for the nine machine guns on the flanks and overlooking the valley, the steep, wooded slope preventing their effective use on the northern firing line. Company commanders placed some of their Chauchat teams where they could cover the flanks of Peabody's guns. There should have been eight Chauchats in each company, but these fragments of companies certainly did not have a full complement, so it is now impossible to determine how many Whittlesey actually had at his disposal. Once he had fortified his isolated position, the major sent word back by runner that Wilhelm had left to cooperate with Lieutenant Knight's containing force at the ravine. He again asked for rations, hoping that men from the Third Battalion, then acting as brigade reserve, could carry them forward.[20]

About 8 A.M., a German airplane circled overhead for a few minutes, then flew off. Thirty minutes later, enemy artillery attempted to shell the position, but because of Whittlesey's decision to dig in on the reverse slope, these shells overshot the Liberty Boys and fell harmlessly in the dirt road, creek, and swamp to the rear. Much more troublesome was a *minenwerfer* that began to lob high-angle trench mortar shells into the American funkholes. At 8:50 the major sent off a message by pigeon that read, "We are being shelled by German Artillery. Can we not have artillery support? Fire is coming from northwest." Lieutenant John G. Teichmoeller, liaison officer for the 305th Artillery, sent a pigeon message to his commanding officer that confirmed the shelling by both trench mortar and 77mm guns located to the northwest, then concluded, "Give us artillery; work quickly." Born in Dayton, Kentucky, and educated at Wittenberg College in Springfield, Ohio, Teichmoeller was drafted into the 324th Field Artillery and became a sergeant before entering officers' training. Commissioned a second lieutenant on July 12, 1918, he first joined Battery D, 305th Field Artillery, on September 10. Unfortunately, Teichmoeller had become confused by the tangled wilderness and gave wrong coordinates for Whittlesey's position, a mistake that would soon prove calamitous.[21]

By the morning of October 3, the attack by the First and Second Battalions of the 308th Infantry had gone according to plan, a rather singular experience during the Argonne campaign. Whittlesey's command had advanced as directed, broken through the German defenses, and taken up a strong position at its assigned objective, all virtually according the schedule drawn up at headquarters. Lieutenant Wilhelm had gone off to assist Lieutenant Knight's two companies and Captain Holderman had brought up reinforcements along the line of runner posts, indicating that this tenuous communication network was still actively in operation. Parties had been started back for rations and Colonel Stacey had sent word that blankets and overcoats would be available. Just as things began to look promising for Whittlesey's command, all hell broke loose.

"Where do we go from here, boys,
Where do we go from here?"
Paddy's neck was in the wreck,
But still he had no fear;
He saw a dead man next to him
And whispered in his ear,
"Oh joy! oh boy!
Where do we go from here?"[22]

Robert Pou, one of the new guys assigned to runner posts, told the story: "A runner from the next post dashed up and said that the Germans had captured or killed the other runners of his post. Before he could finish telling us about it, a bunch of Germans popped up all around us. He and another runner threw up their hands and surrendered. The other runner and myself jumped into the brush, but not before we were fired at several times. We worked our way back through the thick brush opposite the bridge which spanned the creek. Across the creek, and not far from the end of the bridge, lay four stretcher bearers and the two wounded they had been carrying, all dead. They had been killed since I had previously crossed the bridge, just a few minutes before." Fred Evermann, a Minnesotan, was apparently the last runner sent by Whittlesey and, after discovering that the posts had been overrun, he went racing off to report that fact. The combination of reports from Pou and Evermann was cause for serious concern and the major reached an obvious conclusion, "It was feared that the runner lane had been broken." McMurtry concurred. This dismal news was compounded by the return of Lieutenant Leak, who stumbled back to the ridge with all that remained of Company E. He reported that Wilhelm was probably dead and Company E had pretty much ceased to exist. Its effective force consisted of Leak, bleeding from a slight head wound, Lieutenant Harrington who had been with the company just over a day, and seventeen uninjured enlisted men. They had carried back George Chiswell, shot through the body, and Frank Habeck, who had been hit in the wrist and head, but both were permanently out of action. All of those in the ration detail had vanished. Events seemed to confirm information gathered from their lone German prisoner, who finally admitted that his company of about seventy men had arrived the previous evening.[23]

Machine guns from the ridge above the road and Ridge 198 began to rake the slope, whizzing bullets "chirping like a flock of canaries," according to Farland Wade. Then there was that annoying *minenwerfer* that continued to plunk high-explosive shells into the slope, one of them hitting on the right flank and burying the unlucky Harvey Farncomb, who had been wounded crossing the valley and now had to be pulled from an early grave by Otto Volz. To counter this *minenwerfer* threat, Whittlesey dispatched Lieutenant Gordon Schenck with a platoon from Company C to put the troublesome mortar out of action. The situation to the rear would require a more substantial force, since Germans now seemed to be swarming all over Ridge 198. Opting to keep troops from the 308th Infantry together, Whittlesey decided to send Holderman's company, technically not a part of his command, back to reopen communications with the Seventy-seventh Division and, hopefully, connect with those lost units from the 307th. The movement would be a dangerous one, so he strengthened Company K with twenty scouts from McMurtry's battalion.[24]

Captain Holderman set out shortly before noon on October 3, but got no farther than the dirt road in the valley, which was "enfiladed by machine guns on the left flank and snipers on the road and there seemed to be snipers in the rear." After waiting about an hour, he tried again, this time sending the men scurrying across the open ground a few at a time. Despite having three men wounded, Holderman succeeded in reaching the woods on the slope of Ridge 198. As the Americans crossed the open valley, a German yelled from the ridge above the Roman road that the Americans were coming and a voice from Ridge

198 shouted back an acknowledgment. Placing his detachment under cover, Holderman sent three patrols to scour the jungle ahead. They soon returned with news that the Germans had apparently disappeared. Taking advantage of this lull in enemy fire, Holderman reported: "Company 'K' commenced its advance due south, with scouts well out and strong combat groups covering the flanks. After passing the first barbed wire system the company came under galling, flank and frontal machine gun fire and rifle fire."

Undaunted by this ambush, Holderman explained: "The men continued forward, firing as they advanced, and penetrated a second barbed wire system. It soon became evident that the company was completely surrounded by a powerful force of the enemy." He added, "We fought them in there as long as we could. I saw that unless I withdrew the column the company would be completely wiped out as they were coming in on both flanks and on the front." Leaving thirty men under Lieutenant Pool to fight a delaying action, Holderman led the rest of his command, including another five wounded, back across Charlevaux Valley about midafternoon. It was nearly 5 P.M. by the time Pool and his rearguard regained their original funkholes on the right flank of Whittlesey's position. Holderman had earlier sent a runner off to his battalion commander, in addition to a couple of patrols with instructions that they make their way back to the 307th. The runner disappeared, both patrols proved unsuccessful, and now the captain had failed to cut his way through with the entire company. New barbed wire entanglements and machine gun nests blocked the old line of runner posts. Convinced that Whittlesey had been completely sealed off, Holderman officially placed himself under the major's command.[25]

After the morning of October 3, the only way for Whittlesey to communicate with regimental headquarters was by carrier pigeon. This process was awkward at best. Birds from the Pigeon Division were assigned to cotes at the various division headquarters, where new arrivals would spend a week to ten days getting acclimated to their new home. They would be dispatched to the front in wicker baskets or wooden crates carried by men assigned to battalion headquarters, who were responsible for their care and feeding. Pigeons were kept on a "light diet" while at the front, so that when released they would immediately fly back home. When events warranted sending a message, it would be written out in longhand and affixed to a pigeon's leg. The soldier bird would then fly back to the loft at division headquarters, where the dispatch would be telephoned to regimental headquarters. This system was, of course, a one-way affair. No confirmation of a message's arrival could be made and, given the relatively high number of missing birds, there was no guarantee of delivery.[26]

Whittlesey's pigeon message sent off at 10:45 reported that "Germans in small numbers are working to our left rear." They were also everywhere else. A patrol dispatched in search of Americans to the east bumped into Germans, exchanged some rifle fire, and returned. Lieutenant Schenck came back from his sortie against the trench mortar to the northwest and said there were just too many machine guns to make any headway. Men stationed over the crest to the north sent word that they had seen large numbers of the enemy off to the northwest. As the situation worsened, Whittlesey wrote out an order that he and McMurtry personally delivered to the company commanders: "Our mission is to hold this position at all costs. No falling back. Have this understood by every man in your command." Captains and lieutenants dodged from funkhole to funkhole with the order. Cullen visited every man in Company H, encouraging them and handing out the last of his cigarettes. As the lieutenant crawled away from each post, he would say, "Stick to it, boys." The answer invariably was "Don't worry about this post, we'll stick to it alright."[27]

About 3 P.M., a voice from the ridge cried out in a Teutonic accent, "Adolph?" From off to the left came the response, "Hier Eitel!" Then another "Hier" sounded from the south. "Nun alles ist in stellung (Now everyone is in position)!" Dritte Kompagnie alle zusammen (Third Company all together)!" Americans atop the crest came slipping and sliding down the ridge, screaming that the Germans were coming. Shouting for the men to "Stand to!", officers got their men out of the holes and up to the firing line along the roadway just as "a shower of potato-masher grenades fell through the trees." Riflemen and Chauchat teams swept the crest with a torrent of fire and after a few minutes the grenadiers slipped away as swiftly as they had appeared. This scenario would be repeated over and over again. The La Viergettes–Moulin de Charlevaux Road and the upper slope would become a narrow No Man's Land. A few Americans would patrol the crest, while their comrades huddled in holes on the lower slope. During an attack, the Liberty Boys would jump from their holes and, according to McMurtry,

View of the Lost Battalion position (the gray streak on the hillside is the La Viergettes–Moulin de Charlevaux–Binarville Road). From Moore's *U.S. Official Pictures of the World War.*

"form our firing line at the ridge just along the roadway." On rare occasions, some Germans managed to slip past the road, but they were always killed or driven back.[28]

No one summed up the situation on the afternoon of October 3 better than Private Robert Manson, who wrote they were "surrounded on a bleak, unsheltered ravine, with the German Army on a cliff above, and with a powerful German detachment deeply entrenched on the other side of the ravine. Enemy troops were so close that we could hear the calls and orders of the men. If we showed ourselves in the openings of the wooded forest, we could be reached by German machine guns, rifles, and trench-mortars." Snipers became a deadly nuisance on the left flank where Lieutenant Cullen noticed them "getting in closer and closer." On the right flank, Wilbert T. Rumsey, a farmer from Square Butte, Montana, in Captain Holderman's company, must have griped about celebrating his twenty-seventh birthday in such God-forsaken spot. He would not live to celebrate another.[29]

Five of the new replacements in Company H had dug in close together. Three Minnestoans—John McNearney, William Burns, and Nicholas Kurtz—huddled in one hole, while only about four feet away were Richard Hyde, from West St. Paul, and George Nies, a tall, slender farmer from Yellowstone County, Montana. Kurtz had been shot in the forearm by a sniper and went dodging off to seek medical attention. The other four quietly talked back and forth until a powerful explosion rocked the hillside, scattering dirt, rocks, branches, scraps of human flesh, and bits of uniform all over the slope. A trench mortar shell had landed squarely on the funkhole occupied by Hyde and Nies, killing them instantly and stunning their neighbors. McNearney managed to retrieve Hyde's watch and would eventually return it to his mother, but aside from a few handfuls of dirt thrown over the bodies, these dead men would remain unburied in their blood-soaked grave for five days.[30]

At 4:05, Major Whittlesey released a third pigeon, carrying the bad news that he had been unable to reestablish the runner posts and Ger-

Sometimes at night by the lone starlight,
And sometimes at break of day,
We bowed our heads and our prayers we said,
As we packed our dead away.[31]

mans had occupied Ridge 198 "in small numbers," but appeared much more numerous to the west. He also requested 8,000 rounds of rifle ammunition, 7,500 rounds for the Chauchats, 25 boxes of machine gun ammunition, and 250 grenades. After giving some sketchy casualty figures, Whittlesey concluded with the succinct observation, "Situation serious." It took fifty minutes for this information to reach the Seventy-seventh Division's message center. By that time, the Germans had launched an attack that Whittlesey would characterize as "the most severe attempted by the enemy while the Americans were surrounded." Apparently overconfident because of their numerical superiority, the Germans again were not very subtle in their preparations. "Rudolph?" "Hier!" "Heinrich?" "Ich bin hier!" "Nun, alles zusammen!" Another shower of grenades bounced from tree to tree on the left flank and "those damn machine guns," as Lieutenant Cullen called them, criss-crossed their fire on Company H. According to Whittlesey, "The ravine rang with the echoes of machine guns, Chauchats and rifles." American machine gunners did excellent work under the supervision of Second Lieutenant Alfred R. Noon, a Long Island architect who had been married just shortly before being drafted. Twenty-seven years of age and a graduate of Pratt Institute, Noon had been promoted to sergeant, graduated from officers' training school, and received his commission in France. Major Whittlesey would later remark that Noon's machine guns had "worked splendidly" and "the enemy must have suffered heavy losses from this source alone."[32]

Lieutenant Cullen admitted that "between the flat projectory weapon (the machine gun) and the high projectory weapon (the trench mortar) they gave us an awful merry time." Cullen sent Frank Erickson, his new company runner, dashing off through the hurricane of bullets and shells to battalion headquarters for reinforcements. McMurtry gave him eight men, but only three of them reached Company H. Dispatched for additional troops, Erickson started back with twelve more, but lost four under the withering German fire. Cullen's second-in-command was Lieutenant Maurice Griffin, a tiny, almost frail-looking officer from Denver. A North Carolina native, Griffin had started his military career in 1902 with that state's naval reserve. After moving west, he joined the Colorado National Guard in 1906 and was commissioned second lieutenant in 1913. Griffin served on the Mexican border and had been promoted to first lieutenant on December 16, 1917, and assigned to the Fortieth Division. Now the newcomer went down when a machine gun bullet tore through his left shoulder. Griffin

First Lieutenant Maurice V. Griffin, wounded through the left shoulder by a machine gun bullet at 4 P.M. on October 3. From Peterson's *Lost Battalion Survivors from Minnesota and the Northeast.*

tumbled into a shell hole and remained there for another five days, helping to repel future attacks by firing a rifle with his good arm.[33]

Lieutenant Cullen saw Sidney Smith fall when one bullet entered his back and shattered a rib, while another struck his right leg. Smith said he looked down and "seen the hole through the front of my blouse and it looked like I got shot straight through the heart." Despite his wounds, Smith was luckier than the buddy with whom he shared a funkhole, as he later explained: "As soon as I got my breath and got over my shock of being hit, I could see my partner had been shot. When I got to him, the bullet had come straight down his rifle barrel and took both the sights off and hit him right in the temple. He was still alive, and every time he would breathe, a bubble of blood would raise on the side of his head." One of Cullen's "stout-hearted true Americans" from Virginia City, Montana, Smith continued to fire his rifle so fast that shells began to jam. Cullen recalled, "I told him he could go over to Battalion Headquarters and get a safer place, but he answered, 'Hell, I ain't hurt much and can still shoot this gun, so here I stay!'"[35]

Oh, I've been wounded in this fight;
Shot at sunrise, gassed at night,
Outside of that I feel all right.
And I ain't got weary yet.[34]

Private Sidney Smith. A bad eye kept this Montana farmer from enlisting, but that handicap was overlooked when he was drafted. Courtesy of Joanne M. Fritch.

To the right of Company H, Lieutenant Rogers and Company B had a much easier time, subjected mostly to grenades thrown from above the road and bullets that had overshot Cullen's men. Rogers had some good soldiers to steady his line. Foremost among them was Lawrence Osborne, who, because of a critical shortage of officers and sergeants, had been plucked from his duties as supply sergeant and assigned to command a platoon in the advance from the Vesle to the Aisne. Osborne was now second in command of Company B, having previously "displayed absolute disregard for his own safety, exposing himself frequently to shell and machine gun fire to look after his men, and assist them in finding shelter." In the words of a superior, "Sergeant Osborne's indifference to hardship set a high example in his platoon." PFC William Halligan had first been noticed for his attention to duty in the Baccarat Sector, then again in a citation for "gallant and meritorious conduct" under fire: "In the advance from the Vesle to the Aisne and in the Forest of Argonne, this soldier was constantly exposed to shell fire and machine gun fire in performing his duties as company runner. He was wounded slightly by a sniper's bullet but hastened away from the forward dressing station to rejoin his company, informing the Lieutenant in command that he had heard there was to be an attack in the morning and he wished to be on hand."[36]

While directing his men in Company C, Captain Stromee went down with a wound that tore apart his shoulder and Lieutenant Schenck stepped forward to accept a command that should have been his all along. Schenck, too, had some good men under him. Probably the most distinguished was Sergeant Martin Tuite, who, on September 30, had commanded a platoon that "attacked and cleaned out two enemy machine gun positions which had checked the advance" of Whittlesey's First Battalion.[37]

Lieutenant Buhler's consolidated G/A Company came in for its share of action on the right-center of Whittlesey's line. Just as the attack began, Ernest Wornek (G) ran up the slope and rescued a soldier who had been wounded and left behind while returning with a patrol. After his corporal had been killed, Private William Begley (G) took over the squad even though he had been hit in the arm by a machine gun bullet. A native of Brooklyn, Begley had attended St. Mary Star of the Sea School, but at the age of fourteen he began working as a Western Union messenger and soon landed a clerical job. He had been gassed on the Vesle front, but recovered his health just in time for the Argonne drive. Corporal James Dolan, leader of a Chauchat team from Company G, was struck by a bullet in the back, but returned to command his section after having his wound dressed. Corporal Irving Klein, one of Company A's best, was hit in the elbow, but "continued to assist his men in repulsing the attack of an enemy patrol."[38]

The German attack also hit Captain Holderman's Company K. Lieutenant Peabody had placed two machine guns to defend the right flank and rear of the line, where there were open fields of fire into the lower ground. Holderman set out a Chauchat team and riflemen to protect the backs of Peabody's gunners, taking "no chances on leaving any German crawl up within a distance of throwing a hand grenade at our guns." These

He had a pleasant smile, and looked
Clean, decent, just the sort you'd meet
Running a little corner store,
Or carrying tools along the street.
I wish I hadn't shot so quick;
But I was pretty sore. You see,
He came close, yelling "Kamerad,"
And then he threw a bomb at me.[39]

dispositions, combined with the riflemen along the road, allowed Company K to "deliver a terrible burst of small arms fire" upon any force that attempted to approach. Like Cullen's men on the left, Holderman's troops were subjected to "a fierce attack" from grenadiers and snipers, including some who climbed trees for a better view, supported by the deadly *minenwerfer* and some machine guns across the ravine. Dough-boys waited patiently until the Germans came into view, then began a "steady, cool, and deliberate" fire that forced the attackers back in disarray. Holderman reported, "The cries of the enemy wounded could be heard until long after darkness had settled down, when their comrades came and carried both their dead and wounded to the rear." Whittlesey's entire line had repulsed the attackers, whose greatest effort had been concentrated on the American flanks.[40]

Lieutenants Marshall Peabody and Maurice Revnes shared a funk-hole up near the road about in the middle of the position and almost directly up the slope from the PC occupied by Whittlesey and McMurtry. A trench mortar shell exploded on the edge of their hole, blowing off part of Revnes's left foot and tearing apart Peabody's left foot and leg. Both cried out, "First Aid!" but the three first-aid men were too busy to respond right away. Someone put a tourniquet on Peabody's mangled leg and Corporal Joseph Keenan came to help Revnes. The lieutenant pulled out two handkerchiefs and covered the bleeding stump, holding them in place with a bandage from Keenan's first-aid package. Two of Whittlesey's three machine gun officers were now out of action fol-lowing the burst of this single shell. Actual control of the automatic weapons on the right and center fell to Sergeant George Hauck, although Peabody refused to be moved to shelter and attempted to resume command. Hauck received bad news almost immediately. Another trench mortar shell had struck the machine gun of Sergeant Robert Graham, killing him, knocking out the rest of his crew, and destroying the weapon. Major Whittlesey made a mental note to make another attempt to destroy that lethal trench mortar.[41]

James Larney wrote in his diary that *minenwerfer* shells were "raising hell" with Whittlesey's command. One projectile struck close to First Battalion headquarters, fragments tearing the clothing of Walter Baldwin and Robert Manson and smacking Theodore Tollefson in the forehead. Larney was not supposed to be keeping a diary (it could possibly give valuable information to the enemy if he were captured), but he scribbled away from time to time and hid the book in his mess kit carrier. Writing helped to pass the time, because, Larney confessed, "there were long periods when all one did was lie there and hope nothing made a direct hit in your own particular funkhole."[42]

Major Whittlesey and Captain McMurtry with two runners. From Peterson's *Lost Battalion Survivors from Minnesota and the Northwest.*

Whittlesey and McMurtry discussed the command's status that evening of October 3 and it appeared pretty bleak. They had again been cut off from the Seventy-seventh Division, caught inside a ring of German fire for the second time. Two days' fighting had seen the effective strength of the two battalions reduced by about one-fourth. Holderman's company and the machine gunners had also suffered losses. Rifle cartridges remained plentiful, Chauchat clips adequate, machine gun ammunition low, and grenades almost expended. The last rations had been eaten at the noon meal. Smokes were about gone. There was no water supply on the wooded slope. Most of the medical supplies, primarily bandages, had already been used. Nights were growing cold and suffering increased accordingly, especially for the wounded. There were a few positive aspects to their situation. The dense woods and underbrush provided concealment from enemy observation. Most funkholes had been excavated to the dimensions of small dugouts, providing secure cover from all but a direct *minenwerfer* hit. There were still a few pigeons that could carry messages back to the division. Morale remained surprisingly high.[43]

Hunger and thirst had been constant companions for the past week and would remain so. Some men attempted to get water from the stream in the valley, but always drew enemy fire and a few were hit. Water details stumbled upon a spring, but the Boche knew about it and kept a wary eye out in that direction for careless Yanks. After Roland Judd, one of the Camp Upton veterans, was killed while attempting to fill canteens for the wounded, Whittlesey posted a guard to discourage any more such trips during daylight hours. Private Krotoshinsky complained, "We could see water down below and although we were dying of thirst all we could do was to curse the Germans." Uniforms and equipment of dead men, both American and German, were thoroughly searched for food, but without success. Some of the doughboys began to experiment with eating tender leaves and twigs and acorns and roots to relieve their growling stomachs. Nicotine addicts rolled up dry leaves and smoked them to pass the time, wishing for a drag off a real Camel. Lieutenant Cullen saw that "the strain was beginning to tell on the men and their eyes took on an abnormal and peculiar hue."[44]

Amid all this misery and distress, Whittlesey was struck by the attitude of bleeding men, whose "moans and half-suppressed cries" echoed over the dark hillside. He admired their "heroic fortitude," watching helplessly as "they strove to grit the little devils of pain and anguish between their teeth." Loud cries and noises invited a stream of death from "those cursed machine guns," so the injured did their best to remain as silent as possible. When McMurtry stopped to check on a man shot through the guts, he looked up and said softly, "It pains like hell, Captain, but I'll keep as quiet as I can." Officers told their men that help would surely come in the morning, but events of the next few days would, in retrospect, make October 3 look like a walk in the park.[45]

8

TRAPPED

Major Whittlesey was awake before dawn on October 4 after spending a relatively quiet night, sleep being broken only by some half-dozen American shells that inexplicably fell into his position. He busied himself with arrangements for sending out patrols, hoping they might make connection with French troops to the west or with the 307th Infantry to the east. In addition to these small patrols on each flank, the major sent out three larger parties. He conferred with Corporal Holger Peterson, put him in charge of a detachment of Second Battalion scouts, and told the noncom to silently work his way across the valley. Once Peterson had gained the tree line on Ridge 198, his patrol was to infiltrate the German defenses and, hopefully, find a way to reach the 308th Infantry. Whittlesey also sent a twenty-man patrol after the trench mortar that had been harassing his troops. He selected two men from Company B, Corporal Albert Copsey and Private Martin Lokken, both acting sergeants who had already displayed "extreme personal bravery and indifference to hardship," to lead the patrol. Their orders were to reconnoiter to the northwest, attempt to find a path through the machine guns that Lieutenant Schenck had encountered, and destroy the trench mortar.[1]

Ever since their arrival in the pocket overlooking Charlevaux Valley, officers had positioned a few men on top of the ridge above the roadway where they could observe enemy activity and give warning of impending attacks. John Nell explained the predicament of those isolated doughboys: "Our outposts on top of the bank were almost helpless, as they were totally outnumbered by the enemy and within easy reach of grenades. It would have been pure suicide for any of them to fire and give their location away. All they could do was to observe what was going on." Searching for any weakness in the ring of German machine guns that encircled them, Whittlesey also sent Sergeant Herman Anderson and twenty men to the north with instructions to carefully move over the crest beyond this perimeter and probe for a gap in the German line. It was just daylight when Anderson's patrol left their funkholes and scrambled up the steep slope. Private Ralph John remembered: "We had just made it up the hill to the road and were lining up when the machine guns let loose and how the lead did pour in at us for just a minute. Just long enough for us to get out of sight. Those who couldn't jump, rolled or were drug off the road. I jumped and when I hit, I hit rolling, me and the gun all through the brush. When I finally came to a stop, I was pretty well scratched up and my clothes were torn about off." John was one of only three who emerged more or less unscathed. Anderson had been hit by a bullet that "burned the skin in a dark brown line" where it had creased his forehead. Several men were dead, the rest wounded in one way or another, including a friend of John's who "had a finger shot off."[2]

Corporal Peterson fared no better than Anderson. His patrol wormed its way ever so slowly through the oozing swamp, where it seemed "the rattle of every dry stalk, the squish of every knee in the mudhole seemed to fill the silence." Reaching the stream, the Liberty Boys searched for a safe crossing, taking a few steps, then crouching, watching, and listening intently. After they had crossed the creek, there was a tug at Peterson's boot and a pointed finger indicated a silhouette of a German helmet. Americans flattened into the weeds as sounds of men pushing through the brush became louder. A German patrol edged closer and closer, Corporal Peterson keeping his Springfield trained on the helmet-wearer. He fired, the lone shot sounding like the explosion of a 155mm shell in the deathly silent morning, and the German crumpled. Peterson jumped to one side as German rifles cracked a response, then fired at a muzzle flash and was rewarded by cry of pain. A flare flew into the sky, illuminating the valley and a third

German, who seemed transfixed by the light. Peterson shot him too, and, as more flares began to flicker above them, yelled for his men to get the hell out of there. Machine gunners on Ridge 198 began to rake Peterson's patrol as men scrambled back to the safety of their funkholes, one bullet hitting Oscar Wallen in the back. Shortly after the repulse of Anderson and Peterson, Acting Sergeants Copsey and Lokken brought more bad news. Their patrol had gotten close enough to pinpoint the trench mortar's location, but an attempt to neutralize it failed in the face of heavy enemy fire. Sixteen of the twenty men were down, a couple dead, a few badly wounded left behind to their fate, and everyone still mobile straggling back to their holes.[3]

Encouraging word did come from the two small patrols that had been sent east and west along the valley. They returned with news that the Germans appeared to have vanished overnight, but given the repulse of his three larger patrols Whittlesey had his doubts. Hopeful, yet unconvinced, Whittlesey dispatched one of his precious pigeons

Say, why is it heroes
  Is always nice and clean
And tall and swell and handsome—
  Inside a magazine?

It wasn't that way in our crowd
  When shell began to rain.
All our kind of heroes
  Was hell-fire plain.[4]

at 7:25 A.M. and advised regimental headquarters: "Our patrols indicate Germans withdrew during the night. Sending further patrols now to verify this report." His latest message also included additional comments relating to his current situation: "Many wounded here whom we can't evacuate. Need rations badly. No word from D or F Companies." Apparently Whittlesey's small morning patrols had not been too enthusiastic in their scouting, because those sent later to confirm the German departure soon reported that the enemy still remained in force. In fact, about an hour later, Captain Holderman noted that "a new and serious situation arose, which proved very discouraging and distressing to the command." Two more trench mortars began firing from positions to the right front and left front of the Americans, their high-angle trajectories inflicting a "nibbling torture" for the next few days. Whittlesey's men had by now dug deep enough to protect themselves from rifle and machine gun fire, but those "death-dealing, silent-flying trench mortar shells" could strike anywhere without warning. Fortunately, not more than fifteen percent of these shells actually landed among the funkholes, the remainder striking outside the perimeter,

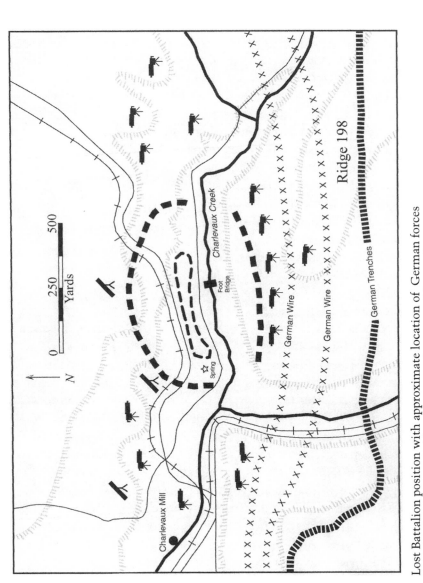

Lost Battalion position with approximate location of German forces
(Based on a map prepared by Captain Nelson M. Holderman)

mainly along the road in the valley. In another stroke of good luck, many of those that did find their mark failed to explode. This errant fire, combined with the large number of duds, led Holderman to remark, "Had all of the trench mortar shells fired by the enemy fallen into the position, then there would have really been a 'Lost Battalion.'"[5]

Most of the work done by men in Whittlesey's command was necessarily performed under cover of night. Procurement of water and food was the most critical of these tasks. A few bold men would each take a handful of canteens and crawl silently down to the muddy stream or the one bubbling spring. Ralph John described how these volunteers "would fill up a few canteens and then beat it back into the brush, protected by a lot of men hidden behind trees at the edge of the clearing." A sudden slip or the careless clatter of a canteen on some exposed rock often summoned a stream of machine gun bullets. Bob Manson told how one doughboy had taken eight canteens for water, but was given "a warm reception by the Hun" and returned with two of his canteens spouting water from bullet holes. On another occasion, when Philip "Zip" Cepaglia, one of the First Battalion runners, took an armload of canteens and crawled toward a shell hole half-filled with brownish water, his foot inadvertently sent a quantity of stones and dirt sliding into the face of another soldier. When the offended individual called Cepaglia a son-of-a-bitch for his carelessness, Zip threw down his canteens, stood up, and started to take off his jacket, yelling, "You wanna make something of it? All right, I fight you right now!" One nearby soldier, afraid that a fistfight would bring unwanted German attention, cried out, "Pipe down and lay down, you crazy wop!" Another added, "If you want to fight, fight the Germans!" The two doughboys called an uneasy truce.[6]

Hungry men also left their funkholes to search German and American bodies for food and ammunition. Ralph John made this attempt once, crawling out to corpses that lay in the valley, but was greeted by a swarm of bullets that seemed to be "coming from all sides." He jumped

My Tuesdays are meatless
My Wednesdays are wheatless
My meals grow more eatless each day.[7]

up and raced for cover, diving into the underbrush where "bullets were close enough to clip the leaves off the trees and low brush so that they would sting the devil out of my face." The pity of men risking their lives for a few morsels of food was that, in nearly every case, they never found any on the dead Germans, who seemed to be as ill-supplied as the trapped Americans.[8]

Shovels were employed for all other nighttime tasks. Latrines had been dug as soon as the Liberty Boys reached the Charlevaux Road and Major Whittlesey insisted that they be used. But at one point, the major discovered a private squatting down and relieving himself at the base of a tree. Angered by this outright disobedience and reprehensible disregard for basic sanitation, Whittlesey ordered him to pull up his pants and use the nearest latrine, threatening to punish any such future act. Despite pervasive hunger and fatigue, the major insisted that the latrines be properly maintained. Whittlesey could not be everywhere at once and it was not long before the hillside became an oversized outdoor toilet. The major also ordered that the dead, who had now started to stink a bit, should be buried every morning before daylight. This order was only half-heartedly obeyed. Digging in the rock-clogged and root-choked soil was exhausting work and men reasoned it would be better to expend their energy on the living rather than on the dead. So soldiers perfunctorily covered corpses with a few shovels full of soil, then spent most of their time digging farther and farther into the slope. One of Lieutenant Cullen's men proved to be the champion excavator, his dugout eventually reaching a depth of seven feet, the entrance protected by heavy logs that he had dragged into position. This man had dug so deep that he encountered a layer of white clay that, when thrown out, covered the green and brown of the hillside below his hole, giving the Germans a prominent target for their machine gun and trench mortar fire.[10]

The Sergeant says my gun is rusty
And I guess he must be right,
But you should see my little shovel,
It is certainly shining bright.[9]

Hours between dawn and dusk seemed an eternity. The division historian remarked simply, "During daylight it was a rash act to stand erect. Positions were changed by crawling along the ground." No one moved unless absolutely necessary, for the slightest movement of foliage prompted a stream of machine gun bullets. Everyone crawled, even Whittlesey, though the major did appear with a freshly shaven face each day, the only man in his force to devote time to tonsorial splendor. Abraham Krotoshinsky and Benjamin Pagliaro had been barbers before the war, but there is no evidence they plied their trade while with Whittlesey's command, although Pagliaro still carried his scissors and razors with him. *Minenwerfers* continued to pound the slope and turned it into "a tangle of twisted shattered trees and splinters" where "showers of mud and gravel fell upon those who were fortunate enough not to come into actual contact with flying shell splinters." Although daytime produced a fresh onslaught of German fire, the sun brought welcome warmth to dispel the bone-chilling cold that kept Americans from getting much sleep.[11]

Like cats with mice, the Germans began to toy with their penned-up foes. This first became apparent when an officer noticed a private emerge from his funkhole and put on his pack. When questioned about what the hell he was doing, the enlisted man responded that word had been passed along the line that the Seventy-seventh Division had been driven back and that Whittlesey had decided to withdraw his command. An immediate inquiry disclosed that some devious English-speaking German had employed this ruse to draw the Americans out of their holes. Emil Peterson admitted that he, too, had been fooled, saying, "I got out once but when a bullet just missed my head I got down in a hurry." Officers summarily cautioned everyone to beware of enemy tricks. Soon after, when a voice cried out "Gaz Masks!" from the under-brush, the doughboys recognized a pronounced German accent and realized there was no such command in the Infantry Drill Regulations. One of them yelled back, "Gas masks hell!" and fired a quick shot, being rewarded by "an unearthly howl" from the concealed Hun. No longer able to fool their opponents with fake American commands, Germans began to shout orders to fictitious bodies of their own troops, such as "Bring up ten machine guns on the left!" and "First, Second, and Third Companies this way!" This was designed to convince Whittlesey of their overwhelming force, but German-speaking Americans shut them up by yelling "Wint Betebren!," loosely translated as "bunch of fart bags."[12]

At 10:55 A.M., Whittlesey, although reduced to but three pigeons, decided to send off another message to headquarters, explaining his worsening situation. He began by stating, "Germans are still around us, though in smaller numbers. We have been heavily shelled by mortar this morning." After giving some incomplete numbers as to his effective strength and losses, Whittlesey continued, "Cover bad if we advance up the hill and very difficult to move the wounded if we change position. Situation is cutting our strength rapidly. Men are suffering from hunger and exposure; the wounded are in very bad condition." The major concluded his message by imploring, "Cannot support be sent at once?"[13]

There was a brief flurry of activity when potato mashers began to fall from the cliff, first on Holderman's flank, then spreading along toward the west. One of the German grenades landed right at the feet of Art Shepard, a Californian in Company G who had lied about his age to get into the California National Guard, and he instinctively jumped on the thing with both feet, driving it into the ground. Luckily for him, it failed to explode. During one grenade attack, a soldier was slashed in the face. When an officer told him to go get his wound dressed, the private glanced up and said, "All right, sir, but I'll be right back." Whittlesey called for the ever-dependable Lieutenant Schenck and sent him clambering up the slope with ten men and a Chauchat to drive off this latest threat. A few bursts from the automatic rifle and several rifle shots neutralized the grenadiers. Riflemen kept a sharp lookout, and occasionally Captain Holderman could see some foolhardy German "come tumbling down from his concealment." The major tried to keep up morale, crawling from man to man and constantly repeating his encouraging message, "Remember, there are two million Americans pushing up to relieve us." Although they never said so to his face, many of the men must have wondered, "Just where the hell are those goddamned two million Americans?"[14]

Men were talking softly among themselves and enjoying a respite from enemy fire when suddenly American shells began to crash onto the northern slopes of Ridge 198. Soldiers began to cheer the explosions, figuring that headquarters knew their position and was now trying to knock out the machine guns and trench mortars that held them captive. Major Whittlesey described this seemingly welcome development: "Increasing in intensity, the barrage crept down the slope, crossed the marshy bottom of the ravine where it hurled mud and brush into the air, and settled directly on our own position." On the right flank, Captain Holderman watched in horror as "shells intended for the enemy's destruction were now registering repeatedly upon the slope" occupied by the Liberty Boys. Geysers of dirt, rocks, fragments of trees, equipment, and body parts erupted all over the hillside. Whittlesey stared helplessly at an "inferno of noise, dust and confusion" as misdirected shells fired by 75mm guns of the 305th Field Artillery tore "huge chunks" of earth from the one position where they were sheltered from

Private Robert Manson, who lost a finger on his right hand while acting as a runner and orderly to Major Whittlesey. From the *American Hebrew and Jewish Messenger.*

German shell fire. Individual funkholes and dugouts for the wounded caved in on top of their occupants. Holderman agreed that it was an "inferno of fire and brimstone," while Lieutenant Eager called it "the most crushing experience of our whole siege." Even the 305th Artillery itself was not immune from the torrent of shrieking death. While firing this barrage, a gun in Battery C had a shell burst prematurely, fracturing the tube, a piece of which killed Private Edgar Blethen.[15]

Doughboys had no idea what to do. Orders could not be heard over the explosions and gleeful Germans watched for Americans to leave their holes before pouring in machine gun fire. Trench mortars added their fire to the carnage. Sergeant Major Ben Gaedeke and Bob Manson were sitting together in their hole about five feet away from Whittlesey when the barrage hit. Manson remembered that suddenly "everywhere about us the ground was heaving and shooting up" and the resulting tumult "had a Wall Street panic beat a hundred different ways." Noticing that the fire seemed less intense toward the left flank, Major Whittlesey yelled for everyone to run to the left and seek shelter there. Manson continued, "Some stayed in their holes, others ran to the left, others to the right." For some reason, Gaedeke ran to the right and was blown apart when a shell exploded at his feet. Manson said tersely that "the only traces we found of the poor lad after the barrage was his hat and gat [helmet and pistol]."[16]

Jack and Bill went up the hill
To get a pail of water;
Along came a shell—Bill ran like hell,
And Jack came humping after![17]

As crashing shells stripped the hillside of cover, Whittlesey yelled for James Larney to put out the white cloth panels used to signal Allied aircraft, then scrambled off to establish his headquarters farther down the slope and to the left. According to regulations, they should have fired off flares to signal "Barrage short" to the artillery, but their flares had been used up days ago. There was little hope that aviators could see the battalion's cloth panels, so a pigeon would have to be dispatched. By now the pigeon handlers had been hard hit. Theodore Tollefson, a youth from Hayfield, Minnesota, had been killed by a shell fragment that carried away part of his skull. Bill Cavanaugh had also been hit by a piece of iron, leaving only Omer Richards to handle the birds. Whittlesey, bleeding from a slight wound on the bridge of his nose, called for a pigeon and Richards reached into a cage to oblige. Overwhelmed by the storm bursting about him, Richards inadvertently allowed one of the two remaining birds to escape.[18]

Whittlesey glared at Richards for a second, then hastily wrote out his last message to regimental headquarters: "We are along the road parallel 276.4. Our own artillery is dropping a barrage directly on us. For heaven's sake, stop it." Richards held the last trembling pigeon, a cock named Cher Ami, perhaps a little too closely as Whittlesey clipped on the message. The pigeon man threw Cher Ami into the air and watched in amazement as his last bird perched calmly on a branch, where it began to smooth its ruffled feathers. Whittlesey, Richards, and others in the immediate area shouted at the stupid bird and, in between shell bursts, threw sticks and rocks to encourage it to leave. All the pigeon did was shift from one branch to another. More drastic action was required, so Richards risked his own life and started to climb the tree, shaking limbs and yelling as he got closer and closer to the winged messenger. Finally Cher Ami took flight, made a few lazy circles above the tornado of exploding shells, and headed for home.[19]

After putting out the signal panels, James Larney saw Bob Manson up near the road and ran to join his friend where the shells did not strike as often. There seemed to be no shell bursts at all on the north side of the road where it had been cut into the hillside, so the pair ran to that place of imagined safety and joined a man they failed to recognize who had the same idea. Although somewhat secure from the shelling, the three men made an easy target for a German machine gunner whose bullets forced all three back into the screaming barrage. Shouting "We've got to get out of here!", Manson went first and lost a finger as he dove down the hill. Larney came next and was hit in the left leg. The third man was shot through the body. Just as they reached cover, Walter Baldwin came staggering along, holding up Sam Feuerlicht of Company C, who had been wounded. A bursting shell nearly disemboweled Feuerlicht. A fragment from the same shell hit Larney in the right arm. Baldwin bound up Larney's wound with strips torn from a shirt and the two rolled downhill, abandoning Feuerlicht, who, to their untrained eyes, appeared to be dead, although he would somehow cling to life for another ten days. The two friends dug a new hole near the bottom of the slope, Larney using a bayonet in his one good hand and Baldwin manning a shovel he had snatched from the body of Paul Andrews.[20]

Ralph John described his experience during the barrage:

My buddy and I were lying in the same dug-out listening to the shells come over. We could tell about where they were going to hit. He would say, 'Here is one that is coming close.' And it did strike—too close for comfort. The dirt was thrown sky high and both of us were nearly buried. I only had one hand out in the open. With this one free hand, I reached my shovel and dug myself and then my buddy out. We had just got ourselves out when another shell hit close by and we were buried again. The third time was too much and we started looking for a safer place. As I was walking around, I stepped on something that wasn't too solid and felt it roll under my feet. I looked down and there were three men lying on the ground covered up with dirt until you couldn't see them. They were still alive but stunned.

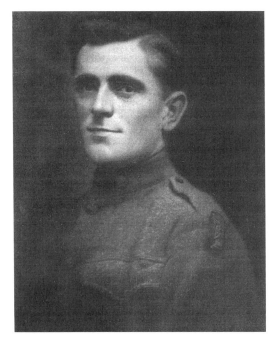

Corporal Walter J.
Baldwin, postwar
secretary of the Lost
Battalion Association.
Courtesy of Thomas J.
Baldwin.

Unable to find an empty hole, John and his buddy lay flat on the ground amid the flying shrapnel, some of it "so close that we could just about feel it whiz by."[21]

Anthony Anastasi, one of the Second Battalion scouts, left a stirring account of how he survived the American barrage. A native of Italy who had declared his intention to become a naturalized American, Anastasi was a Brooklyn tailor before being swept up by the draft. An attempt to claim exemption to support his mother had been denied, so the tall, slender Italian had joined Company F of the 308th at Camp Upton and was now one of the old-timers. When the shelling began, he and two other men shared the same hole. Wounded in the thigh by one of the first shells, Anastasi thought it appeared safer up along the road, so crawled up there and remained about ten minutes until that position came under intense fire. When "hell let loose" along the road, he slid downhill, although partially paralyzed, and landed in an abandoned funkhole. Anastasi resumed his story: "I was content to stay there, but a few minutes after, one of the shells hit above me. All that rubble dropped on top of me, burying me in this hole. The only part of my body that was left exposed was my right leg from the knee down, sticking up. My helmet covered my face and breathing was hard. I tried pushing the weight off my chest but could not budge." Anastasi continued to kick his leg, hoping that someone would rescue him, but he began to suffocate: "I then could see myself going fast; I couldn't breathe anymore and found myself flying into space. At that moment I saw a vision of my Mother appear before me, and at the same time I felt someone pulling me out." After extricating Anastasi, the Good Samaritan ran for cover, leaving the Brooklyn tailor lying on the ground and gasping for air. He never knew who pulled him free, but would always say, "Whoever it was—my sincere thanks to you, and may the good Lord bless you forever." Stephan Honas was shifting positions during the artillery barrage, when he happened to pass by a jumble of debris with a foot sticking out. Honas grabbed hold of the twitching foot and yanked out a dirt-encrusted stranger, who, as he wiped the dirt from his eyes, just managed to blurt out, "I owe you my life." Both men ran for cover and lost track of one another for thirty-nine years. When the pair finally reunited, Max Lesnick, Company C, could finally thank Stephan Honas, Company B, for saving his life.[22]

John Nell described the "dirt and rocks flying high in the air," as "everyone was expecting the next shell to get him." He added, "There were many direct hits blowing men to pieces and wounding dozens more," the funkholes offering no safety from a direct hit. One shell hit the tree where Leonard Glenn and Ray Hammond had dug in, the concussion disorienting Glenn. When he regained his senses, Glenn found that a ten-inch piece of shell had mangled his rifle. Magnus Krogh and Roland Thorbone, both from Company B, had dug in up near the road. Krogh remembered that "sand, rocks, trees, brush, flew all around us." The pair was stunned, awaking next morning to find themselves half-buried with earth and pinned under a tree that had fallen on them. Krogh explained that "we dug ourselves from and under the best we could" and, when they emerged, these replacements "saw legs, arms and bodies lying all around." Krogh's rifle had been "shot to pieces" and a flying splinter had destroyed his pack and mess kit.[23]

For one hour and thirty-five minutes the 305th Field Artillery methodically pounded Major Whittlesey's position. George Walker, one of the three remaining first-aid men, was now himself a casualty with about fifty shrapnel wounds in his back. The surviving members

Private Irving Sirota. A native of
Russia, this former drugstore clerk
served in the 308th Infantry's
medical detachment. Courtesy of
Marvin R. Edwards.

Private James W. Bragg. A West
Virginian whose Lost Battalion
service convinced a judge to dismiss
a bootlegging charge. Courtesy of
Tommy Bragg.

of the medical detachment, Irving Sirota and James Bragg, one a former student at the Brooklyn College of Pharmacy and the other a West Virginia farmer whose weak eyes kept him from being a rifleman, darted back and forth to dress wounds and comfort the injured, but by now they were out of bandages. They had no medicine of any kind. Everything that could be used to bind up wounds was hastily being pressed into service. Alfred Simonson, a Minnesotan in Company B, recalled that the profuse bleeding from a wound in his right cheek could only be stopped by wrapping his head in strips torn from some old underwear.[24]

About thirty minutes after the barrage sputtered out, a small force of Germans crept silently past the outposts above the road and began throwing grenades down into the American position. One grenade landed near Hubert Esch, a replacement in Company C, who remembered, "It tore my pack all to pieces

I know the doctors call us "nuts,"
Oh, yes, I heard them say
We're off for special treatment . . . well,
I'll tell 'em 'bout the day
Artillery was falling short,
And we pushed on anyway.[25]

and splattered my stuff all over the landscape. All I could find after a thorough search was a pair of socks." John Knettel, Joseph Materna, and Joseph Lehmeier shared a hole in the Company K sector. When a grenade suddenly came bouncing down the hill and landed on Materna's back, Lehmeier snatched it up and threw the bomb about twenty feet before it exploded. Lehmeier described the result, "Joe got his ear cut and I got my head full of small particles from it, which made my head bleed considerably." He later said of his quick response, "If I had not thrown it back the three of us would have been killed." This was the second close call for Materna, who had earlier crawled toward some buddies from Montana in hopes of borrowing a few shreds of chewing tobacco. As he approached his friends, a shell exploded squarely in their dugout, killing Roscoe Church, Harvey Cole, and another man who could not be identified in that "hole of blood."[26]

The American barrage had commenced just as Lieutenant Cullen began to interrogate a prisoner brought back by a patrol. As that officer and his German guest huddled in the same hole, Cullen recalled that the shelling lasted "a tremendously long time" and it "came very near ruining the whole detachment." He tried to act nonchalant as shells exploded all around, but a hasty questioning failed to elicit any response beyond "Keine ahnung." Cullen sent the prisoner off to McMurtry,

First Lieutenant William J. Cullen. Although his company endured horrific casualties on the Lost Battalion's left flank, this officer emerged unscathed. From Peterson's *Lost Battalion Survivors from Minnesota and the Northwest.*

then, feeling no reticence about ducking, curled up in the sheltering darkness of his hole "to get what little cover that place offered." He escaped injury during the barrage and the grenade attack that followed had little impact on his company.[27]

Once the fighting stopped, Whittlesey, McMurtry, and Holderman conferred and discussed their options. They had seen no American troops since breaking through the German lines two days earlier, although the sounds of combat could be clearly heard beyond the crest of Ridge 198. Despite repeated messages to regimental headquarters, the savage American barrage indicated that artillery of the Liberty Division, if not the entire division, had no idea of their exact whereabouts. Cher Ami had been the last pigeon (following its release Omer Richards had started to nibble on what remained of the birdseed), so even that one-sided avenue of communication had been shut down. The white battalion panels had been spread out to signal Allied aircraft, but they had continued to fly by unaware of the desperate doughboys huddled below. Soldiers lay flat on their backs, waving towels, underwear, or anything else white in an effort to attract attention, but all in vain. But that evening Whittlesey was convinced that he had managed to signal a French airplane that had circled above their position for a few minutes. He told McMurtry, "I think I got in touch alright enough with that aeroplane." The French pilot supposedly fired off flares to signal that he had seen their panels. Up until now there had been no sign of the Fiftieth Aero Squadron, whose pilots were busy battling faulty sparkplugs while dropping propaganda leaflets over the German lines and heaving out bundles of *The Stars and Stripes* to frontline troops of the Seventy-seventh Division.[28]

After discussing their bleak situation on the evening of October 4, Whittlesey and his officers decided they had no option but to remain in their rabbit warren of holes along the Charlevaux Road. There were a number of factors that were considered in reaching this conclusion. First and foremost was the fact that Whittlesey's command had reached its assigned objective on October 2 and had received no orders either to advance or withdraw from that position. Whittlesey explained that "the present position, although exposed to sniper fire, was well protected from enemy artillery and offered fair protection against the trench mortar to the west." Clear ground along the creek gave the doughboys a wide field of fire that kept the enemy at bay from that direction. Any movement back toward the American lines would bring their troops into contact with the German machine guns, now safely protected by trenches and belts of barbed wire on Ridge 198, as well as expose them to the German artillery. Abandoning their position and striking out in any other direction ran the risk of running into another American barrage. Also taken into account was the large number of wounded, many of whom would have to be abandoned if the command moved elsewhere. That was unthinkable, so Whittlesey's command would have to stay put and wait for the relief that surely must come soon.[29]

Leadership became a problem as casualties among the officers continued to mount. Nineteen other officers had followed Whittlesey into the pocket,

> When will this war be over?
>   When will the gang break through?
> What will the U.S. look like?
>   What will there be to do?
> Where will the Boches be then?
>   Who will have married Nell?
> When's that relief a-comin' up?
>   Gosh, but this thinkin's hell![30]

but that number had already been seriously reduced. Among the senior commanders, Whittlesey had been cut slightly on the nose, McMurtry had received a contusion on his knee that left him hobbling, and Holderman remained in action despite having been cut up several times by shell fragments during the barrage. Captain Stromee had been disabled by a bad shoulder wound. Lieutenant Wilhelm of Company E had disappeared on the morning of October 3. During the barrage, Lieutenants Leak and Harrington sought safety for their men by spreading them out on the right flank. Both had been taken prisoner, leaving Company E under the command of Sergeant Frederick Baldwin. Lieutenant Griffin, second-in-command to Cullen on the critical left flank, was down with a shoulder wound. Lieutenant Buhler had also been hit more than once. Two machine gun officers, Lieutenants Peabody and Revnes, had been severely wounded by shell fragments. Lieutenant Teichmoeller had been deafened by the explosion of a shell during the barrage. Of those remaining unhurt, only one, Lieutenant Cullen, had been an officer at Camp Upton. Harry Rogers, commanding Company B, was a dependable old hand who had enlisted in the Sixth Infantry in August of 1917, rose to the rank of sergeant, then accepted a commission as second lieutenant on July 11, 1918. Other officers were either new arrivals, such as Harrington and Eager, who had been transferred from another regiment; recently promoted graduates from the last officer class at Camp Upton like Schenck and Noon; or reinforcements from the Fortieth Division with no previous battlefield experience.[31]

Many of the new officers literally did not know the names of their men. When later asked how many soldiers he knew in his own company, Lieutenant Revnes, who had been assigned to Peabody's command on September 27, could remember only four names. Leadership would have to come from the senior officers remaining—Whittlesey, McMurtry, Holderman, and Cullen. Of the ranking officers, Whittlesey and McMurtry were both new to battalion command, while Holderman had joined Company K only a few days before the Argonne offensive. Aside from Cullen and Rogers, the remaining lieutenants, learning to fight "on the job," were nothing more than faces in the great army bureaucracy. Old-timers, as well as the western newcomers, looked mainly to their sergeants for direction and encouragement. They were the ones who had always provided continuity as officers continued to move in and out of leadership roles.[32]

From the beginning, the Seventy-seventh Division had been nick-named "The Cosmopolitan Division," but Whittlesey's command was now far more cosmopolitan than when it left Camp Upton. His men

Corporal Martin Becker, a native of Brooklyn, killed just days before his twenty-ninth birthday on October 9. From Haulsee's *Soldiers of the Great War.*

were a cross-section of American life. Many of the New Yorkers had been employed as clerks, salesmen, tradesmen, and laborers, what would be considered the typical city jobs, although a few had worked for well-known firms in the metropolitan area. Martin Becker acted as a chauffeur for Standard Oil in Brooklyn, Ray Blackburn worked as a clerk for Otis Elevator Company in Yonkers, Joseph Fortunato labored as an electrician at the Brooklyn Navy Yard, while Bill Begley started his career at Western Union as a fourteen-year-old messenger. Fred Baldwin ran his own insurance adjusting company, Ed Stringer investigated crimes as a lieutenant of detectives in the New York Police, Alexander Hussey had been a lawyer, John Eichorn owned his own saloon, and Louis Diesel oversaw the books for Franklin Trust Company. At least three men—Joseph Friel, Daniel Tallon, and Samuel Feuerlicht—were post office clerks.[33]

Soldiers from upstate New York were primarily farmers; two exceptions were William Crouse, who had been a machinist at the New York and New England Cement and Lime Corporation, and Arthur Jones, who had acted as a United States custom inspector at Toronto. Although he lived in Sherman, New York, Grant Norton was a student at Allegheny College in Pennsylvania when he signed his draft registration. Replacements from out west included more farmers, but also men with occupations typically associated with frontier life. William Johnson labored

Private William P. Crouse, who
left Columbia County, New
York with the December 15,
1917, draft contingent, bound
for Camp Devens and, ulti-
mately, Camp Upton. From
Haulsee's *Soldiers of the Great
War.*

as a riverman out of Coeur d'Alene, Idaho, Ernest Wornek raised stock,
Henry Luckett worked on commission as a "stallionier"; Frank Lipasti
dug underground for the North Butte Mining Company, and Joseph
Mead cut timber. Other men, from both East and West, were employed
on the railroads that bound the country together. John Ryan was a clerk
for the Railway Mail Service, while Homer Rayson had been employed
by the Buffalo, Rochester & Pittsburgh Railroad and Harold Thomas
served as a brakeman for the Baltimore and Ohio Railroad.[34]

Many of Whittlesey's command were less than perfect physical
specimens when accepted for military service. Some had been rejected
during initial army physical exams, including Otto Volz, who had a
broken arm and shoulder, and George Sims, who had been diagnosed
with tuberculosis in his left lung. Albert Martin, an English alien
working as a Butte miner, had a left leg shorter than his right. Other
men were missing body parts, such as William Johnson, who had lost
the index finger on his left hand, and Farland Wade, who had shot off
a finger in a hunting accident.[35]

No matter what their background or the convoluted manner in
which individuals entered the army and found their way to the Char-

levaux Valley, they were all soldiers now, and damned good ones. Cut off from the American army and trapped in the most hellish place imaginable, discipline remained rock solid and every man did the duty required of him, from Major Whittlesey down to the lowliest replacement. By now the routine had become all too familiar. Send out patrols in the morning and evening. Go for water and search the German dead for food by night. Strip their own dead and wounded friends of clothing that could be used for bandages. Retrieve ammunition from the dead. Try to signal Allied aircraft whenever they appeared, but otherwise stay in their holes during the daylight hours. Talk quietly among themselves about happier times or what they planned to do once the relief came. Hop out of their holes when the officers cried "Stand to!" and fight off German attacks from above the road and from each flank. There was nothing else to do. No food meant no mealtimes to mark the passage of time, so the hours dragged by, enlivened only by German trench mortars and machine guns.[36]

We understand this camouflage,
This art of hiding things;
It's what's behind a soldier's jokes
And all the songs he sings.
Yes, it's nothing new to us,
To us, the rank and file;
We understand this camoflauge
—We left home with a smile.[37]

All previous daytime attacks having been repulsed, the Germans launched a surprise night assault. Captain Holderman described the situation: "About 9 P.M. flares began to shoot all over and around the position, lighting up the entire slope. From all along the slopes to the front hand grenades and potato-mashers began to fall. The enemy rained them onto the position at will." The brunt of this latest German onslaught fell on Lieutenant Cullen's Company H. Again, Americans could hear the Germans crashing through the underbrush, congratulating themselves on closing their trap even tighter. The enemy commander could again be heard shouting, "Eitel?" "Hier!" would come booming from the left. "Adolph?" "Hier!" was the response in Cullen's front. Then their leader yelled, "Sind deiner men da?" The response from all quarters was, "Yah, yah!" At the command "Alle Zusammen!!" potato mashers began to rain down on the Liberty Boys, complemented by a few trench mortar shells. Despite those blazing flares that lit the valley, the Germans remained screened by brush as they cautiously crept forward behind the shower of grenades. Americans waited patiently until the attackers came into view, pouring in a perfect storm of rifle, pistol, Chauchat, and machine gun fire. Next morning numerous pools of dried blood indicated that American bullets had found their mark. During one lull in the grenade throwing, a German officer thought the Americans might surrender, so he called out, "Kamerad vill you?" Cullen gave an unequivocal response, shouting back in German, "Come in and get us, you Dutch bastard!" After the lieutenant had exhausted his repertoire of Germanic curses, Cullen said, "We opened fire on where we thought they might be and gave them hell." The attackers silently withdrew.[38]

They say I'm mad, crazed by the war;
Have you been there, and if so what for?
I for one am damn sick of it all;
"Glory, Democracy," just words that's all.

Fighting for what? "We don't know,"
"Hell of a mess," can tell you that though,
What do we win when we win a fight?
Buddies and Brothers missing at night.[39]

9

No Way Out

October 5 began with a shroud of fog hiding the burial details as hungry and sleep-deprived soldiers threw dirt and rocks over the corpses of what had been buddies. Among those buried that morning was Earl Franklin Jepson, who had been born on Christmas Day, 1891, in Carson City, Nevada. He had been raised in Douglas County, spending his youth working at a variety of jobs that included cook, waiter, farm hand, and railroader, before his dad pulled strings and got Earl a county job. Jepson tried to enlist when America entered the war, but had been rejected by the medical examiners. Snatched up by the draft, he left for Camp Lewis, Washington on June 26, 1918. After being transferred to the Fortieth Division, Jepson received infantry training at Camp Kearny, California, crossed the United States by train, and steamed across the Atlantic, all in less than two months. Earl was one of those replacements sent to reinforce the depleted ranks of Company B of the 308th Infantry and did not then realize he was hustling forward to his death. He was killed on October 4 while on patrol duty.[1]

The entire hillside was a bloody shambles. Roy Lightfoot, an Oregonian in Company C, described the scene: "It was the worst mess I ever saw. Comrades all shot up and lying around under trees and every place you looked. It was worse when you crawled down to the foot of the hill after water. Dead bodies all around the water hole, and

Private Earl F. Jepson, the only soldier from Douglas County, Nevada, to be killed in the war. From Sullivan's *Nevada's Golden Stars.*

the water had lots of blood in it, but it tasted good anyway." Clifford Brown agreed, noting that many of the boys were "mangled beyond description." Stanley Sobaszkiewicz felt bad for a buddy who had been hit up hill and to the right of his own funkhole. Sobaszkiewicz explained, "He got hit in the head and was suffering for three days and three nights before he died." When the wounded man finally expired, Stanley confessed, "It was a relief to us all." John Nell recorded the agonies of two men nearby: "I well remember one poor fellow lay on top of the ground close to the hole I was in. He had a large shrapnel about six inches long buried in his upper leg and a bullet in his stomach. He lay there two days before he passed out. His leg had swollen about twice its normal size. Another man not far from him had shrapnel in his head. He suffered from the afternoon until almost daybreak. Both men suffered tremendously before the reprieve of death overtook them."[2]

Patrols returned with news that the Germans still held their positions and had, in fact, been reinforced by at least two hundred new arrivals that had been spotted from the ridge top as they filtered into positions on Ridge 198. Aside from the usual number of trench mortar shells, October 5 began with an increase in sniping by both rifles and machine guns on the trapped command from all angles as the burial parties completed their work. Arnold Morem began to enlarge his hole by digging deeper into the stony soil, but his movements attracted the attention of a sharpshooter, who promptly sent a bullet into the fresh bank

Private Roy Lightfoot,
Company C, 308th Infantry:
"I was not so much afraid of getting killed or captured as I was of getting all crippled up, as lots of them had arms or legs torn off and would probably have to be carried home in a basket."[3]

of earth he had just excavated. Morem stopped his digging immediately, saying, "That ended the needed improvements for the time being." Ralph John and his buddy knew how dangerous it was to expose oneself now that much of the tree leaves and underbrush had been stripped away by the artillery. John recalled what happened when his comrade playfully put a helmet atop his rifle and raised it into the air: "Immediately the German machine guns started popping away at it. I dug three bullets out of the bank. He said, 'The sons of a gun have sure got us spotted.' I replied, 'Yes, and you had better lie still. That was even too close for me!'"[4]

This constant sniping ended abruptly about 10 A.M. when another American artillery barrage began to fall on Ridge 198, then started to creep down the slope toward the valley. A crescendo of explosions uprooted trees, ripped apart the earth, and tore into German positions as the barrage swept closer and closer to Major Whittlesey's position. For a few minutes, "the air was full of flying Dutchmen and parts of the same." With yesterday's shelling still fresh in their minds, doughboys grabbed their shovels and bayonets and mess gear and began digging feverishly as the 75mm shells dropped closer and closer. Expecting the same result as before, Whittlesey watched in horror as the shells crossed "over the marshland at the bottom of the ravine, tearing out great wads of bushes and undergrowth." Just as it seemed that the shells would strike among the doughboys, this barrage jumped over their position. Whittlesey explained, "Suddenly the barrage lifted and, clearing the anxious funk hole community clinging to the ground below Charlevaux road, it landed directly on the top of the ridge to the north where the enemy formed for his daily attacks."[5]

Private Nell described this latest barrage: "Again the thundering and blasting barrage came down the hill and across the open low land just as it had done the day before. We thought this time it would wipe us out. Just about the time it got to us throwing the mud and dirt high in the air, it seemed to stop a little while, then started again, but this time it was on the top of the hill just above us. We could then breathe a little easier, for it was giving the enemy what we had suffered the day before." Captain Holderman said that after perhaps fifteen or twenty minutes, the friendly barrage "raised and went right over our heads." He continued, "I think this was very much in our favor because we could hear the shouts of the Germans and I believe they were attempting to come over in force at this time." Captain McMurtry concurred, explaining that the shell fire "creeps up to the bottom of our slope and then leap-frogs over us," pounding the Germans with vicious bursts of whizzing shrapnel. Doughboys grinned at the enemy screams that could be plainly heard in between shell bursts as the American gunners offered a belated apology for their error of October 4. But most importantly, according to Whittlesey, "This was proof that the position of the command was understood by the troops fighting forward to make the relief."[6] After comparing the contradictory map coordinates sent back by Major Whittlesey and Lieutenant Teichmoeller with Lieutenant Wilhelm's account of his escape, officers from the Seventy-seventh Division had finally pinpointed the exact location of the cutoff troops.

The French, however, had other ideas. About 3 P.M., a French aircraft circled over the valley amid a torrent of machine gun fire and darted away. Shortly thereafter, a barrage commenced from French guns clustered southwest of Binarville, their 75s methodically pounding Whittlesey's right flank, Captain Holderman remembering many of the shells "striking dead into the position." He later recalled, "They would strike all along the slope, and when groups would attempt to shift to safer ground, the [Germans] would sweep the position with all his fires. No shells seemed to pass over the position and onto the enemy beyond, but either fell short or traveled along the slope occupied by the Americans, and the barrage fell for one hour and thirty-five minutes." By keeping low in their funkholes, Holderman's company suffered few casualties from this second misguided Allied barrage. Captain Holderman would later learn that the French aviator had discovered swarms of Germans where Whittlesey's position was thought to be and mistakenly reported that the Americans had been overrun, prompting the ensuing barrage.[7]

As this shelling tapered off on the right flank, Major Whittlesey and Captain McMurtry were sitting in their newly constructed PC, the first having become too exposed after American shells had stripped away the foliage. Both officers thought this new position, farther up the slope and to the west of the original one, seemed "a pretty good one," but when German machine guns began firing a few bursts from the left, the grievously wounded Lieutenant Peabody yelled out, "I think you have picked out a rather exposed position. You'd better look out!" The two commanders decided Peabody was right and crawled farther to the left, taking shelter behind what McMurtry called "a slight hummock of ground, I should say about six inches high." That officer continued, "The ranging shots became very steady and more continuous this time and Major Whittlesey and I lay down behind this hummock of ground with our heads toward our left flank. We had no more than taken our position on the ground than over come the machine gun barrage, which was most severe. It continued, I should say, for probably sixteen or eighteen minutes." He said the air was filled with "the crackle of the machine guns" and "you could almost feel it in your face." Whittlesey's only comment to McMurtry was, "Most unpleasant!," but he later wrote a more graphic description of the scene: "The hillside fairly crackled with bullets which whistled and moaned to the accompaniment of what sounded like a thousand riveting machines on the surrounding high ground to the rear." On the right flank, Captain Holderman called this "one of the most unpleasant experiences of the siege" as his front was literally "baptized in bullets."[8]

A friend had crawled over to pay a brief visit to Leonard Glenn and Raymond Hammond just before this machine gun barrage. As he crouched across their laps, the machine guns let fly, sending one bullet through the front of his tunic and into his arm. In Company G, one private recalled, "We got flat down in our little holes, trying our best to find cover from these machine guns. They seemed to cover every foot of our ground continuously for about a half an hour." By now, most of Whittlesey's own machine guns had been put out of commission by German trench mortars and machine guns that had targeted the American automatic weapons. Because the machine guns could not be fired from funkholes and the crews were consequently more exposed to enemy fire, all of the original gunners were dead or wounded. Those men now operating the remaining guns had little experience as gunners, having been responsible primarily for loading and toting ammunition boxes. There had been only five boxes per gun to begin with and, despite holding their fire until sure of hitting targets, that supply had almost been exhausted. Whittlesey had high praise for his machine gun detachment: "Our machine gunners were fine. They would withhold their fire until the Boches were near and then let them have it until the cries ceased and the attack was over." Private Sobaszkiewicz described the scene at one of the guns: "There in a little open spot was a machine gun that looked to be out of order but the whole spot looked to me like a wagon wheel composed of dead American soldiers, with the machine gun as the hub."[9]

Sergeant George Hauck, Company D, 306th Machine Gun Battalion: "Lieutenant, I wait for the bastards to get near and then I shoot!"[10]

This intense machine gun barrage was followed by yet another flurry of grenades from the hilltop, many coming tied together in bunches to increase the devastation. One clump of grenades blew the legs off a man up towards the road in the center. As comrades about him beat back the German attack, they could hear him cry over and over, "Mama–Mama–Mama," until he died. Nearby, Thomas Sadler, one of two enlisted men from the 305th Field Artillery who had accompanied Lieutenant Teichmoeller on his liaison mission, fired off a round. Seeing his target fall, Sadler jumped up in celebration, shouting, "I got him! I got him!" Someone in an adjacent funkhole yelled out, "Get down, you damned fool! Do you want to get your head blown off?" Somewhat embarrassed, Sadler flopped down and began firing again. In Company C, PFC Catino Carnebucci, a native of the little village of Monguiuffi in Sicily and a veteran of the Italian army, was shot dead. In Cullen's Company H, Harold Thomas, the railroader from Youngstown, Ohio, received his death wound. Another of Cullen's men, Henry Miller, shared a hole with Isidore Spiegel, who cautioned his friend not to go crawling around in the brush. Spiegel remembered, "Private Miller, in spite of my warnings, decided to reconnoiter and see what he could find. Time passed. Miller did not return and I became apprehensive and started to look for him. I found him severely wounded and I tried to make him as comfortable as possible. I searched for water, but was unsuccessful. Private Miller died in a short while."[11]

The German attackers were soon driven back and Whittlesey knew it was time to send out more men in the heretofore vain attempts to establish communication with regimental headquarters. Everyone wanted to get out of that hell hole, so there were more than enough volunteers for patrol and scouting duty. Whittlesey dispatched only those men whom he considered to be absolutely dependable on the mission of infiltrating the German lines. For the night of October 5, he selected two of his battalion runners who had already proven their courage by repeatedly carrying important messages through heavy fire—George Botelle of Company C and Joseph Friel of Company A. Botelle, well aware that all previous messengers had either been killed, wounded, captured, or stymied in the attempt, had to be coaxed a bit, but felt better after being paired with Friel. Following a short briefing by Whittlesey, the two messengers slipped down the slope and began to crawl across the valley toward Ridge 198. Those ever-present chattering machine guns soon opened fire on the pair, killing Friel instantly and sending Botelle scurrying back to the American position. He had been extremely lucky—a bullet had gone through his helmet and cut a furrow across his forehead, leaving his face smeared with blood. After listening to Botelle's story and examining his ruined helmet, Robert Manson said to himself, "Gee, what a close shave!"[12]

Everything that remotely looked like food had been consumed. Men now ate what previously would have been considered garbage. Omer Richards had polished off the rest of the bird seed. Walter Baldwin carefully used his tongue to extract the last few grains of coffee from a discarded condiment can. Sidney Foss remembered that after the campaign started, he had used a small piece of fatty bacon, less than an ounce in weight, to smear over the small cuts on his hands from the omnipresent barbed wire. Foss pulled the bacon from his pocket, picked off the dirt and lint, carefully sliced it into two pieces, then shared the delicious treat with Sergeant Anderson, his funk-hole mate. Occasionally a blood-stained German corpse would yield a handful of dank, black bread, a veritable feast for the starving Americans. Famished doughboys tried everything. Private Manson said simply, "Some chewed roots of trees, leaves, and tobacco." He tried to eat a pinch of Bull Durham, but confessed, "I felt like a man who is seasick, and wants to throw up, but can't." That evening soldiers heard a rustling in the brush and weeds along the creek. Suspecting a German patrol, they attentively eyed the spot, but were astonished to see a wild boar that had apparently been wounded in the machine gun barrage. A fusillade of bullets erupted from the Springfields. Whittlesey recorded the result: "We tried to get it, and we certainly could have used it, but the attempt failed." There would be no pork for the famished soldiers.[13]

Sergeant Herman Anderson, Company A, 308th Infantry:
"Private Foss picked up one of those condiment cans and there was a little salt and pepper in there mixed together and we stuck our tongues in there now and then to change the taste in our mouths."[14]

Despite Whittlesey's prohibition about going for water during the daytime, men began to sneak down to the creek and spring. Arthur Swanbeck had been hit by shrapnel from an American shell that "broke the bone above the elbow, which left it with a crooked joint." Twenty years later, Swanbeck commented, "The piece of shrapnel went through my arm with such force it might be going yet!" That morning he crept down to a shell hole that had partially filled with water. A German sniper spotted him and "started punching holes in the water," so Swanbeck raced back to safety with his empty canteens. After Hubert Esch, a Minnesota replacement, had made several unauthorized trips for water, Whittlesey found out and forbade him to go again. Lieutenant Maurice Revnes shared a funkhole with Sergeant Anderson and Private Foss about thirty yards above the stream. Unable to leave the hole because of his shattered foot, Revnes tried unsuccessfully to discourage soldiers from exposing themselves along the creek bed. He remembered, "I'd stop them and tell them it was dangerous for them to go and get water. I'd argue with them but they wouldn't reply and most of the men went anyway whether I ordered them or not. They paid no attention to my orders. They were determined to get water and they went." Revnes added that their "faces were very thin and when I'd talk to them they'd sort of listen. Their faces were immobile and no particular smile or anger or anything. They just stared at me." Discipline was starting to fail under the strain of hunger, thirst, sleeplessness, and the ever-increasing casualty list.[15]

Depression hung heavily over Whittlesey's soldiers. Clifford Brown said, "We were waiting—waiting for what seemed to be certain death," and John Nell recalled his comrades remarking, "Well, I guess the sooner the better. We are going to get it anyway." To Nell it appeared "as if we were doomed to die on the spot," and he confessed, "We were literally waiting for our time to die." Death was, indeed, their constant companion. When Private Hans Christensen returned to his funkhole in Captain Holderman's sector after a brief absence, he found it occupied by a stranger who had moved in and made himself at home. Christensen told what happened then: "I was just going to tell him to get out and go dig a hole for himself when I heard a shell come. I lay down right at his feet and the shell burst a little behind him. A piece from the shell entered his back, passed through him, and he died instantly." Burials, performed in the most perfunctory manner, dotted the hillside. Robert Manson observed, "Here and there arms and legs could be seen sticking out of the graves." Many bodies, both those interred and atop the ground, had been chopped, mangled, and horribly dismembered by American artillery and German trench mortars. In some cases, this extreme mutilation prevented the identification of pieces of friends by those dug in only a few yards away.[16]

While no attention was paid to the dead, survivors did everything in their power to alleviate the plight of the wounded, often at the risk of their own lives. Corporal Eiler Bolvig, a native of Denmark who had been married only a few weeks before reporting at Camp Upton, was killed by a German shell while caring for a wounded friend. Each man had been issued two bandages apiece, but these, as well as the supply carried by the first aid men, had long since been used up. Ralph John recalled that "we could do next to nothing for the wounded" and "even shirts, socks and underwear had been torn into rags for bandages." He admitted that everybody "was like a living scarecrow."[17]

Gangrene began to appear and spread its deadly toxins as bloody, makeshift bandages were stripped from the dead and applied to new wounds, the only attempt at hygiene being to turn the dressing material over. Sergeant Lionel Bendheim had been wounded on October 3 by a trench mortar shell that landed squarely on his right leg and shattered it. He would later muse, "How in God's name it

Captain Nelson Holderman: "Bandages were now being taken from the dead and applied to the wounded. Wounds were being wrapped with the spiral puttees worn by the soldiers and taken from the legs of the dead. These proved to be excellent bandages, for the stub of an arm or a leg, or a badly lacerated wound could be securely wrapped with two of these leggins. They were also made of wool and quickly absorbed the blood."[18]

didn't blow me to pieces, I'll never be able to explain." Lack of medical attention and gangrene would cost him the limb. Bendheim shared a hole with Lieutenant Schenck and Sergeant Martin Tuite, both of whom escaped injury when Lionel was hit. These two friends of Sergeant Bendheim found consolation in religion. When not tossing grenades or firing a rifle while driving back attackers or cheering his men while under sniper fire, Lieutenant Schenck spent his time quietly reading a small leather-bound copy of Mary Baker Eddy's *Science and Health*. Sergeant Tuite would silently pray while fingering his rosary.[19]

That evening the distinctive sounds of Chauchats firing could be heard to the south beyond Ridge 198 where the Seventy-seventh Division vainly fought against German defenders. After listening for a few minutes, Major Whittlesey declared that the situation was reminiscent of the bagpipes played by the British relief force that had broken the siege at Lucknow during the Indian Mutiny in 1857. Captain McMurtry reasoned that if the trapped Americans could hear those Chauchats, Whittlesey could signal his continued resistance by firing his own automatic rifles. Whittlesey agreed and instructed Holderman and Cullen, during periods of calm, "to fire bursts of ten shots from their Chauchat rifles." Hopefully, this signal would carry to the advancing troops and pinpoint their location. But firing from the south soon faded and no response came to the regular bursts fired at intervals that night. A couple of American aircraft had been spotted that morning and two more later that afternoon; all of them had tossed out packages that landed in German hands. It was obvious, despite Whittlesey's earlier optimism, that the aviators had not been able to locate him. The major admitted that "hope of being relieved immediately had sunk to a low level."[20]

The weather, which had so far been fairly mild, turned cold and hovered just above the freezing mark, with a rainy drizzle that added to the discomfort of everyone. Whittlesey moved quietly from hole to hole, telling his men that they must stick it out and that those two million Americans were still on the way. He repeated the Lucknow story over and over, explaining how a surrounded British force had held out for forty days against overwhelming odds. He would always conclude with the cheerful observation, "We have been here only four days, so we can stick it out a long while yet." As Whittlesey moved off into the darkness, baffled enlisted men must have looked at one another in amazement and asked what the hell he had meant and where on earth was this stupid Lucknow anyway. As for historical references, Robert Manson said that Whittlesey always reminded him of Lieutenant Colonel George Armstrong Custer riding to his death at the Battle of Little Bighorn. Whatever their personal feelings about the dire situation, they were all pleased that the major expressed a constant interest in their welfare.[21]

October 6 was Sunday, but the trapped doughboys had little to be thankful for as they attempted to keep warm by huddling together under the dripping trees, their predicament being compounded by a mixture of fog, rain, and plummeting temperatures. Those pitifully few blankets and overcoats that had not been left behind covered the most critically wounded. There were no slickers to offer protection from the rain. All excess clothing had long ago been ripped into makeshift bandages. There was no protection whatsoever from the pouring rain that swept the heights along Charlevaux Valley, streaming downhill and filling the funkholes. Hubert Esch remembered that the holes "lower down on the hillside had a lot of water in them and the boys were in bad shape." Feet became swollen and tender from the constant wet, leading officers to believe that trench foot might now be added to the ever-expanding list of worries.[22]

Despite the horrid conditions, apparent hopelessness of the Liberty Boys, and increasing depression, their ability to function as soldiers remained surprisingly high. Captain McMurtry said on October 6: "Although our men were in a weakened

Oh, the grimy mud, the slimy mud,
The cheesy mud, the greasy mud, that
*   filters through your hair,*
You sleep in the mud, and drink it, that's
*   true;*
There's mud in the bacon, the rice and the
*   stew,*
When you open an egg, you'll find mud in it
*   too —*
Sunny France.[23]

state, their spirit was right there and at the word 'stand to' every man came from his funk hole promptly and took his position at the firing point." From his position on the right, Captain Holderman agreed with McMurtry's assessment, saying that the isolation and heavy casualties were "never able to break the morale of the men." He added that "they were not in very good physical condition, although the spirit was very high and you could not see but what they were alright and ready for a fight at any minute." On the left, Lieutenant Cullen confessed that "it began to look pretty dark to me," but he kept crawling from hole to hole, talking to everyone about keeping alert and staying under cover. Cullen greeted everyone with a grin and assured them that "we would get out of this fix," knowing instinctively that he could depend on every man in his company.[24]

Major Whittlesey was a bit more pessimistic than his senior officers. Many enlisted men, hungry and tired and depressed, had spoken to him directly, requesting permission to attempt to break through the German lines. The major always refused these offers, preferring to select the scouts he sent out, but he realized that it would not be much longer before the men would stop asking permission and just leave on their own initiative. Whittlesey summed up the situation on the morning of October 6: "Conditions were growing hourly more serious. The indescribable suffering of the wounded and the seeming failure of troops in the rear to come forward with reinforcements threatened to shake the morale of the command." Whittlesey had inspired confidence from the very beginning with his story about two million Americans coming to their rescue, then later with the Siege of Lucknow tale. Men appreciated his efforts, none more so than Lieutenant Cullen, who said of the major: "He certainly was stout-hearted and as game as they make them. He seemed to be as cool and calm as though we were back at a rest area and my hat goes off to him as being a very good soldier and true American." However, Major Whittlesey and his officers could only do so much. He knew there was a limit to human endurance and at some time in the not too distant future the solid front shown thus far by his command would begin to crack. But where would the first rift appear?[25]

Soldiers had been discussing their situation ever since reaching the Charlevaux Valley, frankly arguing the possibilities of remaining entrenched or breaking out, speculating when relief would appear and whether the Germans would overrun their position in the next attack. These were generally private conversations, the subject being discreetly changed whenever an officer would happen by. It was not that the enlisted men did not share the same opinions as their officers, but they were uncomfortable in speaking their minds to superiors.[26]

Perhaps the most candid conversations had occurred in the funk-hole occupied by Lieutenant Maurice Revnes of the machine gunners, Sergeant Herman Anderson of Company A, and Private Sidney Foss of

Company K. On the morning of October 6 Revnes found himself commanding Lieutenant Peabody's platoon of machine gunners, following the agonizingly painful death of that officer. Son of Alexander M. Peabody, a well-known Wall Street banker, Marshall had been a representative for the Philadelphia banking firm of Brooks, Stokes & Co. when inducted. A graduate of the officer training course at Camp Upton, Peabody had won the respect of everyone in his platoon for close attention to the welfare of the men under his command. Although unable to leave his funkhole after being wounded on October 3, the young lieutenant had kept up the spirits of all within sound of his voice, concealing his own intense pain while encouraging those less seriously wounded than him. During lulls in the firing, those close by could occasionally hear low moaning from Peabody's direction, but he refused to acknowledge how much pain he was in. Only when Whittlesey crawled up to check on him did the false bravado fade for an instant, as he asked, "Can I have some water, sir?"[27]

Due to the death of Peabody and the wounding of Lieutenant Henry J. Williamson, Revnes and Anderson both commanded their respective companies, although the latter was operating as a part of Company G. Sergeant George Hauck had kept Revnes informed as to the status of the machine gun detachment on the right flank, listing current supplies of ammunition and updating casualties that the lieutenant duly noted on his field message pad. During each visit, Revnes, in constant pain with half his foot gone, would ask Hauck what the chances were that they could soon get out. Hauck always responded that they should hope for the best and be as cheerful as possible under the circumstances and be ready to fight and die if necessary. When pressed about how the gunners felt, Hauck responded, "We may get out any day, but we would fight as long as we could hold out." The news had gone from bad to worse for Revnes, isolated from his command. That precise list of killed and wounded would eventually total thirty of the forty-three officers and enlisted men. These appalling casualties, combined with the widespread demoralization resulting from hunger and thirst, brought more urgency to the conversation in Lieutenant Revnes's funkhole.[28]

Revnes began talking about the fix the command was in, wondering aloud, "Would the Germans leave us take the wounded back?" and "Would it be dishonorable to surrender if we weren't relieved at a certain time?" Revnes and Anderson, Foss joining in every now and then, began debating these two questions, as well as whether it would be dishonorable and against regulations to surrender in their current situation. Revnes explained his concerns: "I couldn't figure or see how or what solution the battalion on the hill could come to in getting off the hill or getting rid of the enemy. I felt that they would not leave the wounded around on the hill. They could not really pull off an effective offensive, they could only defend. I heard our friendly troops trying to get to us and then it got fainter. I only assumed that more Germans had gotten in behind us." After much discussion, Revnes and Anderson decided that Major Whittlesey should be informed of their concerns. The lieutenant took out a pencil and wrote a short note on his field message pad, read it back to Anderson, tore it out, and sent Foss crawling off to deliver the memorandum to Whittlesey.[29]

Thrust into the crucible of Charlevaux Valley and, by fate, sharing the same funkhole, Revnes and Anderson were as alike as two sides of a coin. Anderson was from Brooklyn, a big man who had been elevated to sergeant just before the 308th Infantry reached the Baccarat Sector the previous June. He was a combat veteran and had been a duty sergeant until October 1, then was promoted to platoon sergeant after his predecessor had been killed. Acknowledged as the "company pinochle shark" by a comrade, Anderson had been wounded twice, once across the forehead and again on the nose, but kept in touch with the survivors of Company A by daily crawling to their funkholes to check on them and keep up morale.[30]

Although born in New York City in 1889, Revnes had been raised and educated in Philadelphia, where he worked in various capacities for the Philadelphia Opera House. When that establishment closed in 1910, Revnes moved back to New York, where he was employed by a number of theater owners and producers. In 1914, he began to produce one-act plays, such as *Mrs. Avery* and *Kitty Michay*, at the Princess Theater and Castles in the Air. In September of 1917, while his new show, *Hitchi Koo*, was playing at the Princess, Revnes left for Plattsburg, where he had been accepted into the Second Officers' Training Camp. After being commissioned a second lieutenant on November 27, 1917, Revnes reported to Camp Dix and was assigned to the 308th Machine Gun Battalion in the Seventy-eighth Division. Having no machine gun experience, he remembered being relegated to duties such as "building corrals, pulling stumps in camp, officer of the day, and officer of the guard and close order drill of the company."

General J. Franklin Bell had requested that the talented Lieutenant Revnes be transferred to the Seventy-seventh Division. On about February 20, 1918, the stage producer reported to Camp Upton, where he was assigned to the post of camp theatrical director. His new duties included consulting with the Fosdick Commission to discuss which plays were suitable for the soldiers, producing plays on the approved list, and overseeing the construction of the Liberty Theater. While at Camp Upton, Revnes did no military duty. He shipped out with the Seventy-seventh Division, but after only two weeks in France was transferred to Second Corps Headquarters, where he was given the job of supply and transportation officer. In June, he rejoined the Seventy-seventh Division and General Duncan told him to form a "divisional theatrical unit." Gathering musicians, singers, and vaudeville performers from throughout the division, Revnes quickly formed a popular stage company that would eventually become known as the Argonne Players.[31]

Wishing for a more active role in the war, Lieutenant Revnes asked to be transferred to a front-line unit. General Duncan granted his request and in mid-August assigned him to the 306th Machine Gun Battalion. After a couple of weeks as battalion gas officer, Revnes, along with Lieutenant Alfred Noon and some non-commissioned officers, was sent to Gondrecourt for machine gun school. He rejoined the 306th Machine Gun Battalion on September 26, the first day of the Argonne offensive, and the following day was assigned to lead a platoon in Company D, commanded by Lieutenant Peabody. Lieutenant Revnes had been with his company just one week before Whittlesey's command reached the Charlevaux Valley and was a virtual stranger to his men. Given his background as a headquarters officer, his newness to battlefield command, and the oppressive environment in Whittlesey's pocket of resistance, it is not surprising that Revnes was the first man to question openly the decision of his superior.[33]

Vaudeville Routine from the Repertoire of the Argonne Players

"See, General, here is a spy."
"What kind of spy?"
"A mince pie."
"How do you know he is a spy?"
"He has the papers on him."
"Has he got the makin's, too?"
"Yes, sir, sixty bags of Durham."
"My God, the spy is full of bull."[32]

Whittlesey and McMurtry were together in their funkhole when Private Foss crept up and handed over a piece of folded paper. Whittlesey was stunned into speechlessness as he read the following message:

Major W.

    If our people do not get here by noon, it is useless for us to keep up against these great odds. It's a horrible thing to think of, but I can see nothing else for us to do but give up—The men are starving—the wounded, like myself, have not only had no nourishment but a great loss of blood. If the same thought may be in your mind perhaps the enemy may permit the wounded to return to their own lines. I only say this because I, for one, can not hold out longer, when cornered as we are it strikes me that it is not a dishonorable deed to give up.

Revnes

He handed the message to McMurtry, then murmured something to Foss about Lieutenant Revnes being "a little scared." Whittlesey carefully folded the note after McMurtry had finished and placed it in a pocket, then asked the messenger, "Where [does] the lieutenant hang out at?" Foss pointed and said he could show the way, so the major said quietly, "I'll go down there."

The two men slid downhill around tree trunks and bushes until they reached the hole where Revnes lay with his crippled foot. There was a whispered conversation that Foss could not hear completely. Whittlesey asked how the lieutenant was holding up, remarking, "Relief almost got into us there one time, but the Germans made a strong attack and drove them back." He then remarked that everything looked good for reinforcements to get through and "it would be a little matter of time" before they rejoined the division. Just before he left, Whittlesey said something about not being scared. Like a good noncom, Sergeant Anderson kept his mouth shut and let Revnes take the heat for sending off the inflammatory message that had so provoked their commander. Whittlesey said bluntly, "There is going to be no surrender," then launched into his Lucknow soliloquy, muttering, "There have been troops that have been surrounded for forty days. We have been here only five days, so we can stick it out a long while yet." As he was leaving, Whittlesey turned to Sergeant Anderson and gave him a peremptory order: "If you see any signs of anybody surrendering or see a white flag or anything, you shoot him!!" Relieved to avoid the major's ill-concealed wrath, Anderson responded weakly, "Yes, sir."[34]

Whittlesey did what little he could to keep up morale. He and his remaining officers circulated among the soldiers, checking their weapons and fighting condition. His men were obviously too weak and exhausted to bury the dead, but he commanded them to at least cover the corpses with brush and leaves. A couple of rotting bodies that emitted foul-smelling vapors lay just uphill from the major's PC, but it was useless to move elsewhere. Just as no place provided complete safety, no place offered refuge from the nauseating sights and smells.[35]

Early morning patrols failed to penetrate the German lines, so McMurtry noted that the day settled down into the same old routine: "The Germans continued with their usual program—machine guns, sniping and their trench mortars, and kept that up pretty well through the day." There was something different about this day, however. As soon as the rain stopped and the fog cleared, American airplanes came soaring overhead just above the treetops. The white battalion signal panels had already been placed in small openings cut by the American barrage, but most everyone who retained anything of that color began to wave frantically at the air crews. F. M. Mikulewicz, a runner from Company I attached to Second Battalion headquarters, and Captain McMurtry tied together a couple of handkerchiefs and began swinging them wildly. Corporal John Bowden, despite being wounded, went out three separate times under machine gun fire and waved an old towel from Company H's position. Afterwards, Lieutenant Cullen tossed the same dirty towel to Joseph Schanz, who lay on a hump of ground pulling the cloth back and forth across his chest. Packages came tumbling out of the planes, some floating gently to earth under small parachutes and others crashing to earth at blinding speed. But hopeful doughboys watched helplessly as every single package fell into Boche positions. Gleeful Germans cracked open the parcels and those who could speak English shouted down what they had found. "Cheese!" "Cigarettes!" "Canned beef!" "Jam!" "Chewing tobacco!" "Chocolate!!" As might be expected, the Americans replied with a torrent of curses. Captain Holderman, who had been in the military for some fourteen years, said incredulously that he "had never before known that the American soldier's vocabulary contained so much 'enlightening information' and so many 'endearing terms,' and the Germans understood them perfectly."[36]

That afternoon there was yet another grenade attack and advance from the ridge, which was repulsed after about twenty minutes of intense fighting. A trench mortar shell landed on one of the few remaining machine guns on the left, smashing it to junk and killing Lieutenant Alfred Noon. Nearby, James Strickland went down with a shattered thigh. Albert Summers, formerly from Bristol, England, dashed out and dragged Strickland to safety, wrapped up his wound, slid down to the creek for water, and scampered back up to the wounded man—all as bullets continually slammed into tree trunks beside him and clipped leaves overhead. Corporal John Hinchman and Private Stanislaw Kozikowski manned a Chauchat facing south, when suddenly Hinchman fell dead. Kozikowski spotted some movement in bushes along the stream, fired a short burst, and avenged his friend's death. In Company G, PFC William Begley had taken command of his squad after the corporal was killed and, despite a machine gun bullet through his arm, led his men until killed himself during the afternoon's fight. Lieutenant Harry Rogers, the Missourian commanding Company B who had captured that bunch of Germans near l'Homme Mort, received his death wound. The citation for his Distinguished Service Cross would read, "Although under a heavy concentration of fire from enemy machine guns and snipers, by his personal example of calmness he kept his men in order and helped repel counterattacks." When a shell or bundle of grenades burst and wounded William Armstrong, one of his comrades in Company C yelled out, "Come on, they got him! Let's go up there and kill some of those bastards!!" Clifford Brown and his buddy spotted a German who seemed to be directing troops from the hilltop and a couple of well-aimed shots tumbled him from his perch, effectively ending the fighting in front of Lieutenant Schenck's company.[37]

From small a thing as "Gimme a light,"
To laying down his life in a fight,
There was no color, nor was there creed,
Whenever a "Buddy" was in need.[38]

Over on the right flank with Company E, Corporal Daniel Tallon, normally one of McMurtry's battalion clerks, had hitherto displayed "the highest degree of courage and devotion to duty." With *minenwerfer* shells bursting about him, Tailon left the protection of his funkhole to give first aid to a fallen doughboy. After bandaging his wound, Tallon hoisted him to make a dash for safety, but was himself killed by another exploding shell. When a War Department telegram announcing his death arrived at 261 West 114th Street in New York City, Patrick Tallon immediately made arrangements for a memorial mass for his son at the Church of St. Thomas the Apostle. But this tragic news caused Tallon's father to suffer a fatal heart attack, so the memorial was celebrated for both father and son.[39]

Following the German withdrawal, Captain McMurtry joined Whittlesey in their PC. The major saw something odd sticking out of McMurtry's back and gave it a yank. McMurtry screamed out, "Murder! If you do that again, I'll wring your neck!!" Whittlesey had a wry smile on his face as he showed the captain a large sliver from the wooden handle of a German grenade. "Go get it dressed," ordered Whittlesey, then asked incredulously, "Didn't you know you were wounded?"[40]

There were only a few rounds of machine gun ammunition remaining. Rifle ammunition had likewise started to give out, even after scavenging rounds from the casualties. Nothing could be done regarding the former situation, but after dark men slid through the mud to recover rifles and ammunition from those Germans who had died close to the American position. Captain Holderman remembered, "A good supply of rifles and ammunition was obtained, and their rifles made very fine sniping weapons, although they did not compare with the American rifles for long range work." After one such party returned, an enlisted man asked Holderman for permission to go back and thoroughly search the German dead for food. The soldier sported a makeshift bandage on his head, so Holderman at first refused the request, but he relented after repeated appeals. The wounded man crawled out in the darkness and was gone so long that his friends thought he had been captured. When the searcher finally returned, Holderman asked if he had found any rations, whereupon the dough-boy reached into his shirt and pulled something out. "Here, Captain, I have a fine souvenir for you," the man said as he handed over a decorative smoking pipe. Holderman then related how he "proceeded to pull out of his shirt bosom notebooks, looking glasses, shaving utensils, combs, pencils, pens, buttons, ornaments, and other articles too numerous to mention," concluding that "he had not gone out for rations at all, but for souvenirs." No matter how gnawing their hunger, the Americans kept a keen lookout for trophies. Irving Liner pocketed "a shoulder strap of a German who doesn't expect to wear it any more." Magnus Krogh recalled how he and a few others killed four enemy soldiers as they walked along the road and, twenty years later, bragged, "I still have a German mark I got off one of them."[41]

I'm wishin' for things war made me miss,
* A bit of a hug and squeeze and a kiss,*
A loving wife to hold close in my arms,
* Not asking me, "Where's my souvenir charms?"*

And the souvenir that I'm bringin' home,
* It weren't stolen and it's all my own,*
It isn't a relic or a hunk of tin,
* You see, dear wife, it's my own damn skin!*[42]

That night the surviving doughboys went to sleep with but one thought on their minds: "There is nothing before us but death." After completing his nightly funkhole tour, Whittlesey settled down and dozed off next to a young private who had been grievously wounded, the two men huddling together and sharing their body heat to ward off the chill autumn air. Whittlesey slept fitfully, anxiously checking the condition of his sleeping partner in the darkness. Sometime during the night, Whittlesey awoke to find himself cheek to cheek with the wounded soldier, no more than a boy, who had just died in his arms.[43]

10

HELP ON THE WAY

Despite what men in Whittlesey's isolated command thought, other units of the Seventy-seventh Division had been desperately trying to reach them. First to make the attempt were the two companies, D and F of the 308th Infantry, that Whittlesey had left behind. Roused from captured German dugouts at 7 A.M. on the morning of October 2, Lieutenant Knight led them forward an hour later along the west side of the large ravine, where terrain was so steep it was "cumbersome to walking along without any opposition." They were held up by entrenched German forces, so Knight left Company F to hold there and took Company D into the ravine, but judged that any advance along the bottom "would be suicide." As his men began to climb up the southwestern slope of Ridge 198, they met stiff resistance from Jerrys who showered them with grenades. One member of the company said that "it was impossible to see them [Germans] though they were just above us, but they must have had a wonderful view of us." In order to save his company, Lieutenant Knight pulled it back to the west slope of the ravine. During this withdrawal, Lieutenant Charles Turner's platoon became detached from the main body and surrounded by the enemy. Although encircled by machine guns and snipers, in addition to being exposed to German artillery, Lieutenant Turner "ridiculed the thought of surrender." A few weeks earlier, he had written home, "If it is God's will I shall return, but if I die, which I think I will, you may always rest assured that it was for the country and the folks I love so well." Turner and his men held out to the bitter end, only a corporal and three privates escaping alive from the twenty-man platoon.[1]

Did you ever think as the hearse rolls by,
That the next trip they take they'll be layin' you by
With your boots a swingin' from the back of a roan,
And the undertaker inscribing your stone?[2]

When no one from Whittlesey's force came back to link up with Knight's "containing force," the lieutenant launched a series of attacks designed to reach the combined battalions somewhere up ahead. His two companies managed to press forward less than one kilometer, but came to a standstill and entrenched on the western slope of the ravine under heavy fire. Informed that Whittlesey had been cut off, Knight sent out a twelve-man patrol under Sergeant Mike Davis with a message for the major from regimental headquarters. Davis gathered his men together and explained their mission, one patrol member relating that "he told us if he was bumped off, one of us must take the message through."[3]

Setting out at 1 A.M. on October 5, "a horibal darck night," according to one of Davis's men, the patrol discovered that German snipers, seemingly everywhere, fired at the slightest noise. One doughboy remembered that "we twisted around through the brush, and wound down a canyon, making no nois scarcely, we passed by some jery dug outs. I was the last man in the column, and I see a jerry in the door of a dug out with his back to us." Sneaking up the steep incline, Davis and his men got within sight of Major Whittlesey's position, although they did not know it at the time. Ridge 198 suddenly erupted with "horibal gun fire." A soldier slumped to the ground, shot through the head, while everyone else jumped for cover "in shell holes, under bushes, and behind logs." Shouts of "Kamerad!" echoed across the hill as shadows disappeared with the rising sun, but Davis had no intention of surrendering. He and his men stuck it out all day, sniping at enemy riflemen that ventured too close, sheltering themselves from return fire, and enduring a brief flurry of shells directed on their position. After nightfall, the Americans wormed their way back toward the main body of Company D, successfully eluding German patrols and machine gun nests. Sergeant Davis reported that, despite losing over one-half of his patrol, he had been unable to make contact with the cut-off troops.[4]

Although German riflemen were unable to dislodge Davis's patrol, they did find three soldiers who had been hiding on Ridge 198 ever since Lieutenant Wilhelm's ill-fated breakout on October 3. Corporal Irving Goldberg had pulled two seriously wounded men—his first sergeant, Harold Kaplan, and Saul Marshallcowitz, from the regimental medical detachment—into a particularly dense part of the forest, where they lay undetected for over two days, trapped between Whittlesey's position and the division's main line. There they remained, without food or water, a native-born Gotham salesman tending the wounds of two Russian immigrants, Kaplan, a former Marine and rubber worker, and Marshallcowitz, a tailor from Broome Street. Germans seeking out the stubborn American patrol finally stumbled upon the trio, who would finish the war in prison camp.[5]

About dawn on October 5, the Germans attacked Lieutenant Knight and his two depleted companies, now numbering about one hundred men, one of whom recalled, "All day long the scrap continued, our men showing plainly the effects of their long days of continuous advance, holding out purely through the force of will power." After repulsing several attacks, Knight initiated his own advance, but found that after seven hours of fighting he had only gained a hundred yards. Dead and wounded, both American and German, littered the battlefield when units from the 307th Infantry came forward and relieved the two battered companies. Two days later, Company D could muster only 26 soldiers of the 214 who had gone over the top on September 26 and it was acknowledged that the condition of these few survivors "was pretty bad." Company F had suffered just as severely. Lieutenant Knight had been unable to link up with Whittlesey as Colonel Stacey's original plan had intended, but it was not for lack of trying.[6]

The French Groupement Durand, which had been assigned to act as liaison on the left of the Seventy-seventh Division, had simply vanished after proving to be woefully inadequate for the task assigned to it. The right of Groupement Durand, held by the 368th Infantry, did not align with the left of the Seventy-seventh Division and, as troops advanced into the Argonne, this original gap between the French and Americans gradually widened to a distance of eight hundred meters. This divergence had allowed the Germans to slip in around Major Whittlesey's battalion when it was first cut off on September 29–30. The situation got even worse on October 1, when the 368th was withdrawn completely and transferred to the French XXXVIII Corps. Just as Whittlesey had broken through a gap between two German corps, the Germans had now surrounded Whittlesey by penetrating this breach between the French and American armies.[7]

At Seventy-seventh Division headquarters, General Alexander seemed pleased that Major Whittlesey had reached his objective on the evening of October 2, but was also concerned that French advances had been halted south of Binarville. Fearing for the safety of his left flank, Alexander began shifting his reserves in that direction. He instructed General Evan Johnson to move the Third Battalion, 308th Infantry, held in brigade reserve, up to protect the exposed flank of Whittlesey's two battalions. But Alexander was irate when he discovered that "instead of being posted as to cover Whittlesey's left, in contact with him and facing northwest, that battalion was posted in a body and facing north," at least one kilometer from Whittlesey's position. Enemy patrols quickly discovered this gaping hole in the division line and aggressive German commanders sent troops to surround Whittlesey with truckloads of barbed wire and dozens of machine guns. In the process of doing so, the Germans naturally overran the American line of runner posts that connected Colonel Stacey with his advance battalions. News of this latest development reached General Alexander at about 2 A.M. on October 3, but he later confessed that "the information did not, at the time, make a very deep impression," since similar reports about losing contact with various units had been made almost daily in the past week. These situations always rectified themselves as other units of the division caught up with those supposedly cut off.[8]

General Alexander naturally assumed that the 307th Infantry would be able to push forward through the forest later that day and link up with Whittlesey. After all, Captain Holderman had gotten Company K forward past the German defenders, so Alexander reasoned the remainder of the regiment could also fight its way through. However, the division's primary goal still remained to advance wherever possible, relief of Whittlesey's command being only a secondary concern since the resulting progress would surely free him from encirclement. The division commander fully expected General Evan Johnson, commander of the 154th Brigade, to get enough troops forward to relieve Whittlesey. Johnson intended to do just that, telling his officers, "This is a family affair and, as such, we will handle it ourselves." The relief of Whittlesey's command really was a family affair for Sergeant Arthur Diesel, whose brother Louis was one of the machine gunners dug in along the Charlevaux Road.[9]

The relationship between the two generals responsible for rescuing Whittlesey was somewhat strained. When the initial advance of the 154th Brigade had been held up on the morning of October 2, General Alexander left a telephone message for his subordinate: "You tell General Johnson that the 154th Brigade is holding back the French on the left and is holding back everything on the right and that the 154th Brigade must push forward to their objective today. By 'must' I mean must and by 'today' I mean today and not next week. You report heavy machine gun fire, but the casualty lists do not substantiate this. Remember that when you are making these reports." After receiving this message, which was based on faulty information, Johnson contacted Alexander to explain the true situation. He attempted to point out that on the left the French were actually five or six hundred meters to his left rear and the 153rd Brigade was well behind on the right. But Alexander would have none of that and Johnson remembered being "told by him in a most peremptory way, that I must push on at once and everything on my right and left was ahead and I was holding back everything and that if I could not do this he would get someone that could!"[10]

That afternoon, after Whittlesey's command had captured machine guns and taken prisoners during its breakthrough, General Johnson sent a status report to J. R. R. Hannay, Alexander's chief of staff, and appended a message for the general himself. He again explained that the French were "actually back of my line," this information fresh from a corps observer, and the 153rd Brigade was "not only relatively but actually behind my troops." Johnson then added in frustration, "My Brigade is, and has been, away ahead of anything on my right or left. If he will look at the map he will see it." Johnson concluded by stating, "I know what I am talking about." As soon as the news of Whittlesey's apparent success reached division headquarters, Hannay telephoned Johnson and said, "General Alexander says 'Congratulations.'" Johnson, by now completely indignant, responded icily, "I do not consider it a matter for congratulations, but I wish to put him absolutely in possession of the facts."[11]

Although the Third Battalion, 308th Infantry, had been transferred from brigade reserve, it was employed to hold the regimental sector, leaving Companies D and F to contend against the enemy west of the north-south ravine. Lieutenant Knight's two companies were reinforced and eventually relieved by the Second Battalion, 307th Infantry, which operated along both sides of the north-south ravine under the direction of Colonel Stacey. This battalion, actually Companies E, G, H, and L, had been relaxing at Depot de Machines, where the men washed in the small creek, fought the cootie war, and enjoyed their first cooked meal in nine days. The first attack by Companies G and L occurred about 3:30 P.M. on October 4 on the eastern slope of the ravine where "they came under a fire from both flanks and the front, and they looked at the work before them—a steep and narrow ravine, its sides choked with brush and wire, the crests to right and left held with machine guns, rifle and hand grenades, a long-distance machine gun fire sweeping down its length from the north and the first ranging shells wailing in from across the hills." It was a good place to die.[12]

All for a dollar a day,
All for a dollar a day,
Kill sixty Germans before you mess,
Can't get your coffee for killing less.
Count all the Germans you slay
Each night before hitting the hay,
Then when you're through with your duties,
Sit down and count up your cooties,
All for a dollar a day.[13]

Company L went into line on the left of G and made only a minimal gain before dark, despite the loss of the battalion commander, all three company officers, and a number of infantrymen. Colonel Stacey placed a lieutenant from the 308th Infantry in charge of Company L, but he, too, was wounded before morning. Word reached Captain Edward Grant of Company H that now he commanded the Second Battalion. A native of Franklin, Massachusetts, Grant had graduated from Harvard in 1905 and went on to play professional baseball. He started off in the minor leagues, but joined the National League with the Philadelphia team in 1911. After a year in Cincinnati, Grant joined the New York Giants and spent two years playing third base at the Polo Grounds, where he was praised as "a clever third sacker and a fair hitter." Following his retirement in 1915, Grant began a law career in Boston, but joined the Officers' Training Camp at Plattsburg when America entered the war. Now the former big-leaguer was utterly exhausted. Witnesses swore that he was "literally too weary" to lift a cup of coffee to his lips. As he walked along the railroad in the bottom of that hotly contested ravine to oversee the operations of Companies G and L, a German shell killed a couple of men and wounded his adjutant. The popular Eddie Grant cried out, "Flop, everybody!" but remained standing to call for a stretcher for the adjutant, and was struck in the side by a second shell that killed him instantly. He was succeeded as battalion commander by Lieutenant Weston Jenkins of Company E.[14]

When informed that another attack had been ordered for the morning of October 5, Colonel Cromwell Stacey, "an officer of the regular army of over twenty years service," refused to "assume the responsibility" for this new assault. He complained to General Johnson that his men were completely worn out and incapable of doing the job, later explaining: "I do not believe that at any time during the fighting in the Argonne Forest, the Brigade and Division Commander had a correct appreciation of the enormous difficulties encountered . . . [and] I could tell from the impatient and unreasonable messages and orders I received that they had no idea of the actual conditions." Stacey asked to be relieved and sent to the rear, where he might be assigned to some supply post. Given the critical nature of the advance, Johnson refused to accommodate him, but did report Stacey's actions to General Alexander. The division commander thought Stacey's actions and remarks to be "weak in the extreme" and ordered Johnson to relieve him immediately, not wishing to retain an officer "whose will power and nerve had completely forsaken him." Johnson protested and pointed out that regimental command would then necessarily fall to Captain Lucien Breckenridge, since Major Whittlesey was not available to assume that post. Alexander was adamant and told Johnson that "the command of the regiment was immaterial so long as the officer at its head could and would fight." Colonel Stacey was relieved of command on the morning of October 5 and sent to the evacuation hospital at Vaubecourt, where doctors diagnosed him as suffering from neurasthenia, now commonly referred to as a nervous breakdown. Exhibiting a decidedly jittery appearance, Stacey could not remember things that had recently happened, which seemed to heighten his nervousness. The chief of staff for the First Corps sent Captain Albert Rich to inquire into Colonel Stacey's fitness. Although unable to interview the colonel himself, Rich's questioning of medical personnel led him to determine that Stacey was "both physically and mentally affected before reaching the hospital." Rich concluded that "the actions of Colonel Stacey indicate that he does not possess the necessary qualifications to command a combat unit in action."[15]

To coordinate the attack of October 5, General Alexander got on the telephone and ordered General Johnson to go forward and personally direct the troops. He had been unimpressed with Johnson's performance, even going so far as to complain that his brigade had "seemed to be very much at sea as to the locations of its constituent elements." Johnson seemed incredulous at this order from his superior and explained that, should he lead the attack, he would lose track of the overall situation and be out of communication with both brigade and division headquarters. But Alexander was adamant and Johnson got together four companies from the 307th, about 250 men, and headed them north along both sides of the deadly ravine. Captain Rainsford described the impossible situation: "The companies and battalions were by now thinned and merged beyond definition. New lieutenants, coming up from the rear as replacements, were put in charge of whatever elements were at hand and launched upon whatever attack was under way. Few who took part in those continuous assaults can give any consecutive account of them. Officers returned wounded to hospital never knowing with what troops they had fought, and the men moved to obey their orders half-drugged with exhaustion."[16]

Troops could make no significant headway on either slope of the ravine, so Johnson sent a platoon from Company E creeping like Indians north along the bed of the ravine. He followed behind at a respectful general's distance. Johnson rounded a bend of the creek and saw all but one of the platoon lying dead, ambushed by machine gun crews concealed on the slopes. The sole survivor, though wounded through both legs, continued to fire his rifle at a machine gun posted right on the narrow-gauge railroad. As General Johnson watched in horror, "another burst from it tore him to pieces." Johnson, "tired, worn, but not downhearted," carefully crawled to the rear and went off to report his latest failure to division headquarters. The presence of a general on the extreme front had made no difference, although some benefit did come from Johnson's exposure to enemy bullets and whizzing shell fragments. One of his enlisted men explained, "We just said to ourselves, if our General can take such a chance, I guess we can and we went ahead. And how the news spread! Every man in the brigade was proud of that act. You could hear such remarks as: 'Hear what our General did? He went out to the line just like any Lieutenant, took things just like the men did, and got away with it. Some General, eh?'"[17]

General Johnson reported to division headquarters that the ravine had been swept by German artillery, machine guns, and intense rifle fire. His advance had been stopped by acres of barbed wire and carefully constructed trenches on both slopes, while machine guns now occupied the very bottom of the valley where Whittlesey had broken through. Johnson said that he was "pushing for all I am worth," and then, to appease General Alexander, added, "Personally directing." Alexander's only response was that Johnson should "push forward" as hard as he could and "cut through" to his troops in front. It was impossible to obey this order and Johnson's attack finally ground to a halt about 5 P.M. The Argonne campaign had thus far cost the 154th Brigade at least sixteen hundred killed and wounded and, in Johnson's opinion, his troops were "in no condition to go forward owing to physical exhaustion."[18]

Despite constant pleas from headquarters about maintaining liaison with the French, there were never any coordinated attacks between the Allied armies. There was often no coordination among companies from the same regiment.

> *If through entangled wires and mud,*
> *Charging the Boche, we madly run,*
> *With comrades dropping, dyed with blood,*
> *And sickening sights and sounds that stun,*
> *And in death's duel meet the Hun*
> *'Midst shell holes, smoke, and battle flame,*
> *Steel clashing steel and gun to gun—*
> *God give us guts to play the game.*[19]

The division historian would later explain: "Companies would proceed for a way, side by side, then suddenly a deep ravine would step in between them. Supports, in as good order as permitted by the wild growth they were struggling through, would be following somewhere behind the front line, when suddenly they would find themselves floundering in a swamp. Runners and connecting patrols were called upon to accomplish the feats of Iroquois Indians." Guides operated by instinct, especially after dark when the briefest flare of a match would bring chattering death in an instant. Footpaths led straight into German ambushes and crashing through the underbrush would always get a man killed. Patrols, platoons, and companies moved in single file, with orders being relayed up and down the line, although this form of communication seemed completely undependable. An order to "Watch out for holes" in a matter of minutes would be perverted into "Wash out your clothes." Rusted wire was everywhere—barbed wire protecting trench systems, chicken wire covering the endless machine gun nests, and trip wires waiting to flatten any unwitting doughboy and alert lurking German snipers. It was quite literally a jungle, part natural and part manmade, where corporals and sergeants, not generals and colonels, gave the orders that got men killed.[20]

Attitude meant everything. One doughboy from the Liberty Division had been carried into an advanced dressing station, where he stoically smoked a cigarette as the doctors probed and dressed several wounds. As they worked, the doctors inquired how he came to be shot up so badly. He explained, "Well, we came to a clearing in the woods and there was a nice wide stretch of marsh and soggy field to charge across before we could get at the Hun, who was peppering us from the opposite trees. Our lieutenant said 'deploy' and we did. We got over a hundred yards of that clearing when shells and machine gun bullets began to find us, so our lieutenant ordered 'take cover.'" When the injured doughboy indicated that the grass was only a few inches high, a wide-eyed doctor asked, "Well, what did you do?" The veteran reached up and pulled his helmet down over one eye, saying, "That's all and kept on going."[21]

On the right of the Seventy-seventh Division, General Alexander's other brigade, the 153rd, ran into stiff German resistance along a ridge in the Bois de la Naza. Diagonal gaps had been slashed through the timber by German defenders, who used them as avenues to fire into the advancing Americans. The 306th Infantry occupied the front line of General Edmund Whittenmyer's brigade and one of its officers recalled the only safe way to traverse these murderous alleys was "either to dash or to crawl on our stomachs." Doughboys tried repeatedly to break through what they described as "this dense line of machine guns," but could make no headway "through that black, slimy wilderness, with German machine guns hid in the roots of trees and the whole terrain fiendishly laid off with wire and paths." There were so many Maxims that any attack on one gun would be easily repulsed by those on either flank. One officer saw that his men had finally killed a machine gun crew dug in at the base of a tree, but only after eight of them had been killed in the attempt. Following three days of nerve-shattering combat that saw no appreciable gain, the 306th was relieved by the 305th Infantry.[22]

Word reached Whittenmyer's brigade that Whittlesey's command had been cut off somewhere out to their left front, but the soldiers cared not for the romantic term "lost battalion," saying simply, "To us it was simply that some of our buddies had gotten into a jam." Try as they might, soldiers from the 305th Infantry could make no headway against the Germans in the Bois de la Naza. Captain Frank Tiebout explained why: "The undergrowth in this portion of the forest was so dense that individuals could in some places with difficulty worm their way unobserved to within a few yards of the enemy by making extraordinarily careful use of cover, and by patiently avoiding the small clearings or traps cut in the forest by the Germans, where a false move would be certain to call forth enemy fire, point blank." At some points, machine guns would occupy pits not more than twenty feet apart. Americans crept forward in their gang formations "inch by inch, one man at a time, crawling ever closer and closer to the enemy until fired at point blank by the opposing gunners—then digging for dear life." At times the air would be "blue with bullets," doughboys sliding gas masks from their chests to their backs in order to get a few inches closer to the ground.[23]

Day after day, the 305th Infantry attacked without hope of success. Captain Tiebout wrote with disgust, "Those in higher command could not or would not appreciate the unspeakable difficulties of the situation and demanded that the opposition be shattered at once." Doughboys prayed for artillery support, but got very little of it. Americans and Germans were too closely intermixed and division headquarters refused to even consider a minor tactical withdrawal to allow Allied heavy guns to pound enemy targets. Rifle grenades could not be used in the dense underbrush. Officers tried to employ Stokes Mortars, but that meant some forward observer must be, to all intents and purposes, within the barrage he was directing. Division headquarters would accept no excuses and kept demanding that troops be thrown at the "impregnable line of machine guns" that soldiers now began referring to as "Dead Man's Hill" and "Suicide Hill."[24]

A soldier from Company F described one assault: "At 3:30 we lined up our gangs and

There are ships that carry President Wilson—
They are mightly giants of the foam;
But I'd trade them all for just a row boat,
If that row boat would carry me home.[25]

started over that most terrible hill. We were at once under direct machine gun fire, the worst yet, and it seemed as if the air was so full of bullets that a man could not move without being hit. A man standing upright would have been riddled from head to foot. That's what happened to Lieutenant Gardner, leading E Company. We were approaching the crest of Suicide Hill, advancing very slowly on our bellies. The only order that could be heard was 'Forward,' and Company F was game. It was awful. The poor boys were getting slaughtered as fast as sheep could go up a plank. No one could ever describe the horror of it." There were no reserves; every man had been committed to the battle. Coordination was impossible and commanders had no idea where their troops were or what they were doing. General Whittenmyer, "Old Witt" to his men, was personally directing the attacks, but it made no difference and the result could have been easily predicted: "The dead lay thick in the brambles and shrubbery; the wounded came back in droves." Companies, already seriously under strength, could muster no more than a handful of survivors. After one particularly costly attack, Old Witt removed his helmet, wiped the sweat from his forehead, and remarked quietly, "Well, anyone who says he likes war is either a damn fool or a damn liar."[26]

Artillery occasionally did fire to support the infantry attacks, with all too familiar results. Floyd Smith, fighting with the 305th Machine Gun Battalion, made the following diary entry: "Stockton wounded; also the Chaplain. Sergeant Goerse killed. Our own artillery fire got them." Captain Tiebout wrote with obvious disgust that "we got artillery 'support,' but it fell short and must have knocked out as many of our own men as those of the enemy." The 306th Field Artillery received word at midnight on October 6 that it was to begin immediately a slow barrage in support of Whittlesey's command—"to help some of our doughboys who had got themselves in trouble" was how the officers explained it—firing 125 rounds over the next four hours. At 4 A.M. the big guns began to intensify the barrage, sending off three rounds per battery each minute, so that over the next two hours 360 155mm rounds slammed into the German lines. At least that was the plan. Reports reached division headquarters that some of these monster shells had actually fallen on French troops and General Johnson's brigade, killing several men, including Lieutenant Harold Fiske of the 306th Machine Gun Battalion. Alexander called this "inexcusable if correctly reported" and launched an investigation. After reviewing the evidence, including fragments of the shell that killed Fiske, Lieutenant Colonel James Galloghy concluded that the barrage had been "well directed upon the target assigned to it" and "carefully conducted with due precaution as to safety, and certainty of firing" and that Fiske actually had been killed by a German shell. The necessity of even convening such an inquiry speaks volumes regarding the problem of employing artillery in the Argonne Forest.[27]

To counter the overwhelming German fire power, General Alexander began to push his own machine gunners into the front lines. Some elements of the 306th Machine Gun Battalion had occupied German huts near l'Homme Mort, where they did nothing more military than clean each individual bullet, so that the grease would not cause stoppages while firing, and wash out carbon from the barrels. They moved into position on the night of October 5 and supported American patrols probing the German lines. As the patrols started off, Charles Minder said that "little red flashes like fireflies could be seen all over the place." American gunners fired through burlap screens to hide their guns' flashes and shifted positions frequently, but still lost men to enemy fire. Minder explained, "The rifle shots were popping constantly. It's a queer sound when they whistle thru the air. They sound like—PING! As each one flew past me last night, it gave me a sickening feeling to think how near I was to being hit each time." Everyone seemed exhausted and "pale as sheets," but kept to their work. PFC Minder could barely recognize his wraithlike friends, none of whom now looked like "the red-cheeked, fat fellows they used to be." But the infantry had it worse and when one runner came by he seemed little more than a skeleton, carrying news that the companies were being shot to pieces. One of the Argonne veterans explained the way they all felt: "I didn't care whether I got hit or not. It's funny, but when you feel like that, nothing seems to hit you. It's the fellow who is scared the most that gets hit first."[28]

Summing up the operations of the Liberty Division from October 3 to 6, General Alexander admitted that "although the Division attacked each morning none of those attacks made any impression upon the resistance in our

One more sunrise, one more sunrise,
Spatters blood across the skies.
Soon the mourning world will surely wake,
Maddened men their vengeance take,
I and many more will die,
I and many more will die.[29]

front." Everyone not essential in the rear echelons had been given rifles and hustled forward to replace the horrendous losses that had seen companies shrink to the size of platoons. In Alexander's opinion, "the

154th Brigade was about exhausted." The 153rd Brigade was occupied with continuing attacks on the Bois de la Naza and could not spare troops to assist General Johnson's brigade. Despite some outrageous claims about successful advances, including one flamboyant story that a French officer had actually reached Whittlesey, the French had made no significant gains and made little attempt to coordinate their attacks with the Americans'. Except for the return of Lieutenant Wilhelm and Sergeant Callahan on October 3, no one had seen Major Whittlesey or any of his men since they had punched through the German lines on October 2 and all communication with the isolated command had ceased after the arrival of Cher Ami two days later. Undoubtedly embarrassed by his inability to reach Whittlesey, Alexander ordered his brigades to attack again on October 7.[30]

At 7:30 that morning, General Johnson told Alexander, "I cannot see or locate the French. At this hour I have therefore ordered my troops to assault without them." To impress his superior that he would personally supervise the attack, Johnson added, "I shall be beyond wire communication for awhile." About thirty minutes later, Johnson sent the division commander an update on the current attack: "Am attacking. Artillery fire apparently has had no effect. Wire not cut. Machine guns and high explosive shells being used against command. French on our left not attacking." Although the Twenty-eighth and Eighty-second Divisions had started to creep forward to the east and north as the Germans began to withdraw under heavy pressure, the Seventy-seventh Division could make no progress against the hills and trenches in its front.[31]

But there was a small glimmer of hope. On the afternoon of October 6, General Alexander had begun a walking tour of his division front, commencing at 153rd Brigade headquarters, where he offered encouragement to General Whittenmyer. Alexander then walked westward behind the lines to Depot de Machines, where he encountered Lieutenant Colonel Eugene Houghton, commanding the 307th Infantry. Houghton informed General Alexander that one of his patrols had just spotted a small break in the enemy wire and his men were at that moment beginning to inch through the gap one by one. This infiltration continued all night, although there was no "premature demonstration" to bring attention to the movement. By morning, the bulk of several companies had managed to wriggle through the opening, the first penetration of German defenses since Whittlesey had disappeared. Before concluding his walking tour, Alexander consulted with Johnson and told him of Houghton's success in finding a way through the maze of wire. The generals agreed that this development appeared "to promise good results" and both expressed confidence that Whittlesey, although obviously beleaguered and probably short of ammunition, had not yet surrendered.[32]

General Alexander had finally turned to the Fiftieth Aero Squadron for help late on October 4. He sent four identical messages to the Chief of Air Services for the First Army Corps, requesting that an airplane be dispatched next morning, "at the earliest possible moment that observation can be secured," to drop those messages to Whittlesey. Explaining that this mission had become "vitally necessary," Alexander said it was imperative that the pilot "endeavor first to locate his position with extreme accuracy, then to attract his attention and then to drop the messages so as to insure that at least one of the messages will reach Major Whittlesey." He also cautioned that "they be dropped so near him as to avoid the danger of their falling into the hands of the enemy." Visibility was poor that morning and it was almost noon before aircraft could go aloft with the cryptic messages, all of which read: "Defend yourself in your present position. Help is coming to you." Four airplanes, two about noon and two later in the evening, swooped over the Argonne and dropped these messages, as well as small packages of cigarettes and chocolate. But the thick woods made "orientation even on the ground very hard" and the dispatches fell nowhere near Whittlesey's position, one being dropped over the supply company of the 307th Infantry, somewhere south of l'Homme Mort.[33]

In fairness to the pilots and observers, the Argonne was "a sea of green" that had no points of reference, except for an occasional glimpse of one of many small streams that flowed "deep in the recesses of a cavernous ravine." Add to this nondescript topography Alexander's comment that "our observers were anything but expert nor did the training of our air service develop along really profitable lines" and it is easy to see how American air crews failed to locate Whittlesey's position. More planes went up on October 6 and began to drop packages of food, ammunition, and medical supplies on the coordinates of the Charlevaux Valley, where Whittlesey had last been reported to have dug in. Lumbering DeHavillands skimmed along scarcely above the hilltops in a continuous series of flights that dropped about one-half ton of supplies during the day. Pilots also carried new orders to Whittlesey from General Alexander, who had now completely reversed his previous instructions:

> Retire with your forces to Regimental P.C. The attention of the enemy in your rear is being held by our rifle and machine gun fire. This should enable you to locate the enemy by his fire and strike him in the rear and flank.

To reopen communications with the trapped Americans, small parachutes were removed from aerial flares and attached to baskets of pigeons, the birds floating gently to earth "with surprising efficiency."[34]

Lieutenants Harold Goettler and Erwin Bleckley had been the first to leave the Remicourt airfield, which had been shrouded in fog that "covered the field like a drab blanket." Goettler's plane "looked like a lean grey ghost" as he flew north to the Argonne, where the "interminable fog and mist" hid objects below "as they would have been by darkness." Goettler swooped down to a mere two hundred feet above Charlevaux Valley; German machine guns actually fired down on the DeHavilland while it roared by in search of Whittlesey's position. Seeing no sign of the Americans, Bleckley threw out his bundles of food on their third pass and Goettler headed back to Remicourt, where the airmen counted over forty bullet holes in their plane.[35]

Just before noon, Lieutenant Pickerell and his observer, Lieutenant Alfred George, headed for Charlevaux Valley, where visibility "as usual was very poor." Pickerell recalled, "Every one of us that went over that day got bullet holes. I know my plane had several in it, but they didn't hit any vital spots, so we didn't go down." Other crews were not so lucky. Lieutenants George Phillips and Michael Brown saw one bullet pass through their windshield, another through the altimeter, and a third knocked out the engine, although Phillips was able to land northeast of Binarville. About an hour later, Lieutenants Allen Bird and William Bolt crash-landed near Vienne le Chateau, their plane full of holes from a storm of German rifle and machine gun fire. Everyone at Remicourt was alarmed when these two planes failed to return, but Whittlesey must be found somehow. Lieutenants Goettler and Bleckley suited up for a second mission, but there was a mechanical problem with their own plane, so they set off in Pickerell's machine, flying into the maelstrom of German fire that now swept the skies over Charlevaux

Valley. Their DeHavilland was hit repeatedly as they flew over the valley just over the treetops, but Goettler managed to fly to Binarville before crashing. He was killed instantly and Bleckley died before reaching a hospital, a double tragedy for the Fiftieth Aero Squadron. Goettler and Bleckley would each receive posthumously a Medal of Honor.[36]

Lieutenants Maurice Graham and James McCurdy flew over the treetops on the last flight of the day and spotted several soldiers emerge from a dugout at the exact coordinates of Whittlesey's supposed location. Assuming they were Americans, McCurdy leaned over to drop a crate of pigeons just as a German raised his rifle and shot him in the neck. Graham safely piloted the aircraft back to its base, where the airmen reported that, based on their experience, the "inference was that the Huns had overpowered our men and were 'mopping up' the dugouts." Tragically, none of the messages or supplies dropped for Whittlesey ever reached him or his starving troops. It was not until 11:30 A.M. on October 7 that Lieutenant Woodville Rogers, an observer in a DeHavilland piloted by Lieutenant Robert Anderson, finally spotted a battalion signal panel and two small infantry panels put out by Whittlesey's men, positively identifying their location.[37]

As troops from the Seventy-seventh Division continued their efforts to reach Whittlesey's command, newspaper correspondents got word of the story. Fully one-third of the reporters covering the Argonne campaign worked for New York newspapers, soldiers from other divisions enviously referred to these

When this fucking war is over,
Oh how happy I will be.
When I leave this God damned army,
For my home across the sea.
No more dress parades on Sunday,
No more asking for a pass,
We will tell our damned old top kick,
To go and kiss our ass.[38]

correspondents as "volunteer press-agents" for the Seventy-seventh Division. Additionally, as New York City was the largest metropolitan area in the United States, whatever impacted it reverberated throughout America and the world. Thomas M. Johnson, one of those many correspondents, explained: "Whatever its polyglot National Army Division might do, would be interesting. When its tenement dwellers became backwoodsmen, and pretty good backwoodsmen, in a Robin Hood's Forest, the story was as good as Charles A. Dana's famous, 'If a man bites a dog.'"[39]

The Argonne campaign quickly became *the* American newspaper story of the entire war. One of the first stories was filed on the evening of September 26, when a single correspondent went forward in the wake of the advancing Seventy-seventh Division. Amid the miles of barbed wire, camouflaged trenches, shattered dugouts, and hundreds of machine gun nests, he encountered far more. Thomas Johnson explained: "He saw German prisoners with helmets camouflaged with leaves, cartridges with bullets filed across sickeningly to make dum-dums, brought in by merchants of bananas and push-carts, crapshooters and subway guards, lawyers from Park Avenue, gangsters from Avenue A, not a woodsman nor a lumberjack among them, intermingled with some cowboy replacements, Americans all, attacking a forest, the strongest single natural obstacle on the Western Front." After filing his report, the cat was out of the bag and other correspondents scurried to cover the Argonne fight, although when many naïve Americans first heard the news, they wondered why on earth the United States Army was battling Germans in the "Oregon Forest."[40]

Newspapermen were responsible for making Major Charles Whittlesey a household name back in the States. Kidder Mead, press officer of the First Corps and formerly reporter for the *New York World*, wrote twice-daily press releases that went by motorcycle to Bar-le-Duc, where they were posted on a central bulletin board. Mead's updates, as befitted his background, read like exciting news stories rather than dry military documents. One of the reporters following events in the Seventy-seventh Division was Fred Ferguson of the United Press, who on October 3 sent a cable with news of Whittlesey's plight. Harold Jacobs, his cable editor, responded, "Send more on Lost Battalion," an innocent reference that gave the cut-off command a name that still lives on in historical literature. Every dispatch now bore the name "Lost Battalion" and Kidder Mead "played it up heavily," as did Major Bozeman Bulger, another former *World* associate who was General Pershing's chief press officer. Newspaper readers in America and around the world eagerly snatched up the latest editions to keep up with the Lost Battalion story. Thomas Johnson admitted, "It was the sort of story that a correspondent could write with every bit of his imagination working—and still fall short of the whole truth."[41]

11

RELIEF AT LAST

As the sky began to lighten on the morning of October 7, Major Whittlesey had trouble finding men with enough strength left to conduct the daily patrols, but there were more than enough volunteers for the task of attempting to break through to the American lines. Robert Manson explained that, overall, "things looked pretty blue" and "we were in a desperate fix." In his opinion, "It was death to stay and the chances of getting back to our lines were one in a hundred." Given the appalling condition of everyone in the pocket, one chance in one hundred seemed to be a pretty good choice. A lieutenant started out with four men before dawn, but quickly returned after two of his men had been killed. Whittlesey wanted the best men possible for another attempt and asked Captain Holderman for a recommendation. He selected one of the old-timers, Abraham Krotoshinsky, a fragile-looking Polish Jew, described as "a small, emaciated young man with large, limpid blue eyes," whose bad posture made him look less than the trained soldier he actually was. Two other men agreed to accompany him, but their names have been lost over the years. Krotoshinsky would later say of them, "One of the other fellas is a replacement fella. His name I do not remember. The other is a Irish fella. He has a Irish name." Krotoshinsky described his feelings just before setting out that morning: "I started at sun-up on a gray, gloomy day, already weak from lack of food and already convinced that death would be the only outcome. I didn't care. After five days of being fired at, hope was gone, and all I wanted was peace."

The three scouts set out after dawn, Whittlesey, McMurty, and Holderman hoping that sending men out in the daylight would be more successful than dispatching them in the dark of night. Krotoshinsky, followed by the other two volunteers, slipped down toward the swamp, then ran across thirty feet of open ground as German machine gunners squeezed off their first rounds of the morning. He remembered, "I could feel the bullets whistle all around me but I didn't get hit once." They all split up, but the other two soon returned, reporting to Whittlesey that the fire was too heavy and that Krotoshinsky had probably been killed. But the Polish barber was not dead. When the Germans opened fire, he ducked behind a stump and remained quiet. After what seemed like an eternity of silent waiting, Krotoshinsky began to crawl on his belly through the undergrowth for several hundred yards. He then began a series of short dashes from one piece of cover to another—stumps, logs, thickets, tree roots—anything that would offer a temporary hiding place. Following the valley, with the stream always on his left and the ridge to his right, the New Yorker doggedly continued his irregular line of travel.

The scout from Company K had one close call early that morning, writing later, "They were looking for me everywhere. I just moved along on my stomach, in the direction I was told, keeping my eyes open for them. The brush was six feet high and often that saved me. Once a squad of Germans passed right by my hiding place jabbing their bayonets into the thicket and swearing like the devil. One big fellow nearly stepped on my hand." Krotoshinsky continued his tale: "Every minute I thought they would get me, I expected death, but I thought of it only as a physical thing, nothing more. I thought of nothing but the necessity of getting that message through. Home, friends, memories, those things one thinks of in less dangerous places were all forgotten. I was kept busy retracing my route and making detours in the effort to throw the Germans off the track." Slowly, ever so slowly, Private Krotoshinsky made his way through barbed wire and past German positions, so close to the enemy that he could distinctly hear their conversations, as he sought to locate American soldiers.[1]

Following two seemingly unsuccessful efforts to get messengers out that morning, Whittlesey asked Lieutenant Schenck for a couple

Private Abraham Krotoshinsky. One of the original Camp Upton draftees, he crawled through the German lines in search of help. From the *American Hebrew and Jewish Messenger.*

of volunteers from Company C for yet another attempted break-through. Stanislaw Kozikowski, the Polish Chauchat gunner who was still looking to avenge the death of his friend Hinchman, and Clifford R. Brown, one of those upstate New York farmers from Chautauqua County, agreed to try. Whittlesey gave the two men a short talk: "Boys, you know the conditions as well as I do. You know what you are up against. If you get thru, just tell them that we have not surrendered, but that we must have help at once." Brown responded, "We'll get thru, because we're trusting God to get us back."[2]

The pair stripped off extra equipment, but were immediately stopped by one of the new lieuten-

> The Colonel calls the Major when he wants something done,
> And the Major calls the Captain, and starts him on the run.
> The Captain then gets busy, and tries to make it suit
> By shifting all the baggage on a Shave Tail Second Lieut.
> The said Lieutenant ponders and strokes his downy jaw,
> Then calls a trusty sergeant and to him lays down the law.
> The sergeant calls a corporal, explains how it must be,
> Then the corporal calls a private, and that poor private's ME.[3]

ants who would not allow them to leave that way. Brown exploded, saying, "I'm certainly not going out there loaded down with full equipment!" They crawled back and protested to the major, who told them, "You boys are doing this, go any way you please." Brown remembered that he and Kozikowski finally got started at about 1:30 that afternoon. They had not gone far before loud crashing could be heard in the brush behind them and the doughboys drew their pistols in anticipation of a fight. Two American soldiers came into view and announced to Brown and Kozikowski that they had decided to come along. This was no place for a crowd, especially when two of them seemed as secretive as the proverbial bull in a china shop, so the original messengers tried to split off from the newcomers, but they kept following Brown and Kozikowski like a couple of lost puppies. Finally, they ducked into a thicket and watched incredulously as the tagalongs came plunging through the bushes and disappeared out of sight. Neither Brown nor Kozikowski had recognized the pair and never saw them again; their fate and identity remain a mystery.

After this scary encounter, the two scouts soon heard noises all around, "like cattle when the flies are after them" was how Brown described it. They ducked under cover just as a German water party, all of them carrying canteens, headed for the creek. The scouts now decided to separate, moving about twenty yards apart, so that if one man was taken prisoner the other might still get through. Dodging away from the German water detail, the Americans stumbled upon a narrow road that had been cut through the forest and, as they walked along this open area, almost ran into two Germans strolling down to the valley. Brown said they jumped behind some bushes, but admitted, "I was afraid they would hear my breathing." Abandoning the roadway, the two men crawled up the ridge and halted just short of a German trench line that overlooked the Lost Battalion position. Brown explained what happened next: "I saw a big German standing guard on top of the parapet. But again I was lucky. I saw him before he saw me. I dropped flat on the ground in some tall grass and laid there for two and a half hours until dark, scarcely stirring the meanwhile." Brown could see that the Germans "had machine guns planted about every two rods on top of the parapet" and that they had worn a path from there downhill to the stream. Brown and Kozikowski had agreed by hand signals to follow this path over the trench after dark. Rain began to fall and the night was "black as ink." After starting out, they encountered no Germans, who had obviously sought shelter from the rain, but did run into a barbed wire entanglement. Brown explained how they got through the web of wire: "I would have to put my foot down cautiously and then put my hands down to spread the wires while I lifted my foot up and advanced it, repeating the same operation all over again." He then said, "If it had not been for the inky darkness and the noise of the falling rain to cover up noises made by us, I'm afraid we would never have made it." But Brown and Kozikowski, like Krotoshinsky before them, had managed to break through the German lines that surrounded Major Whittlesey's position.[4]

Shortly after Whittlesey dispatched the morning messengers, he decided to personally lead a patrol up to the Charlevaux Road, where it would attempt to sneak through the encirclement. A few soldiers "who were able to navigate" went with the major, including Private Ralph John, who said, "Our back-bones and our stomachs were rubbing." John admitted to being pretty weak and found it almost impossible to climb the steep hillside. As he pulled himself along by grabbing tree roots, Major Whittlesey passed the private and said, "Come on, Jack, this may be our last battle." Although gasping for breath, Private John responded, "I'm a game son-of-a-bitch!" and kept climbing. The patrol reached the roadway and rested there, scanning the woods and brush for signs of the enemy. Suddenly a German soldier broke from cover and started to run across the road. Catching this movement out of the corner of his eye, John wheeled around and fired, the muzzle of his rifle only a few feet from Whittlesey's shoulder. The major jumped and yelled, "What the hell is coming off?" Private John simply pointed at the German tumbling down the slope. Whittlesey glanced at the body, turned to John, and said simply, "Good work, boy." The major's patrol quickly determined that the Germans remained in force and the doughboys slid back down to their funkholes to await further developments.[5]

Early that morning, Emil Peterson, a private in Company H, had gone to the creek to fill a canteen for a wounded buddy, receiving as a thank-you a few scraps of tobacco. Peterson then settled into his funkhole and was sleeping when someone called out his name. Seeing a bunch of other men from his company rushing down into the creek bottom, he assumed they were running after some packages of food that had been dropped by an airplane. Jumping from his hole, Peterson dashed to the creek. Among those already there was Private Lowell

Hollingshead, who had joined several other men in an attempt to cut through the German lines, supposedly on Whittlesey's orders. Hollingshead had been having recurring dreams of eating an unending bounty of steak and potatoes, so went along in hopes of at least finding a food package if the small party could not break through to the regiment. Shielded by the ever-present morning fog, hungry men splashed across the creek and raced for the shelter of trees on the south bank. There they halted to catch their breath, being joined by Peterson as a machine gun opened fire somewhere off to the right.[6]

They had seen no food parcels, so talked things over for a minute and decided to expand their search farther into the woods. Peterson recalled that they had unanimously agreed "to shoot it out with the Germans." Hollingshead, a replacement who had joined Company H just before the Argonne fight, decided to go along even though he did not know the names of his comrades. He was a resident of Mt. Sterling, Ohio, when he enlisted on January 2, 1918. After training at Camp Jackson, South Carolina, the eighteen-year-old Buckeye served with the First Corps Artillery Park until transferred to the 308th Infantry. Promoted to corporal on March 13, 1918, young Hollingshead had been busted to private just a week before his transfer. It is reasonable to assume that the infraction that led to his demotion also contributed to his being assigned to the infantry.[7]

Since their "very lives hinged on every wrong or right move that was made," they selected Robert Dodd, a full-blooded Paiute from Nevada, to lead them. Although unable to write his name, the tall, slender Dodd inspired confidence and the others fell into line behind him. Hollingshead explained how their guide seemed to be doing a good job: "After resting awhile we started up a path in the forest with the Indian now leading us. He only permitted us to go short distances and then take rests to preserve what little strength we had left. We moved very carefully, going quite a bit of the way on our hands and knees. It was right after one of these rest periods when we were again moving that the Indian stopped short and motioned for the rest of us to halt by raising his hand high above his head, and I knew then the Indian had scented danger." They all hesitated amid a silence "so dense you could hear your own heart beat" and waited. Bullets began to rip through the leaves and chip bark from the trees as machine guns began chattering from all around the party. Hollingshead said that the skies

Private Robert Dodd, a Paiute Indian
from Nevada, who led a group of
Company H men into an ambush
on the morning of October 7.
Courtesy of the William
Hammond Mathers Museum,
Indiana University.

"fairly rained lead" and he watched helplessly as "little spurts of dirt"
kicked up before and around him.

It was a massacre. Dodd went down with bullets in his shoulder
and leg. Hollingshead felt a bullet tear through his left thigh just above the knee and saw the soldier ahead of him, with "jagged bullet holes in his head," die without a struggle. Emil Peterson took two bullets through his left leg, but managed to half-stumble into a nearby shell hole that offered shelter from the hail of gunfire. Another

*When the final taps is sounded and we lay aside
    life's cares,
  And we do the last and gloried parade, on
    Heaven's shining stairs,
And the angels bid us welcome and the harps
    begin to play
  We can draw a million canteen checks and
    spend them in a day.
It is then we'll hear St. Peter tell us loudly with
    a yell
  "Take a front seat, you soldier men, you've
    done your hitch in Hell!"*[8]

bullet struck Cecil Duryea in the right leg and he crawled into a
thicket to hide. After the machine guns stopped chattering, half of the

Private Henry Chin. Drafted in 1917, he was the first resident of New York's Chinatown to be killed in the war. From Haulsee's *Soldiers of the Great War.*

Americans lay dead and the rest had been wounded seriously. Among the killed was Henry Chin, a member of the Young China Association in New York City and the first resident of Chinatown to be killed in the war. When informed of Henry's death, his father, Dr. Chin Hing Lang, remarked stoically, "I thank the spirits of his ancestors that he went as I would have him go. He went—a real American. My boy is lost, but his country and my country still live."[9]

Sheltered in a shell hole, Peterson tried to dress his wounds as the firing died down. He watched as the Germans came into sight, covered the American dead with branches, broke their Springfield rifles, and carried off the wounded. One of the Germans spotted him and tossed a grenade that exploded harmlessly, but the wounded man threw away his rifle and the Germans captured him as well. A Jerry relieved Peterson of his watch and tobacco before they carried him and Duryea over to a nearby machine gun, where they deposited the Americans on each side as a sort of rude shield.[10]

Hollingshead did not know what to do and played dead until a German emerged from the brush about six feet away and pointed a Luger pistol at him. The barrel of the pistol seemed to be "as large as a shotgun," so the wounded man shouted out the only German word he knew, "Kamerad!" As visions of Mom, Dad, home, and his childhood swirled through Hollingshead's mind, the German lowered his pistol and smiled. The kindly German private came over to Hollingshead and began speaking in English, pointing to the blood staining his pants leg. He put his arm around the doughboy and both men stumbled back to where one of the machine guns had fired on the American party. After the Germans sent a man running off to the rear, the wounded Ohio boy had a rather bizarre experience—the gunner who had shot him kindly showed how they worked their machine gun and even fired off a few bursts toward Whittlesey's position to illustrate his skill. The enemy runner returned and directed that the four surviving Americans be taken to the rear. Hollingshead, who was able to hobble along, soon outdistanced the others, who had to be carried, and never saw them again. He said, "I felt more God-forsaken than ever without my Buddies."[11]

Back in the pocket, Whittlesey knew that time was running out because his worst fears were starting to be realized. Cracks had started to appear in the solid discipline that had characterized his command ever since being trapped on October 2. Although Whittlesey had quickly quashed the sentiments expressed by Lieutenant Revnes, an overwhelming despair had gripped the enlisted men, who now seemed willing to do anything to escape their prisonlike environment. A couple of them had ducked away from their funkholes to follow Brown and Kozikowski, but the worst incident occurred when men from Lieutenant Cullen's company just up and left their position in search of food. The tale told by survivors of following a mysterious sergeant's order was nothing more than a dodge to avoid court-martial for deserting their posts. Even those who retained their sense of discipline had seemed to lose all hope and appeared resigned to their fate. Robert Manson told how they spent the empty hours of October 7: "Some of us wrote short messages, each entrusting his to some pal on the chance that his pal might get through alive. There were some thanks whispered for the little-chronicled deeds of kindness the week had witnessed. Here and there men promised to kill each other rather than be taken prisoner."[12]

James Larney explained how the strain affected one soldier, who "jumped to his feet shouting, and started galloping madly in a small circle, swearing viciously in Italian. Several times he went around our funkhole, slightly crazed. 'Get down! Get down! You'll get bumped off sure!' yelled his comrades. And, slowly, he relapsed into his funkhole."[13]

The major circulated among his remaining officers, encouraging them to redouble their efforts to keep up morale, and dodged from funkhole to funkhole repeating his stale refrain of two million American soldiers coming to their rescue and the too-oft told tale of the British Army holding out at Lucknow. Whittlesey's public happy face had no effect on Captain Leo Stromee, whose wounds kept him confined to a hole where he would scratch a few words in his diary each day. On October 6 the Californian wrote simply, "No relief all supplies cut off and condition desperate." Next day he noted, "Men in awful shape." Here and there among the funkholes, starving scarecrows could be seen licking the grease from captured German rifles. Without Whittlesey actually saying what was on his mind, Captain Holderman knew what was expected of every man under his command still able to fight. This unspoken message was quite simply that "if the Germans captured the hillside they would find there the last of its defenders, dead at his post." Events had taken this defensive stand way beyond Lucknow. The major now thought in terms of Leonidas dying with his Spartans at Thermopylae, Eleazer ben Yair and the Jewish zealots killing one another instead of surrendering at Masada, and Paladin Roland fighting to the death while commanding Charlemagne's rearguard at Ronces-valles. Whittlesey's personal code of honor would not allow the thought of surrender to enter his mind, so the only option was to fight to the last man.[14]

Artillery from the Seventy-seventh Division again fired in support of those troops trying to reach Whittlesey, but too many of these shells went astray and struck among the funkholes inside his perimeter. Captain Stromee noted that this latest barrage lasted about three hours, a rather terrifying way to pass the morning hours. Even Whittlesey admitted to feeling "discouragement" at this latest shelling. This demoralization was compounded by the sound of American gunfire, which sounded no closer than on previous days, an indication that the Liberty Division had as yet achieved no success against the German defenders. Shortly before noon, grenades began falling from the ridge, accompanied by long-range machine gun fire, but the grenadiers did not press their attack and desperate doughboys fought them off with well-aimed rifle fire.[15]

By the afternoon of October 7, Captain Holderman had been hit eight times and would later say of his injuries, "My wounds were very slight. I was struck in the right foot with a piece of shell; in the left calf; in the right thigh; the right wrist; both hands; on the nose and the right side of the face." In Holderman's opinion, he had received "three

Private Robert S. Yoder, who enlisted on
July 1, 1917, and trained at Camps Lewis and
Kearny before joining Company E, 308th
Infantry as a replacement. From *In the
Service: The Great World War Honor Roll,
Southwest Washington.*

flesh wounds, that you might call wounds, but the rest of them were
small particles," although most of them were now exhibiting the
symptoms of gangrene. Despite his own physical distress, Captain
Holderman remained a steadying influence on the right flank. William
Johnson, a Minnesotan in Company K, remarked that Holderman "was
one great fellow" who gave his men orders "to shoot anything we saw
moving and which looked like a German." On one occasion, Holderman came sliding through the bushes and asked, "Anybody here that
can stop some of that sniping?" Even Holderman's suggestions had the
force of orders, so Robert Yoder, a
slim young man from Centralia,
Washington, piped up, "I'll try,
sir!" George Newcom volunteered
to accompany his friend from Company E and the two crawled up to
the roadside, taking up a position at
the base of a tree. Yoder would keep
careful watch and invariably shoot
any German rifleman careless

> *I've got a rifle,*
>   *It's always ready to sight.*
> *Sniping Huns is a fad of mine*
>   *When I'm out on the firing line.*
>
> *Click! Bang! Biff!*
>
> *Whene'er I can contrive one.*
>   *I've often said to myself, I've said,*
> *"Cheer up, Bill! There's a German dead,*
>   *And he's more use than a live one."*[16]

enough to disclose his hiding place to the young American sniper. Not all
of Holderman's men were as proficient as this sharpshooter from the
Evergreen State. George Speich said simply, "If we saw a movement anywhere in range we would take a crack at it, primarily however, to keep
them off us rather than with any hope of inflicting very serious damage."[17]

While their comrades huddled on the same stinking hillside, all four survivors from the party that had deserted from Company H had been taken to German dugouts, where they were given a slice of dark bread and a cigarette. Lieutenant Heinrich Prinz began to interrogate them individually. When he asked Emil Peterson how many Americans were still alive and how much ammunition they had, the wounded doughboy answered defiantly that they had "plenty of ammunition" and would "never surrender." Prinz inquired about the fate of a captured German soldier and Peterson said the man was in good shape, although he had no idea whom the officer was talking about. Prinz then asked how many Americans there were in France, so the private boldly proclaimed "about ten million!" These answers tended to confirm the information given Prinz by the two captured lieutenants, Leak and Harrington, who had been taken on October 4. Left alone for a few minutes by their captors, they had agreed on a fanciful story that they belonged to a three-thousand-man command, well supplied with ammunition, which had easily walked through the German lines. Hoping to keep some pressure off Whittlesey and those few remaining scarecrows in the pocket, Leak and Harrington told the few enlisted men taken with them to stick to that tale if questioned. Prinz, as well as his superiors, was perplexed by these responses.[18]

The German officer hoped to learn more from Private Lowell Hollingshead, the only ambulatory prisoner then in his possession. Hollingshead had been blindfolded before reaching a headquarters dugout and, when the blindfold was removed, he was amazed to find himself in a huge underground apartment, boasting board floors and walls. There were a number of rooms, all of them well furnished, and the youngster was led into one that contained a few chairs, a couch, an office table, a typewriter, and a phonograph. Heinrich Prinz, whom he described as "well dressed and handsome," greeted him cordially. "How long since you have eaten?" asked the officer. "Five days," responded Hollingshead. "Poor devil, you must be starved." "I certainly am." Prinz bade him lie down on the couch and dispatched an orderly for food and a doctor, then offered his prisoner a gold-tipped cigarette. Somewhat confused by his kind treatment, Hollingshead said that "we were for all the world like host and guest rather than an officer and captured enemy soldier."

Private Emil A. Peterson, wounded in the left leg and captured by Germans on the morning of October 7. Courtesy of Orvin A. Peterson.

A doctor came in and dressed his leg; then an orderly reappeared with a loaf of black bread and a pail full of vegetables and meat drenched with vinegar. While Hollingshead dug into the chow, Prinz and several other officers started asking questions, but quit when they found the American more interested in eating than talking. After this hasty meal, Prinz began to interrogate his prisoner by first gaining his confidence. When he learned that Hollingshead was from Ohio, Prinz said that before the war he had occasionally visited Cincinnati while working for a tungsten firm based in Spokane, Washington. He also remarked that he admired the Americans' courage, but felt sorry for those wounded whose cries could be heard in the German lines. Prinz then asked how many men were on the hillside, how much ammunition remained, and other questions of a military nature. When Hollingshead refused to answer these inquiries, Prinz walked him to the mouth of the dugout, handed him a pair of binoculars, and asked if he could see the American position. Although he could plainly see some of the funkholes, the Ohioan claimed to be unable to locate his comrades.

Moving back inside, Prinz motioned for Hollingshead to rest on the couch, then began working at the typewriter. Following the war Lieutenant Prinz would admit, "The Germans felt it absolutely suicidal for the American detachment to persist in its defense, and for that reason I sent the message requesting surrender." He concluded, "One of the most depressing things our troops encountered was the lack of 'nerves' shown by the American troops. But our troops' nerves were badly shaken."

After a few minutes, the lieutenant asked his captive if he would be willing to carry a message to the American position. Hollingshead said sure, if he could read it first. After scanning the document, he wrote his name in two blank spaces and agreed to deliver it, but only after he got some rest. Prinz roused the American after a short nap, telling him, "If you are to get the message back before dark you must start now." Hollingshead rubbed the sleep from his eyes and responded, "I am ready." Prinz tucked his letter into the private's pocket, then generously gave him a cane, saying, "This will aid you in walking." Prinz offered a flag of truce, nothing more than a stick with a white cloth attached, gave Hollingshead two packages of cigarettes and the rest of his German loaf of bread, affixed the blindfold, and said goodby. A German soldier guided him to the Charlevaux Road, removed his blindfold, and pointed toward the American position. Carrying his white flag aloft, he slowly hobbled in that direction, leaning on his new cane while blood flowed from his wound, until halted by an American outpost. Someone asked who he was and what he wanted. Hollingshead replied that he had just returned from the German lines with an important message for Whittlesey. A lieutenant came up and escorted him to the headquarters hole.[19]

It was about 4 P.M. when Hollingshead limped up to where Major Whittlesey and Captain McMurtry sat in their funkhole. They had just been joined by Captain Holderman, who made a habit of reporting personally to the major some three or four times each day and now squatted just outside the PC. After he had accepted the note from Prinz, McMurtry somewhat hotly asked why the private had left his position with Company H. Hollingshead briefly poured out his whole story—went after food parcels, ambushed, four killed, four wounded, questioned by Germans, and sent back to the Americans with this message. Hollingshead later remembered, "Major Whittlesey told me

Private Lowell R. Hollingshead.
Wounded in the left thigh and
taken prisoner, he carried the
German surrender demand to
Major Whittlesey on the
afternoon of October 7. From
McCollum's *History and
Rhymes of the Lost Battalion.*

to go lie down and rest, so I went to my funkhole and immediately fell
unconscious." Another account has more of the ring of authenticity
about it and has Whittlesey saying, "You had no business to leave your
position under any circumstances without orders from your officer. Go
back where you belong." Cullen was anything but happy to see this
derelict private and, when Hollingshead dropped into a hole with Harold
Neptune and started to relate his adventures, the lieutenant promptly
told him to keep quiet or he would shut him up with a bullet.[20]

Apparently unaware that Charles Whittlesey was the senior officer
with the American force, Lieutenant Prinz had mistakenly addressed
his letter, "neatly typewritten on a sheet of good quality paper," to the
commander of the Second Battalion "Jaeger Rifles," but McMurtry
prompted turned it over to the major. Whittlesey's jaw dropped when
he read:

> To The Commanding Officer of the 2nd Batl. J. R. 308
>   of the 77th American Division.
> Sir.
>   The Bearer of the present, Lowell R Hollingshead has been
> taken prisoner by us on October

He refused to the German Intelligence Officer every answer to his questiones and is quite an honourable fellow, doing honour to his father-land in the strictest sense of the word.

He has been charged against his will, believing in doing wrong to his country, in carrying forward this present letter to the Officer in charge of the 2nd Batl. J. R. 308 of the 77th Div. with the purpose to recommend this Commander to surrender with his forces as it would be quite useless to resist any more in view of the present conditions.

The suffering of your wounded man can be heared over here in the German lines and we are appealing to your human sentiments.

A withe Flag shown by one of your man will tell us that you agree with these conditions.

Please treat the Lowell R Hollingshead as an honourable man. He is quite a soldier we envy you.

The German Commanding Officer

After he had read the document, Whittlesey handed it to McMurtry, who remembered it as "the only funny thing that I know of connected with the pocket." McMurtry handed it over to Holderman, who read it and looked up at the other two. Holderman later explained, "There was not a great deal said, we just looked at each other and kinder smiled." McMurtry said that "there was a good smile all around among the crowd of us." As for the major, he would write of the event: "The three officers looked at one another *and smiled*. For there was humor, both sardonic and typically Teutonic, in those words: 'We are appealing to your humane sentiments.' A strange appeal it seemed from the enemy who for five days had killed or wounded more than fifty per cent of the besieged command!"[21]

Fred Evermann was close by and would always claim that Whittlesey's only verbal response to Prinz's note was, "No, Sir, by God, never!" Others said they heard him remark, "We're Americans—we can't surrender!" He did say quietly, "Go back to your posts," so Holderman went dodging off to the right flank, while McMurtry hurried off to inform Cullen what had happened. A few inquisitive sergeants quickly learned what had transpired and began to spread the word from funkhole to funkhole. When one private inquired of Whittlesey whether the surrender demand was true, the major said it was. The private pushed up his helmet and muttered, "Why, the sons of bitches!" The German missive had been a serious miscalculation. Starving and dispirited Americans now found a focus for their agony and anger. Holderman heard several men say, "I wonder what they think we are," but mostly he listened to a torrent of the most loathsome curses ever flung about on a battlefield. The shattered hillside resounded with shouts of "Go to hell!" "Kiss our American asses!!" and "Come over and get us, you Dutch sons of bitches!!!" in addition to many more vulgar and novel expletives. Every American on that steeply sloping piece of purgatory was now just plain pissed off. Five days of suffering and torture had reduced them to the most basic of instincts and one of Whittlesey's soldiers explained, "You become like an animal." He then asked, "Does one wild animal surrender to another?" All over the hillside men could be seen grimly honing their bayonets on stones, sharpening them to a razor's edge. Wounded men crawled from their holes, picking up rifles and pistols and spare cartridges for the attack that would soon come. This next fight would be to the death.[22]

Whittlesey was typically low key. Later he wrote, "No answer whatever, written or verbal, was made to the German commander's letter." One of his friends would joke that the major was simply "conserving white paper" when he refused to acknowledge the surrender demand. Whittlesey's only response was to order someone to bring in the white battalion signal panels, so they could not be misconstrued as a sign of surrender. Irving Liner secured the First Battalion panel, while William Powers folded up that belonging to the Second Battalion. Anyone who had been trying to signal low-flying aircraft with dirty white rags immediately hid them from view. Newspapermen would pounce on this episode and, taking their cue from an offhand remark by General Alexander, telegraph reports that Whittlesey had sent the Germans a three-word response: "Go to hell!" That story circulated freely at the press center in Bar-le-Duc and within hours readers around the world began reading about the famous "Go

> *Keep your head down, Fritzie boy,*
> *Keep your head down, Fritzie boy.*
> *Last night, by the pale moonlight,*
> *We saw you, we saw you.*
> *You were mending broken wire,*
> *When we opened rapid fire.*
> *If you want to see your father in your Fatherland,*
> *Keep your head down, Fritzie boy![23]*

244 BLOOD IN THE ARGONNE

to Hell" Whittlesey. Damon Runyon would later investigate the incident and conclude, "Whittlesey says he did not say it, but that it covered his thoughts at the time, anyway." The major's only concern at the time was to keep his men on their toes for the ensuing attack. When he first heard the "Go to Hell" story, Sergeant Martin Tuite made the comment, "What he really told us was to fix bayonets and set ourselves."[24]

After waiting about thirty minutes for a reply, the Germans launched yet another attack. First there were questions shouted down from the crest, asking if the Americans would surrender. German-speaking doughboys yelled back, "Hell, no!!" Trench mortars began to pound the area with shells. Machine guns opened fire from Ridge 198 and both flanks. Bundles of grenades came tumbling down the hill among the funkholes. One four-inch fragment from a mortar shell crashed into Arnold Morem's left side, breaking a couple of ribs. Corporal Harry Schaffer pulled it out, covered the jagged hole with a rag, and went back to firing. Another shell killed Lieutenant Gordon Schenck, one of Whittlesey's stalwart officers during the siege. Sharing a funkhole with Lionel Bendheim and tending the sergeant's gangrened limb, Schenck died instantly when his back was shredded by shrapnel, while Bendheim, only inches away, sustained only a slight wound in his good leg. Someone would later disclose that Schenck had been wounded in the foot before Whittlesey's command was cut off, but he refused to mention his injury for fear of being evacuated. The adjutant of the 308th Infantry would say of Schenck: "He was in command of a Company, steadied them, and without thought of personal danger went back and forth on his defenses helping, offering advice, and cheering his men. He was a splendid example to them, never losing heart when all was blackest and no relief was in sight, and he gave the most glorious sacrifice a man can give. The officers and men of the 308th Infantry are proud of the way he fought and died, and are proud to have known and been associated with him." Colonel Averill told Schenck's family that "he would climb up the bank in view of the Germans, throw grenades at them, and fire his rifle, helping his men to drive them back. The men were broken-hearted when they learned of his death."[25]

As the enemy began to close in, officers cried out, "Stand to!" and men scrambled from their holes to fight off the attackers. The heaviest blows came in the center and on the right flank, where Captain Holderman said Company K withstood "the fiercest attack of the entire siege."

Albert Kaempfer agreed, saying that "the bullets came thick and fast" and "men dropped all around." Moving about from hole to hole, shifting men to resist each new enemy thrust, Holderman nearly burst with pride at what he witnessed: "Men too weak to stand, and men severely wounded, drew themselves up to the firing line, took deliberate aim and fired into the advancing enemy. Those who could not fire loaded rifles for their comrades." That scene was repeated all along the Charlevaux Road. In Buhler's company to the left, John Nell noticed that "many of the boys [were] almost too weak and nervous to load and handle their rifles." Unable to move his shattered left shoulder, Lieutenant Griffin could be seen firing a rifle with his good right arm. Nell said that despite a shortage of cartridges, soldiers from Company G "gave them all we had" and watched in relief as the grenade tossers finally disappeared.[26]

Lester Griswold, one of Schenck's men, had been hit by a bullet that cut a groove from his left eye to the ear. He thought that side of his face had been paralyzed, but remarked, "It didn't bother me a bit." Griswold had no chance to tend his wound, explaining, "The way those Huns attacked us we either had to fight or die." Robert Gafanowitz had been firing a Chauchat on the Company G front until struck by grenade fragments that smashed his right forearm. Although unable to operate his weapon, Gafanowitz refused to leave the team and shifted over to pass ammunition for the man who replaced him as gunner. Henry Erickson had spent the morning exchanging shots with German snipers, but finally went down with a hole in his thigh. Instead of calling for assistance, Erickson continued to fire his rifle and helped repulse this latest attack. Lawrence Osborne, the former supply sergeant who had assumed command of Company B following the death of Lieutenant Rogers, was killed by a trench mortar round. Corporal Holger Peterson, who had led several of Whittlesey's patrols, fell dead. A mortar shell claimed the life of William Halligan, who had left a hospital bed to join his company in the Argonne. Men fell by the dozens as trench mortars, grenades, machine guns, and rifles raked the American position.[27]

Over with Company K, Private Kaempfer saw German soldiers firing only fifty feet away. Thinking they had gained an advantage, German officers sent forward two men with flamethrowers to administer a coup de grace on the two right flank companies, hoping to cause enough confusion that the Americans would be driven down into the valley where they could be cut down by machine guns. Liquid fire sizzled through brush, setting alight everything with which it came in contact. Ludwig Blomseth and his buddy jumped up and ran for their lives as the stream of living flame licked at their backs. Blomseth turned to see if they were being followed and fell into an abandoned funkhole, with his friend tumbling in on top of him. The clothing of both men was on fire, so they rolled about on their backs like upended turtles until the flames were extinguished. One American ran back, flames engulfing his uniform and inflicting third-degree burns that proved fatal. Enraged doughboys jumped up, screaming obscenities, and shot down the Huns operating those infernal machines, turning them into human torches. Sergeant James Carroll took careful aim and killed an enemy sergeant who appeared to be in charge of the flame-throwers. Then these crazed Americans—gaunt with starvation, unshaven, ragged, filthy, and sporting bloody bandages on their wounds—did something totally unexpected. Despite being so weak they could barely walk, exhausted doughboys began a counterattack, driving back the Germans with a storm of rifle fire and moving in for the kill with those gleaming bayonets. Veterans avenged their dead friends by the numbers: "Charge bayonets!" "Advance!!" "Thrust!!!" Untrained in the use of the bayonet, replacements swung rifle butts and trench knives. They took no prisoners. They just wanted to kill. Wounded Jerrys were murdered where they fell. To the Germans, it must have seemed like the end of the world when those frenzied apparitions—bearded, bleeding, and roaring their defiance—rose from the earth and came at them like resurrected warriors on Judgment Day. After firing a few desultory shots, the Germans turned and fled.[28]

Following this German retreat, James Larney noted in his secret diary a brief conversation between Whittlesey and Sergeant George Hauck: "Machine gun non-com reports to Major Whittlesey liquid fire came out of a clump of bushes and he turned machine gun in there and heard no more of it. Major tells him he had done right thing and if it shows up again do the same."[29]

Whittlesey figured that this latest attack had lasted only about twenty frantic minutes, perhaps longer on Holderman's flank where the pressure had been heaviest. After receiving reports from his company commanders, the major knew that the situation had gone from dire to hopeless. Fewer than 250 men had enough strength remaining to be counted on in battle. Five of the six machine guns in Lieutenant Peabody's platoon had been destroyed. No matter, there were only forty-eight rounds remaining anyway. Survivors of Lieutenant Noon's detachment also had just one gun in action. Despite gleaning the hillside for German weapons and cartridges, men were sharing ammunition so that everyone had at least a few rounds. Grenades had long since been used up. There was no sound of battle from the south. No airplanes had been seen since about noon. There would be no stopping another enemy assault, no matter how feeble. As darkness fell and moans from the wounded filled his ears, Whittlesey pondered how he could keep his men alive for just one more day. One of his men wrote, "We began another horrible and dreadful night, not knowing if this would be our last on earth." Whittlesey and McMurtry settled into their funkhole to discuss their options and mull over reports from Holderman that the Germans seemed to be particularly active, although there was little firing.[30]

Unknown to the two officers, some of those promised two million Americans were finally on their way to relieve the beleaguered command. By noon on October 7, Colonel Houghton had gotten several companies through that tiny gap in the German wire. Success had finally been achieved by the 308th Infantry along the railroad in the north-south ravine, as well as on the 153rd Brigade's front. Attacks farther west by other divisions of the American First Army had led to a strategic withdrawal all across the Seventy-seventh Division's front, although enough Germans remained as a rear guard to make any hasty advance somewhat perilous. Lieutenant F. A. Tillman led Company B of the 307th as it moved northwest, supported by Companies A and M. They slipped cautiously along a wilderness trail, crossed a stream, and suddenly encountered about seven or eight Germans loaded with grenades. In the fading light, Tillman's men killed most of them. Just a few yards beyond the German bodies lay the Charlevaux Road.[32]

As a nauseating stench overwhelmed his senses, Lieutenant Tillman fell into a hole and landed on someone who let out a cry of surprise. A

Lieutenant Maurice Revnes, Company D, 306th Machine Gun Battalion:
"Some of the wounded cried continuously, they cried that they were in great pain. The most of the wounded were lying flat in funkholes and when it was quiet and there was no firing, you could hear moaning all over the hill."[31]

shadowy form lunged at the officer with a bayonet, which he just managed to dodge. Tillman yelled, "What's the matter with you? I'm looking for Major Whittlesey." One of Holderman's men replied, "I don't give a damn who you are and what you want. You just step on my buddy again and I'll kill you!" Tillman identified himself and said those words that the besieged soldiers had dreamed of hearing: "You're relieved, and we'll have food up for you right away." The soldier apologized and lifted up his wounded buddy, saying, "See? We're relieved. You're going to be all right." The frail casualty could only manage a weak cheer, before slumping back into the hole.[33]

About the time Tillman reached Whittlesey's command, his last set of scouts, benefiting from the German withdrawal, reached units from the Seventy-seventh Division. First to arrive was Abraham Krotoshinsky. It was nightfall when he crawled into an abandoned trench and tried to get his bearings. While resting there, Krotoshinsky heard American voices in the distance, but began to worry about his reception: "I was coming from the direction of the German lines and my English is none too good. I was afraid they would shoot me for a German before I could explain who I was." With tears in his eyes, he weakly called out, "Hello! Hello!" American voices responded, "Who the hell are you and what do you want?" A patrol quickly located Krotoshinsky and took the dog-tired private back to some officer's headquarters, where he related his story. Doughboys gave him hot coffee and bully beef, the best food he had ever tasted in his life. Early next morning he guided several relief companies back to the pocket, where "the men were like crazy with joy," and rejoined his buddy Art Fein, who offered the tearful welcome, "Gee, I never thought I'd see you again."[34]

Brown and Kozikowski had managed to wriggle free, but now they were afraid of being shot by American guards because they would be coming from the German lines without the current password. They finally decided to just walk along and talk as if they had a right to be there. Luckily they stumbled upon a guard who shouted "Halt!" instead of shooting first. Brown recalled, "Altho skeptical at first and keeping us covered, we finally convinced him who we were." A runner took the two men back to regimental headquarters, where Captain Breckinridge spread out a map and asked, "Can you tell us exactly where the Lost Battalion is?" When they did so, Breckinridge responded, "Good, this is the first time we've known exactly where to look for you," then got on the phone to alert General Johnson. After devouring some bread, beans, and chocolate, Brown and Kozikowski washed and shaved for the first time in two weeks before lying down on "the best bed in the place." Krotoshinsky, Brown, and Kozikowski each received a Distinguished Service Cross, the citation for which read that he had "volunteered to carry a message through the German lines, although he was aware that several unsuccessful attempts had been previously made by patrols, the members of which were either killed, wounded, or driven back. By his courage and determination he succeeded in delivering the message and brought relief to his battalion."[35]

Whittlesey and McMurtry were talking softly when a runner came gliding up and reported that an officer leading an American patrol had just arrived on the right flank and needed to speak with the major. Whittlesey said quietly, "I will go up and see just what this is," and crawled away. McMurtry remained for some ten minutes, then came to his senses and went scrambling after Whittlesey. Following the road, McMurtry found the major eating a sandwich while he talked with a stranger. The captain blurted out, "For God's sake, give me a bite of that!" After a few hurried mouthfuls of food, McMurtry learned that the newcomer was an officer "from the 307th Infantry, who had moved in on our right flank with his patrol and that just behind him were three companies of the 307th Infantry and that it was an actual fact that we were relieved!" Lieutenant Tillman had already committed a serious mistake by the time McMurtry arrived on the scene. When the lieutenant said something about being happy to rescue the trapped men, Whittlesey lashed out with the curt observation, "Rescue, hell. If you had come up when we did, you wouldn't have put us in this fix." After directing Tillman and the other officers to place their men as a protective screen on the heights above the road, Whittlesey and McMurtry began to supervise the distribution of about sixty cans of corned beef hash carried by the relief column. Officers and noncoms "counted every can and measured out each mouthful with their spoons," so that everyone got an equal share.[36]

As he made arrangements for the wounded to be fed first, Whittlesey enjoyed the wonderful sight that greeted his eyes: "In the grim darkness of the shadows above Charlevaux brook, haggard men with bleary eyes and muddy stubble on their chins rose from the holes they had expected would be their graves, and grasped one another's hand silently.

They crawled to the side of those heroic wounded, and whispered the news that relief had come, that food was on the way to the position at that very moment, and that it was all over but the shouting which would have to be deferred until later. If tears flowed, the darkness concealed them."[37]

> **Captain George McMurtry,**
> **2nd Battalion, 308th Infantry:**
> *"One man would turn to the other and would shake him by the hand and like that, but you would not put it down as indescribable. It was fine to be relieved, but they didn't go crazy over the thing.*[38]

John Nell noticed an abnormally large number of men walking around his funkhole and finally asked, "What's up?" A stranger replied, "Relief has come in on our right and more is coming in behind them." Nell confessed, "It was like being reborn." Noncoms came along with cans of meat and, although there was only enough for a few spoonfuls per man, it was wonderful stuff. Robert Manson remembered, "It was the happiest moment of my life. I was hysterical. I laughed and cried for joy. I felt like a cat having nine lives." When the corned beef hash came around, Manson admitted, "I ate it from my hands covered with blood and dirt. I'll tell the world it tasted like sirloin steak smothered with onions." Lieutenant Cullen was sound asleep when Frank Erickson, his company runner, woke him. Thinking it was another German attack, Cullen jumped up to do battle, but Erickson said that relief had come and presented the lieutenant with a sack containing some bread and hash. Cullen sent his compliments to Major Whittlesey, then made the rounds of his company funkholes, spreading the good news and giving each man a forkful of hash. After that, Cullen boasted, "We were ready to go on for another six days then."[39]

> *And if I ever break away*
> *I'm going to gorge myself each day*
> *On porterhouse and apple pie with real ice cream*
> *'N everything.*[40]

After about an hour, rations had been passed around and the 307th was in position. For the first time since October 2, not a single shot disturbed the soldiers, who could sleep soundly if they wished. Many chose not to do so. They stayed awake in their filthy holes, surrounded by the stench of death, and kept their wounded buddies company. Men hardened by their wartime experiences miraculously regained their humanity. Having survived this incredible ordeal, they had seen enough of death. Doughboys could not ease the pain of gangrened wounds, but they could provide comfort. Rough, calloused hands, smeared with dried blood but more gentle than any mother's, caressed mud-caked hair and smoothed bloody uniforms. In hushed tones, bearded friends talked of the future and girls and parents and of how life would be so great back in the States. But over and over again could be heard the same whispered words, "Hang on, buddy, hang on." "Just a few more hours." "Hang on. Hang on." But some of the wounded were too far gone and there, on that isolated French ridge so far from home, a few slipped away forever. Each of them died a free man.[41]

12

LIVING LEGENDS

As relief columns began to pour into Charlevaux Valley, soldiers were immediately engulfed by a nauseating stench from human compost that filled the air around Major Whittlesey's Lost Battalion position. They first encountered an irregular ring of corpses, German soldiers who had fallen too close to the American lines and could not be retrieved, now blackened by exposure and decomposition. Within this circle of death were the American bodies, many partially stripped as the living frantically tore apart clothing of the dead for use as bandages. Counting some few who had not made it through the night, there were over one hundred bodies, most hastily covered by a thin layer of earth or a few tree branches, more to screen them from view than to provide any sort of burial. Here and there lay body parts that had been scattered about by American artillery and German trench mortars. Added to this overpowering stink were the more subtle smells of blood and the rot of gangrened wounds. An odor of hundreds of thousands of expended cartridges lent a sulfury tinge to the polluted atmosphere. Overall hung the reeking smell of a gigantic outdoor toilet. One of the relieving officers said of this place, "My God! It was pitiable. Those fellows had been through a hell that made our drive through to relieve them seem like a pleasure excursion."[1]

From his comfortable dugout, General Evan Johnson ordered staff officers to rush forward food, medical supplies, and overcoats at first light, following up personally to assess the situation and reorganize the brigade. Accompanied by a number of newspaper reporters, General Alexander left his cozy division headquarters and hurried forward to meet Whittlesey. While everyone waited for medical supplies and rations and useless generals, Lieutenant Tillman walked around the ghastly battlefield and was appalled at what he found: "The sheer horror of that strip of hillside is unimaginable. The stench was unbearable. Bits of flesh, legs and arms, parts of bodies, were all about. The hillside in their position had been literally blown to pieces—hardly a spot that had not been struck." As for the soldiers, Tillman noted that they "sat and stared with drawn faces, burning eyes, tense jaws, but with the idea of resistance fixed in their minds." Impassive faces clearly displayed their determination, and Tillman wrote later of his sense that, "they could have given in and got relief, but they had elected gallantly to stay there, to die there, to rot there, if necessary, rather than to give in." He continued, "That's all there is to it. If they couldn't go on, they at least held on, until going on was possible again. They had no idea of retreat." Now all they wanted was food, rest, and lots and lots of cigarettes.[2]

When he awoke on the morning of October 8, Corporal Olof Nelson said that his stomach "growled like a piece of machinery without oil." Major Whittlesey began to solve that problem, personally handing out coffee, hash, bread, and jam as fast as it could be carried forward. James Larney noted, "We received butter, syrup, bread, canned beans, and the fellows just dove for it and were smeared with butter and syrup in their haste to bolt it down." David Tulchin would recall with unconcealed glee, "I got hold of a whole pound of butter!" Captain Stromee wrote in his diary, "Day of great joy relief at last and bukoo rations for half starved men." Amid the pure joy surrounding these first few bites of food, General Alexander stepped out of his staff car on the Charlevaux Road. Sliding down the slope with a retinue of nicely-dressed staff officers and reporters, Alexander began shouting for Whittlesey. Robert Manson happened to be sitting in his funkhole enjoying a bit of breakfast and did not fancy this intrusion, yelling out, "Who the hell is calling the Major now?" Glancing up, Manson saw a stranger with two stars on his campaign hat and scrambled to the position of attention, saluted, and reported that Whittlesey had gone over to Captain Holderman's company. "Shall I call him, sir?" "No! No! I'll go to him," said Alexander, as he started carefully picking his way through the debris.[3]

The division commander greeted Whittlesey with news that he had been promoted to the rank of lieutenant colonel, replacing Fred Smith, who had been killed only a few days earlier. Glancing up at the canopy of green, General Alexander commented, "Well, I can see why the airplanes couldn't find this place." Overhearing this remark, Private Cepaglia burst out, "General, the artillery certainly found it!" Alexander shot back that it was French artillery that had fired into their position, so Cepaglia, unwilling to engage in a shouting match with the division commander, prudently shut up. General Alexander failed to mention this little exchange when he later wrote his recollections of that morning: "Seated about the little shelters which they had so gallantly defended or attending to the wants of their many wounded comrades they showed their confidence in themselves in their Cause by every word and act." He also said, "I endeavored to express to all of them something of the admiration felt by the whole American army for their determined stand against superior forces." Nobody really cared what Alexander thought or said and they just wanted him to go away. Maybe his soldiers would have shown more interest if he had been passing out bottles of beer.[4]

Mad-moiselle from Armentieres,
Parlez-vous.
Mad-moiselle from Armentieres,
Parlez-vous.
The General won the Croix de Guerre,
But the son of a bitch wasn't even there!
Hinky-dinky, parlez-vous![5]

Coming to his senses, General Alexander finally noticed that hundreds of men lay waiting patiently for medical attention. He sent staff officers racing off with orders to immediately set up an advanced ambulance station to remove Whittlesey's casualties and to dispatch a convoy of ten trucks to evacuate those uninjured. Alexander also had them make arrangements for billets, delousing equipment, and new uniforms at Depot de Machines. While everyone waited, officers and noncoms began to tally the horrendous losses, but the true story of casualties could never be told. Captain Holderman, who would later try to compile a complete list of the dead and wounded, explained why: "It was impossible to make the determination from company records, as during the eighteen days the Division was in that dense forest it was utterly impossible to keep an

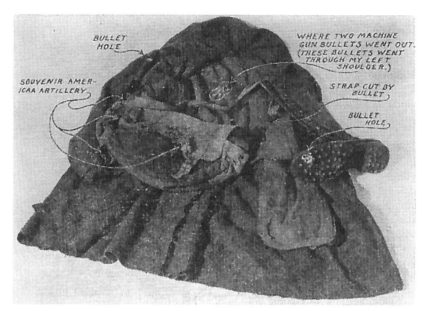

Battle damage to Lieutenant Griffin's overcoat and boot. From Peterson's *Lost Battalion Survivors from Minnesota and the Northwest.*

entirely accurate check on the personnel. The companies were well filled for the initial thrust, but considering the deaths, wounded, stragglers, and men detailed on various duties, no accurate record would be obtained." In Holderman's opinion, any figures presented "would be only *fairly accurate*," a sentiment echoed by Captain L. Wardlaw Miles in his *History of the 308th Infantry*.[6]

Besides, numbers do not tell the whole story. Consider the case of Lieutenant Maurice Griffin, who had been shot through the left shoulder. He gave a complete description of his condition in a letter home: "I have four bullet holes in my overcoat, and my trousers were torn to pieces by a grenade, but I only had my knees cut besides the bullet in my shoulder. The strap to my field glasses was cut by a bullet, my gas mask was cut in half by shrapnel, and my helmet has a dent from a bullet." To top it off, Griffin told his wife, "The picture I have of you has a hole in it from a piece of shell." Some men had been hit so often by bullets and shell fragments that they were simply listed as "wounded, multiple." Others were like Sergeant John Colasacco, a bear of a man who could normally hold six men on his shoulders, but who now, although unwounded, lacked strength to stand up and could only crawl about on his hands and knees. In his post-battle report, Major Whittlesey listed the "effectives," including both officers and enlisted men, who remained in his command: First Battalion, 308th Infantry, 87; Second Battalion, 308th Infantry, 109; Company K, 307th Infantry, 35; and Companies C and D, 306th Machine Gun Battalion, 21; a total of 252. Well over 400 soldiers had either been killed, wounded, captured, or had succumbed to disease or otherwise been put out of action by the Germans—more than sixty per cent of his total force.[7]

As officers worked to compile their losses, detachments from the 307th and 308th Ambulance Companies began to arrive. These men had been following behind the advance of the 154th Brigade as it tore through the Argonne, but since ambulances were useless without roads, every available person had been sent into the forest to carry stretchers. Their efforts had been supplemented by musicians from the regimental bands, who proved to be remarkably out of shape for such strenuous duty. But it took four men at least twelve hours to carry a patient five kilometers, so everyone not on the firing line was converted into a stretcher bearer. Following the capture of Depot de Machines, these ambulance companies began to evacuate their wounded along the narrow-gauge German railway running north and south through that transportation center.[8]

Delbert Davis was with the 307th Ambulance Company when it reached the scene and he recorded his impressions of the shocking sight that he encountered, beginning with the comment, "What a spectre met our eyes!" He continued: "Scores of dead and wounded lay stretched out in the swampy forest, indicating to a certain extent the misery endured by these men during their imprisonment in the Annex of Hell." Although avoiding mention of the most gruesome details, Davis did state that no orator, no artist, and no playwright could ever hope to "set forth the suffering, hardships, misery, and that which is preeminent, beyond precedent, the display of courage of the Beleaguered Battalion." William Conklin was struck by the composure of the wounded, many of whom "sat along the side of the road, wrapped in blankets, each of them looking like a cross between a specter and a hobo, waiting their turn without a murmur."[9]

As doctors began to tag the wounded for removal, they bypassed Sidney Smith, who still lay in a muddy funkhole with his mortally wounded buddy. Afraid of being left behind, Smith shouted, "Ain't you going to give me a tag?" He was shocked by the blunt response, "Why, you're going to die before long." Smith's loud protests convinced the doctor to reconsider his original diagnosis, so he asked the wounded man if he could walk. When Smith said yes, he responded, "There's a boy, 18 years old, who had his hand shot off. You take care of this boy." Smith looked after the youngster until a first-aid man came along, smelled gangrene in the stump, and marked the boy for immediate removal. Despite a bullet wound through his body and another in his leg, Smith would have to wait to be evacuated until the seriously injured had been transported.[10]

Those most severely wounded either crawled or were carried up to the Charlevaux Road, where they were placed into rickety Ford ambulances and taken to the division triage station at La Chalade. Wounded in the left arm and right leg, James Larney was laboriously climbing uphill, "swinging from tree to tree," when Captain Breckenridge came up behind him, grabbed his belt, and hauled him up to the waiting ambulances. Sergeant Conklin remembered, "By packing the cars to the limit, with the less serious cases clinging to the running boards, we got this big evacuation job done by 2:00 in the afternoon." Those less seriously hurt either walked or were carried back on stretchers to the German railway, where they were loaded onto small flatcars and pushed by hand back to Depot de Machines. Conklin was impressed by one of these patients: "He was a young fellow, hardly more than a boy, who had been wounded and taken prisoner by the Germans. In their haste they had left him behind. We picked him up and found he had a probable leg fracture and other wounds. He said the Boches had been quite decent to him." Conklin said that boy was "the most chipper stretcher case I ever saw." Many of the wounded had been unconscious when removed from the battlefield, including Joseph Giefer, who said, "The first I remember was when they were cutting off my shoes at the first aid station." Nearly all of Whittlesey's wounded passed through the 308th Field Hospital, where conditions became so chaotic that almost three dozen men had their condition listed as "Not Yet Determined" before being shipped to evacuation hospitals for proper diagnosis and treatment. Lieutenant Colonel R. W. Kerr, chief division surgeon, reported that during the first ninety minutes of frenzied activity, about 140 of Whittlesey's men had passed through the field hospital. The 307th Ambulance Company reported the evacuation by litter of about three hundred patients in six hours, while the 308th Ambulance Company took away over one hundred and thirty more in Ford and mule-drawn ambulances. More than three hundred survivors would eventually be hospitalized, most of them suffering from "exhaustion and inanition," in addition to their wounds.[11]

As litter bearers carried away the wounded, Whittlesey ordered that the dead be buried. Few had strength enough to respond, but John McNearney did throw more dirt over the remains of Richard Hyde and George Nies, his friends who had lain in their funkhole since being killed on October 3. James Slingerland wrote that his pal, Lauren G. Reid, had been hit by a piece of shrapnel during the last attack on October 7 and "died in the hole after a day and night." Slingerland had helped bind up Reid's wound and "felt sure that he would be strong enough to last until they could get him to a hospital, but he was too weak" and died during the night. Slingerland said, "We buried him on a little hillside with hundreds of other boys the morning after we were rescued." Clyde Hintz also helped to inter dead Americans, but because everyone was so exhausted, "they were buried where they had fallen, usually in the hole where they had dug in." On the following day, a sergeant leading an intelligence gathering patrol in search of dead Germans came upon a cluster of about thirty of these graves, including that of Lieutenant Schenck. Those burials had been incomplete, the lieutenant being only "partially covered with earth." Chaplain James J. Halligan, who had just missed going forward with Whittlesey because he had been giving Last Rites to a dying German soldier, commandeered the 308th Regimental Band to assist in the grisly task. On behalf of the mothers and wives, Halligan carefully compiled a list of burials and made a map of each grave, "showing the location and direction as to how to reach it and identify the spot." The real burials came a few days later when Headquarters Company of the Fifty-third Pioneer Infantry set up shop at Moulin de Charlevaux and began the systematic interment process, carrying bodies down to a temporary cemetery in the bottom of the ravine.[12]

While the body snatchers (slang for stretcher bearers) and grave-diggers worked, Whittlesey led everyone else down into the valley where they sprawled out in the sunshine and enjoyed some fresh air. The major recalled that "the first hot food which the men received was the cocoa supplied by the Y.M.C.A.," two members, Stephen Burrows and Harry Blair, being attached to the 308th Infantry. As "white and exhausted" soldiers smoked cigarettes and sipped hot chocolate, reporters located Whittlesey, "a tall, slim, youngish man, wearing glasses, very tired, sitting on a stump in a little clearing." Newsmen began to quiz him, but Whittlesey waved his hand and stopped them, saying, "Don't write about me, just about these

We'll write to her tomorrow and this is what we'll say,
He breathed her name in dying; in peace he passed away –
No words about his moaning, his anguish and his pain,
When slowly, slowly dying. God! Fifteen hours in dying!
He lay a maimed thing dying, alone upon the plain.[13]

men." One writer asked how the replacements had fared alongside the veteran New Yorkers. The major replied, "Well, they're bigger men physically, you know, and more used to outdoor life and they were fine—but they were all fine. One of my finest was a New York Jew, a runner, named Liner." He introduced Private Irving Liner, a Company D man attached to battalion headquarters, who commented, "Just to think—a year ago I was studying law, and I had every comfort, too. Now, I have been lousy for two weeks." When pressed about how he had managed to hold out so long, Whittlesey responded, "It was kind of hard to stick it out sometimes, especially when we heard them trying to get through to us, getting nearer and nearer, then being driven back. It was hard not to have a wash, too. In fact, when they did get through, it was quite a relief." Somewhat embarrassed by this last remark, Whittlesey said shyly, "I wasn't trying to make a pun." As they interviewed some of the survivors, one of them said simply, "*We* held out because *he* did. We was all right if we could see him once a day." While their commander answered questions, some bored men wandered over toward the life-saving spring. John Nell discovered where a single German machine gun had been positioned behind a U-shaped barricade of railroad ties and estimated that the pile of empty brass cartridges would fill about sixty bushel baskets. He then filled his canteen, "got out my Gillette and proceeded with a shave and washed my face and hands, all of which were badly needed."[14]

A doughboy from the 307th Infantry at a forward observation post had been startled before dawn on October 6 by a staff officer accompanied by "a skinny fellow" wearing "a strange uniform." This stranger was

Damon Runyon, famed correspondent for the *New York American*, who had come forward to write up the Lost Battalion story. He stayed with that outpost for two days, getting little sleep and only a few bites of food, until moving forward with the relief columns. The doughboy thought Runyon was crazy and told him, "You're a sucker. Go back where it's comfortable." The newsman responded, "I've got a lot of circulation back home. This is a good story." Now Runyon was in his glory, talking to survivors and making copious notes for his next column, noting the major as "a tall, lean-flanked fellow around forty years old. He has a funny little smile." The newsman had first encountered some of these soldiers at Camp Upton, where he remembered them "all jabbering in their own language at once." He noted with admiration that "the one-time counter-jumpers, brokers, clerks, gangsters, newsboys, truck drivers, collegians, peddlers and what not held the positions which they had been ordered to take," burrowing in the ground "like moles." He was particularly struck by "a little chap who used to sell newspapers around Times Square." Now the soldier, caked with mud and barely able to keep his eyes open, "was grinning broadly." All of the survivors were "infinitely proud of their gallant stand."[15]

Everyone waited patiently until midafternoon for that phantom truck convoy which never arrived, so they would have to leave on foot. It was about three o'clock when Whittlesey and McMurtry assembled their battalions on the dirt road in the valley for a march back to Depot de Machines. Thomas Johnson, one of the correspondents, witnessed the departure and noticed that every spectator had tears in his eyes. He wrote that the survivors "walked heavily, numbed by utter exhaustion, clothes tattered and filthy, faces like drawn masks of putty, with the fixed stare of determination. Worn out, dirty, hungry, thirsty, they would not give in. The eyes told that. Those of us who were there and saw them, as the Pioneers turned the first spadeful of earth for the others, knew that here was indeed a holy place." Other doughboys from the Liberty Division had gathered to welcome them as they marched west, then turned south toward regimental headquarters, but the demonstration failed to materialize. One soldier who had come to bid them hearty congratulations, could not bring himself to glorify the procession: "I couldn't say anything to them. There was nothing to say anyway. It made your heart lump up in your throat just to look at them. Their faces told the whole story of their fight." Reporters were already lauding them as American heroes, but the survivors all knew that was crap. Arnold Morem admitted, "We didn't feel like heroes but we did feel very lucky to be still alive." When Martin Lokken's son later asked if he was a hero, the Argonne veteran said honestly that he was "simply another scared soldier who did his job and was lucky enough to survive." Everyone who marched away from Charlevaux Valley knew in his own heart that the only real heroes were those who never left.[16]

Survivors of Company C spotted Clifford Brown standing among the crowd gathered to witness Whittlesey's return and burst out: "Brown, we knew you'd do it! We

Good-bye, old Pal,
I've been to hell and back again;
There's where you fell, in mud and blood and rain.
Sure, we won—you paid the bill;
You swapped your life for that green hill;
Good-bye, old Pal.[17]

knew you'd do it!" The successful messenger smiled and waved, but took note of their appearance: "What a sight those boys were! Their clothes were torn; they were unkempt, the mud in which they had laid had frozen to their bodies." Years later when interviewed about the incident, Brown said slowly, with tears streaming down his cheeks, "I can't describe my emotions of that moment. But—well, I'll tell you, it made a fellow feel pretty good."[18]

Rolling kitchens had been deployed at Depot de Machines and the order was to give the men as much food as they wanted, starting with beef stew and coffee. They all tried to eat too much at first. After filling up on bread, jam, and chocolate bars, Otto Novotny admitted that he "became very sick." John McNearney confessed that he "could not eat more than a bite at a time," gagging every time he tried to swallow more. Martin Lokken got so sick from downing a handful of chocolate bars that he "wouldn't eat another Hershey bar" the rest of his life. Ralph John left a complete account of his encounter with real food: "I can well remember the first thing I had to eat was a big white onion, and, boy, did I bite into it. Next I had some red molasses and bread. There were prunes, tomatoes, spuds, rice and coffee, a banquet if I ever looked at one. I would eat a few bites or rather gobble it down, then I would have to run aside and I'd vomit it all up. I'd go back and eat some more, then lost it. This was the way I tried to eat my supper, with darned little staying down." Billets in the German dugouts failed to materialize and everyone slept in the rain. Private John got little sleep, admitting, "I'll bet I made forty trips to the bushes—with both ends operating!"[19]

Robert Manson, one of the less seriously injured soldiers, described his first encounter with the outside world at the La Chalade hospital: "The place was a beautiful abbey and was built by pious hands nine hundred years ago. All was dark outside, for we were in constant dread of air attacks. The interior was lit by candles. The place was so beautiful, that it reminded me of 'Alice in Wonderland.' It was like going from hell to heaven. There the Red Cross served us with bread, hot tomato soup, hot coffee, chocolate, and cigarettes." James Larney wrote of his visit to La Chalade: "At Division Field Hospital in empty church somewhere I got soup and cigarets. Vomited the soup. Couldn't hold it." From this advance dressing station, wounded soldiers were taken to evacuation hospitals. Anne Hardon was a Red Cross worker stationed at Bourges when some of the Lost Battalion men arrived. Like all the other casualties, they came in "covered with dust and a many days' beard which evidently embarrassed them." At first, hospital staff could not tell officers from enlisted men. Hardon was amazed to find that some of Whittlesey's men were "so chipper that I had to see the great green gashes in their bodies to believe they were wounded." One man told her that "when he looked at his wound that morning there were worms in it." New arrivals were fed, washed and shaved, then funneled through a pre-operative ward, the operating room, and on to a general ward for their recovery, followed by convalescence in base hospitals.[20]

Many of the wounded were in terrible shape following their ordeal. Irving Klein, a Jewish native of Kassa, Hungary, living in Oakland, California, had been struck in the left elbow by a machine gun bullet on October 3. The projectile tore apart the joint, destroying the end of the humerus and the top of the radius. Corporal Klein was admitted to A. R. C. Hospital 110 at midnight on October 8, where an operation was conducted to save his arm. After five days of recuperation, he was transferred to Base Hospital 47 at Beaune, where he underwent two more operations. Klein arrived in New York on January 5, 1919 where he suffered through a fourth operation at General Hospital 1 in the Bronx. Doctors were able to save his arm, but he would never be able to bend the limb. Pistoria Bonaventura was not so lucky and doctors had no choice but to amputate his left leg above the knee. Despite his missing limb, the young Italian kept a good attitude. When a reporter discovered him aboard a troopship in New York Harbor, the veteran piped up, "I come-a from New York. Bronx. Name-a Pistoria. I'm-a the Lost Battalion. They tell-a me lost. I did-a not know."[21]

From a hospital bed, Sergeant Lionel Bendheim wrote to his mother and sister on October 11, telling them cheerily, "Well, dears, as they say in the army, 'they got me.'" Bendheim went on to describe his experiences and explain how he had lost his right leg, then continued: "Now, then, brave women, this is the time to show your wonderful spirits. Even though I'll need crutches to navigate, I'm sure I'll be able to work O.K. Think of the thousands that have so willingly laid down their lives. I am coming home, and I'll be just as fine and dandy and cheerful and happy as you always knew Lionel to be. I'll pinch you on the knee, mother dear, and make you say ouch three times." He concluded his message: "Be brave, be good, and trust in God. May He bless and keep you well and happy, so that I get a great big smile from the both of you. Now, don't worry; everything will be all right. Lots and lots of love and kisses." Sergeant Lionel Bendheim made the most of his hospital stay and eventually married Betty Smith, his army nurse.[22]

George Mayhew, a Nevada private in Lionel Bendheim's company, also wrote to the folks at home of his experiences, admitting, "They sure killed them off fast when we went through the Argonne forest." Mayhew explained the situation after being

I don't want to get well, I don't want to get well, / I'm in love with a beautiful nurse. / Early ev'ry morning, night and noon, / The cutest little girlie comes and feeds me with a spoon. / I don't want to get well, I don't want to get well, / I'm glad they shot me on the fighting line. / The doctor says I'm in bad condition, / But oh, oh, oh, I've got so much ambition, / I don't want to get well, I don't want to get well, / For I'm having a wonderful time.[23]

cut off by the Germans: "We got in a trap and staid in for seven days without anything to eat. You talk about a hard looking bunch. We sure were it. We were so weak we could hardly walk and we had to do some hard fighting to save our bacon. I do not know whether or not I looked as tough as the rest but I expect I did." James Slingerland, another Nevada boy, wrote, "They gave us hell and killed a lot of our boys, and we fought back all the time, keeping the Boches jumping."[24]

Survivors were already beginning to tell tall tales, amplifying their already astounding story with outright lies. Abe Krotoshinsky told how enemy officers "dressed up squads of Germans in American uniforms and tried to surprise us." Another of Whittlesey's soldiers told a gullible Nurse Hardon that the Germans "took one boy prisoner and cut his wrists and put poisoned rags on the cuts and sent him back to the captain telling him that they would all be treated the same way if they didn't surrender." In reality, the Germans treated their American prisoners with civility. A lone man from Captain Holderman's company crept down to the water hole to fill his canteen, but was shot during the attempt and disabled. Captain Rainsford told what happened to him: "There a bombing-party of the enemy later found him, dressed his wound with care, and offered him his choice of being carried back with them as a prisoner or left to be found by his friends. He chose the latter, and was known to the company as their best-bandaged casualty." Rainsford said it was simply an "act of chivalry."[25]

Legends began to grow. Privates in the little ruined La Chalade church began to talk about one of their lieutenants, claiming that he emerged from the siege "with eighteen machine gun bullet holes in his clothes, but without a scratch. He had one bruise from a bullet which had killed a man behind him. A machine gun fired at this lieutenant from a distance of thirty feet and the lieutenant's gas mask was cut away, but the officer was uninjured." Another rumor about the German surrender demand, quoted as "an unquestioned legend" (whatever that is!) by a *Stars and Stripes* reporter, claimed that "Major Whittlesey's answer was in three words on a piece of crumpled paper, wrapped around a stone, and thrown into the German lines, and that those three words were 'Go to hell.'" All of the legends, however, would be dwarfed by the tale of Cher Ami, the pigeon that carried Major Whittlesey's last message from the pocket. Although Cher Ami would make several additional flights, he was eventually shot, hopefully by *German* gunfire but one never knows, on October 27, while returning to division headquarters from the front. He was struck in the breast and lost a leg on this last mission. The New York press carried Cher Ami's story when he returned to the United States in 1919 aboard the *Ohioan*. But the public had become so enamored with the Lost Battalion story that facts were completely ignored and ever since, in both popular and scholarly lore, Cher Ami is said to have been nearly killed while heroically carrying the message that saved the Lost Battalion. He became the most famous bird in the world.[26]

While the stories began to grow, Captain Holderman took Company K off to rejoin the 307th and the machine gunners returned to their battalion, saying good-by to old friends from the past week. In the 308th Infantry, Lieutenant Cullen admitted to feeling "pretty tired and worn out," writing to business associates in New York that "sleeping in mud a couple of inches deep and eating bully beef and drinking coffee when you can get it, is not conducive to corpulency." The campaign had been tough on everyone. Ralph John explained that he had weighed 185 pounds on the day he left New York, but was down to 135 when admitted to a hospital about a week after being relieved. Private John gave an account of what he did at Depot de Machines: "We tried to shave but had only cold water and with three weeks whiskers on, besides plenty of clay that had massed on our faces, you can imagine what agony we went through with trying to scrape all this off with a safety razor. Some of the yells were like the coyotes back in Dakota. We got a clean bath and clean clothes. . . . Our underclothes were as stiff from dirt as if they had been starched." In addition to the physical comforts now enjoyed by Whittlesey's men, the sun was actually shining and John admitted, "Boy, did we feel wonderful."[27]

Newly commissioned Lieutenant Colonel Whittlesey was the only surviving officer from the First Battalion aside from Lieutenant Knight, but on the afternoon of October 8 regimental headquarters sent him twenty brand-spanking-new second lieutenants, "most of them a corking lot of fellows." Whittlesey assigned the most promising to command companies and set the rest up as platoon leaders. After Captain McMurtry's departure for the hospital, Captain J. H. Prentice from the 307th Infantry took over the Second Battalion of the 308th. He too was inundated by lieutenants, but his crowd at least included Karl Wilhelm, who showed up with his hand bandaged to assume command of Company E and noted that the Lost Battalion survivors "presented a hideous spectacle." Bodies were desperately needed at the front, so survivors of the Second Battalion were told to be ready to march early on October 9. One day of recuperation would have to suffice! A new lieutenant was given the unenviable task of waking some of them at 2 A.M. He remembered, "I felt I was taking my life in my hands to give them the news of the hike ahead of them. As I looked at them asleep, one on top of the other, on mud and stones, comfortable, despite all this, because

Survivors of the Lost Battalion photographed on October 12, 1918. From the National Archives.

Sure, a bit of shrapnel fell from out the sky
one day
  And it nestled in my shoulder in a quaint
  and loving way,
And when the doctor saw it, it looked so
sweet and fair,
  He said, "Suppose we leave it for it looks so
  peaceful there."
Then he painted it with iodine to keep the
germs away,
  It's the only way to treat it, no matter what
  they say.
But early the next morning he changed his
fickle mind,
  And he marked me down for duty and he
  sent me up the line.[28]

safe, I hesitated. It seemed a heartless thing to do." But orders were always orders, so he roused them for the march and was greatly surprised that "the men did not grumble nor was there a suspicion of hostility" as they hoisted their battle packs and started back north into the forest. The lieutenant did notice, however, that veterans from the Lost Battalion prudently carried "as much corned willy and hardtack as their packs could hold." Whittlesey received orders to assume command of the division reserve, a portion of which would be his old First Battalion. Those lucky men got two days of rest before going back to work.[29]

Events were already in motion to recognize publicly those who had performed "above and beyond the call of duty" during the siege. Lieutenant Colonel Whittlesey was by now an international celebrity. After a few days with the division reserve, followed by a couple of weeks at regimental headquarters performing "some regular lieutenant coloneling," as he put it, Whittlesey was off for America. Reaching New York in mid-November, just after the Armistice, he found himself proclaimed America's greatest war hero, a role that made him extremely uncomfortable. His first priority was a trip to Pittsfield, Massachusetts, for a reunion with his parents, Mr. and Mrs. Frank Whittlesey. Only then did the shy warrior return to New York City for the adulation awaiting him. Classmates from Williams College hounded him into making an appearance at a special "War Night" affair on November 21. When F. T. Woods, president of the alumni club, introduced Whittlesey (Class of 1905) that night, he referred to the "Go to hell" message, saying, "It was a command, a malediction and a prophecy combined." But the lieutenant colonel refused to talk about himself.[30]

Although Charles Whittlesey would become the international symbol of his Lost Battalion, he preferred to share that honor with others. A New York Sun reporter frantically scribbled down his remarks, as Whittlesey shared a personal observation: "You don't hear enough of the enlisted men in France. I'm afraid we didn't think much about them at first. They were just ordinary American boys when they went over, but now they've changed and the officers have adopted a different attitude toward them. I can't describe the fondness that we acquired for them as we saw them day after day doing their work without complaint. It makes you proud of America to think of these common soldiers of ours. And remember that those who have been picked out for special praise are the symbols of the men behind them. No man does anything alone. It's the chaps you don't hear about that make possible the deeds you do hear about." No matter how hard members of the audience tried to coax him into talking about his experience in leading the Lost Battalion, Whittlesey assumed his typical reticence and refused to say anything further.[31]

Lieutenant Colonel Whittlesey would later offer a public tribute to the officers and men of the Lost Battalion: "In a forest in northeastern France in a cold and damp October, without rations, without surgical attention, cut off, as they supposed, from the notice of their fellow men, they gave to the day's hardships and duties a courage and plain human kindness that will always make one proud of the record of the American soldier. Such achievements are not attributable to any officer or group of officers or leaders. They arise from brave men working unselfishly together with faith in the cause which they serve. When an individual shows courage under stress, we feel a thrill at his achievement, but when a group of men flash out in the splendor of manliness we feel a lasting glow that is both pride and renewed faith in our fellow man." Whittlesey concluded his tribute by writing, "I feel a bond of understanding and fellowship for the American soldier in every place and every time, doing his job simply and finely, asking neither sympathy nor praise."[32]

American civilians did not understand the military mentality and needed heroes to help them reconcile the country's staggering loss during the last three months of the war. Whittlesey would do quite nicely. He had been in line to command a new regiment, but the end to fighting led to his honorable discharge at Camp Dix on December 5 as the army began to implement plans for demobilization. That same day, the War Department announced its first list of men to win the Medal of Honor in the Great War, former Lieutenant Colonel Whittlesey and Captain George McMurtry being two of those recipients. The commander of the Lost Battalion would officially be presented his medal in Boston Common on Christmas Eve, 1918, by Major General Clarence Edwards, commander of the Northeast Department.[33]

Now a certified war hero, Whittlesey was invited to speak on December 15 at a Union Peace Jubilee hosted by an association of New York Episcopal churches at the Sixty-ninth Regiment Armory. Secretary of the Treasury William McAdoo spoke first, but the crowd estimated to number at least six thousand had come to see and hear the Medal of Honor winner. Presented by the event's chairman as "a modern Cincinnatus who had laid aside his sword to go back to the pursuits of peace," Whittlesey was greeted by a standing ovation. Dressed in civilian clothes, he "stood uneasily, shifting his weight from one foot to the other waiting for the enthusiastic outburst to subside." He then spoke from the heart: "The American soldiers are not going to come back hating the Germans. No man who has been out in the front line trenches facing the enemy is going to return with malice in his heart. The paramount trait of the American soldier is kindliness. If he met the Kaiser on the road he would be as willing to share his cigarette with him as with anyone else." Whittlesey continued, "Mind you, I do not want to let the Germans off too easily. I merely want to see justice done. Germany after the war, it must be remembered, is going to be part of our world community." The audience, which had come to hear a rousing war tale, sat in stunned silence. Blushing at this unexpected reaction, Whittlesey vowed to keep silent on the war and thereafter would attend Liberty Loan drives or Red Cross fundraisers only if he could avoid making speeches. But he did not shy away from unpopular topics. Writing in the *New Republic* on the subject of military pre-paredness in the United States, Whittlesey argued against pacifism and said bluntly, "As an infantry officer who saw the simple realities of training and fighting with the man of the line, I know, with a certainty which needs no reinforcing, that America was unprepared, even at the end!"[34]

While Charles Whittlesey was making an uneasy adjustment to civilian life, men from his command still had to close out the war. The Liberty Division continued crashing through the Argonne on its impetuous course toward the Meuse River and Sedan. By October 10, the Germans had been pushed out of the Argonne Forest and the Seventy-seventh Division was sprinting toward the towns of St. Juvin and Grand Pré on the Aire River, both of which were firmly in American hands by October 16. General Alexander's division was then relieved by the Seventy-eighth Division and withdrew for rest and reorgani-zation in corps reserve until called upon for the final American drive on November 1. This latest advance had not been without cost to Lost Battalion survivors, some of whom sustained wounds that finally ended their days of combat. Slightly wounded in the pocket, Corporal Arthur Doherty was hit again, this time by German shrapnel on October 11. Sidney Foss emerged unscathed from Charlevaux Valley only to be seriously wounded in the attack on Grand Pré. About that same time Ralph John inhaled mustard gas and was evacuated. He remembered being "so badly burned I couldn't see and could hardly walk" and "felt as if I were on fire all inside and outside too." He finished the war in a Bordeaux hospital. John Nell had been gassed shortly after the relief, then came down with influenza because of his weakened respiratory system. While in the hospital, safely tucked away from the constant terror at the front, Nell confessed that he "came very near to having a complete nervous and mental breakdown." He tried to relax, but complained that "the sights and sounds I had lived with for the past weeks all came back to me." Flashbacks to those horrors in the pocket would torment him for the rest of his life.[35]

Events spun dizzily towards a conclusion of the war, rumors of an armistice circulating freely for about a month before a surrender document was actually signed. Taking its place again in the front line, the Liberty Division joined the great American push to the Meuse River. Doughboys began passing through dozens of French towns with unpronounceable names, occasionally riding in trucks, but always part of a torrent of Americans pouring toward Germany. Corps headquarters announced a race to the Meuse and a new brigade commander predicted that if "any damned brigade in the American Army" got through, this one would!" Exhausted and hungry men would pay the price for generals' egos. The last attack by Charles Whittlesey's old First Battalion occurred at 6:30 A.M. on November 5 near the village of Stonne. It was not an easy one. An artillery liaison officer was killed, the supporting 37mm gun broke down, and one of two machine guns was destroyed by an enemy shell, yet by noon, despite moderate enemy resistance, the 308th Infantry had captured the town. The only two German prisoners had been taken by Private Earle Wolfe, a Lost Battalion man from Company C. Held in reserve thereafter, men from the 308th contented themselves with raiding German gardens. On November 7 in Haraucourt there was a grand feast of German food—boiled turnips, cabbages and beets, served up with thousands of loaves of pumpernickel bread. Scuttlebutt of a German surrender swept through the division, but so many rumors had failed to come true that this latest "news" was completely dismissed. Precisely at eleven o'clock on the morning of November 11, the war came to an end. Brought to a state of complete indifference to anything, weary soldiers refused to believe the announcement and then displayed little emotion when the story was confirmed by division headquarters. One soldier commented that "reaction to the news was not of a startling nature," explaining, "we uttered no shrieks of joy, we waved no flags, we flourished no bunting, and we made no comments on the salvation of the world." What the veterans did was simply resume normal operations, "some picking up cigarette butts, some peeling potatoes, some grooming horses, some sweeping out billets, some saluting officers, some cursing the army, and some cursing each other." It was almost as if no one cared.[36]

Oh, won't it be great to get back to the States,
And back to home life again;
To be able to go to a telephone
And call up a regular Jane.

To be able to sit and look in her eyes,
While you tell her of No Man's Land,
And to know she believes you're not telling her lies,
By the way she is squeezing your hand.[37]

The rest of November was spent marching hither and yon across northern France until the Seventy-seventh Division finally reached its assigned training area near Chaumont in the Haut-Marne Department. One soldier said that here, "for the first time in the history of training, drill was superseded by soap." Once the men were clean and free of cooties, police details scoured the streets and villages. Then came a barrage of "countless memoranda and bulletins," telling veterans the proper way to assault a machine gun and how to act during a gas attack, lessons that had already been learned in actual service. General Headquarters ordered an endless series of combat scenarios and always seemed pleased with the results. Officers and soldiers listened attentively to instructions, then ignored the silly exercises.[38]

There had been talk of the Liberty Division being home for Christmas, but that proved to be just another latrine rumor. Thanks to a $5,000 donation from the 308th Infantry Association, that regiment had a superb Christmas

Company Commander: Hostile band of wild women sighted on horizon to the south. What to do?
Battalion Commander: Capture and hold women. Battalion PC will be located there.[39]

holiday. Representatives of the various service agencies assigned to the Seventy-seventh Division scoured France for delicacies for a huge Christmas celebration. Village church bells tolled out carols, while French children danced around "real Christmas trees gayly decorated with swinging lanterns, paper dolls, puppets, cornucopias full of candy, cakes, and various dainties, and an individual present for each child." Doughboys watched sporting events during the day and enjoyed entertainers imported from Paris for the evening. The absolute best part of the holiday was Christmas dinner. Liberty Boys of the 308th Infantry had apparently cornered the entire turkey market in that region of France, which, "added to what the limitless ingenuity of fifteen unscrupulous mess sergeants could devise," made dinner "little short of heaven." On Christmas Day, President Wilson came to Langres to watch picked companies of the Seventy-seventh Division march by, another one of those "firsts" that the Liberty Boys always boasted about, this affair being "the first time that American troops passed in review before, and were addressed by, a President of the United States on foreign soil."[40]

Following the Armistice, there was much to tidy up. General Evan Johnson had considered court-martialing Whittlesey on some trumped-up charge to rehabilitate his own reputation. No one in authority would authorize such a rash act against America's most famous war hero. Jealous Regular Army officers had little use for Whittlesey, but they were unwilling to risk their own careers by taking a public stand against the Plattsburg graduate. Lieutenant Maurice Revnes was not so fortunate. He was hauled before a court-martial in January 1919 and charged with a violation of the Seventy-fifth Article of War. Specifically, it was alleged that he did "misbehave himself before the enemy, in that he sought to induce Major (now Lieutenant Colonel) Charles W. Whittlesey, 308th Infantry, then and there commanding, shamefully to surrender himself, and the force of which he was in command, to the enemy." The court, composed of officers from the Seventy-seventh Division, found Revnes guilty of the charge, although it agreed that he had not done so "shamefully," and sentenced him to be dismissed from the service. Copies of the court's paperwork were forwarded to General Pershing's headquarters for review. The conviction of Revnes was overturned at army headquarters by the following endorsement: "In the foregoing case of 2d Lieut. Maurice S. Revnes, 306th Machine Gun Battalion, the evidence shows that the accused gallantly performed his duty for many days under the most trying circumstances; that he was wounded and had for a long time been without food. The sentence is disapproved."[41]

Among those testifying at the Revnes court-martial were McMurtry, Holderman, and several enlisted men who had been with the Lost Battalion. Whereas Whittlesey's receipt of the Medal of Honor had been front-page news around the world, McMurtry admitted during testimony that he learned of his own Medal of Honor from brother officers who had read a notice of it in the newspaper. Regimental headquarters somewhat belatedly confirmed his award. As for Whittlesey, he knew full well that his friend deserved that medal and would always say, "I don't know what I would have done without Captain George C. McMurtry." Captain Holderman would have to wait until 1921 for his Medal of Honor. It would come only after an impassioned plea from Whittlesey, describing how Holderman, "though wounded early in the siege and suffering great pain continued throughout the entire period leading and encouraging the officers and men under his command." On October 6, "he rushed through enemy machine gun and shell fire, and carried two wounded comrades to a place of safety." Next day, during the last attack, Captain Holderman and another man, armed only with pistols and captured enemy grenades, succeeded in driving off a German platoon that tried to encircle Company K. When informed by the War Department that his recommendation for Holderman's medal had been approved, Whittlesey said it was "the finest news in the world."[42]

A number of other soldiers received Distinguished Service Crosses, including Lieutenants Cullen, Schenck, and Rogers; James Bragg and Irving Sirota from the medical detachment; and the three men who had successfully escaped from the pocket on October 7, Krotoshinsky, Brown, and Kozikowski. Sixteen other enlisted men received a DSC Lieutenants Eager, Griffin, and Williamson were cited in division orders as "having distin-

Doughboy Definition:
D. S. C.—"Decent Suit of Civvies"[43]

guished themselves by gallant and meritorious conduct," along with a bunch of sergeants, corporals, and privates. Many of these honors were made posthumously. Some men entitled to similar recognition were overlooked because no officer from their company had survived to certify their courageous conduct. Company B seems to be underrepresented because of the death of Lieutenant Rogers and his successor, Sergeant Osborne. Not a single machine gunner received so much as a mention, due not to their lack of devotion to duty but rather to the fact that Lieutenants Peabody and Noon had been killed, while Revnes, in addition to his shattered foot, had his legal problems. Most of those who received awards would have agreed with Irving Liner, who confessed, "I don't remember doing anything so wonderful."[44]

In January, Liberty Boys received shoulder patches for their uniforms, appropriately the Statue of Liberty embroidered in yellow on a blue ground. V-shaped gold chevrons for wounds and foreign service were also passed out. Each chevron worn on the right sleeve represented one wound, while a chevron on the left sleeve indicated six months served overseas. Soldiers from other divisions ridiculed the new Statue of Liberty shoulder patch. One man from the Rainbow Division exclaimed, "I thought it was a French Mademoiselle with a candle huntin' for your 'Lost Battalion!'"[45]

General Pershing reviewed the Seventy-seventh Division on February 24. It was a grand affair, all of that panoply of war that civilians go crazy over, with the great general first riding by the assembled troops, then dismounting and inspecting each company. After the inspection, Pershing presented Distinguished Service Crosses to 126 officers and men. At the command, "Pass in Review," Henry Smith told how the various units, "after standing all day, with just a bacon sandwich to sustain us," formed for the procession that would march by the commanding general and his staff. Everyone witnessing the show pronounced it an unqualified success. Those doing the marching had another perspective, since the review ground had recently been stripped of vegetation and plowed. Smith noticed that "the men in the infantry regiments, trying to keep rifles on shoulders, were floundering and falling in all directions. Sometimes bayonets came down first into the ground and it was a wonder that somebody wasn't hurt."[46]

An officer said that "the period of demobilization was fast developing into a period of demoralization" as soldiers continued military life with no apparent purpose. So many men went on sick call that one artillery officer complained in exasperation that they should have taken the company guidon with them. An enlisted man explained how bored soldiers passed their time, "We stood inspections galore; we stood in the mud for mess; and we stood guard over every stick and stone and every well in Dancevoir. We discussed the chances of getting home, discussed the futility of drilling, and discussed the villainy of the officers."[47]

Sick of the smell of billets –
Sick of the chow—
Wanta leave France and put on long pants!
Wanta go NOW!![48]

After an eternity of drill, athletics, and inspections, the order finally came for the Seventy-seventh Division to go home. The 308th Infantry and a good chunk of the 307th Infantry embarked on April 19, 1919, aboard the aptly named *America*, a confiscated German liner, which was anchored in the harbor at Brest. Among those who gathered along the rail and watched the French shoreline recede into the distance was Lee McCollum of Company A, 308th Infantry. He offered his impressions of the moment: "Laughingly we had first boarded these boats bound for France, youth looking for adventure, soldiers on parade. Now less than a year later we were returning home no longer laughing, light-hearted boys in our 'teens and early twenties, but men old beyond our years. Each of us was bringing home an uninvited guest, a guest that would live with us through the rest of our days, who would sit with us at our tables and would wake us from our earned nights of rest, to force us to walk step by step with him, over and over again, across the battlefields of France."[49]

Following nine days at sea that no one seems to have said much about, boys aboard the *America* caught sight of Rockaway Point and Coney Island and screamed out, "Land! Land!!" just as fervently as sailors under Christopher Columbus had done. When their ship passed by the Statue of Liberty, many soldiers waved to her and shouted, "You'll never see me again, lady, unless you do an about face!" The ship docked at Hoboken, where excited doughboys streamed down gangplanks to the cheers of tens of thousands of relatives who waved from behind a large screen fence. Occasionally, a soldier would recognize a face in the throng and race to the fence to exchange kisses with a wife or girlfriend. Most of the men just waited in long lines to board the ferryboats that would convey them to Long Island City, where trains would carry them to Camp Mills. After being assigned to barracks, the men went through a final delousing (politely referred to as a "sanitation process" in the States) and received two-day passes. It was a joyous time for all.[50]

While enjoying these two days of freedom, overseas veterans heard how their families had been

Home, boys, home, is the place we want to be,
Home, boys, home, in the land of liberty,
Then we'll hoist Old Glory to the top of the pole,
And all enlist again, in a pig's asshole!!![51]

"crammed full of bunk" about the war in France. They tried to explain what had really happened, but quickly discovered that the civilians "resented having the myths exploded. They wanted to believe the foolish and improbable things they did believe." So it was with the Lost Battalion. General Alexander said of it, "This command was neither 'lost' nor 'rescued'" and "Major Whittlesey and his command held the position to which they had proceeded under my order and were found by me on the very early morning of Oct. 8, an organized command, in good order, and in excellent spirits." George McMurtry would later argue, "Our regimental, brigade and division headquarters always knew exactly where we were." He then explained why: "As soon as we reached our objective we sent several written messages back by way of our runner posts before they were shot up, and after we were surrounded by the enemy we sent five messages back by carrier pigeons, and every one of these messages clearly stated the correct map co-ordinates of our position." Eventually, even General Pershing would be called upon for his opinion and he would conclude that "the battalion was not lost in the sense that we did not know where it was. It was cut off." No one in America wanted to listen to any debunking of the Lost Battalion myth. Nor did anyone admit the awful truth that Whit-tlesey's courageous stand had played no part in the ultimate success of General Pershing's Meuse-Argonne campaign. Although troops from the Lost Battalion had successfully repulsed attacks by some second-rate German units (portions of the 252nd and 254th Reserve Infantry, 122nd Landwehr, a squad of storm troopers, and a collection of hastily-summoned pioneer companies), relief could not, and did not, come until other divisions forced the enemy withdrawal.[52]

Upon reaching New York, Chaplain Halligan went to the 308th Infantry Association, where he spoke to "a sad and brave little company" of mothers and wives of the dead and missing. The ladies talked with Halligan individually, each hoping for some scrap of information about what had happened to her boy or husband. Aside from lengthy typewritten lists of names and burial sites, the chaplain could offer little comfort. He told relatives of the Lost Battalion dead, "Few of the boys had an opportunity to send any last messages. They were all trying so hard to keep up their courage for the sake of comrades lying beside them. They kept their pain to themselves and their knowledge that they were going west when they were aware of this, which was not always, so as not to lower the courage of their comrades. We can all be proud of their gameness for I don't know a single one of those boys who did not play the game to the last minute." Grieving widows and mothers had waited months for even this bit of news and all seemed satisfied with Chaplain Halligan's kindness.[53]

Family members were afraid that their boys had been corrupted by army life and would retain the worst traits of a soldier—a vigorously profane language, a desire to steal anything a man desired, the twin addictions of gambling and drunkenness, and even a tendency for senseless violence. Chaplain Halligan rushed to assure them that the veterans would be fine and that the doughboy was "a reverent being toward God. He may be blasphemous toward other things—and he really doesn't mean it—but never toward God. We know him in the front line when God and the doughboy are close to each other. There the soldier is stripped of the trimmings of civilian life and he comes to just the essential things of life." Unerring in his judgment of other soldiers, a doughboy from the Liberty Division always respected another man's religious beliefs and expected the same tolerance in return. Major Joseph Fogerty said that the war had "not stifled religion in them, nor is it a foundation for predictions of a religious revival," although the old soldiers would be a problem for organized religions of every denomination. Now they would filter doctrines, dogma, and sermons according to "the true underlying values they discovered in the presence of death."[54]

Fogarty predicted "there will be no wave of dissipation, no overflow of immorality and drunkenness," even during a short period of celebration, because the doughboys had returned as better men. American mothers had watched their sons march off in 1917, half-afraid "they would come back brutalized by the things they would have to do and see." But instead, soldiers had found "a faith in humanity they never knew before." They had learned to love and missed the warmth and tenderness of America. Fogerty insisted, "I do know that every last man of us pictures paradise in his own mother's home or in the home some girl is going to help him establish and cannot for one moment see himself separating from that fireside." Veterans from the Argonne would never again take anything for granted and had learned the immense value of those little things in life—a drink of cold water—a bed—a bite of food. After what they had been through, America seemed to be heaven on earth.[55]

That idealized vision of home would soon lead to widespread disappointment. Lee J. Levenger, a New York chaplain, captured the essence of the combat experience on French battlefields: "For the fact is that the soldiers, especially those who have gone through the actual fighting, have achieved a brief but intense glimpse into the eternal mysteries of life and death. Without their own desire they have come face to face with God. They have dropped, for a time, thought of social distinctions, of money and what it can buy, of luxury, of comfort even; they have lived like beasts of prey, burrowing into the ground for shelter, killing that they might live, caring for little except enough food to keep themselves alive and for their precious steel helmets and gas masks and their still more precious rifles. They have seen their friends die by their side and have gone forward, carrying on as soldiers must." To counter this intense experience, scared young men created an ideal remembrance of a home that had never really existed. The reality of civilian life with family and friends in America would prove to be dull and commonplace. Of course, there would be physical comforts, but there would not be, nor could there be, any true sympathy or understanding for veterans of the war.[56]

After a few days of idleness at Camp Mills, it was time for a parade. Victorious armies always paraded and New Yorkers wanted to see their sons marching in a monstrous homecoming spectacle. As for the soldiers, they detested "the idea of being heroes on parade." When a reporter asked one company of veterans, "Do you fellows want to parade?" the response was "a volley of no's." In spite of their aversion to hiking through city streets, the public got its parade. Over one million spectators gathered on May 6 to watch the Seventy-seventh Division, New York's Own, march over the five-mile route. Precisely at 10 A.M., General Robert Alexander, "mounted on a beautiful black horse and looking for all the world as proud as a conquering Caesar," started up Fifth Avenue. More than twenty-five thousand soldiers emerged from the side streets, moved effortlessly into column, following their commander and "turning the great highway into a river running bank-full with olive drab and steel." The men marched in massed formation, filling the wide thoroughfare from curb to curb, at 128 steps per minute, the entire division passing by in just under forty-five minutes. One veteran remembered, "The day was clear and cool, the pace was brisk, and the men marched with superb snap and swing. Sidewalks and grandstands which extended along the entire route were filled with proud relatives and friends who cheered lustily as the regiments tramped by with bands playing, the colors fluttering in the breeze and the artillery's guidons gleaming in the sun."[57]

One civilian noted that the parade was "human rather than military" and "the boys forgot how to march." He explained: "They were home, and were glad to show it. Their faces were aglow. Happiness was reflected in every sun-browned face." Soldiers did an "Eyes left!" at the reviewing stand on the steps of the Public Library on Forty-second Street, catching a glimpse of what some of them thought were "tawdry" military decorations adorning the building. After passing Central Park, where huge grandstands had been erected, General Alexander turned aside and reviewed the troops as they passed by for the last time. The grand parade ended at 116th Street where units disbanded and took subway cars to their original rendezvous points. Next morning those from the West would be sent home for discharge, while soldiers from New York and the eastern states would report to Camp Upton.[58]

Camp Upton was not the same. One veteran machine gunner remarked sadly, "Now it was peopled by strangers who were not interested in us, particularly, and somehow there was a feeling that the old camp had

And we'll grin, grin, grin,
While we're marching down the Avenue,
Grin, grin, grin,
When the crowd begins to yell
For the 77th's home again,
Nevermore to roam again,
Loosen up your jaws a bit and grin like hell.

So we'll grin, grin, grin,
While the girls we love are loving us;
Grin, grin, grin,
With the girlies we adore.
Think of sunny France again,
Dance and sing, and dance again,
Grin because we'll never have to go there any more.[59]

slipped from us and that we didn't belong." There were also too many memories associated with Camp Upton, too many friends who had been bosom buddies during those training days, who now occupied graves in France. But the last night in barracks was identical to that first night way back in September of 1917. Rowdies threw shoes, brooms, and pieces of equipment at random targets. Anyone caught dozing off became the victim of a vicious pummeling. Bunks mysteriously collapsed on their occupants. Men were wrapped into mattresses and tossed downstairs amid hoots of laughter. A barrage of tasteless body noises, screams, animal calls, and whizzbang imitations filled the air. Men who chattered like a machine gun found themselves stalked by the numbers and rushed by a gang of roughnecks. These were no longer the Argonne veterans who had wallowed in blood and gore while trying to carry out impossible assignments. The boys of 1917 had come home.[60]

FADING AWAY

In the public mind, Charles Whittlesey became the human symbol of the Lost Battalion story and he was showered with honors. At the annual commencement exercises for Harvard University held on June 19, 1919, Whittlesey received an honorary Master of Arts Degree. Four days later he accepted a similar award from Williams College, his alma mater. When veterans from the 308th Infantry organized an American Legion Post with headquarters in the old Astor Library on Lafayette Street, Whittlesey's name was on the roster. He returned to his former law partnership, but in 1920 became an associate with the firm of White and Case, which had more work in his chosen specialty of banking law. Most of his spare time was devoted to veterans' issues. Feeling obligated to those common soldiers who still suffered because of wartime trauma, Whittlesey acted as chairman of the Red Cross Roll Call in New York. Requests for him to appear numbered in the thousands and he made as many appearances as possible so as not to disappoint ex-soldiers and their families. These constant reminders of the war began to take a toll, but the public would not allow Charles Whittlesey to make a successful transition to civilian life.[1]

There was an odd attempt to retell the Lost Battalion story in a silent film that showed in the summer of 1919. A mixture of documentary footage and fictionalized script, *The Lost Battalion*, in an attempt to portray the events realistically, employed a number of the veterans as actors. Among those playing themselves in the film were Robert Alexander, Charles Whittlesey, George McMurtry, William Cullen, Arthur McKeogh, Philip Cepaglia, Abraham Krotoshinsky, Jack Hershkowitz, and John Monson. The film, produced by Edward A. MacManus, was first screened for Lost Battalion survivors in the Ritz Carlton ballroom on the evening of July 2. It began with men from every stratum of New York society as they walked into the "recruiting offices" as the division came into being at Yaphank. In addition to soldiers, there were society maidens and stenographers: "Each had a service star close to their hearts and after fevered knitting and anxious waiting they all shared in the honor and glory of the victory." Everyone seemed pleased with the production. When the film was released publicly in September, a reviewer for the *New York Times* wrote a scathing critique. He enjoyed the first part of the movie that dealt with the soldiers being gathered together at Camp Upton, saying that portion was "uncommonly interesting and well-made." But he found the reproduction of Argonne battle scenes to be "an elaborate and painstaking fabrication, . . . unconvincing and, considering the materials at hand, surprisingly undramatic." The reviewer said that director Burton King "appears to have labored under the impression that the beleaguered battalion fired continuously for six days." He concluded his review with the observation that George McMurtry could be spotted "darting through the shell-swept pocket in extraordinarily flossy and shiny boots." Despite the use of actual veterans, *The Lost Battalion* was a flop in New York, although American Legion posts across the country embraced the movie as a proven fundraiser for many years. In Gastonia, North Carolina, the film was advertised as "the greatest picture of its kind—an epoch in screen history," while in Ironwood, Michigan, it was hailed as "the world's most astounding picture."[2]

Memories of the war came crashing back to Whittlesey on July 12, 1921, when the New York press reported that John J. Monson, recent movie actor and one of the men who had received a Distinguished Service Cross for bringing relief to Whittlesey's command when first cut off in the Argonne, was awaiting burial in Potter's Field on Blackwells Island. After receiving his discharge from the 308th Infantry, Monson enlisted in Company A, Sixty-first Infantry and was stationed at Camp Jackson, South Carolina. In March of 1921 he returned to New York

282 BLOOD IN THE ARGONNE

City on furlough, but fell ill there with tuberculosis, a complication of being gassed during the war. Whittlesey's old runner was taken first to New York Hospital, then transferred to Bellevue, where he died on July 8 without mentioning his wartime service to the hospital staff. When no one claimed the body, Monson's remains were taken to the city morgue, where they lay for four days. The identity of this forgotten man was finally established through a box of medals that were included in some effects that he had requested be sent to a former landlady.

As though embarrassed by this tawdry treatment of a former war hero, New Yorkers fell all over themselves to honor a hometown war hero who had come so close to being buried in an unknown grave. Although he was technically a deserter at the time of his death, the army expedited some paperwork so that Monson could be buried in Cypress Hills National Cemetery. Officers from Governors Island provided a uniform and casket, as well as a caisson pulled by a team of black horses, a firing squad, and bugler to play "Taps" over the grave. Floral arrangements from total strangers packed the Church of the Ascension. Official delegations from organizations as diverse as the Knights of Columbus, Longshoreman's Union, and the Daughters of the Grand Army of the Republic attended a mass and listened to Chaplain James J. Halligan's eulogy. Members of the 308th Infantry Post of the American Legion packed the pews. It was an impressive sendoff for poor John Monson, who, according to one *New York Times* reader, was just one of "the sick, the wounded, the insane young veterans who are lost in the No Man's Land of our ignorance, indifference and neglect." Charles Whittlesey got up from a sick bed to attend Monson's funeral and walked directly behind the hearse in the cortege. Friends said this was typical of Whittlesey, risking his own life to pay tribute to a common soldier.[3]

Only one month later, Whittlesey felt compelled to accept command of the newly reorganized 308th Infantry, United States Army Reserve, another reminder of the horrible events of the Great War. Repeatedly forced to confront memories of his combat service in official capacities, Whittlesey turned into America's most reluctant warrior. Colonel Nathan Averill, his old commander, said of him, "Constantly called upon for aid and advice by the mothers and widows of the dead and missing, he gave everything he had, everything that was in him—not only to them but to all the men of the regiment, wounded and in trouble—who found in him a ready friend, counselor and aid." Unable to leave behind the horrors of the battlefield, a deep depression settled over the sensitive officer. Work for the Red Cross left him immersed "in a sea of woe," where he would "go to two or three funerals every week, visit the wounded in the hospitals, and try to comfort the relatives of the dead."[4]

This depression would be intensified following events that occurred on October 24, 1921, in the city hall of Chalons-sur-Marne, France. At eleven o'clock in the morning, Sergeant Edward F. Younger, a wounded and decorated soldier from the United States Army of Occupation who had fought in the Chateau-Thierry, St. Mihiel, Somme, and Meuse-Argonne campaigns, entered a room containing four identical steel gray caskets, sitting atop flag-draped shipping cases. Each casket contained the remains of an unknown American soldier exhumed from the cemeteries at Belleau Wood, Bony, Thiaucourt, and Romagne-sous-Montfaucon. By the time Sergeant Younger arrived, all paperwork relating to the exhumations had been burned and the bodies and caskets had been repeatedly mixed so that no trace of their origin remained. Carrying a bouquet of white roses, Sergeant Younger circled the caskets three times, then suddenly stopped and placed the flowers over the body of what would thenceforward be known as America's Unknown Soldier.

The soldier selected by Younger was removed and placed in an ebony and silver coffin, bearing the eloquent inscription: "An Unknown American Who Gave His Life in the World War." After lying in state for several hours, a huge funeral cortege marched to the village railroad station, where a special train waited to carry the Unknown to Havre, at which point he would be transferred to the *Olympia* for the long voyage to America. The *Olympia* reached Washington Navy Yard on November 9 and the Unknown was taken to the United States Capitol where he lay in state for two days. On Armistice Day, November 11, President Warren G. Harding pinned a Medal of Honor on the flag-covered coffin just before it was interred in Arlington Cemetery on a hill overlooking Washington, D.C. Among those who participated in this impressive ceremony was Lieutenant Colonel Charles W. Whittlesey, who returned home "deeply affected" by the ceremony. A family friend said, "He was the sort of man who would say: 'Look at that poor fellow, and think of all the poor boys who were killed. What right have I to be alive?'" Whittlesey was undoubtedly tormented by the possibility that the Unknown Soldier might be one of his own men, maybe even the youngster who had died in his arms.[5]

Each life must have its crosses,
And a soldier gets his share.
From a trip across the ocean
To the envied Croix de Guerre.

There are crosses by the Censor
Far too many, so it seems;
There are crosses in the letters
From the girlie of his dreams.

There's a cross that's worn by heroes,
Who have faced a storm of lead;
There's a cross when he is wounded,
There's a cross when he is dead.[6]

On November 20, Whittlesey attended a reception for Marshal Ferdinand Foch at the New York Hippodrome, sharing the stage with crippled men missing arms and legs. He was in poor health, suffering from what others described as "a racking cough" that often awoke other residents in his home. By Wednesday, November 23, Whittlesey knew what he must do. He called in a stenographer and dictated a will, in which he left all his property to his mother.

Whittlesey stayed late at work that night, bringing up to date all the paperwork relating to a dozen law cases on which he had been working. Next day was Thanksgiving and he spent the holiday afternoon with the family of John B. Pruyn, his former law partner, and seemed to be "in unusually cheerful spirits." On Friday, he walked to the American Express Office on Broadway and purchased a ticket to Havana on board the United Fruit Company ship *Taloa*. That afternoon, Whittlesey telephoned his housekeeper and asked that his breakfast be ready at 8 A.M. next morning, telling her, "I'm going away to be alone for a few days. I am tired." Although a confirmed bachelor, he took a lady friend to the theater before going home.

Shortly after the *Taloa* left port on Saturday, Whittlesey presented himself to Captain Farquhar Grant, who remembered that they talked about an hour during the day, mostly about the Army–Navy football game that was being played that afternoon. The lieutenant colonel was apparently an avid football fan and never missed an important game unless called away by urgent business. He ate at the captain's table that evening, then wandered into the smoking room where he struck up a conversation with a businessman from Cuba named Maloret. A veteran of the Puerto Rican campaign during the Spanish-American War, Maloret recalled that Whittlesey "had none of the bearing of a man with a heavy load on his mind" and "spoke of the war with apparent calmness." The two men had a drink together, then, after about an hour, the conversation lagged. At 11:15, Whittlesey abruptly arose, said, "Good night," and left the smoking room. He walked calmly to the ship's rail engulfed in a heavy fog, the same kind of fog that had hung so thickly over the hillside in Charlevaux Valley. Then Lieutenant Colonel Charles W. Whittlesey, war hero, Medal of Honor recipient, and tormented soul, stepped overboard to join the dead of the Lost Battalion.[7]

Whittlesey's suicide was front-page news in the United States. Total strangers expressed shock and horror at his sudden demise, but those who knew him best were not surprised. He had kept too much bottled up inside for far too long until he could no longer stand the pain and anguish. Old comrades and college friends naturally held a public memorial service, with members of the Lost Battalion helping to swell the crowd. Everyone agreed with Colonel Averill, who said that he was "convinced that his death was in reality a battle casualty and that he met his end as much in the line of duty as if he had fallen by a German bullet on the Vesle or in the Argonne." Averill added, "The scars of conflict or the wounds of battle are not always of the flesh." The colonel concluded his remarks with a fervent prayer that "God, who in His Infinite Wisdom saw fit to take from our midst Charles Whittlesey, may give to his soul that peace and quiet for which he so longed."[8]

William Cullen rendered the most heartfelt eulogy of his former commander: "Citizen Whittlesey, helping a deceased soldier's family, visiting a wounded buddy in a hospital, hurrying to the assistance of a man in trouble or conducting a drive for some auxiliary—out of the army, true, but still in the service. No shell-racked towns nor war-torn roads, nor midnight marches, nor late patrols, but empty sleeves and missing limbs or steel-braced members tautly held, and the sturdy heart of America's son cracks in the presence of the greater price. The grim determination that scorned an enemy's insolent request quailed in contemplation of neglected comrades. Envious of their plight and disappointed in that he was not permitted to pay an equal price—Citizen Whittlesey died—but to his comrades, Whittlesey, 308th Infantry, is just missing in action."[9]

By the time of Charles Whittlesey's death, some of his old comrades had already been disinterred and returned to America. Dead soldiers from the Lost Battalion had originally been buried where they fell, although Pioneer squads had dug them up for reburial in a small plot of ground at the bottom of Charlevaux Valley, identities being listed with the Graves Registration Service. Early in 1919, the Quartermaster Corps began the arduous task of consolidating American bodies from French battlefields into large, centrally-located cemeteries. Remains from the Charlevaux graveyard were dug up again and trucked ten miles to the Meuse–Argonne Cemetery at Romagne-sous-Montfaucon, the majority being buried for a third time in Plot B. But grieving families wanted their dead boys close by, so many dozens were exhumed once again during the early 1920s and shipped to and scattered all across America for a fourth burial. That is why Benjamin Hofstetter and Samuel Jolly are buried in Arlington National Cemetery; Ancel Fassett is now in Keokuk, Iowa; Arthur Jones lies in French Creek Cemetery in Chautauqua County, New York; David Gladd rests in Cypress Hills National Cemetery; and Thomas J. Lyon waits for Judgment Day in Bethany Baptist Church Cemetery in McCormick County, South Carolina.[10]

"A noble death," you say? Ah, well –
But I'm his mother, and my tears
Blot out all thought of how he fell,
Or where. Dear God! his tender years . . .

My boy! The first dread shock of grief
Has left my heart a thing of lead.
What matters Country; what Belief?
What matters anything? He's dead![11]

Owen Wister visited the battlefields and cemeteries of France in 1921 and bemoaned the fate of these transplanted American war dead, so many of whom had been "dispersed over a wide continent that did not witness their sacrifice or share their conflict. They lie apart from each other, instead of in a place consecrated especially to them, and they will be inevitably forgotten when those who mourn them now are followed to the tomb themselves and in their turn forgotten." In Wister's opinion, France was "the true home of them all, and to her dust does their dust belong." He imagined each of the silent doughboys vainly protesting his removal: "Mother, did no one tell you that I said I wanted to stay with the boys?"[12]

Some mothers listened to those impassioned, ghostly pleas and allowed their boys to remain at peace, including Edith G. Rochester, whose son Nat had been killed on October 3 in Lieutenant Wilhelm's attempted breakout. Edith spoke for many mothers when she offered this sentiment: "I think it is better to let our boys who have given their lives 'over there' rest where they are—but I should want to know that their resting place was properly cared for and marked." To assure

Private Ancel E. Fassett, a rancher from Lismas, Montana, killed on October 5. From Haulsee's *Soldiers of the Great War.*

grieving family members that this last wish had been respected, the United States government arranged a series of expense-paid pilgrimages to the French battlefields and cemeteries for Gold Star mothers. Yet a few mothers who desired to make the arduous journey to Europe would not even have a grave to visit. When Sarah Halligan requested information regarding a pilgrimage to see the final resting place of her son William, she received the following explanation from an officer of the Quartermaster Corps: "While it is regretted to advise [you] that the remains of your son have not been located and you will understand no grave can be shown you as that of your son, there is more than an even chance that his remains have been recovered and, lacking means of identification, been interred in the Meuse-Argonne American Cemetery in France under a cross inscribed: 'Here Rests in Honored Glory an American Soldier Known but to God.'" The bodies of William C. Halligan, Walter L. Domrose, Charles B. Jeffries, Arthur H. Jones, Henry Miller, Grant S. Norton, Lawrence M. Osborne, and Harold H. Thomas were never identified and their names are inscribed on tablets in a memorial chapel on the cemetery grounds.[13]

Although bodies could be removed from their battlefield, no living soldier from the Lost Battalion ever truly escaped from the pocket along Charlevaux Creek. Just as his memories had tormented Charles Whittlesey into suicide, recollections of those momentous October days would haunt survivors until the day they died. When Lars Olson read of Whittlesey's suicide, he became irrational and violent. After an

Private Grant S. Norton, a resident of Chautauqua County, New York, killed a week before his twenty-third birthday. From Haulsee's *Soldiers of the Great War.*

extended hospitalization, Olson was released and fled to Denmark in an attempt to escape the past. Some veterans turned to alcohol for solace, while a few others, such as Wilbur Whiting, took their own lives. It was tough adapting to civilian life. Sidney Smith confessed: "When I got married my wife was afraid to sleep with me for a long time. We lived close to the railroad where the trains would come screaming by, and I'd wake in the night thrashing. I was awful nervous." Jacob Loendorf could never burden a woman with his emotional baggage and spent the rest of his years living by himself in a one-room shack on the Montana prairie.[14]

For a while, at least, Whittlesey's veterans received special treatment, none more so than the former medic, James W. Bragg. Hauled before a federal judge in West Virginia on a charge of "possessing property designed for making liquor," Bragg produced his Distinguished Service Cross and accompanying citation. Impressed by this wartime service, the judge dismissed Bragg's bootlegging charge. Treated as heroes by their family and friends and communities for the first few months at home, Whittlesey's men soon found that Lost Battalion stories could only be told so often before listeners began to lose interest. Free drinks in neighborhood taverns began to dry up and newspapers no longer carried their story, so the heroes from France went back to earning a living. Uniforms were mothballed in closets and medals tucked safely away in drawers, taken out only when children begged to play with them. During the war they had gone everywhere and done everything asked of them, but now the country wanted its veterans to quietly disappear and become productive members of society. In the words of Ralph John, "people forget too easily."[15]

After being discharged from the army, survivors of the Lost Battalion scattered across the length and breadth of the United States. Employment came in a number of areas. George McMurtry made a

I've pillowed my head in a stable,
I've slept with my back in the mud,
And I've lain down at night
Full of cooties and fright
With my feet in another man's blood.[16]

fortune as a New York stockbroker, but Clyde Hintz farmed and operated a popcorn wagon in the Hutchinson, Minnesota, city park during summer months. Nelson Holderman served as commandant of the Soldier's Home in Yountville, California. Clarence Roberts ran a cattle ranch in Montana, while Sherman Eager went on to teach physics at Oklahoma Agricultural and Mechanical College. Raymond Flynn co-authored a history of Company E, then worked for Radio Station WBZ in Boston from 1932 to 1935 as the French-Canadian "Joe La Flamme" on the show "Joe and Bateese." He then moved to Hollywood and did bit and extra work in films. Harold Neptune ended up in Sun Valley, California, and could boast that he "worked in pictures for several years, in most of the big horse operas, such as The Gaucho, with Fairbanks, Army Girl, Gunga Din, Marco Polo, Duel in the Sun and Gone With the Wind—to mention just a few."[17]

While memories of the Lost Battalion faded, Thomas M. Johnson, the *New York Sun* correspondent who had watched Whittlesey's command march out of the pocket on the morning of October 8, never forgot what he had seen. Although numerous accounts, often inaccurate, had appeared in various newspapers and magazines, Johnson wanted to tell the story to a wider audience. He wrote an article titled "The Lost Battalion" for the November, 1929, issue of the *American Magazine*, which boasted a circulation of over two million. Still intrigued by the tale of Whittlesey's command, Johnson teamed up with Fletcher Pratt, a popular military historian, to write a more in-depth history of the event. After interviewing some survivors, corresponding with others, and examining archives in both Washington and Germany, Johnson and Pratt completed work on *The Lost Battalion*. This book was

Private Raymond E. Flynn. After the war he coauthored a history of Company E, 308th Infantry, and acted in Hollywood movies. From Hussey's *History of Company E, 308th Infantry (1917–1919)*.

published by the Bobbs-Merrill Company in 1938, the year that marked the Lost Battalion's twentieth anniversary, but the authors did not let facts get in the way of a good story.[18]

In addition to telling a more expanded version of the story, Johnson and Pratt's book prompted two important developments. First of all, their narrative concentrated almost exclusively on the New Yorkers, much to the chagrin of veterans originally from the Fortieth Division, who, despite their late arrival, had done just as well as their eastern comrades. Although Johnson and Pratt had declared an intention "to get and tell the full truth," they simply had not done so. Carl J. Peterson, an AEF veteran himself and brother of Emil A. Peterson of the Lost Battalion, was one of those upset at how the western men had been slighted in published accounts and he set out to correct the record. In his spare time, Peterson began to contact Lost Battalion survivors in Minnesota and other western states, soliciting their stories of events in the pocket. Partly to balance the emphasis on New Yorkers in Johnson and Pratt's 1938 book, Peterson published a pamphlet titled *Lost Battalion Survivors from Minnesota and the Northwest* in 1939.

He included excerpts from recollections of survivors west of the Mississippi River, supplemented by dozens of wartime photographs. Peterson's ultimate goal was to publish a book of personal narratives by these forgotten soldiers, his pamphlet being issued, in part, "to help bring in others that I have, as yet, not been able to contact and to hurry up those who have not sent in their stories." Unfortunately, Peterson never completed his project.[19]

Secondly, Johnson and Pratt's book prompted the formation of a Lost Battalion Survivors Association in New York City. Although some friends had kept in touch over the years, many had lost track of comrades and were eager to make contact with those who had shared their wartime experiences. By the fall of 1938, about 125 survivors had been located and 51 attended a reunion in the Seventy-seventh Division Clubhouse that year to commemorate the twentieth anniversary of the Argonne campaign. Yearly reunions followed at the Murray Hill Hotel until 1946, when the annual meeting was held at the Williams Club, subsequent meetings being at the Hotel Shelburne. George McMurtry picked up the tab for the entire affair each year until his death in 1958, while Walter J. Baldwin compiled the mailing list, sent out invitations and newsletters, and kept track of the deaths of members.

Each meeting followed the same format. Men would arrive, sign the register, and receive a badge, then mingle with old friends. Promptly at one o'clock the meeting was called to order and George McMurtry would lift his glass and offer a toast, "To the dead of the Lost Battalion!" As old veterans raised glasses and drank in silence to long-departed friends, their eyes instinctively glanced toward the only decoration allowed in the hall. On a table in front of an empty chair always sat an elaborate bouquet sent by the fiancée of Lieutenant Marshall Peabody. As long as there was a Lost Battalion reunion, there was always a bouquet, sometimes dahlias and sometimes gladiolas, but always this one simple, mute remembrance of a true love who had failed to return. Following this emotional ceremony, a luncheon was served, the good food (creamed turkey and apple pie one year) being complemented by a few war stories and updates on family matters. The meal was followed by cigars and glasses of beer, as McMurtry made a short inspirational speech. Then each survivor was called upon to rise, state his name and company and where he came from, a special badge being given to the man who had traveled the farthest. After a recap of the previous year by Walter Baldwin and the reading of telegrams and letters of regret, the meeting would adjourn with all vowing to see one another the next year, "the good Lord willing."[20]

It might be assumed that these men who had shared such an intense experience would spend their time talking about life in the pocket, but such was not the case. At one reunion, Robert Manson explained to an outsider, "We've hashed and rehashed the incident; we prefer to forget it, it wasn't pleasant, too much tension every time we talk about it." Abe Krotoshinsky, when interviewed in 1940 about his daring escape from the pocket, confessed, "Mostly I forgot already. I don't talk so much about it no more." Besides, there was a new battle for these veterans to fight. As the years continued to roll on, those young soldiers, who had marched so tall and proud through the streets of New York in 1918 and 1919, noticed that their hair was mysteriously disappearing just as their waistlines seemed to be expanding and stamina seemed to vanish. Physical ailments began to appear or seemed to intensify. Men began to approach that magic age of sixty-five and retirement loomed in the not-too-distant future. Everyone began to agree with Joseph Heuer, who noticed that "the weeks and months go by faster." They also saw family members and old comrades begin to fall by the wayside. As Raymond Blackburn put it, "Some of my best friends have passed on." It was time for the survivors of the Lost Battalion to confront their own mortality.[21]

Having seen too much of death, men from the Lost Battalion embraced life and became devoted to their families. Letters between old army buddies always noted joyous occasions, such as weddings, births, anniversaries, moves into new homes, and retirements. They all made the transition from fathers to grandfathers with obvious pride. James Carroll put it into perspective when he said, "All of us I am sure have had many trials and tribulations over the years—many of which may have seemed impossible to overcome—yet I wonder whether any of us were ever in a spot quite as rugged as those October 2d to 7th days in 1918. In my book we are just forty years to the good and for that alone we should indeed be grateful." Carroll was right. Nothing that life threw at them could ever be as bad as those five October days, but there was just one thing that came close.[22]

While the boys of 1917 had gone overseas and kicked the Kaiser's ass, as they had promised to do when entering Camp Upton, there was always a lingering doubt as to whether they had kicked his ass hard enough. The answer, sadly, was no. The rise of Adolf Hitler and consequent advent of World War II tore the very hearts out of veterans of the Argonne, for America's sons, *their own sons*, would have to go back to Europe and do it all over again. Emulating their fathers, sons of the Lost Battalion stepped forward and did their part, although most steered clear of the infantry. Both of Olaf Nelson's sons went off to serve and Frank Erickson's boy flew thirty-six bombing missions over Germany in a B-17. Jack Tucker's son, Milton, put in two years in the Air Force. Anthony Anastasi's only son lost his life during the war. One of Philip Kornely's boys died when his bomber crashed in England. Sidney Smith's son died during the Battle of the Bulge. The list goes on and on. Even a few of the survivors themselves pitched in to fight the war. Called up from the reserves, William Cullen and Sherman Eager both served on active duty again.[23]

Ralph John had a son old enough to fight in World War II and felt compelled to record his recollections of "five days of horror and bloodshed for what we, as soldiers in the Lost Battalion, thought was a just cause." His story was a gritty, first-hand account that pulled no punches about conditions in the pocket. John's narrative also revealed much about an old soldier's thoughts in the days before the diagnosis of posttraumatic stress disorder. At one point he confessed, "Sometimes my eyes get so full of tears that I can hardly write and my thinker quits thinking, just halted on those dreadful scenes that I ran into hundreds of times each day." He gave additional details of his tortured existence: "You may think it is an easy job to write about it all, but I write a while and my eyes get so filled with tears at the memory of it all that I just have to quit. Then something big comes up in my throat and chokes me. I try to lie down and rest but I can't rest nor sleep. If, after exhaustion, I do sleep it is only to live it all over again in dreams, seemingly more real than when I'm awake. Now after more than twenty years, the memory carries an indelible copy of those miserable days in the pocket, that will never be blotted by good times or other troubles I may have."[24]

At first glance, the Lost Battalion story was a tale of courage and determination against great odds, the tale resonating particularly with civilians, who cheered Major Whittlesey's leadership and his men's endurance well beyond the normal call of duty. Over time, the Lost

Battalion has rightly taken a place in the pantheon of American military history that celebrates such small-unit actions as Colonel William Travis's defense of the Alamo, Major George Forsyth's fight at Beecher's Island, and Lieutenant Colonel George Custer's action on the Little Bighorn River. Rightly proud of their success, Lost Battalion survivors nevertheless had nagging doubts about their celebrated affair and rightly so.

Corporal Walter J. Baldwin, 308th Infantry:
Come on home, nothing's too good!
When we came out of the Argonne Wood.
The bands played loud, the banners waved,
In old New York, for our parade.

They soon forget as the years roll by,
As we get older, you and I.
We struggle on, try hard to smile,
While we wonder, "Was it all worth while?"[25]

In fact, the entire Lost Battalion episode was a scathing indictment of the American army and its commanders. The Seventy-seventh Division wasted months of training on how to live and fight in the trench warfare then being waged in France, although it had absolutely no instruction on how to conduct combat operations in the war of movement later fought on the Vesle and Argonne fronts. This initial mistake was compounded by a temporary assignment to the British front, where doughboys exchanged their American arms and equipment for British counterparts, wasting even more precious weeks in training and familiarization with weapons they would never use. When desperately needed reinforcements finally arrived in late September, they proved to be woefully undertrained, many never having fired their rifles. Newcomers were paired off with veterans and simply told to watch the old-timers and follow their lead.

Combat operations in the Argonne Forest exposed serious deficiencies in the Seventy-seventh Division. To counter the effectiveness of German machine guns, frontline commanders has been given one-pounder guns and Stokes Mortars, while infantrymen had been issued rifle grenades. Artillery support was also available. Out in the forest, not one of these weapons worked as anticipated, so attacks essentially consisted of American infantry against German automatic weapons. Headquarters published a new set of tactics for attacking German machine guns on September 5, only three weeks before the Argonne campaign began, so many troops never had a chance to practice them. Once the battle started, quartermasters were unable to keep pace with the battle line, leaving troops chronically short of both food and ammunition. If the Seventy-seventh Division had not unexpectedly captured the German narrow-gauge railroad, this supply problem would have assumed critical proportions.

Once the Argonne campaign began, cooperation between the left flank of the American army and the right flank of the French army was nonexistent. This allowed German units to penetrate into the gap between the two, then swing around and encircle a portion of the 308th Infantry not once, but twice. A continued failure to secure the left flank of the Seventy-seventh Division was matched by negligence in failing to seize the initiative offered when Major Whittlesey's command broke through the German lines on October 2. This blundering at division headquarters was matched by a lack of continuity at headquarters of the 308th Infantry. Colonel A. F. Prescott, who had led the regiment for less than six weeks, was relieved of command on September 27, the second day of the campaign, being succeeded first by Lieutenant Colonel Frederick Smith, then by Colonel Cromwell Stacey. After General Alexander ordered Stacey's removal on October 5, Major Whittlesey was the regiment's senior officer, although he was cut off and unable to assume command. Captain Lucien Breckinridge took over at headquarters for the next three days. Given the lack of proper training, an inability to counter the threat posed by German machine guns, a constant scarcity of rations and ammunition, and lack of competent leadership at the regimental level and above, it is remarkable that Major Whittlesey and his command were able to survive their terrible ordeal in the Argonne Forest.

Lost Battalion soldiers grew old with memories of the Charlevaux Valley swirling about their brains. Paul Schwartz admitted that, after thirty-nine years, events in the pocket "seem like they happened only yesterday." Paul Segal agreed, writing to Walter Baldwin, "All I can say is that forty years is a long while to look ahead but a short while to look back." Isidore Spiegel stated, "When a man becomes aged, tired and worn out, he tends to reminisce. I look back at those years and recall as vividly as ever the time we were lost in the Argonne Forest." Twenty years after the fact, Arnold Morem confessed, "I can still smell the awful odor that came from the dead bodies lying around." When someone asked Abe Krotoshinsky whether he ever watched war movies, such as *All Quiet on the Western Front*, he answered, "I don't like such movies. It makes me all upset."[26]

The war was always with these old soldiers, shadowing their every move. They always teetered on the brink of 1918. An automobile back-firing could be a *minenwerfer* shell. The far off rat-tat-tat of a woodpecker sounded like a distant machine gun. A chicken killed for Sunday dinner turned into a wounded buddy flopping in his own blood. But it was the dreams that were the worst because they were so realistic and so random. Awakening in a pool of sweat, scared and trembling, men would literally be afraid to sleep. Scars were mute evidence of physical wounds that had healed, but the emotional wounds remained raw and jagged forever. It was not that the veterans were afraid of death. They knew from bitter experience that dying was an intensely personal journey that must be undertaken alone, whether surrounded by family and friends in a clean bed at home after a lingering illness or in the blink of an eye while huddled alone in a muddy funkhole. But the old soldiers also realized that for them the journey was not as long as for others. Some part of them had already died on that steep hillside bordering Charlevaux Valley, a lonely spot in the gloomy Argonne Forest that had been made forever American with their own blood.

PHOTOGRAPHS

A Cross-section of Soldiers
from the Lost Battalion

Private Bernard J. Lee. A native of Perth, Ontario who was enrolled as a theological student in Tewksbury, Massachusetts, before entering the service. From Haulsee's *Soldiers of the Great War.*

Private Hyman Gallob, a native of Kiev, who was a Manhattan shipping clerk before being drafted. From Haulsee's *Soldiers of the Great War.*

Private Lauren G. Reid, a Nevada native who was mortally wounded by shrapnel during the last German attack on October 7. From Sullivan's *Nevada's Golden Stars.*

Private Bert L. Blowers, an upstate farmer from Wyoming County, New York, who was wounded while fighting on the left flank with Company K, 307th Infantry. From Haulsee's *Soldiers of the Great War.*

Private Jesse J. Mendenhall, a stock raiser from Red Bluff, California, who was killed on October 5. From Haulsee's *Soldiers of the Great War*.

Private Carl A. Rainwater, the last of four brothers who left Great Falls, Montana, for military service. From *Honor Rolls Containing a Pictorial Record of the Gallant and Courageous Men from Cascade County, Montana, USA, Who Served in the Great War, 1917–1918–1919*.

Private John F. Damcott, formerly a milk inspector from Clymer, New York, who fought under Lieutenant Schenck until his death on October 5. From Haulsee's *Soldiers of the Great War*.

Private Ralph Brinkema, a native of Holland, wounded in the left shoulder while fighting with Company K, 307th Infantry. From *In the World War, 1917–1918–1919*.

Private Arnold M. Morem was wounded by a shell fragment, and his rifle struck by three bullets. From *In the World War, Fillmore County, Minnesota.*

Private George M. Benthagen, a resident of Borup, Minnesota, who was killed while holding the middle of the line with Company G, 308th Infantry. From Haulsee's *Soldiers of the Great War.*

Appendix

SOLDIERS OF THE
LOST BATTALION

This list is based upon the roster published in *History of the 308th Infantry*, but has been expanded to include all soldiers who broke through the German lines with Major Whittlesey on October 2, 1918. The original roster has been supplemented by published sources, unpublished material, reunion rosters, and manuscript records at the National Archives in College Park, Maryland. Only one name, John Gehris, has been removed from the original roster. Whenever possible, names are listed as they were in 1918. For example, Saul Marshallcowitz later changed his surname to Marshall, but is listed here under the original form.

[Maj. = Major, Capt. = Captain, 1 Lt. = 1st Lieutenant, 2 Lt. = 2nd Lieutenant, Sgt. Maj. = Sergeant Major, 1 Sgt. = 1st Sergeant, Sgt. = Sergeant, Cpl. = Corporal, PFC = Private First Class, Pvt. = Private, Bug. = Bugler, Mech. = Mechanic, Wag. = Wagoner. NYD = Not Yet Determined.]

Adams, Charles F.	Pvt.	Co. K, 307th Infantry	NYD
Adams, Charles I.	Pvt.	Co. K, 307th Infantry	W'd, multiple
Ahlstedt, Reuben H.	PFC	Co. G, 308th Infantry (runner)	W'd, right thigh
Albis, Stanislaus	Pvt.	Co. B, 308th Infantry	W'd, right leg
Altiera, Samuel A.	Pvt.	Co. K, 307th Infantry	NYD
Amatteti, Bart	Pvt.	Co. B, 308th Infantry	NYD

Anastasi, Anthony	Pvt.	Co. F, 308th Infantry (scout)	W'd, left leg
Anderson, Carl A.	Pvt.	Co. K, 307th Infantry	
Anderson, Gus	Pvt.	Co. K, 307th Infantry	Killed
Anderson, Herman G.	Sgt.	Co. A, 308th Infantry	W'd, head
Anderson, Joseph J.	Pvt.	Co. D, 308th Infantry	
Andrews, Paul F.	PFC	Co. G, 308th Infantry	Killed
Armstrong, William W.	PFC	Co. C, 308th Infantry	W'd
Arnold, Harold V.	PFC	Co. F, 308th Infantry (scout)	Killed
Baker, David H.	Pvt.	Co. B, 308th Infantry	W'd
Baker, Edward	Pvt.	Co. K, 307th Infantry	W'd, right thigh
Bakker, Dick W.	Pvt.	Co. E, 308th Infantry	Killed
Baldwin, Frederick W.	Sgt.	Co. E, 308th Infantry	
Baldwin, Joseph K.	Cpl.	Co. C, 308th Infantry	
Baldwin, Walter J.	Cpl.	1 Bat'n, 308th Infantry	
Bang, John	Pvt.	Co. K, 307th Infantry	Killed
Baskin, Louis	Pvt.	Co. C, 308th Infantry	Constipation
Becker, Gustave A.	Pvt.	Co. C, 306th MG Bat'n	Killed
Becker, Martin	Cpl.	Co. D, 306th MG Bat'n	Killed
Bedrna, William	Pvt.	Co. ?, 308th Infantry (scout)	
Beebe, Leonard	Pvt.	Co. K, 307th Infantry	W'd, multiple
Beeson, Leonard R.	Pvt.	Co. K, 307th Infantry	W'd, right shoulder
Begley, William A.	PFC	Co. G, 308th Infantry	Killed
Bejnarowicz, Joseph	Cpl.	Co. C, 308th Infantry	
Bendheim, Lionel	Sgt.	Co. C, 308th Infantry	W'd, both legs
Benson, Arthur E.	Pvt.	Co. C, 308th Infantry	
Bent, Elmer E.	Pvt.	Co. H, 308th Infantry	
Benthagen, George M.	Pvt.	Co. G, 308th Infantry	Killed
Berg, Louis	Pvt.	Co. K, 307th Infantry	
Berkowitz, Michael	Pvt.	Co. E, 308th Infantry	Prisoner
Berlev, Floyd	Pvt.	Co. K, 307th Infantry	W'd, NYD
Beske, Arthur A.	Pvt.	Co. B, 308th Infantry	Killed
Bickmore, Harry	Pvt.	Co. B, 308th Infantry	
Bivalace, Giovanni	Pvt.	Co. K, 307th Infantry	W'd
Blackburn, Raymond	Sgt.	Co. C, 308th Infantry	
Blanchard, Alonzo D.	Cpl.	Co. K, 307th Infantry	
Bland, Charles J.	Pvt.	Co. E, 308th Infantry	Killed
Blomseth, Ludwig	Pvt.	Co. G, 308th Infantry	

Blowers, Bert L.	Pvt.	Co. K, 307th Infantry	W'd, died disease, Dec.
Boden, John	Pvt.	Co. G, 308th Infantry	Killed
Bolvig, Eiler V.	Cpl.	Co. H, 308th Infantry	Killed
Bonaventura, Pistoria	PFC	Co. B, 308th Infantry	W'd, left leg
Botelle, George W.	Pvt.	Co. C, 308th Infantry (runner)	W'd, head
Bowden, John	Cpl.	Co. H, 308th Infantry	W'd, left leg, foot
Bradford, Robert F.	Cpl.	Co. K, 307th Infantry	
Bradshaw, Stanley O.	Pvt.	Co. B, 308th Infantry	W'd, left shoulder
Bragg, James W.	Pvt.	Med. Det., 308th Infantry	NYD
Brennan, George H.	Pvt.	Co. D, 306th MG Bat'n	
Brennan, Harold	Pvt.	Co. E, 308th Infantry	
Brennen, Thomas	Cpl.	Co. C, 308th Infantry	W'd
Brew, William F.	Pvt.	Co. K, 307th Infantry	W'd, NYD
Brice, James A.	Pvt.	Co. E, 308th Infantry	NYD
Bringham, Victor L.	Pvt.	Co. K, 307th Infantry	W'd, left femur
Brinkoma, Ralph	Pvt.	Co. K, 307th Infantry	W'd, left shoulder
Brody, Irving	Pvt.	Co. B, 308th Infantry	W'd, left leg
Bronson, Emery	Pvt.	Co. B, 308th Infantry	W'd, right leg, hand
Bronstein, Benjamin	Pvt.	Co. E, 308th Infantry	Prisoner, died a POW
Brown, Clifford R.	Pvt.	Co. C, 308th Infantry	
Brown, Edwin C.	Sgt.	Co. H, 308th Infantry	W'd, right arm
Brown, Gilbert E.	Pvt.	Co. K, 307th Infantry	Died of w'ds, Oct. 15
Bruton, James	Pvt.	Co. G, 308th Infantry	Killed
Bueskins, Herbert	Pvt.	Co. K, 307th Infantry	W'd, left arm
Buhler, Fred, Jr.	2 Lt.	Co. G, 308th Infantry	W'd, multiple
Burns, William C.	Pvt.	Co. H, 308th Infantry	
Buth, Harry O.	Pvt.	Co. H, 308th Infantry	Killed
Cadieux, Henry J.	Pvt.	Co. B, 308th Infantry	W'd, head
Caldwell, Louis B.	Pvt.	Co. H, 308th Infantry	
Callahan, William	Sgt.	Co. E, 308th Infantry	
Cappiello, Savino	Pvt.	Co. C, 308th Infantry	NYD

Carnebucci, Catino	PFC	Co. C, 308th Infantry	Killed
Carroll, James B.	Sgt.	Co. K, 307th Infantry	
Cassidy, Henry C.	Pvt.	Co. C, 308th Infantry	W'd, left shoulder, hand
Castrogiovanne, Samuel	Pvt.	Co. C, 308th Infantry	Killed
Cathcart, Joseph E.	Pvt.	Co. H, 308th Infantry	
Cavanaugh, William M.	Pvt.	Co. E, 308th Infantry	W'd, NYD
Cavello, Thomas	Pvt.	Co. H, 308th Infantry	Killed
Cella, Innocenzo	Pvt.	Co. A, 308th Infantry	NYD
Cepaglia, Philip	Pvt.	Co. C, 308th Infantry (runner)	
Chamberlain, James	Cpl.	Co. K, 307th Infantry	
Chambers, Joseph H.	Pvt.	Co. H, 308th Infantry	W'd, neck
Charlesworth, Percy W.	Pvt.	Co. C, 308th Infantry	W'd, left leg
Chavelle, Charles H.	PFC	Co. B, 308th Infantry	W'd, left arm
Chin, Henry	Pvt.	Co. H, 308th Infantry	Killed
Chiswell, George H.	Pvt.	Co. E, 308th Infantry	W'd, right wrist, head
Christ, Charles F.	Pvt.	Co. K, 307th Infantry	
Christensen, Hans W.	Pvt.	Co. K, 307th Infantry	
Christenson, Philip	Pvt.	Co. K, 307th Infantry	W'd, right chest
Christian, Robert E.	Pvt.	Co. H, 308th Infantry	Killed
Christianson, Enoch	Pvt.	Co. A, 308th Infantry	
Christopher, Joseph J.	Pvt.	Co. K, 307th Infantry	W'd, multiple
Chupp, Ammon	Pvt.	Co. ?, 308th Infantry (runner)	W'd, left knee
Church, Roscoe G.	Pvt.	Co. K, 307th Infantry	Killed
Clark, Raymond O.	Pvt.	Co. H, 308th Infantry	Killed
Clark, Nathan	Pvt.	Co. D, 306th MG Bat'n	Killed
Clay, Thomas H.	Pvt.	Co. H, 308th Infantry	W'd, NYD
Clemons, Melvin E.	Pvt.	Co. G, 308th Infantry	
Coatney, Arthur F.	Pvt.	Co. H, 308th Infantry	W'd, right thigh
Coe, Richard R.	Pvt.	Co. H, 308th Infantry	W'd, left arm
Cohen, Morris	Pvt.	Co. D, 306th MG Bat'n	W'd, right shoulder
Colan, James	Cpl.	Co. G, 308th Infantry	W'd, back
Colasacco, John G.	Sgt.	Co. C, 308th Infantry	
Cole, Harvey R.	Pvt.	Co. K, 307th Infantry	Killed
Collins, John	Pvt.	Co. A, 308th Infantry	W'd, left knee
Condon, James T.	Pvt.	Co. C, 308th Infantry	NYD

Conneally, John	Pvt.	Co. G, 308th Infantry	
Connelly, John	Pvt.	Co. K, 307th Infantry	W'd, right foot
Connelly, Timothy	Pvt.	Co. K, 307th Infantry	
Conrad, James M.	Pvt.	Co. D, 306th MG Bat'n	Killed
Copsey, Albert V.	Cpl.	Co. B, 308th Infantry	
Cornell, Charles B.	Cpl.	Co. H, 308th Infantry	
Cornell, Henry C.	Pvt.	Co. C, 306th MG Bat'n	W'd, left ear, neck
Covert, Parley J.	Pvt.	Co. E, 308th Infantry	Prisoner
Crosby, John A.	Pvt.	Co. C, 308th Infantry	W'd
Crotty, Martin J.	Pvt.	Co. D, 306th MG Bat'n	W'd, left hip
Crouse, William P.	Pvt.	Co. K, 307th Infantry	Killed
Cullen, William J.	1 Lt.	Co. H, 308th Infantry	
Cummings, Roy	Pvt.	Co. H, 308th Infantry	
Cunningham, Niles F.	Pvt.	Co. C, 308th Infantry	NYD
Curley, Edward T.	Pvt.	Co. C, 308th Infantry	W'd, left side
Dahlgren, Gust A.	Pvt.	Co. G, 308th Infantry	W'd, NYD
Damcott, John F.	PFC	Co. C, 308th Infantry	Killed
Damon, Harry P.	Pvt.	Co. H, 308th Infantry	
Daomi, Patrick	Pvt.	Co. E, 308th Infantry	Killed
Dayo, Harrison	Pvt.	Co. ?, 308th Infantry (scout)	
Deaderick, Osro	Pvt.	Co. G, 308th Infantry	
Deahan, James A.	Sgt.	Co. K, 307th Infantry	
Del Sasso, John L.	Pvt.	Co. E, 308th Infantry	Died of w'ds, Oct. 20
Delgrosso, Frank	PFC	Co. G, 308th Infantry	W'd, head
Delmont, John	Pvt.	Co. H, 308th Infantry (scout)	NYD
Delserone, John	Pvt.	Co. H, 308th Infantry	W'd
Devanney, Patrick	Pvt.	Co. E, 308th Infantry	Died of w'ds, Oct. 11
DeWitt, Roy	Pvt.	Co. E, 308th Infantry	Killed
Diesel, Louis	PFC	Co. D, 306th MG Bat'n	Killed
Dimmick, Frank C.	Pvt.	Co. D, 306th MG Bat'n	Killed
Dingledine, Elliott N.	Pvt.	Co. D, 306th MG Bat'n	Died of w'ds Oct. 9
Dodd, Robert	Pvt.	Co. H, 308th Infantry	W'd, shoulder, leg
Doherty, Arthur F.	Cpl.	Co. E, 308th Infantry (runner)	W'd

Domrose, Walter L.	Pvt.	Co. E, 308th Infantry	Killed
Dorr, Donald E.	Pvt.	Co. H, 308th Infantry	Killed
Downs, Lee H.	PFC	Co. C, 308th Infantry	W'd
Drake, Herbert M.	Pvt.	Co. H, 308th Infantry	
Dubbin, Frederick L.	Pvt.	Co. K, 307th Infantry	
Duffy, George W.	Cpl.	Co. B, 308th Infantry	Sprained ankle
Dunham, Ralph O.	Pvt.	Co. F, 308th Infantry (runner)	
Dunnigan, Thomas	Pvt.	Co. B, 308th Infantry	
Duryea, Cecil L.	Pvt.	Co. H, 308th Infantry	W'd right leg, prisoner
Dyrdal, Joseph B.	Pvt.	Co. B, 308th Infantry	Killed
Eager, Sherman W.	2 Lt.	Co. G, 308th Infantry	
Edlund, Herman	Pvt.	Co. G, 308th Infantry	
Edwards, Lyle J.	Pvt.	Co. H, 308th Infantry	
Eggleston, George	Pvt.	Co. D, 306th MG Bat'n	
Eichorn, John	Pvt.	Co. ?, 308th Infantry (runner)	Bruised left heel
Eifert, Otto H.	Pvt.	Co. E, 308th Infantry	Prisoner
Elkin, Gabe	Pvt.	Co. H, 308th Infantry	
Ellbogen, Martin	Cpl.	Co. F, 308th Infantry (scout)	W'd, left shoulder
Elliott, Frederick	Pvt.	Co. G, 308th Infantry	W'd
Engen, Conrad	Pvt.	Co. H, 308th Infantry	W'd
Englander, George M.	Bug.	Co. G, 308th Infantry	W'd, right leg
Erdahl, Olaf	Pvt.	Co. H, 308th Infantry	
Erickson, Alfred E.	Pvt.	Co. H, 308th Infantry	Killed
Erickson, Arthur	Pvt.	Co. G, 308th Infantry	
Erickson, Frank G. S.	Pvt.	Co. H, 308th Infantry	
Erickson, Henry	Pvt.	Co. A, 308th Infantry	W'd, right thigh
Esch, Hubert V.	Pvt.	Co. C, 308th Infantry	
Estes, Frank R.	Pvt.	Co. H, 308th Infantry	
Euteneuer, Albert A.	Pvt.	Co. K, 307th Infantry	
Evans, Peter	Pvt.	Co. B, 308th Infantry	W'd, left face
Evermann, Fred	Pvt.	Co. B, 308th Infantry	
Fairbanks, Truman P.	Pvt.	Co. G, 308th Infantry	W'd, multiple
Fare, John	Pvt.	Co. K, 307th Infantry	W'd, right leg
Farncomb, Harvey M.	Pvt.	Co. K, 307th Infantry	W'd, left ankle

Fassett, Ancel E.	Pvt.	Co. H, 308th Infantry	Killed
Feeney, Francis	Pvt.	Co. B, 308th Infantry	
Fein, Arthur E.	Pvt.	Co. K, 307th Infantry	W'd, back, right arm
Felton, James P.	Pvt.	Co. K, 307th Infantry	W'd, left arm
Feuerlicht, Samuel	Pvt.	Co. C, 308th Infantry	Died of w'ds Oct. 14
Fitzgerald, Peter A.	Pvt.	Co. G, 308th Infantry	W'd, right leg, left hand
Flack, Earl A.	Pvt.	Co. H, 308th Infantry	
Flaming, Henry P.	Pvt.	Co. H, 308th Infantry	
Flower, Leo A.	Pvt.	Co. C, 306th MG Bat'n	NYD
Flynn, John T.	Pvt.	Co. B, 308th Infantry	NYD
Flynn, Raymond E.	Pvt.	Co. E, 308th Infantry	Diarrhea
Fortunato, Joseph C.	Mech.	Co. C, 308th Infantry	
Foss, Sidney, J.	Pvt.	Co. K, 307th Infantry	
Francis, William E.	Pvt.	Co. H, 308th Infantry	W'd, left wrist
Fredette, Frank D. S.	Pvt.	Co. F, 308th Infantry (runner)	
Freeman, Harry	Sgt.	Co. G, 308th Infantry	W'd, right shoulder
Friel, Joseph	Pvt.	Co. A, 308th Infantry (runner)	Killed
Frink, Charles W.	Pvt.	Co. C, 308th Infantry	W'd
Gaedeke, Benjamin F.	Sgt. Maj.	1 Bat'n, 308th Infantry	Killed
Gafanowitz, Robert	PFC	Co. G, 308th Infantry	W'd, right forearm
Gallagher, Dennis A.	Pvt.	Co. G, 308th Infantry	W'd
Gallob, Hyman	PFC	Co. B, 308th Infantry	Killed
Gaupset, Sigurd P.	Pvt.	Co. H, 308th Infantry	W'd, right leg
Gavin, George M.	Pvt.	Co. B, 308th Infantry	Killed
Geanekos, Agel	Pvt.	Co. B, 308th Infantry	
Gibbons, Peter	Pvt.	Co. K, 307th Infantry	
Gibson, Herbert B.	Pvt.	Co. H, 308th Infantry	W'd, forearm
Gibson, Fred	Pvt.	Co. B, 308th Infantry	Killed
Giefer, Joseph	Pvt.	Co. D, 308th Infantry	W'd, head, finger
Giganti, Joseph A.	Pvt.	Co. C, 308th Infantry	Constipation
Gill, Thomas H.	Pvt.	Co. K, 307th Infantry	
Gillece, Bernard	Cpl.	Co. E, 308th Infantry (scout)	

Gilley, George	Cpl.	Co. K, 307th Infantry	
Gitchell, Leonard C.	Pvt.	Co. H, 308th Infantry	Killed
Gladd, David E.	PFC	Co. C, 308th Infantry	Killed
Glenn, Leonard N.	Pvt.	Co. B, 308th Infantry	
Goldberg, Irving R.	Cpl.	Co. E, 308th Infantry	Prisoner
Goldhorn, Henry W.	Pvt.	Co. H, 308th Infantry (scout)	NYD
Graham, Robert J.	Sgt.	Co. D, 306th MG Bat'n	Killed
Greally, Michael J.	Sgt.	Co. G, 308th Infantry	Killed
Green, Bert M.	Cpl.	Co. K, 307th Infantry	NYD
Greenfield, Barney	Pvt.	Co. B, 308th Infantry	Influenza
Greenwald, Irving W.	PFC	Co. E, 308th Infantry (scout)	W'd, femur, right foot
Griffin, Maurice V.	1 Lt.	Co. H, 308th Infantry	W'd, left shoulder
Griswold, Lester	Pvt.	Co. C, 308th Infantry	W'd, left eye
Gross, Herbert	Pvt.	Co. E, 308th Infantry (runner)	
Grossberg, Percy	Pvt.	Co. G, 308th Infantry (scout)	
Gudis, Peter C.	Cpl.	Co. E, 308th Infantry	
Habeck, Frank	PFC	Co. E, 308th Infantry	W'd, left rib
Hagerman, Mark C.	Sgt.	Co. G, 308th Infantry	
Halligan, William C.	Pvt.	Co. B, 308th Infantry	Killed
Hamilton, John R.	Pvt.	Co. ?, 308th Infantry (runner)	
Hammond, Raymond E.	Pvt.	Co. B, 308th Infantry	
Hanson, Theodore	Pvt.	Co. H, 308th Infantry	Killed
Hanson, Walter	Pvt.	Co. B, 308th Infantry	
Harch, ?	Pvt.	Co. D, 306th MG Bat'n	
Harkleroad, Lee C.	Pvt.	Co. C, 306th MG Bat'n	W'd, multiple
Harlin, Albert D.	Pvt.	Co. D, 308th Infantry (runner)	
Harrington, Victor A.	2 Lt.	Co. E, 308th Infantry	W'd, prisoner
Harris, Thomas	Pvt.	Co. B, 308th Infantry	
Hatch, Boyd S.	Sgt.	Co. K, 307th Infantry	
Hatcher, Otto R.	Pvt.	Co. C, 308th Infantry	
Hauck, George E.	Sgt.	Co. D, 306th MG Bat'n	
Havens, George E.	PFC	Co. E, 308th Infantry	Killed
Hazen, Louis N.	Pvt.	Co. C, 308th Infantry	W'd, shoulder, left foot
Healy, Jeremiah	Sgt.	Co. G, 308th Infantry	W'd, right leg

Hearty, James H.	Pvt.	Co. B, 308th Infantry	W'd, right wrist
Hecker, Arthur J.	Pvt.	Co. H, 308th Infantry	
Held, Jacob	Cpl.	Co. C, 308th Infantry	
Hendrickson, Alfred	Pvt.	Co. K, 307th Infantry	W'd, left leg
Hepworth, Clyde	Pvt.	Co. H, 308th Infantry	W'd, rheumatism
Hermsdorf, Harry J.	Sgt.	Co. B, 308th Infantry	
Heuer, Joseph P.	Sgt.	Co. K, 307th Infantry	
Hicks, Arthur	Pvt.	Co. K, 307th Infantry	W'd, left leg
Hicks, Stacy M.	Pvt.	Co. C, 308th Infantry	
Hiduck, Anthony	Pvt.	Co. A, 308th Infantry	W'd, head
Hildenbrand, Carl	Pvt.	Co. B, 308th Infantry	Killed
Hinchman, John A.	Cpl.	Co. C, 308th Infantry	Killed
Hintz, Clyde C. A.	Pvt.	Co. B, 308th Infantry	
Hission, William	Pvt.	Co. C, 308th Infantry	
Hoadley, George	Pvt.	Co. K, 307th Infantry	
Hofstetter, Benjamin J.	Pvt.	Co. H, 308th Infantry	Killed
Hogue, Frank D.	Pvt.	Co. K, 307th Infantry	Diarrhea
Holbert, Edward	Pvt.	Co. H, 308th Infantry	
Holden, Wyatt L.	Pvt.	Co. C, 308th Infantry	
Holderman, Nelson M.	Capt.	Co. K, 307th Infantry	W'd, multiple
Holliday, William M.	Pvt.	Co. B, 308th Infantry	Killed
Hollingshead, Lowell R.	Pvt.	Co. H, 308th Infantry	W'd, left thigh
Holt, James M.	Pvt.	Co. D, 306th MG Bat'n	
Holt, John	Pvt.	Co. B, 308th Infantry	Died of w'ds Oct. 13
Holzer, William E.	Pvt.	Co. G, 308th Infantry	W'd, left leg
Honas, Stephen M.	Pvt.	Co. B, 308th Infantry	W'd, multiple
Hott, John	Pvt.	Co. E, 308th Infantry	Prisoner
Hoven, Sylvester	Pvt.	Co. B, 308th Infantry	Killed
Hudlow, Reuben	Pvt.	Co. A, 308th Infantry	W'd, left hand
Huff, George	Pvt.	Co. K, 307th Infantry	
Huntington, Lloyd A.	Pvt.	Co. H, 308th Infantry	W'd, left humerus
Hussey, Alexander T.	Pvt.	Co. E, 308th Infantry	
Hyde, Richard W.	Pvt.	Co. H, 308th Infantry	Killed
Iltz, Henry	Pvt.	Co. C, 306th MG Bat'n	NYD
Indiana, Domineck	Pvt.	Co. C, 308th Infantry	
Ingram, Theodore W.	Pvt.	Co. F, 308th Infantry (scout)	
Iraci, Alfio	Pvt.	Co. E, 308th Infantry	Killed

Irwin, James	Pvt.	Co. C, 308th Infantry	
Jacob, William	Sgt.	Co. C, 308th Infantry	
Jacobson, Charles	Pvt.	Co. C, 308th Infantry	
Jacoby, Leo J.	Pvt.	Co. C, 308th Infantry	
Jeffries, Charles B.	Pvt.	Batt D, 305th Field Artillery	Killed
Jepson, Earl F.	Pvt.	Co. B, 308th Infantry	Killed
John, Ralph E.	Pvt.	Co. A, 308th Infantry	
Johnson, Charles A.	Pvt.	Co. K, 307th Infantry	Killed
Johnson, Edward	Pvt.	Co. G, 308th Infantry	Killed
Johnson, Grover C.	Pvt.	Co. A, 308th Infantry	
Johnson, Louis N.	PFC	Co. C, 306th MG Bat'n	Killed
Johnson, Maurice E.	Sgt.	Co. D, 306th MG Bat'n	
Johnson, Raymond	Pvt.	Co. C, 308th Infantry	W'd
Johnson, William F.	Pvt.	Co. K, 307th Infantry	
Johnson, William J.	Pvt.	Co. A, 308th Infantry	Killed
Jolly, Samuel	Pvt.	Co. H, 308th Infantry	Killed
Jones, Arthur H.	PFC	Co. B, 308th Infantry	Killed
Jones, David O.	Pvt.	Co. K, 307th Infantry	W'd, left arm
Jorgensen, Arthur F.	Pvt.	Co. F, 308th Infantry (scout)	
Jorgensen, Herbert	PFC	Co. G, 308th Infantry (scout)	W'd, right arm
Joyce, Joseph	Pvt.	Co. H, 308th Infantry	W'd, neck
Judd, Roland W.	Pvt.	Co. A, 308th Infantry	Killed
Kaempfer, Albert O.	Pvt.	Co. K, 307th Infantry	W'd, right arm
Kandel, Benjamin	Pvt.	Co. E, 308th Infantry	Missing
Kaplan, Harold	1 Sgt.	Co. E, 308th Infantry	W'd, prisoner
Karalunas, John	Pvt.	Co. K, 307th Infantry	W'd, left arm, chest
Karpinsky, Frank	Pvt.	Co. B, 308th Infantry	W'd
Kaspirovitch, Jacob	Pvt.	Co. E, 308th Infantry	W'd, left hip, side
Kaufman, Emil	Pvt.	Co. C, 308th Infantry	
Keegan, James A.	Pvt.	Co. B, 308th Infantry	Influenza
Keenan, Joseph C.	Cpl.	Co. D, 306th MG Bat'n	
Keeney, ?	Pvt.	Co. C, 306th MG Bat'n	
Keim, George	Pvt.	Co. C, 308th Infantry	
Kellogg, Ernest	Pvt.	Co. E, 308th Infantry	Killed
Kelly, Joseph D.	Pvt.	Co. D, 306th MG Bat'n	W'd, left leg
Kelly, Kennedy K.	Pvt.	Co. A, 308th Infantry	Killed

Kelly, Michael	Pvt.	Co. E, 308th Infantry (scout)	
Kelmel, William	Pvt.	Co. K, 307th Infantry	
Kennedy, Edward A.	Pvt.	Co. D, 306th MG Bat'n	W'd, back, neck, side
Kennedy, Joseph C.	Cpl.	Co. G, 308th Infantry	
Kiernan, Joseph	Cpl.	Co. E, 308th Infantry (scout)	NYD
King, Joseph R.	Pvt.	Co. C, 308th Infantry	W'd, left knee
Kirchner, Gerard	Sgt.	Co. H, 308th Infantry (scout)	
Klein, Irving	Cpl.	Co. A, 308th Infantry	W'd, left elbow
Knabe, William H.	PFC	Co. K, 307th Infantry	W'd, multiple
Knapp, John	Pvt.	Co. E, 308th Infantry	Killed
Knauss, Daniel M.	Pvt.	Co. H, 308th Infantry	
Knettel, John J.	Pvt.	Co. K, 307th Infantry	
Knifsund, Otto M.	Pvt.	Co. C, 308th Infantry	
Knott, Carlton V.	Pvt.	Co. B, 308th Infantry	Killed
Koebler, George	PFC	Co. H, 308th Infantry (scout)	Killed
Koernig, George C.	Pvt.	Co. H, 308th Infantry	Killed
Kolbe, Charles A.	Pvt.	Co. C, 306th MG Bat'n	W'd, left shoulder, back
Kornely, Philip A.	PFC	Co. B, 308th Infantry	W'd, right leg
Kostinen, Frank J.	Pvt.	Co. C, 308th Infantry	
Kozikowski, Stanislaw	Pvt.	Co. C, 308th Infantry	
Krantz, Walter J.	Pvt.	Co. C, 308th Infantry	
Krogh, Magnus B.	Pvt.	Co. B, 308th Infantry	W'd
Kronenberg, Max	Pvt.	Co. E, 308th Infantry	Prisoner
Krotoshinsky, Abraham	Pvt.	Co. K, 307th Infantry	NYD
Kurtz, Nicholas	Pvt.	Co. H, 308th Infantry	W'd, right forearm
Landers, Patrick J.	Sgt.	Co. H, 308th Infantry	
Langer, Julius	Pvt.	Co. H, 308th Infantry	
Larkin, Archie F.	Pvt.	Co. C, 308th Infantry	
Larney, James F.	Pvt.	1 Bt'n, 308th Infantry	W'd, right arm, left leg
Larson, Erik	Pvt.	Co. C, 308th Infantry	
Lauder, Frank N.	Pvt.	Co. C, 308th Infantry	
Lavine, Joseph	Pvt.	Co. E, 308th Infantry (scout)	

Layman, Ray E.	Pvt.	Co. G, 308th Infantry	
Leak, James V.	1 Lt.	Co. E, 308th Infantry	W'd, prisoner
Lee, Bernard J.	Pvt.	Co. C, 308th Infantry	Killed
Leflaer, Len L.	Pvt.	Co. H, 308th Infantry	
Lehmeier, Joseph	Pvt.	Co. K, 307th Infantry	W'd, head
Lekan, Michael	Wag.	Co. K, 307th Infantry	Killed
LeMay, Adlare J.	Pvt.	Co. D, 308th Infantry	W'd, prisoner
Lesley, James E.	Pvt.	Co. H, 308th Infantry	
Lesnick, Max	Pvt.	Co. C, 308th Infantry	W'd, left shoulder
Lightfoot, Roy H.	Pvt.	Co. C, 308th Infantry	
Lima, Sigurd	Pvt.	Co. G, 308th Infantry	Killed
Lindley, Gilbert L.	Pvt.	Co. G, 308th Infantry	W'd, rheumatism
Liner, Irving L.	Pvt.	Co. D, 308th Infantry (runner)	
Lipacher, Isaac	Pvt.	Co. K, 307th Infantry	W'd, head
Lipasti, Frank	Pvt.	Co. K, 307th Infantry	Killed
Little, Robert G.	Pvt.	Co. H, 308th Infantry	Killed
Loendorf, Jacob	Pvt.	Co. C, 308th Infantry	W'd, forehead, back
Lokken, Martin O.	Pvt.	Co. B, 308th Infantry	
Lonergan, James E.	Pvt.	Co. D, 306th MG Bat'n	W'd
Long, Patrick	Pvt.	Co. K, 307th Infantry	
Looslie, Daniel H.	Pvt.	Co. B, 308th Infantry	Killed
Lovell, Arthur R.	Pvt.	Co. G, 308th Infantry	
Lowman, Cecil O.	Pvt.	Co. C, 308th Infantry	
Luckett, Henry C.	Pvt.	Co. H, 308th Infantry	Killed
Lucy, William J.	Pvt.	Co. H, 308th Infantry	
Lukas, Michael J.	Pvt.	Co. E, 308th Infantry (runner)	
Lund, Engval	Pvt.	Co. C, 308th Infantry	NYD
Lynch, James A.	Pvt.	Co. H, 308th Infantry	Killed
Lyon, Thomas J.	Pvt.	Co. H, 308th Infantry	Killed
Lyons, Frank J.	Pvt.	Co. K, 307th Infantry	
Lysen, Chester	Pvt.	Co. C, 308th Infantry	
Macali, Joseph	Pvt.	Co. B, 308th Infantry	W'd, left wrist
Magnusson, David	PFC	Co. F, 308th Infantry (scout)	W'd, right foot
Mahoney, Marion E.	Pvt.	Co. C, 308th Infantry	
Main, Fred T.	Sgt.	Co. C, 308th Infantry	
Mandell, Fred A.	Pvt.	Co. C, 308th Infantry	W'd, multiple

Mann, Sydney C.	Pvt.	Co. H, 308th Infantry	Trench foot
Mannion, Thomas J.	Pvt.	Co. K, 307th Infantry	NYD
Manson, Robert	Pvt.	Co. B, 308th Infantry (runner)	W'd, right hand
Marchlewski, Stephen	Pvt.	Co. C, 308th Infantry	
Marcus, Samuel	Sgt.	Co. B, 308th Infantry	Neuritis
Marcy, Leo W.	Cpl.	Co. D, 306th MG Bat'n	Killed
Mares, Rito	Pvt.	Co. G, 308th Infantry	Missing
Marion, Roy L.	Pvt.	Co. C, 308th Infantry	W'd, right chest
Marshallcowitz, Saul	Pvt.	Med Det, 308th Infantry	W'd, prisoner
Martin, Albert E.	Pvt.	Co. K, 307th Infantry	W'd, right leg
Martin, Wayne W.	Pvt.	Co. A, 308th Infantry	
Martin, William H.	Pvt.	Co. G, 308th Infantry	Died of w'ds Oct. 24
Materna, Joseph	Pvt.	Co. K, 307th Infantry	W'd
Mathews, Andrew	Pvt.	Co. H, 308th Infantry	
Mathews, Richard W.	Cpl.	Co. B, 308th Infantry	NYD
Mauro, Frank	Pvt.	Co. H, 308th Infantry	W'd, left foot
Mayhew, George	Pvt.	Co. C, 308th Infantry	
McCabe, John	Pvt.	Co. C, 308th Infantry	
McCallion, John J.	Pvt.	Co. E, 308th Infantry (runner)	Missing
McCauley, Jesse J.	Pvt.	Co. G, 308th Infantry	
McCoy, Bert C.	Pvt.	Co. A, 308th Infantry	W'd
McElroy, Joseph A.	Pvt.	Co. I, 308th Infantry	NYD
McFeron, Olin	Pvt.	Co. C, 308th Infantry	
McGowen, Joseph L.	Pvt.	Co. C, 308th Infantry	
McGrath, Eugene M.	Pvt.	Co. C, 308th Infantry	Killed
McMahon, Martin	Cpl.	Co. B, 308th Infantry	W'd, right hand
McMullin, William	Pvt.	Co. E, 308th Infantry	Prisoner
McMurtry, George G.	Capt.	2 Bat'n, 308th Infantry	W'd, left knee, shoulder
McNearney, John A.	Pvt.	Co. H, 308th Infantry	
Mead, Joseph P.	Pvt.	Co. C, 308th Infantry	Killed
Mears, Robert L.	Pvt.	Co. C, 308th Infantry	
Medboe, Joseph	Pvt.	Co. C, 308th Infantry	W'd, right hand
Mele, Michael	Pvt.	Co. G, 308th Infantry	W'd, multiple
Melvin, Harry J.	Pvt.	Co. F, 308th Infantry	
Mendenhall, Jesse J.	Pvt.	Co. H, 308th Infantry	Killed
Merry, Ernest S.	Cpl.	Co. E, 308th Infantry	W'd

Mettam, Nie B.	Pvt.	Co. A, 308th Infantry	NYD
Meyerowitz, Tobias	Pvt.	Co. K, 307th Infantry	
Meyers, Charles	Pvt.	Co. B, 308th Infantry	
Mikulwicz, F. M.	Pvt.	Co. I, 308th Infantry	
Miller, Fernnau	Pvt.	Co. H, 308th Infantry	
Miller, Henry	Mech.	Co. H, 308th Infantry	Killed
Miller, Henry I.	Pvt.	Co. E, 308th Infantry	Killed
Miller, Nathaniel	Pvt.	Co. G, 308th Infantry	W'd, NYD
Miney, Patrick	Pvt.	Co. E, 308th Infantry	W'd
Monan, Robert F.	Pvt.	Co. K, 307th Infantry	
Monk, William	Pvt.	Co. C, 308th Infantry	W'd, chin, left knee
Morem, Arnold M.	Pvt.	Co. E, 308th Infantry	W'd, left side
Morris, Albert	Pvt.	Co. C, 308th Infantry	
Morris, Louis	PFC	Co. B, 308th Infantry	W'd, left thigh
Morrow, Bert B.	Sgt.	Co. C, 308th Infantry	NYD
Munson, Gustave	Pvt.	Co. H, 308th Infantry	W'd, right hand
Murphy, James J.	Sgt.	Co. K, 307th Infantry	
Murphy, John	Pvt.	Co. C, 308th Infantry	
Murray, Fred	Pvt.	Co. F, 308th Infantry	W'd, left hand
Murray, Kenneth	Pvt.	Co. K, 307th Infantry	
Murray, Thomas	Pvt.	Co. K, 307th Infantry	W'd, head
Myers, Tobias S.	Cpl.	Co. K, 307th Infantry	
Mynard, Edwin S.	Sgt.	Co. D, 306th MG Bat'n	
Nauheim, Alfred P.	Cpl.	Co. A, 308th Infantry	W'd, bayonet (acc)
Nell, John W.	Pvt.	Co. G, 308th Infantry	
Nelson, Arthur G.	Cpl.	Co. H, 308th Infantry (scout)	W'd, right foot
Nelson, Olaf	Cpl.	Co. H, 308th Infantry	
Neptune, Harold B.	Pvt.	Co. H, 308th Infantry	W'd, right leg
Newcom, George H.	Pvt.	Co. E, 308th Infantry	
Nies, George W.	Pvt.	Co. H, 308th Infantry	Killed
Noon, Alfred R.	2 Lt.	Co. C, 306th MG Bat'n	Killed
Norton, Grant S.	PFC	Co. B, 308th Infantry	Killed
Novotny, Otto	Pvt.	Co. F, 308th Infantry	
O'Brien, Lewis	Pvt.	Co. C, 308th Infantry	
O'Connell, James P.	Cpl.	Co. D, 306th MG Bat'n	
O'Connell, John	Pvt.	Co. E, 308th Infantry	Prisoner
O'Connor, Patrick J.	Pvt.	Co. G, 308th Infantry	Killed

Ofstad, Gile	Pvt.	Co. K, 307th Infantry	W'd
O'Keefe, John J.	Pvt.	Co. E, 308th Infantry (scout)	W'd, left foot
O'Keefe, Thomas C.	Bug.	Co. D, 306th MG Bat'n	Killed
Oliver, Walter T.	Pvt.	Co. D, 306th MG Bat'n	W'd, right arm
Olson, Fred	Pvt.	Co. C, 308th Infantry	
Olson, Lars	Pvt.	Co. C, 308th Infantry	
Olstren, Andrew	Pvt.	Co. K, 307th Infantry	
Orlando, Angel	Pvt.	Co. H, 308th Infantry	W'd
Osborne, Lawrence M.	Sgt.	Co. B, 308th Infantry	Killed
Ostrovsky, Isadore	Pvt.	Co. H, 308th Infantry	
Ostrow, I.	Pvt.	Co. H, 308th Infantry	
Oxman, Charles	Pvt.	Co. C, 308th Infantry	
Pagliaro, Benjamin	Pvt.	Co. G, 308th Infantry	W'd, influenza
Pardue, Robert M.	Pvt.	Co. E, 308th Infantry	W'd
Parker, George W.	Pvt.	Co. F, 308th Infantry	
Patterson, Clarence	Pvt.	Co. ?, 308th Infantry (runner)	
Payne, Andrew	Pvt.	Co. C, 308th Infantry	W'd, head
Peabody, Marshall G.	2 Lt.	Co. D, 306th MG Bat'n	Killed
Pennington, Joseph R.	Pvt.	Co. E, 308th Infantry	W'd, left thigh, butt
Perea, Enrique	Pvt.	Co. H, 308th Infantry	
Perrigo, Myron D.	Pvt.	Co. G, 308th Infantry	W'd, right eye (acc)
Pesetti, Salvatore	Pvt.	Co. K, 307th Infantry	
Peters, Clarence	Pvt.	Co. B, 308th Infantry	W'd, neck, face, left leg
Peterson, Emil A.	Pvt.	Co. H, 308th Infantry	W'd, left leg, prisoner
Peterson, Holger	Cpl.	Co. G, 308th Infantry	Killed
Peterson, Walter S.	Pvt.	Co. B, 308th Infantry	W'd, left eye
Peterson, William L.	Pvt.	Co. E, 308th Infantry	Killed
Petti, Alfred J.	Pvt.	Co. H, 308th Infantry (scout)	
Phelps, Harry L.	Pvt.	Co. C, 308th Infantry	Killed
Phelps, Jacob C.	Pvt.	Co. K, 307th Infantry	W'd, right leg
Phillips, Henry	Pvt.	Co. E, 308th Infantry	Prisoner
Pierson, John L.	Pvt.	Co. K, 307th Infantry	W'd
Pinkstone, Charles W.	Cpl.	Co. C, 308th Infantry	W'd, left foot
Pollinger, Frank J.	Pvt.	Co. G, 308th Infantry	W'd, right foot

Pomeroy, Lawrence	Pvt.	Co. B, 308th Infantry	
Pool, Thomas G.	1 Lt.	Co. K, 307th Infantry	W'd, right side
Pope, Calegere	Pvt.	Co. K, 307th Infantry	
Potter, Oscar	Pvt.	Co. G, 308th Infantry	W'd, arthritis
Pou, Robert E.	Pvt.	Co. E, 308th Infantry	
Powell, Josephus	Pvt.	Co. H, 308th Infantry	W'd, back
Powers, William J.	Pvt.	1 Bat'n, 308th Infantry	
Probst, Louis M.	Mech.	Co. E, 308th Infantry (scout)	NYD
Prusek, Joseph	Pvt.	Co. K, 307th Infantry	
Pugh, Charles J., Jr.	Pvt.	Co. E, 308th Infantry (runner)	
Puniskis, Joseph H.	Pvt.	Co. C, 308th Infantry	
Radant, Silas L.	Pvt.	Co. G, 308th Infantry	W'd
Rainwater, Carl A.	Pvt.	Co. G, 308th Infantry (runner)	
Rank, Lloyd	Pvt.	Co. B, 308th Infantry	
Ratonda, Herman E. H.	Pvt.	Co. D, 308th Infantry	W'd
Ratto, Vito	Pvt.	Co. E, 308th Infantry	
Rauchle, Frank	Cpl.	Co. C, 306th MG Bat'n	NYD
Ray, Guy W.	Pvt.	Co. B, 308th Infantry	
Raygor, Earnest E.	Pvt.	Co. E, 308th Infantry	Killed
Rayony, Spiro	Pvt.	Co. ?, 308th Infantry (runner)	
Rayson, Homer	Pvt.	Co. G, 308th Infantry (scout)	Died of w'ds Oct. 19
Recko, Jack	Pvt.	Co. H, 308th Infantry	
Rector, Frank C.	Cpl.	Co. D, 306th MG Bat'n	
Regan, William	Pvt.	Co. G, 308th Infantry	Died of disease Dec. 18
Reid, Lauren G.	Pvt.	Co. G, 308th Infantry	Killed
Reiger, John	Pvt.	Co. B, 308th Infantry	W'd
Renda, John	Pvt.	Co. H, 308th Infantry	W'd, left leg
Revnes, Maurice S.	2 Lt.	Co. D, 306th MG Bat'n	W'd, left foot
Reynolds, John	PFC	Co. C, 308th Infantry	Killed
Rhoads, Solomon E.	Pvt.	Co. H, 308th Infantry	
Rice, Chauncey I.	Cpl.	Co. D, 306th MG Bat'n	
Richards, Omer	Pvt.	1 Bat'n, 308th Infantry	
Richardson, ?	Pvt.	Co. C, 306th MG Bat'n	
Richter, Morris	Pvt.	Co. C, 308th Infantry	NYD
Ridlon, Ernest J.	Pvt.	Co. G, 308th Infantry	W'd, right hand

Name	Rank	Unit	Status
Rissi, Bernard	PFC	Co. G, 308th Infantry	Killed
Ritter, Charles	Pvt.	Co. H, 308th Infantry	W'd, right thigh
Roberts, Benjamin	PFC	Co. K, 307th Infantry	W'd, back, right leg
Roberts, Clarence	Pvt.	Co. B, 308th Infantry	
Robertson, Arch	Pvt.	Co. H, 308th Infantry	
Rochester, Nathaniel N.	PFC	Co. E, 308th Infantry	Killed
Rodriguez, Alfred	Pvt.	Co. ?, 308th Infantry (scout)	
Roesch, Clarence R.	Sgt. Maj.	2 Bat'n, 308th Infantry	
Rogers, Harry	2 Lt.	Co. B, 308th Infantry	Killed
Ronan, Maurice H.	Pvt.	Co. C, 306th MG Bat'n	
Rosby, Thorvald	Pvt.	Co. K, 307th Infantry	W'd, arms, leg
Rose, Sidney	Pvt.	Co. E, 308th Infantry	W'd, forehead
Rosenberg, Samuel	PFC	Co. H, 308th Infantry	Died of w'ds Oct. 12
Ross, Albert A.	Pvt.	Co. G, 308th Infantry	Killed
Rossum, Haakon A.	Cpl.	Co. G, 308th Infantry	W'd
Royall, Joseph	Pvt.	Co. H, 308th Infantry	
Rudolph, Aloysius J.	Pvt.	Co. E, 308th Infantry	Killed
Rugg, Hiram M.	Pvt.	Co. H, 308th Infantry	W'd, head, back
Rumsey, Wilbert T.	Pvt.	Co. K, 307th Infantry	Killed
Ruppe, John F.	Pvt.	Co. H, 308th Infantry (scout)	Killed
Ryan, John F.	Cpl.	Co. D, 306th MG Bat'n	Killed
Sackman, Julius	Sgt.	Co. D, 306th MG Bat'n	W'd, left side, abdomen
Sadler, Thomas G., Jr.	Pvt.	Batt D, 305th Field Artillery	W'd, left leg
Sands, Lester T.	Pvt.	Co. H, 308th Infantry (scout)	
Santillo, Anthony T.	Pvt.	Co. D, 306th MG Bat'n	Killed
Santini, Guiseppe	Pvt.	Co. G, 308th Infantry	
Scanlon, John H.	Pvt.	Co. D, 306th MG Bat'n	W'd, left back, hip
Schaffer, Harry L.	Cpl.	Co. H, 308th Infantry	W'd, face
Schanz, Joseph A.	Pvt.	Co. G, 308th Infantry	
Schenck, Gordon L.	2 Lt.	Co. C, 308th Infantry	Killed
Schettino, Lememe	Pvt.	Co. K, 307th Infantry	

Schmidt, John H.	Mech.	Co. G, 308th Infantry	W'd, left leg
Schmitt, Frederick F.	PFC	Co. D, 306th MG Bat'n	Killed
Schmitz, Joseph J.	PFC	Co. D, 306th MG Bat'n	W'd, right femur
Schultz, Otto J.	Pvt.	Co. E, 308th Infantry	Died of w'ds Nov. 7
Schultz, William	Pvt.	Co. G, 308th Infantry	
Schwartz, Paul A.	Cpl.	Co. K, 307th Infantry	NYD
Scialdone, Guiseppe	Pvt.	Co. K, 307th Infantry	W'd, leg
Segal, Paul	Pvt.	Co. C, 308th Infantry	
Selg, Eugene	Pvt.	Co. G, 308th Infantry	
Semenuk, Harry	Pvt.	Co. C, 308th Infantry	
Senter, Henry H.	Pvt.	Co. H, 308th Infantry	W'd, left knee
Shea, James E.	PFC	Co. H, 308th Infantry	Killed
Shepard, Arthur H.	Pvt.	Co. G, 308th Infantry	
Sica, Rocco	Pvt.	Co. E, 308th Infantry	Killed
Simonson, Alfred	Pvt.	Co. B, 308th Infantry	W'd
Sims, George P.	Cpl.	Co. K, 307th Infantry	
Sirota, Irving	Pvt.	Med. Det., 308th Infantry	Trench foot, NYD
Sketson, Orlander	Pvt.	Co. B, 308th Infantry	Missing
Slingerland, James E.	Pvt.	Co. G, 308th Infantry	
Smith, Sidney	Pvt.	Co. H, 308th Infantry	W'd, left side, right leg
Sobaszkiewicz, Stanley	Pvt.	Co. H, 308th Infantry	W'd
Solomon, Arthur	Pvt.	Co. F, 308th Infantry (scout)	
Spallina, Joseph	Pvt.	Co. K, 307th Infantry	W'd, right hand
Speich, George F.	Cpl.	Co. K, 307th Infantry	W'd, injured knee
Spiegel, Isidore	Pvt.	Co. H, 308th Infantry	
St. Cartier, Lucien F.	PFC	Co. C, 308th Infantry	Killed
Stamboni, Joseph	Pvt.	Co. D, 306th MG Bat'n	W'd
Stanfield, John A.	Pvt.	Co. H, 308th Infantry	
Steichen, Albert N.	Pvt.	Co. H, 308th Infantry	Rheumatism
Stenger, W.	Pvt.	Co. H, 308th Infantry	
Stingle, Frank	Pvt.	Co. K, 307th Infantry	W'd, face, right thigh
Stoianoff, Blaze	Pvt.	Co. H, 308th Infantry	
Strickland, James R.	Pvt.	Co. H, 308th Infantry	W'd, right femur

Stringer, Edward	Pvt.	Co. E, 308th Infantry (runner)	W'd, spine
Stromee, Leo A.	Capt.	Co. C, 308th Infantry	W'd, shoulder
Stumbo, Leroy A.	Pvt.	Co. K, 307th Infantry	W'd, head
Sullivan, Jerry	Pvt.	Co. E, 308th Infantry	Prisoner
Summers, Alfred E.	Pvt.	Co. H, 308th Infantry (scout)	
Sundby, Melvin G.	Pvt.	Co. H, 308th Infantry	Died of disease Oct. 15
Surgo, Benedetto	Pvt.	Co. C, 308th Infantry	
Swanbeck, Arthur	Pvt.	Co. K, 307th Infantry	W'd, right arm
Swanson, Edward	Pvt.	Co. H, 308th Infantry	
Swanson, Olaf W.	Pvt.	Co. E, 308th Infantry	Killed
Swanson, Sigurd V.	Pvt.	Co. B, 308th Infantry	NYD
Swartz, John B.	Pvt.	Co. H, 308th Infantry	W'd
Sweeney, Bernard J.	Pvt.	Co. D, 306th MG Bat'n	W'd, left wrist
Swenson, Oscar A.	Pvt.	Co. G, 308th Infantry	Killed
Taasaas, Andrew J.	Pvt.	Co. H, 308th Infantry	
Talbot, William R.	Pvt.	Co. E, 308th Infantry	Killed
Tallon, Daniel B.	Cpl.	Co. E, 308th Infantry	Killed
Teichmoeller, John G.	1 Lt.	Batt D, 305th Field Artillery	Deaf
Test, Pietro	Pvt.	Co. K, 307th Infantry	W'd, chest, rt shoulder
Thatcher, Lee	Pvt.	Co. C, 308th Infantry	
Thomas, Clifford	Pvt.	Co. K, 307th Infantry	W'd
Thomas, Harold H.	Pvt.	Co. H, 308th Infantry	Killed
Thompson, Arthur A.	Cpl.	Co. D, 306th MG Bat'n	
Thorbone, Roland	Pvt.	Co. B, 308th Infantry	
Thorsen, Harry	Pvt.	Co. G, 308th Infantry (runner)	W'd
Tiederman, Herbert	Pvt.	HQ Co, 308th Infantry	
Todisco, Amos	1 Sgt.	Co. G, 308th Infantry	W'd, left hand
Tollefson, Theodore	Pvt.	1 Bat'n, 308th Infantry	Killed
Tolley, Courtney W.	Pvt.	Co. D, 306th MG Bat'n	
Torpey, Leslie C.	Pvt.	Co. D, 306th MG Bat'n	
Trainor, Leo W.	2 Lt.	Co. C, 308th Infantry	W'd
Travers, John H.	Pvt.	Co. D, 306th MG Bat'n	Died of w'ds Oct. 17
Treadwell, Ray	Pvt.	Co. K, 307th Infantry	NYD
Trigani, Antonius	Pvt.	Co. G, 308th Infantry	

Tronson, Melvin C.	Pvt.	Co. E, 308th Infantry	Prisoner
Tucker, Jack	Cpl.	Co. C, 308th Infantry	
Tuite, Martin F.	Sgt.	Co. C, 308th Infantry	
Tulchin, David	Pvt.	Co. C, 308th Infantry (runner)	
Tumm, Charles G.	Cpl.	Co. H, 308th Infantry	Killed
Turnquist, Benjamin E.	Pvt.	Co. K, 307th Infantry	
Underhill, Lester	Mech.	Co. K, 307th Infantry	
Untereiner, Hugo E.	Pvt.	Co. H, 308th Infantry	
Vitkus, Joseph	Pvt.	Co. E, 308th Infantry	
Vittulli, Constantine	Pvt.	Co. C, 308th Infantry	W'd, abdomen
Volz, Otto M.	Pvt.	Co. K, 307th Infantry	W'd, lower cheek
Voorheis, John L.	Cpl.	Co. C, 308th Infantry	NYD
Wade, Farland F.	Pvt.	Co. G, 308th Infantry (scout)	W'd, head
Walker, George	PFC	Med Det, 308th Infantry	W'd, multiple
Wallace, Dosia W.	Pvt.	Co. G, 308th Infantry	W'd, left eye
Wallen, Oscar	Pvt.	Co. G, 308th Infantry	W'd
Wallenstein, Charles	Pvt.	Co. C, 308th Infantry	NYD
Weaver, Glenn H.	Pvt.	Co. G, 308th Infantry	W'd, right arm
Weiner, Walter	Pvt.	Co. ?, 308th Infantry (scout)	
Weinhold, Fred	Pvt.	Co. E, 308th Infantry	Prisoner
Wenzel, Edward L.	Pvt.	Co. H, 308th Infantry (scout)	Prisoner
Wheeler, Otto	Pvt.	Co. H, 308th Infantry	Killed
White, Peter H.	Pvt.	Co. F, 308th Infantry (runner)	
White, Scott R.	Pvt.	Co. H, 308th Infantry	Influenza
Whiting, Wilbur C.	Cpl.	Co. H, 308th Infantry	
Whittlesey, Charles W.	Maj.	1 Bat'n, 308th Infantry	W'd, nose
Wilber, Frederick L.	PFC	Co. G, 308th Infantry	W'd, face
Wilhelm, Karl E.	2 Lt.	Co. E, 308th Infantry	W'd, hand
Williamson, Henry J.	2 Lt.	Co. A, 308th Infantry	W'd, toe
Willinger, Isadore	Pvt.	Co. K, 307th Infantry	Prisoner
Willis, Oscar	Pvt.	Co. H, 308th Infantry	W'd, left leg
Witschen, Vincent	Pvt.	Co. K, 307th Infantry	

Witthaus, Albert R.	Pvt.	Co. H, 308th Infantry	W'd, left shoulder
Wolf, Samuel	Pvt.	Co. B, 308th Infantry	
Wolfe, Earle I.	Pvt.	Co. C, 308th Infantry	
Wondolowsky, Stephen	Pvt.	Co. A, 308th Infantry	
Woods, James R.	Pvt.	Co. G, 308th Infantry	
Workman, William J.	Pvt.	Co. H, 308th Infantry	Killed
Wornek, Ernest	Pvt.	Co. G, 308th Infantry	W'd, left heel
Wright, William J.	Pvt.	Co. D, 306th MG Bat'n	
Yoder, Robert S.	Pvt.	Co. E, 308th Infantry	
Zeman, Louis	Pvt.	Co. H, 308th Infantry	Killed
Ziegenbalg, William	Pvt.	Co. B, 308th Infantry	

NOTES

CHAPTER 1: THE DRAFT

1. Tryon, "The Draft," p. 344; Harbord, *American Army*, pp. 24–25.
2. Eisenhower, *Yanks*, pp. 4–6, 9–10.
3. Tryon, "The Draft," pp. 340–44; Field, *Battery Book*, p. 4.
4. Herschell, *The Kid*, p. 1.
5. *New York Times*, August 12, 1917, sec. 6; Field, *Battery Book*, p. 4; Showalter, "America's New Soldier Cities," pp. 439, 449–50.
6. Batchelder, *Camp Upton*, pp. 4–5; *New York Times*, July 17, 1917.
7. *77th Division*, p. 11; *306th Infantry*, p. 1; *New York Times*, August 12, 1917, sec. 6, and August 21, 1917.
8. *77th Division*, pp. 162–63; Batchelder, *Camp Upton*, p. 6; *New York Times*, September 23, 1917, sec. 1.
9. "Civilian workmen swarmed": Howard, *304th Field Artillery*, p. 6; Miles, *308th Infantry*, pp. 3–5; "Myriad of sweating": Tiebout, *305th Infantry*, p. 13; "It wore an air": *305th Field Artillery*, p. 5; *77th Division*, p. 12.
10. Howard, *304th Field Artillery*, p. 8; Field, *Battery Book*, p. 18; *305th Field Artillery*, pp. 13–14.
11. *New York Times*, September 10, 1917; Dwyer, "Camp Upton," p. 31; Batchelder, *Camp Upton*, p. 12; *77th Division*, p. 13; Field, *Battery Book*, p. 6; Miles, *308th Infantry*, p. 7; Crump, *Conscript 2989*, p. 4.
12. Merrill, *Uncommon Valor*, p. 308.
13. Batchelder, *Camp Upton*, p. 14; Merrill, *Uncommon Valor*, pp. 298–99; Field, *Battery Book*, p. 6.

14. *77th Division*, p. 13; "Fifth Avenue": Howard, *304th Field Artillery*, p. 9; *306th Field Artillery*, p. 7.

15. *305th Field Artillery*, p. 16.

16. *77th Division*, p. 13; Hunt, *Blown In*, pp. 12–16; *306th Field Artillery*, p. 7; *305th Field Artillery*, p. 15.

17. Dwyer, "Camp Upton," p. 32; "Melting-Pot Division," p. 89; *306th Infantry*, p. 7; *Hickoxy's Army*, p. 13; Rainsford, *Upton to the Meuse*, p. 4; Sullivan, *History of New York*, 4:1333.

18. *305th Field Artillery*, p. 18; Rainsford, *Upton to the Meuse*, pp. 3–4; *77th Division*, p. 13.

19. Byers, "Camp Upton," p. 15; Hunt, *Blown In*, pp. 60–65, 325–37; *New York Times*, September 6, 1942, sec. 7.

20. Hussey, *Company E*, p. 5.

21. Merrill. *Uncommon Valor*, p. 300; Tiebout, *305th Infantry*, pp. 14–15; Davis, *307th Ambulance*, p. 11; *New York Times*, July 25 and August 16, 1917; September 13, 1917.

22. *New York Times*, September 10 and 21, 1917; Dwyer, "Camp Upton," p. 55; Tiebout, *305th Infantry*, p. 14; *305th Field Artillery*, p. 19; "midst of awful crowd": Boyer, "Army Bandsman," p. 189.

23. *New York Times*, September 13, 1917; Dwyer, "Camp Upton," p. 55; Howard, *304th Field Artillery*, p. 11; Field, *Battery Book*, p. 7; Tiebout, *305th Infantry*, pp. 15–16; Davis, *307th Ambulance*, pp. 12–13.

24. Merrill, *Uncommon Valor*, p. 307; *New York Times*, September 13, 1917; Field, *Battery Book*, p. 7; Tiebout, *305th Infantry*, p. 16; Shookhoff, *Machine Gun Company*, p. 1; "it felt more like": Davis, *307th Ambulance*, p. 10; Rindge, "Uncle Sam's Nephews," p. 281.

25. *306th Field Artillery*, p. 68; Batchelder, *Camp Upton*, pp. 16, 46; Teibout, *305th Infantry*, p. 21; *New York Times*, September 13, 1917; October 5, 1917; *308th Infantry Rumor*, p. 3.

26. Batchelder, *Camp Upton*, p. 36; Field, *Battery Book*, pp. 8–9; Howard, *304th Field Artillery*, p. 20.

27. Berry, *Make the Kaiser*, p. 360.

28. *New York Times*, September 15, 1917; "viewed from distance": *306th Field Artillery*, p. 8; *306th Infantry*, p. 10; *305th Field Artillery*, p. 20; Shookhoff, *Machine Gun Company*, p. 1.

29. *New York Times*, September 10, 1917; September 21, 1917; Merrill, *Uncommon Valor*, p. 303; "Boys from the docks": Sweeney, *History of Buffalo*, p. 152; *77th Division*, p. 15; "diverse and interesting": Sullivan, *History of New York*, 4: 1334; Howard, *304th Field Artillery*, p. 22.

30. *New York Times*, September 24, November 19, December 16, 1917, sec. 1.

31. *77th Division*, p. 14; Miles, *308th Infantry*, p. 11; Tiebout, *305th Infantry*, p. 19; *New York Times*, September 29, sec. 1; and December 9, sec. 1; *New York Sun*, March 30, 1919, sec. 6; Field, *Battery Book*, pp. 22–24.

32. Tiebout, *305th Infantry*, p. 26; Rindge, "Uncle Sam's Nephews," p. 282.

33. Hussey, *Company E*, p. 1; *302nd Engineers*, p. 19; Field, *Battery Book*, p. 10; Howard, *304th Field Artillery*, p. 7; Batchelder, *Camp Upton*, p. 18; *305th Field Artillery*, pp. 21–22.

34. Batchelder, *Camp Upton*, p. 38; Crump, *Conscript 2989*, p. 30; Merrill, *Uncommon Valor*, p. 303.

35. Batchelder, *Camp Upton*, p. 38.

36. *77th Division*, p. 14; Dwyer, "Camp Upton," pp. 33–34; Biggs quote: *New York Times*, October 14, 1917, sec. 1.

37. Crump, *Conscript 2989*, p. 54.

38. Batchelder, *Camp Upton*, pp. 24, 26; *New York Times*, December 16, 1917, sec. 1; Dewan, "From Long Island to Over There," www.lihistory.com; Dwyer, "Camp Upton," p. 34.

39. *306th Field Artillery*, p. 10; Tiebout, *305th Infantry*, p. 18; Howard, *304th Field Artillery*, p. 23; *77th Division*, p. 15; "men standing": *New York Times*, October 9, 1917.

40. *New York Times*, October 29, 1917; November 1, 1917.

41. *306th Infantry*, p. 11; Hunt, *Blown In*, pp. 108–13; *308th Infantry Rumor*, p. 6.

42. *New York Times*, October 14, 1917, sec. 1; Hunt, *Blown In*, pp. 352–60.

43. Hunt, *Blown In*, pp. 345–52.

44. Ibid., pp. 282–86.

45. Ibid., pp. 53–59.

CHAPTER 2: CAMP UPTON

1. Field, *Battery Book*, pp. 15, 18.

2. Field, *Battery Book*, p. 16; Dickson, *War Slang*, pp. 83, 95; Tiebout, *305th Infantry*, p. 20.

3. "Looking back": *302nd Engineers*, p. 20; "our own colossal": Field, *Battery Book*, pp. 15–16.

4. *New York Times*, September 29, sec. 1; October 9, December 16, 1917; "more concerned over": Rainsford, *Upton to the Meuse*, p. 10; *77th Division*, pp. 15–16.

5. *New York Times*, March 18, 1919.

6. MS 3144, Frank A. Partridge, Gordon Collection.

7. *New York Times*, March 10, 1918.

8. Johnson, "Students," pp. 44–47.

9. *New York Times*, March 18, 1919; Johnson, "Students," pp. 47–48; *306th Infantry*, p. 9.

10. *305th Field Artillery*, p. 21; Tiebout, *305th Infantry*, p. 12.

11. Cray, *Erotic Muse*, p. 229.

12. Davis, *307th Ambulance*, p. 21; *Hickoxy's Army*, p. 17; "which for minuteness": *77th Division*, p. 16; Miles, *308th Infantry*, p. 15; *306th Infantry*, p. 13.

13. *306th Infantry*, p. 13; Miles, *308th Infantry*, p. 115; Whittlesey described: *New York Times*, September 25, 1938, sec. 7.

14. *305th Field Artillery*, p. 35.

15. *77th Division*, p. 16; Miles, *308th Infantry*, p. 16; Rainsford, *Upton to the Meuse*, pp. 14–15.

16. Tiebout, *305th Infantry*, p. 23; *306th Infantry*, p. 17; Berry, *Make the Kaiser*, p. 344.

17. Davis, *307th Ambulance*, pp. 23–24.

18. MS 3144, Frank A. Partridge, Gordon Collection.

19. Shookhoff, *Machine Gun Company*, p. 3,

20. Whitman quote: *New York Times*, February 8, 1918; Miles, *308th Infantry*, pp. 5, 17–18; *77th Division*, p. 17.

21. *77th Division*, p. 17; Tiebout, *305th Infantry*, p. 28; *305th Field Artillery*, p. 53; Rainsford, *Upton to the Meuse*, p. 15; "From sidewalk to sky-line": *306th Infantry*, p. 21.

22. *Literary Digest* quote: Sullivan, *History of New York*, 4:1334–35; *306th Infantry*, p. 20–21; Minder, *This Man's War*, p. 140; *306th Field Artillery*, p. 65.

23. The nickname "Statue of Liberty Division" proved to be unwieldy in the columns of New York newspapers, so editors generally shortened it to simply "Liberty Division," apparently unaware that the same name had already been applied to the Seventy-ninth Division, then being formed at Camp Meade, Maryland. See *77th Division*, p. 17; *New York Times*, March 14, 1918; Tiebout, *305th Infantry*, p. 28; Miles, *308th Infantry*, p. 19; Hussey, *Company E*, p. 81; "Melting–Pot Division," p. 85.

24. Tiebout, *305th Infantry*, p. 27; Miles, *308th Infantry*, p. 18; quotes appear in Field, *Battery Book*, pp. 22–23; Davis, *307th Ambulance*, p. 30.

25. Davis, *307th Ambulance*, pp. 29–30.

26. *77th Division*, pp. 19, 162; *306th Infantry*, p. 22; Miles, *308th Infantry*, p. 14.

27. *305th Field Artillery*, pp. 32–34; Rainsford, *Upton to the Meuse*, pp. 6–7, 18; *306th Field Artillery*, p. 11.

28. Blowers, *Roundtrip*, pp. 3–4, 6, 11.

29. *77th Division*, p.19; Smith, *305th Machine Gun Battalion*, pp. 7–9.

30. *New York Sun*, March 30, 1919, sec. 6; Smith, *305th Machine Gun Battalion*, pp. 8–9, 11.

31. *302nd Engineers*, pp. 26–27.

32. Ibid., pp. 28–29; Smith, *305th Machine Gun Battalion*, pp. 9–10.

33. *Stars and Stripes*, April 12, 1918.

34. Hussey, *Company E*, pp. 8–9; Miles, *308th Infantry*, p. 22; Ranlett, *Let's Go*, pp. 8–9; Blowers, *Roundtrip*, p. 9.

35. Hussey, *Company E*, p. 9; Shookhoff, *Machine Gun Company*, p. 5; Ranlett, *Let's Go*, p. 9; Rainsford, *Upton to the Meuse*, pp. 18–19; Blowers, *Roundtrip*, p. 9.

36. Stevenson, *Poems*, p. 668.

37. Shookhoff, *Machine Gun Company*, p. 7; Miles, *308th Infantry*, p. 23; Rainsford, *Upton to the Meuse*, p. 19; Blowers, *Roundtrip*, p. 9; "like a file of ants": Ranlett, *Let's Go*, p. 10.

38. Hussey, *Company E*, p. 10; Miles, *308th Infantry*, p. 24; Shookhoff, *Machine Gun Company*, p. 8; quotes: Rainsford, *Upton to the Meuse*, pp. 20–21.

39. Miles, *308th Infantry*, p. 25; Hussey, *Company E*, p. 12; Rainsford, *Upton to the Meuse*, p. 23; Blowers, *Roundtrip*, pp. 9–10; Berry, *Make the Kaiser*, p. 344.

40. Hussey, *Company E*, p. 12; Rainsford, *Upton to the Meuse*, p. 23; Miles, *308th Infantry*, pp. 26–27; Blowers, *Roundtrip*, p. 10; Ranlett, *Let's Go*, p. 19.

41. Davis, *307th Ambulance*, pp. 34–35.

42. Tiebout, *305th Infantry*, p. 30.

43. Ibid., p. 33; *306th Infantry*, p. 24.

44. Minder, *This Man's War*, p. 6; Davis, *307th Ambulance*, p. 37; Tiebout, *305th Infantry*, pp. 34, 36; *306th Infantry*, pp. 23–25, "Everybody turn in" quote on p. 24.

45. Minder, *This Man's War*, pp. 9, 18.

46. *Stars and Stripes*, April 5, 1918.

47. *306th Infantry*, p. 26; Davis, *307th Ambulance*, p. 38; Minder, *This Man's War*, pp. 9, 12, 13, 14–17.

48. Minder, *This Man's War*, pp. 9, 16, 20, 21; Davis, *307th Ambulance*, p. 43; Tiebout, *305th Infantry*, pp. 34, 37.

49. Field, *Battery Book*, pp. 33, 35–37; *Hickoxy's Army*, p. 18; *306th Field Artillery*, pp. 11–12.

50. *Hickoxy's Army*, pp. 18–19; Field, *Battery Book*, p. 38.

CHAPTER 3: OVER THERE

1. Ranlett, *Let's Go*, p. 114; Crump, *Conscript 2989*, p. 53; *77th Division*, p. 20; *306th Infantry*, p. 26; Smith, *305th Machine Gun Battalion*, p. 11; Davis, *307th Ambulance*, p. 45; Miles, *308th Infantry*, p. 29; Berry, *Make the Kaiser*, pp. 344–45.

2. Minder, *This Man's War*, pp. 23–24; Ranlett, *Let's Go*, pp. 21–22; Miles, *308th Infantry*, p. 28; *306th Infantry*, p. 26; Smith, *305th Machine Gun Battalion*, p. 11; Tiebout, *305th Infantry*, p. 37; Davis, *307th Ambulance*, pp. 45–46.

3. Minder, *This Man's War*, pp. 23–24; Rainsford, *Upton to the Meuse*, pp. 23–24; Miles, *308th Infantry*, p. 28; Davis, *307th Ambulance*, p. 46.

4. Miles, *308th Infantry*, p. 29; *306th Infantry*, p. 26; "From the appearance": *77th Division*, p. 20; Shookhoff, *Machine Gun Company*, p. 12; Minder, *This Man's War*, pp. 26–27; *302nd Engineers*, p. 30; Dickson, *War Slang*, p. 93.

5. Tiebout, *305th Infantry*, p. 39; Smith, *305th Machine Gun Battalion*, p. 12; "A salute": *306th Infantry*, p. 28.

6. Dickson, *War Slang*, pp. 56, 62–63, 88–89, 93, 103; Fraser, *Soldier and Sailor Words*, p. 81.

7. Dickson, *War Slang*, pp. 44, 62, 68, 70, 73, 99; Smith, *305th Machine Gun Battalion*, p. 23.

8. Blowers, *Roundtrip*, p. 11; Miles, *308th Infantry*, p. 30; *77th Division*, p. 20; Ranlett, *Let's Go*, p. 29, Chavelle quote on p. 31; Shookhoff, *Machine Gun Company*, p. 12; Smith, *305th Machine Gun Battalion*, p. 13; Tiebout, *305th Infantry*, p. 39; Davis, *307th Ambulance*, p. 53; Sullivan, *History of New York*, 4: 1336.

9. Sullivan, *History of New York*, 4: 1335–36.

10. Dickson, *War Slang*, p. 37.

11. Davis, *307th Ambulance*, p. 53; Smith, *305th Machine Gun Battalion*, p. 13.

12. *77th Division*, p. 21; *306th Infantry*, p. 30; Smith, *305th Machine Gun Battalion*, pp. 16–17; Blowers, *Roundtrip*, p. 11; Ranlett, *Let's Go*, p. 33.

13. Davis, *307th Ambulance*, p. 55; Smith, *305th Machine Gun Battalion*, p. 14.

14. *Stars and Stripes*, February 8, 1918.

15. "Numerous searchlights": Miles, *308th Infantry*, p. 31; Tiebout, *305th Infantry*, pp. 39–40.

16. Shookhoff, *Machine Gun Company*, p. 13; Hussey, *Company E*, p. 16; *302nd Engineers*, p. 34; Miles, *308th Infantry*, p. 31; Howard, *304th Field Artillery*, p. 52; Minder, *This Man's War*, p. 42.

17. Minder, *This Man's War*, p. 42.

18. Tiebout, *305th Infantry*, p. 42.

19. Tiebout, *305th Infantry*, p. 42; "so vividly pictured": Shookhoff, *Machine Gun Company*, p. 13; Miles, *308th Infantry*, p. 78; Smith, *305th Machine Gun Battalion*, p. 15; Blowers, *Roundtrip*, p. 13.

20. *77th Division*, p. 23; Smith, *305th Machine Gun Battalion*, p. 16; Tiebout, *305th Infantry*, p. 47; Dickson, *War Slang*, pp. 51, 65, 80.

21. Smith, *305th Machine Gun Battalion*, p. 17; Davis, *307th Ambulance*, p. 64; Tiebout, *305th Infantry*, p. 44; Blowers, *Roundtrip*, p. 12.

22. *77th Division*, p. 21; Blowers, *Roundtrip*, p. 11; Minder, *This Man's War*, p. 34; Hussey, *Company E*, p. 17; Shookhoff, *Machine Gun Company*, p. 13.

23. Rainsford, *Upton to the Meuse*, pp. 31–32, 35; Miles, *308th Infantry*, p. 36.

24. Rainsford, *Upton to the Meuse*, pp. 32–33.

25. "A huge sport": *77th Division*, p. 22; Rainsford, *Upton to the Meuse*, p. 26; Hussey, *Company E*, p. 19; Miles, *308th Infantry*, p. 36; Tiebout, *305th Infantry*, pp. 45–46, quotes on p. 46.

26. Berry, *Make the Kaiser*, p. 346.

27. Tiebout, *305th Infantry*, p. 43.

28. Miles, *308th Infantry*, pp. 39–41; Hussey, *Company E*, p. 19; *Stars and Stripes*, January 17, 1919.

29. Tiebout, *305th Infantry*, p. 50; Blowers, *Roundtrip*, p. 15; Hussey, *Company E*, pp. 19–20; *77th Division*, p. 21.

30. Minder, *This Man's War*, pp. 52, 77.

31. *77th Division*, p. 165; Miles, *308th Infantry*, pp. 41–42.

32. Fraser, *Soldier and Sailor Words*, p. 64; Dickson, *War Slang*, p. 57; Shookhoff, *Machine Gun Company*, p. 35; Tiebout, *305th Infantry*, pp. 42–43.

33. *New York Times*, November 10, 1929, sec. 5.

34. Blowers, *Roundtrip*, pp. 14, 15, 17.

35. *77th Division*, p. 23; Shookhoff, *Machine Gun Company*, p. 18; Smith, *305th Machine Gun Battalion*, pp. 23, 27; Tiebout, *305th Infantry*, p. 49; Davis, *307th Ambulance*, pp. 64–65.

36. MS 3144, Frank A. Partridge, Gordon Collection.

37. Smith, *305th Machine Gun Battalion*, p. 24; Tiebout, *305th Infantry*, pp. 48, 51–52.

38. Shookhoff, *Machine Gun Company*, pp. 18–19; Ranlett, *Let's Go*, p. 74; Hussey, *Company E*, p. 21; Rainsford, *Upton to the Meuse*, p. 57; Miles, *308th Infantry*, pp. 43–44.

39. Schweinickle, *Thousand Laughs*, np.

40. Berry, *Make the Kaiser*, p. 346.

41. *77th Division*, p. 32; Miles, *308th Infantry*, p. 49; Dickson, *War Slang*, p. 90.

42. *77th Division*, p. 43; *302nd Engineers*, p. 43; Miles, *308th Infantry*, pp. 45–46.

43. Minder, *This Man's War*, pp. 43–44; Miles, *308th Infantry*, pp. 48–49; Berry, *Make the Kaiser*, p. 347; *New York Times*, September 25, 1938, sec. 7.

44. Hussey, *Company E*, p. 22; Berry, *Make the Kaiser*, p. 347; "Good lads": Miles, *308th Infantry*, p. 48.

CHAPTER 4: BACCARAT AND THE VESLE

1. Rainsford, *Upton to the Meuse*, p. 44.

2. Ibid., pp. 44–45, "whispered consultations" on p. 45; Smith, *305th Machine Gun Battalion*, p. 27; Tiebout, *305th Infantry*, pp. 63–64, "I was cautious" on p. 63.

3. *77th Division*, p. 32; *306th Infantry*, p. 36; Rainsford, *Upton to the Meuse*, p. 49; Miles, *308th Infantry*, pp. 49, 53.

4. Miles, *308th Infantry*, pp. 54–56, "most cosmopolitan" on p. 59; *306th Infantry*, p. 38; Minder, *This Man's War*, p. 139; Ranlett, *Let's Go*, pp. 95–96.

5. Miles, *308th Infantry*, pp. 56, 59–60; Flood quote: *New York Sun*, April 6, 1919, sec. 6; Rainsford, *Upton to the Meuse*, pp. 49–50; *Jamestown (N. Y.) Evening Journal*, April 7, 1931.

6. Miles, *308th Infantry*, pp. 63–66; *New York Sun*, April 6, 1919, sec. 6.

7. Rainsford, *Upton to the Meuse*, pp. 48–54, "a few charred" on p. 50; *Through the War*, p. 9.

8. *New York Times*, November 10, 1929, sec. 5.

9. Miles, *308th Infantry*, p. 66; *St. Lawrence University*, p. 253; Minder, *This Man's War*, p. 140; *Company D, 308th Infantry*, p. 14; *77th Division*, p. 34.

10. Ranlett, *Let's Go*, p. 102.

11. *306th Infantry*, p. 40; Smith, *305th Machine Gun Battalion*, p. 31.

12. Hussey, *Company E*, p. 26; Smith, *305th Machine Gun Battalion*, pp. 37–38.

13. Smith, *305th Machine Gun Battalion*, pp. 37–39; Miles, *308th Infantry*, p. 68; Blowers, *Roundtrip*, pp. 14–15.

14. *302nd Engineers*, pp. 49–51; Miles, *308th Infantry*, p. 69.

15. Goodman quotes: *306th Field Artillery*, pp. 15, 17; Field, *Battery Book*, p. 46.

16. *New York Times*, May 4, 1919, sec. 4; Field, *Battery Book*, pp. 48–49, "many divisions" on p. 49; *Hickoxy's Army*, p. 24.

17. *306th Field Artillery*, p. 21; *Hickoxy's Army*, pp. 28–29, "Out of neighboring house" on p.29; Field, *Battery Book*, p. 57.

18. Rainsford, *Upton to the Meuse*, pp. 60–61; McKeogh quote: *New York Sun*, April 6, 1919, sec. 6; *New York Times*, May 4, 1919, sec. 4.

19. *New York Times*, November 10, 1929, sec. 5.

20. *77th Division*, pp. 37, 39, "those great men" on p. 39; *302nd Engineers*, pp. 50–51; *New York Sun*, April 6, 1919, sec. 6.

21. *New York Sun*, April 6, 1919, sec. 6.

22. *77th Division*, pp. 40–42, "Lorraine was only" on p. 40; Howard, *304th Field Artillery*, p. 104.

23. *306th Infantry*, pp. 43–44.

24. McKeogh, *Victorious 77th Division*, p. 15.

25. Smith, *305th Machine Gun Battalion*, p. 44; *306th Field Artillery*, p. 106.

26. *77th Division*, p. 42; Tiebout, *305th Infantry*, pp. 91–96, "The dugouts" on p. 92; Miles, *308th Infantry*, p. 74.

27. Howard, *304th Field Artillery*, pp. 100–1.

28. McKeogh, *Victorious 77th Division*, p. 16; *New York Sun*, April 6, 1919, sec. 6; *302nd Engineers*, p. 53; Graham quote: Sullivan, *History of New York*, 4: 1345.

29. *77th Division*, p. 43; Fraser, *Soldier and Sailor Words*, p. 129; "smaller guns": Sullivan, *History of New York*, 4: 1344.

30. Miles, *308th Infantry*, pp. 77, 79–81.

31. Shookhoff, *Machine Gun Company*, p. 96.

32. Rainsford, *Upton to the Meuse*, pp. 75–77; Howard, *304th Field Artillery*, p. 105; Smith, *305th Machine Gun Battalion*, p. 49; Miles, *308th Infantry*, p. 98; Davis, *307th Ambulance*, p. 123; Tiebout, *305th Infantry*, p. 100; "our drinking water": *Jamestown (N. Y.) Evening Journal*, April 7, 1931.

33. Smith, *305th Machine Gun Battalion*, p. 48.

34. Davis, *307th Ambulance*, pp. 119–21.

35. Tiebout, *305th Infantry*, pp. 93, 100, 105–6; Smith, *305th Machine Gun Battalion*, pp. 51–53; Minder, *This Man's War*, p. 274.

36. Field, *Battery Book*, p. 83.
37. Miles, *308th Infantry*, pp. 85–89.
38. Ibid., pp. 89–93.
39. *302nd Engineers*, pp. 57–60.
40. Ibid., p. 72.
41. Field, *Battery Book*, pp. 76, 78.
42. *77th Division*, p. 45; "with appalling speed": Rainsford, *Upton to the Meuse*, p. 71.
43. *77th Division*, p. 47; *306th Field Artillery*, pp. 28, 105.
44. *77th Division*, pp. 47–48; *306th Infantry*, pp. 51–53; *New York Sun*, November 24, 1918, sec. 4; April 13, 1919, sec. 6; McKeogh, *Victorious 77th Division*, p. 17.
45. *77th Division*, p. 48; Rainsford, *Upton to the Meuse*, pp. 89–94.
46. Niles, *Songs Mother Never Taught*, p. 190.
47. *77th Division*, pp. 161–62, 212.
48. Miles, *308th Infantry*, pp. 97, 100; Palmer quote: Sullivan, *History of New York*, 4: 1347.
49. Miles, *308th Infantry*, p. 100; *Through the War*, p. 12; "It lost one third": *New York Times*, September 25, 1938, sec. 7.

CHAPTER 5: AISNE AND ARGONNE

1. *77th Division*, p. 53; *302nd Engineers*, pp. 63–65; Miles, *308th Infantry*, p. 100; Rainsford, *Upton to the Meuse*, pp. 105–6, quote on p. 111.
2. Rainsford, *Upton to the Meuse*, pp. 110–11; Miles, *308th Infantry*, pp. 101–3, "men were so tired" on p. 102.
3. Minder, *This Man's War*, pp. 273–74.
4. Ibid., p. 274.
5. Shookhoff, *Machine Gun Company*, p. 95; Rainsford, *Upton to the Meuse*, pp. 112–13; "They were exhausted": *Through the War*, p. 15; Minder, *This Man's War*, pp. 277, 284; *306th Field Artillery*, p. 31.
6. *77th Division*, p. 57; *302nd Engineers*, pp. 68–70; McKeogh quote: *New York Sun*, April 13, 1919, sec. 6.
7. *Through the War*, p. 13; Smith, *305th Machine Gun Battalion*, p. 57.
8. Rainsford, *Upton to the Meuse*, pp. 113–16.
9. Miles, *308th Infantry*, pp. 104–5; "Send more men": McKeogh, *Victorious 77th Division*, p. 19.
10. Minder, *This Man's War*, p. 277.
11. Rainsford, *Upton to the Meuse*, pp. 120–22.
12. Ibid., pp. 124–25.
13. Miles, *308th Infantry*, pp. 57–58, 106–9; McKeogh quote: *New York Sun*, April 13, 1919, sec. 6.
14. Tiebout, *305th Infantry*, pp. 121–23.
15. Ibid., p. 123.
16. Ibid., pp. 126–30.
17. *306th Infantry*, pp. 54–58.

18. Field, *Battery Book*, p. 87; Tiebout, *305th Infantry*, p. 139.

19. Field, *Battery Book*, p. 181.

20. *77th Division*, p. 58; *306th Infantry*, p. 58; Tiebout, *305th Infantry*, p. 135.

21. Rainsford, *Upton to the Meuse*, pp. 130–33.

22. Smith, *305th Machine Gun Battalion*, pp. 58–59; *306th Field Artillery*, p. 33; Miles, *308th Infantry*, p. 110, Whittlesey quote on pp. 116–17.

23. Miles, *308th Infantry*, p. 117; Tiebout, *305th Infantry*, pp. 135–36; *Company D, 308th Infantry*, p. 18; "came out of the lines": *Through the War*, p. 15; Rainsford, *Upton to the Meuse*, p. 153.

24. McKeogh, "Whittlesey," p. 111.

25. *77th Division, Summary of Operations*, p. 23; Sullivan, *History of New York*, 4:1351–52; Pershing, *My Experiences*, 2: 280–81.

26. Rainsford, *Upton to the Meuse*, p. 154; "Without illumination": Tiebout, *305th Infantry*, pp. 136–37; Smith, *305th Machine Gun Battalion*, p. 61.

27. Tiebout, *305th Infantry*, pp. 137–38; "His hair is matted": Field, *Battery Book*, p. 98.

28. *New York Sun*, March 30, 1919, sec. 6.

29. Pershing, *My Experiences*, 2:282–83, 290–91.

30. *New York Times*, November 10, 1929, sec. 5.

31. *77th Division*, p. 59; Miles, *308th Infantry*, pp. 118–19, Whittlesey quote on p. 119.

32. *40th (Sunshine) Division*, pp. 25–26, 37–38; Gordon, "Sidney Smith," p. 29.

33. *40th (Sunshine) Division*, pp. 38, 65; McCollum, *Our Sons*, pp. 34–35; Nettleton, *Yale in the War*, pp. 146–47; *Brooklyn in the War*, p. 176; Stromee Diary.

34. John, "Lost Battalion," TS; Ralph John Draft Registration.

35. Herschell, *The Kid*, p. 56.

36. "Took the jump-off": Miles, *308th Infantry*, p. 120; Stacey, "My Experience"; Rainsford, *Upton to the Meuse*, pp. 156–57; *306th Infantry*, p. 60; Tiebout, *305th Infantry*, pp. 143–45, "were quick to absorb" on p. 145; Gordon, "Sidney Smith," p. 30.

37. Weston Jenkins Interview, October 6, 1918, Drum MS.

38. *Combat Instructions, September 5, 1918*, pp. 3–5.

39. Ibid., pp. 5–8.

40. McKeogh, *Victorious 77th Division*, p 5.

41. McKeogh, *Victorious 77th Division*, p. 6.

42. McKeogh, "Whittlesey," p. 111.

43. Peterson, *Lost Battalion*, "Joseph B. Dyrdal."

44. *302nd Engineers*, pp. 77, 80, 83.

45. *77th Division*, pp. 61–62; Ottosen, *Trench Artillery*, pp. 127–29, Reid quote on p. 128; *New York Times*, February 24, 1919.

46. *77th Division*, pp. 62–64, Alexander quote on p. 64; Dyke quote: *306th Field Artillery*, p. 36.

47. *77th Division*, p. 61; Pickerell quote: Ruffin, "They Found," p. 15.

48. *77th Divison*, p. 63; Miles, *308th Infantry*, p. 122; *77th Division, Summary of Operations*, pp. 29–30.

49. McCollum, *Our Sons*, pp. 58–59.

50. Rainsford, *Upton to the Meuse*, p. 165; Demaree, *Company A*, p. 70; Miles, *308th Infantry*, pp. 121–22.

CHAPTER 6: OVER THE TOP

1. *77th Division*, p. 64; "'Bang' goes a howitzer": *New York Times*, March 30, 1919, sec. 1.

2. Howard, *304th Field Artillery*, p. 172.

3. *306th Field Artillery*, p. 50; McCollum, *Our Sons*, pp. 70, 74.

4. Vogel, *World War I Songs*, p. 399.

5. McCollum, *Our Sons*, p. 70; "One literally could not": Rainsford, *Upton to the Meuse*, p. 167; McKeogh, *Victorious 77th Division*, p. 22; Lewis, "Argonne," pp. 9, 29; Smith, *305th Machine Gun Battalion*, p. 64.

6. Rainsford, *Upton to the Meuse*, pp. 158–59; Tiebout, *305th Infantry*, p. 148; *New York Times*, March 18, 1919.

7. McKeogh, "Lost Battalion," p. 5; *New York Sun*, April 17, 1919, sec. 6; Gordon, "Sidney Smith," p. 30.

8. Rainsford, *Upton to the Meuse*, p. 171; Lewis, "Argonne," p. 9; Sweeney, *Buffalo in the War*, p. 244; McKeogh, *Victorious 77th Division*, p. 22; Tiebout, *305th Infantry*, p. 150; *Lima (Ohio) News*, September 19, 1937.

9. *New York Times*, November 10, 1929, sec. 5.

10. *New York Sun*, November 22, 1918; Miles, *308th Infantry*, pp. 115–16; *Williams College*, p. 205.

11. McKeogh, "Whittlesey," pp. 111–12; Miles, *308th Infantry*, p. 115.

12. McKeogh, "Whittlesey," p. 111.

13. Ibid., p. 112.

14. Miles, *308th Infantry*, p. 115; McKeogh, "Whittlesey," p. 111.

15. McKeogh, "Lost Battalion," p. 6; Thomas Pool Draft Registration.

16. Minder, *This Man's War*, pp. 331–32.

17. Miles, *308th Infantry*, p. 127; Demaree, *Company A*, p. 72; McKeogh, *Victorious 77th Division*, p. 2; Lewis, "Argonne," p. 32.

18. Miles, *308th Infantry*, p. 127; Demaree, *Company A*, pp. 72–73; *Company D, 308th Infantry*, p. 26; Maguie, "Private Krotoshinsky," p. 327; Tjentland, "Martin O. Lokken."

19. *New York Times*, March 30, 1919, sec. 1.

20. Hussey, *Company E*, p. 47; Miles, *308th Infantry*, pp. 129–32; Lewis, "Argonne," p. 32.

21. Lewis, "Argonne," pp. 32–33; *Company D, 308th Infantry*, pp. 28, 31–32; Miles, *308th Infantry*, pp. 130–32; Gordon, "Sidney Smith," p. 32.

22. *77th Division*, p. 72; Miles, *308th Infantry*, pp. 129–30; Smith, *305th Machine Gun Battalion*, p. 65.

23. Rainsford, *Upton to the Meuse*, pp. 179–81, 185–86.

24. McCollum, *Our Sons*, p. 97; *77th Division*, pp. 69, 71.

25. John, "Lost Battalion," TS.

26. Brophy, *Long Trail*, p. 56.

27. Miles, *308th Infantry*, p. 132; McKeogh, *Victorious 77th Division*, p. 22; McKeogh, "Lost Battalion," p. 6; Demaree, *Company A*, p. 73; Hussey, *Company E*, pp. 48–49; Sweeney, *Buffalo in the War*, p. 244; *Lima (Ohio) News*, October 3, 1937.

28. Bellows, "Medal of Honor," pp. 487–88, Whittlesey quote on p. 487; Sweeney, *Buffalo in the War*, pp. 244–45; Miles, *308th Infantry*, pp. 135–37.

29. McKeogh, "Lost Battalion," pp. 6, 18.

30. Ibid., p. 18; Berry, *Make the Kaiser*, pp. 354–55.

31. McKeogh, "Runner Quinn," p. 154.

32. McKeogh, "Lost Battalion," pp. 18, 22, 24; Berry, *Make the Kaiser*, pp. 354–55; *New York Sun*, October 17, 1918; Miles, *308th Infantry*, pp. 335, 337–38, 291, 294.

33. Whittlesey's Messages nos. 4 and 5, September 29, 1918, 77th Division Field Orders; Miles, *308th Infantry*, pp. 133–34; Johnson and Pratt, *Lost Battalion*, p. 19. The original copy of this message in the records of the Seventy-seventh Division in the National Archives reads, "It is very slow trying to clean up this rear area from here by small details when this pricking sack of machine guns can be used by the enemy." L. Wardlaw Miles, in his *History of the 308th Infantry*, rewrote the same sentence to read, "It is very slow trying to clean up this rear area from here by small details when this trickling back of machine guns can be used by the enemy."

34. "Aided by our": Demaree, *Company A*, p. 74; McCollum, *Our Sons*, p. 74; "snapping of twigs": *77th Division*, pp. 69, 71.

35. *New York Sun*, November 24, 1918, sec. 4.

36. Miles, *308th Infantry*, pp. 140–41; *New York Times*, November 24, 1958; Hussey, *Company E*, pp. 83–84; "I don't believe": Eager, "Lost Battalion," p. 3.

37. Rainsford, *Upton to the Meuse*, pp. 178, 182; *Company D, 308th Infantry*, p. 33; *77th Division*, pp. 40–41; Maguie, "Private Krotoshinsky," p. 327.

38. Nell, *Lost Battalion*, pp. 82–83.

39. *302nd Engineers*, pp. 92–94.

40. Miles, *308th Infantry*, pp. 140–41; Stromee Diary; Hussey, *Company E*, p. 50; Demaree, *Company A*, p. 75; *Company D, 308th Infantry*, p. 34; Nell, *Lost Battalion*, p. 84.

41. Brophy, *Long Trail*, p. 34.

42. McCollum, *Our Sons*, p. 99; John, "Lost Battalion," TS: Gordon, "Sidney Smith," p. 32.

43. Demaree, *Company A*, pp. 74–75; McCollum, *Our Sons*, pp. 99–101; John, "Lost Battalion," TS.

44. Sweeney, *Buffalo in the War*, pp. 244–46.

45. Demaree, *Company A*, pp. 74–75; McCollum, *History and Rhymes*, p. 51; Miles, *308th Infantry*, p. 142; Hussey, *Company E*, p. 57; Lewis, "Argonne," p. 34.

46. *Notes on Recent Operations*, p. 14.

47. Miles, *308th Infantry*, p. 142; Nell, *Lost Battalion*, p. 85; (Cooperstown, N. D.) *Sentinel-Courier*, November 10, 1927; Sigurd Lima and Carl Michaelson Draft Registrations.

48. Nell, *Lost Battalion*, p. 85; *Lima (Ohio) News*, October 3, 1937.

49. Eager, "Lost Battalion," pp. 2–3.

CHAPTER 7: BREAKTHROUGH

1. Whittlesey quote: Miles, *308th Infantry*, p. 148; 308th Infantry, Supplementary Report, Drum MS; *Company D, 308th Infantry*, pp. 36–37; Revnes Court Martial Transcript, p. 76.

2. Miles, *308th Infantry*, p. 149; Revnes Court Martial, pp. 76, 95, 101, 102, 223.

3. Miles, *308th Infantry*, p. 149; Revnes Court Martial, pp. 76–77, 184, 232, 240; *New York Sun*, November 15, 1918; McCollum, *Our Sons*, pp. 117–18.

4. Sweeney, *Buffalo in the War*, p. 246.

5. *Stars and Stripes*, May 3, 1918.

6. Nell, *Lost Battalion*, pp. 85–86; Miles, *308th Infantry*, p. 150, 239 (Cullen quote); 308th Infantry, Supplementary Report, Drum MS; Johnson and Pratt, *Lost Battalion*, pp. 31–32.

7. Nell, *Lost Battalion*, pp. 86–87; Peterson, "Lost Battalion," p. 5; John, "Lost Battalion," TS; Eager, "Lost Battalion," pp. 3–4; Brown and Whittlesey quotes: *Jamestown (N. Y.) Evening Journal*, April 7, 1931.

8. Miles, *308th Infantry*, p. 150; 308th Infantry, Supplementary Report, Drum MS; Revnes Court Martial, p. 77.

9. *77th Division*, p. 201; Miles, *308th Infantry*, p. 151; 308th Infantry, Supplementary Report, Drum MS; Johnson and Pratt, *Lost Battalion*, p. 39; Nell, *Lost Battalion*, p. 88; Eager, "Lost Battalion," p. 4; Peterson, *Lost Battalion*, "Herbert Tiederman," "Charley Meyers."

10. Revnes Court Martial, pp. 77 (McMurty quote), 185; Miles, *308th Infantry*, p. 151; Peterson, *Lost Battalion*, "Julius Langer," "Leonard N. Glenn"; Nell, *Lost Battalion*, p. 90.

11. Peterson, *Lost Battalion*, "Herman E. H. Ratonda," "Clyde Hintz," "Adlare LeMay."

12. Johnson and Pratt, *Lost Battalion*, pp. 40, 45–46; Hussey, *Company E*, p. 153.

13. Powers quote: Johnson and Pratt, *Lost Battalion*, p. 46; Miles, *308th Infantry*, pp. 150–52, 240 (Cullen quote), 344–45; Holderman, "Operations," pp. 11–12; *Lima (Ohio) News*, October 3, 1937.

14. Adams, *Our Company*, "The Fight of the Lost Battalion."

15. Miles, *308th Infantry*, p. 152; Johnson and Pratt, *Lost Battalion*, pp. 66–67; Revnes Court Martial, p. 77.

16. Miles, *308th Infantry*, p. 153; Sweeney, *Buffalo in the War*, pp. 246–47; Hussey, *Company E*, pp. 52–53; *Brooklyn in the War*, p. 97; Johnson and Pratt, *Lost Battalion*, p. 79.

17. Foreman, *Service Record*, 1:635–38.

18. *New York Times*, September 25, 1938, sec. 7; Holderman, "Operations," pp. 13, 16; Revnes Court Martial, p. 124; *40th (Sunshine) Division*, pp. 62–63; Johnson and Pratt, *Lost Battalion*, p. 50; Statement of Thomas G. Pool, April 23, 1929, ABMC Records; Thomas Pool Draft Registration.

19. Holderman, "Operations," p. 16; Revnes Court Martial, p. 122; Johnson and Pratt, *Lost Battalion*, pp. 52–53; Peterson, *Lost Battalion*, "Peter P. Koshiol."

20. Holderman, "Operations," pp. 17–18; Revnes Court Martial, pp. 77–78; Miles, *308th Infantry*, 107, 152–53, 161–62, 164; Maguie, "Private Krotoshinsky," p. 327.

21. Holderman, "Operations," pp. 18–19; Johnson and Pratt, *Lost Battalion*, pp. 73–77, Whittlesey and Teichmoeller messages, pp. 73–74; *305th Field Artillery*, p. 272, 360; *Ohio in the War*, 17:17228.

22. Howard Johnson and Percy Wenrich, "Where Do We Go From Here?" 1917. Sheet music in author's collection.

23. Peterson, *Lost Battalion*, "Robert Pou," "Fred Evermann"; Miles, *308th Infantry*, p. 153; 308th Infantry, Supplementary Report, Drum MS; Holderman, "Operations," p. 17; Johnson and Pratt, *Lost Battalion*, 78.

24. Johnson and Pratt, *Lost Battalion*, pp. 79–80, 81; Miles, *308th Infantry*, pp. 153–54; Revnes Court Martial, p. 78.

25. Holderman, "Operations," pp. 20–21; Revnes Court Martial, pp. 121–22.

26. Miles, *308th Infantry*, pp. 154–55; *New York Sun*, April 17, 1919; *New York Times*, May 28, 1919; *Stars and Stripes*, February 22, 1918; Johnson and Pratt, *Lost Battalion*, p. 73.

27. Miles, *308th Infantry*, pp. 154 (Whittlesey's order), 240–41; Johnson and Pratt, *Lost Battalion*, pp. 82 (Whittlesey's message), 89.

28. *77th Division*, p. 202; McMurtry quote: Revnes Court Martial, p. 79; Miles, *308th Infantry*, p. 156.

29. Manson, "Through Hell," p. 400; Miles, *308th Infantry*, p. 240; Wilbert T. Rumsey Draft Registration.

30. Peterson, *Lost Battalion*, "John A. McNearney," "Nicholas Kurtz."

31. Adams, *Our Company*, "Memorial."

32. Miles, *308th Infantry*, pp. 156–57 (McMurtry quote), 240; 77th Division, Messages Sent and Received, Pigeon Message, October 3, 1918, Drum MS; *Brooklyn in the War*, p. 107.

33. Miles, *308th Infantry*, pp. 240 (Cullen quote), 322; Peterson, *Lost Battalion*, "Frank G. H. Erickson"; *77th Division*, p. 202; Johnson and Pratt, *Lost Battalion*, p. 110; Dukehart, *My Heritage*, p. 142.

34. Peat, *Legion Airs*, p. 33.

35. Miles, *308th Infantry*, p. 241; Shore, *Montana in the Wars*, p. 88; Gordon, "Sidney Smith," p. 33.

36. Miles, *308th Infantry*, pp. 318, 320.

37. Stromee Diary; Johnson and Pratt, *Lost Battalion*, p. 100; "attacked and cleaned out": Miles, *308th Infantry*, p. 327.

38. Miles, *308th Infantry*, pp. 283–86, 292, 300; *Brooklyn in the War*, p. 99.

39. York, *Mud and Stars*, p. 114.

40. Revnes Court Martial, pp. 122, 166; Holderman, "Operations," pp. 23–24; Maguie, "Private Krotoshinksy," p. 327.

41. Revnes Court Martial, pp. 159–60, 325–26; Johnson and Pratt, *Lost Battalion*, p. 102.

42. *Lima (Ohio) News*, October 3, 1937.

43. Miles, *308th Infantry*, p. 157; Revnes Court Martial, p. 79; Holderman, "Operations," pp. 24–25.

44. Revnes Court Martial, pp. 96–97; Cullen quote: Miles, *308th Infantry*, p. 241; Nell, *Lost Battalion*, p. 93; John, "Lost Battalion;" Johnson and Pratt, *Lost Battalion*, p. 103, Krotoshinksy quote: Maguie, "Private Krotoshinsky," p. 327.

45. Miles, *308th Infantry*, pp. 157–58, 241.

CHAPTER 8: TRAPPED

1. Miles, *308th Infantry*, pp. 158, 329; Johnson and Pratt, *Lost Battalion*, p. 111.

2. Revnes Court Martial, p. 79; Nell, *Lost Battalion*, pp. 92–93; John, "Lost Battalion" TS.

3. Johnson and Pratt, *Lost Battalion*, pp. 116–18; Miles, *308th Infantry*, pp. 329–30.

4. *Hickoxy's Army*, p. 114.

5. Whittlesey message: Miles, *308th Infantry*, pp. 158–59; Holderman, "Operations," pp. 25–26.

6. Miles, *308th Infantry*, p. 157; John, "Lost Battalion," TS: Manson, "Through Hell," p. 400; Johnson and Pratt, *Lost Battalion*, p. 123.

7. York, *Mud and Stars*, p. 8.

8. John, "Lost Battalion," TS.

9. York, *Mud and Stars*, p. 88.

10. Johnson and Pratt, *Lost Battalion*, p. 159; Miles, *308th Infantry*, pp. 159, 242–43; John, "Lost Battalion," TS.

11. "A tangle of twisted": *77th Division*, p. 204; *New York Times*, November 26, 1927; and October 5, 1938; *New York Sun*, September 22, 1944.

12. *77th Division*, pp. 202, 204; Peterson, "Lost Battalion," p. 7.

13. Miles, *308th Infantry*, p. 159.

14. *Lost Battalion Survivors, 1958*, p. 10; Johnson and Pratt, *Lost Battalion*, p. 124, 131–32 (Whittlesey quote); Rainsford, *Upton to the Meuse*, p. 220; Holderman, "Operations," pp. 26–27.

15. Whittlesey quote: Miles, *308th Infantry*, p. 160; Holderman, "Operations," p. 27; Eager, "Lost Battalion," p. 4; *305th Field Artillery*, p. 275.

16. Holderman, "Operations," p. 27; Manson, "Through Hell," p. 400.

17. *Stars and Stripes*, March 22, 1918.

18. Johnson and Pratt, *Lost Battalion*, pp. 135, 137; Peterson, *Lost Battalion*, "Theodore Tollefson," "William M. Cavanaugh."

19. Johnson and Pratt, *Lost Battalion*, pp. 135–37.

20. Johnson and Pratt, *Lost Battalion*, pp. 137–39.

21. John, "Lost Battalion," TS.

22. Anastasi quote: *Lost Battalion Survivors, 1958*, p. 6; Anthony Anastasi Draft Registration; *New York Times*, September 30, 1957; *Lost Battalion Survivors, 1957*, p. 5.

23. Nell, *Lost Battalion*, p. 94; Peterson, *Lost Battalion*, "Leonard N. Glenn," "Magnus B. Krogh."

24. Miles, *308th Infantry*, pp. 160, 284, 297, 344–45; Newspaper clipping, Edwards MS; James W. Bragg Draft Registration; Peterson, *Lost Battalion*, "Alfred Simonson."

25. *New York Sun*, December 22, 1918.

26. Miles, *308th Infantry*, pp. 159, 161; Peterson, *Lost Battalion*, "Hubert V. Esch," "Joseph Lehmeier," "John J. Knettel."

27. Miles, *308th Infantry*, p. 241.

28. Whittlesey quote: Revnes Court Martial, pp. 93–94; Miles, *308th Infantry*, pp. 159, 161, 163; Nell, *Lost Battalion*, p. 94; John, "Lost Battalion," TS; Sweeney, *Buffalo in the War*, p. 248; Johnson and Pratt, *Lost Battalion*, p. 140; Morse, *50th Aero Squadron*, pp. 42–43.

29. Miles, *308th Infantry*, pp. 159, 161 (Whittlesey quote); Holderman, "Operations," p. 33.

30. *Stars and Stripes*, February 18, 1918.

31. Hussey, *Company E*, p. 54; Revnes Court Martial, p. 85; Harry Rogers, Service Card, Office of the Adjutant General, State of Missouri; Johnson and Pratt, *Lost Battalion*, p. 254.

32. Revnes Court Martial, p. 252; Johnson and Pratt, *Lost Battalion*, pp. 128–31. The list of officers in the pocket is as follows: Maj. Charles W. Whittlesey, commanding 1st Battalion, 308th Infantry; 2nd Lieut. Henry J. Williamson, Co. A; 2nd Lieut. Harry Rogers, Co. B; Capt. Leo A. Stromee, 2nd Lieut. Gordon L. Schenck, and 2nd Lieut. Leo W. Trainor, Co. C; Capt. George G. McMurtry, Co. E, commanding 2nd Battalion, 308th Infantry; 1st Lieut. Karl E. Wilhelm, 1st Lieut. James V. Leak, and 2nd Lieut. Victor A. Harrington, Co. E; 2nd Lieut. Fred Buhler, Jr., and 2nd Lieut. Sherman W. Eager, Co. G; 1st Lieut. William J. Cullen and 1st Lieut. Maurice V. Griffin, Co. H; Capt. Nelson M. Holderman and 1st Lieut. Thomas G. Pool, Co. K, 307th Infantry; 2nd Lieut. Marshall G. Peabody and 2nd Lieut. Maurice S. Revnes, Co. D, 306th Machine Gun Battalion; 2nd Lieut. Alfred R. Noon, Co. C, 306th Machine Gun Battalion; and 2nd Lieut. John G. Teichmoeller, Batt. D, 305th Field Artillery, liaison officer.

33. Martin Becker, Joseph Fortunato, Ray Blackburn, John Eichorn, Joseph Friel, Daniel Tallon, and Samuel Feuerlicht Draft Registrations; *Brooklyn in the War*, pp. 99, 115; *New York City Directory, 1917*, pp. 302, 1050, 1881.

34. *Columbia County in the War*, p. 185; *Brooklyn in the War*, p. 110; *New York Times*, November 21, 1918; Homer Rayson, Harold Thomas,

Joseph Mead, William Johnson, Grant Norton, Ernest Wornek, Henry Luckett, Frank Lipasti, and Arthur Jones Draft Registrations.

35. Otto Volz, George Sims, Albert Martin, William Johnson, and Farland Wade Draft Registrations.

36. *77th Division*, p. 204.

37. York, *Mud and Stars*, p. 5.

38. Holderman, "Operations," pp. 28–29; Cullen quote: Miles, *308th Infantry*, pp. 241–42.

39. McCollum, *History and Rhymes*, p. 24.

CHAPTER 9: NO WAY OUT

1. Manson, "Through Hell," p. 400; Sullivan, *Nevada's Golden Stars*, pp. 140–41.

2. Peterson, *Lost Battalion*, "Roy H. Lightfoot," "Stanley Sobaszkiewicz;" *Jamestown (N. Y.) Evening Journal*, April 7, 1931; Nell, *Lost Battalion*, p. 95.

3. Peterson, *Lost Battalion*, "Roy H. Lightfoot."

4. Miles, *308th Infantry*, pp. 162–63; Peterson, *Lost Battalion*, "Arnold Morem"; John, "Lost Battalion," TS.

5. Whittlesey quote: Miles, *308th Infantry*, p. 163; *77th Division*, p. 205; Revnes Court Martial, pp. 80, 98.

6. Nell, *Lost Battalion*, p. 95; Revnes Court Martial, pp. 80 (McMurtry quote), 123 (Holderman quote); Whittlesey quote: Miles, *308th Infantry*, p. 163.

7. Holderman, "Operations," pp. 30–31.

8. Revnes Court Martial, p. 80; Whittlesey quote: Miles, *308th Infantry*, p. 163; Johnson and Pratt, *Lost Battalion*, p. 180; Holderman, "Operations," p. 35.

9. Peterson, *Lost Battalion*, "Raymond E. Hammond," "Stanley Sobaszkiewicz"; "We got flat": Nell, *Lost Battalion*, p. 96; Revnes Court Martial, pp. 163, 233–34, 245; *New York Sun*, November 15, 1918.

10. Revnes Court Martial, p. 257.

11. Johnson and Pratt, *Lost Battalion*, pp. 181–82; Putnam, *Gold Star Record*, p. 220; *Ohio in the War*, 17:17307; Spiegel quote: *Lost Battalion Survivors, 1958*, pp. 10–11.

12. Revnes Court Martial, p. 81; Miles, *308th Infantry*, pp. 284, 289–90; Johnson and Pratt, *Lost Battalion*, pp. 186, 196; Manson, "Through Hell," p. 400.

13. Johnson and Pratt, *Lost Battalion*, pp. 158, 191; Revnes Court Martial, p. 172; Manson, "Through Hell," p. 411; Whittlesey quote: *New York Sun*, November 15, 1918.

14. Revnes Court Martial, p. 152.

15. Peterson, *Lost Battalion*, "Arthur Swanbeck," "Hubert V. Esch"; Revnes Court Martial, pp. 236–37.

16. *Jamestown (N. Y.) Evening Journal*, April 7, 1931; Nell, *Lost Battalion*, p. 96; Peterson, *Lost Battalion*, "Hans Wm. Christensen"; Manson, "Through Hell," p. 400.

17. *New York Times*, December 14, 1918; Sweeney, *Buffalo in the War*, p. 248; John, "Lost Battalion," TS.

18. Holderman, "Operations," p. 32.

19. Ibid.: 37; Miles, *308th Infantry*, p. 165; Bendheim quote: *New York Times*, May 4, 1919, sec. 9; Johnson and Pratt, *Lost Battalion*, p. 176.

20. Revnes Court Martial, pp. 109, 117; Whittlesey quote: Miles, *308th Infantry*, p. 164; Morse, *50th Aero Squadron*, p. 43.

21. 77th Division, Operations, October 6–7, 1918, Drum MS; Revnes Court Martial, pp. 117, 140; Manson, "Through Hell," p. 411.

22. Irving Sirota, one of the medical detachment, was one of those who contracted trench foot. See *77th Division*, p. 205; Miles, *308th Infantry*, p. 164; Peterson, *Lost Battalion*, "Hubert V. Esch."

23. York, *Mud and Stars*, p. 53.

24. Revnes Court Martial, pp. 81 (McMurtry quote), 131; Holderman, "Operations," p. 22; Cullen quote: Miles, *308th Infantry*, p. 242.

25. 308th Infantry, Supplementary Report, Drum MS; Miles, *308th Infantry*, pp. 165 (Whittlesey quote), 242 (Cullen quote).

26. Johnson and Pratt, *Lost Battalion*, pp. 128–29.

27. Revnes Court Martial, p. 167; Johnson and Pratt, *Lost Battalion*, pp. 104, 190; *New York Times*, November 15, 1918.

28. Revnes Court Martial, pp. 154, 158, 160, 162, 166.

29. Ibid., pp. 169, 170, 263.

30. Ibid., pp. 141, 151, 153; Adams, *Our Company*, "Extras."

31. Revnes Court Martial, pp. 210–15.

32. Woollcott, *Command Is Forward*, p. 154.

33. Revnes Court Martial, pp. 215–17.

34. Ibid., pp. 86, 140, 144, 171, 174, 175.

35. Miles, *308th Infantry*, p. 165; Revnes Court Martial, p. 81.

36. McMurtry quote: Revnes Court Martial, p. 81; Miles, *308th Infantry*, p. 324; *77th Division*, p. 205; Johnson and Pratt, *Lost Battalion*, p. 201; Morse, *50th Aero Squadron*, p. 45; Peterson, *Lost Battalion*, "F. M. Mikulewicz," "J. A. Schanz"; Holderman, "Operations," pp. 34–35.

37. Miles, *308th Infantry*, pp. 165, 283, 296 (Rogers citation), 298; Johnson and Pratt, *Lost Battalion*, p. 207; *Jamestown (N. Y.) Evening Journal*, April 7, 1931.

38. McCollum, *History and Rhymes*, p. 111.

39. Miles, *308th Infantry*, p. 320; *New York Sun*, December 11, 1918; *New York American*, December 15, 1918.

40. Revnes Court Martial, p. 85; Johnson and Pratt, *Lost Battalion*, p. 185. Johnson and Pratt claimed that this incident occurred on October 5, while McMurtry stated positively that it happened in "late afternoon of the 6th."

41. Holderman, "Operations," pp. 36–37; Liner, "Five Days," p. 251; Peterson, *Lost Battalion*, "Magnus B. Krogh."

42. McCollum, *History and Rhymes*, p. 115.

43. 77th Division, p. 205; *New York Times*, November 30, 1921.

CHAPTER 10: HELP ON THE WAY

1. *Company D, 308th Infantry*, pp. 36–39; *Brooklyn in the War*, p. 40; *New York American*, November 29, 1918.

2. Niles, *Songs Mother Never Taught*, pp. 188–89.

3. *Company D, 308th Infantry*, pp. 39–42, 50.

4. Ibid., pp. 50–51.

5. Irving R. Goldberg Questionnaire, American Jewish Historical Society; Conlin, *First Aid*, p. 7; Irving Goldberg, Harold Kaplan, and Saul Marshallcowitz Draft Registration.

6. *Company D, 308th Infantry*, pp. 42–45.

7. *77th Division, Summary of Operations*, pp. 30, 39, 45.

8. Alexander, *Memories*, pp. 213–14.

9. Ibid., p. 214; Johnson quote: McKeogh, *Victorious 77th Division*, p. 23; *Brooklyn in the War*, p. 115.

10. Evan Johnson Testimony, October 6, 1918, Drum MS.

11. Ibid.

12. Rainsford, *Upton to the Meuse*, pp. 197–98.

13. Woollcott, *Command Is Forward*, pp. 153–54.

14. Rainsford, *Upton to the Meuse*, pp. 200–1; *New York Sun*, October 22, 1918; Woollcott, *Command Is Forward*, pp. 133–35.

15. Alexander, *Memories*, pp. 218–19; Albert T. Rich, Report of Inspection of the 77th Division, October 8, 1918, Drum MS; Stacey, "My Experience."

16. Rainsford, *Upton to the Meuse*, pp. 201–2.

17. Ibid., p. 202; *New York Times*, November 10, 1918, sec. 2; Evan Johnson Testimony, October 6, 1918, Drum MS.

18. Evan Johnson Testimony, October 6, 1918; Robert Alexander Testimony, undated; Messaged Sent and Received, Headquarters, 77th Division, 3h0, October 5, 1918, 16h05 October 5, 1918, Drum MS.

19. *Rookie Rhymes*, p. 37.

20. *77th Division*, pp. 74–75.

21. Ibid., pp. 75–76.

22. Ibid., p. 74; *306th Infantry*, pp. 70–75; "this dense line": *New York Times*, May 5, 1919, sec. 6.

23. Tiebout, *305th Infantry*, pp. 153–55; Smith, *305th Machine Gun Battalion*, p. 69.

24. Tiebout, *305th Infantry*, pp. 156–57.

25. York, *Mud and Stars*, p. 100.

26. Tiebout, *305th Infantry*, pp. 157–58.

27. Smith, *305th Machine Gun Battalion*, p. 68; Tiebout, *305th Infantry*, p. 167; Field, *Battery Book*, p. 107; Galloghy quote: *306th Field Artillery*, p. 52; Report of Operations, 306th Field Artillery, October 4–7, 1918; Report of 152nd Field Artillery Brigade, October 1–8, 1918; Alexander quote: Albert T. Rich, Report of Inspection of the 77th Division, October 8, 1918, Drum MS.

28. Minder, *This Man's War*, pp. 335, 343–44, 347, 348, 350, 351–52.

29. Jantzen, *Hooray For Peace*, p. 219.

30. Alexander, *Memories*, pp. 220–21, 223; Johnson and Pratt, *Lost Battalion*, pp. 116, 141.

31. Alexander, *Memories*, pp. 224–27.

32. Ibid., pp. 221–23.

33. Messages Sent and Received, Headquarters, 77th Division, Alexander to Whittlesey, 22h20 October 4, 1918; Alexander to Chief of Air Service, 1st Army Corps, 21h00; Robert Alexander Testimony, Drum MS; Morse, *50th Aero Squadron*, p. 43.

34. Alexander, *Memories*, p. 221; Miles, *308th Infantry*, p. 253; Messages Sent and Received, Headquarters, 77th Division, Alexander to Whittlesey, 17h15, October 5, 1918, Drum MS; Morse, *50th Aero Squadron*, p. 45.

35. Richardson, "Rescue," pp. 9–10.

36. Ruffin, "They Found," pp. 16 (Pickerell quote), 17; Morse, *50th Aero Squadron*, pp. 45–46, 49, 51; Richardson, "Rescue," pp. 10, 62.

37. Morse, *50th Aero Squadron*, p. 46; "inferrence was": Richardson, "Rescue," pp. 62–63.

38. York, *Mud and Stars*, p. 88; Peat, *Legion Airs*, p. 142. Both of these versions contain expurgated lyrics.

39. Johnson, *Without Censor*, p. 206.

40. Ibid., pp. 206–07.

41. Ibid., pp. 234–35; Johnson and Pratt, *Lost Battalion*, pp. 265, 309; Johnson, "Lost Battalion," p. 86.

CHAPTER 11: RELIEF AT LAST

1. Miles, *308th Infantry*, pp. 165–66; Manson, "Through Hell," p. 400; *New York Times*, February 2, 1940; Maguie, "Private Krotoshinsky," p. 338; McCollum, *History and Rhymes*, pp. 84–85; Johnson and Pratt, *Lost Battalion*, pp. 222–23, 250–51; *Jamestown (N. Y.) Evening Journal*, April 7, 1931.

2. Whittlesey quote: *Jamestown (N. Y.) Evening Journal*, April 7, 1931; Downs, *History of Chautauqua County*, 2: 616.

3. York, *Mud and Stars*, p. 27.

4. *Jamestown (N. Y.) Evening Journal*, April 7, 1931.

5. John, "Lost Battalion," TS.

6. Peterson, *Lost Battalion*, "Emil A. Peterson"; McCollum, *History and Rhymes*, pp. 66–67; Johnson and Pratt, *Lost Battalion*, p. 204.

7. Peterson, *Lost Battalion*, "Emil A. Peterson"; McCollum, *History and Rhymes*, pp. 67–68; *Ohio in the War*, 8: 7783.

8. York, *Mud and Stars*, p. 22.

9. Hollingshead described their leader as "a full–blooded Indian from Montana," but evidence now points to Robert Dodd, from Lovelock, Nevada as the individual who led the group. It should be expected that, as a newcomer to Company H, Hollingshead would be unclear as to men's names and backgrounds. Peterson, *Lost Battalion*, "Emil A. Peterson"; McCollum,

History and Rhymes, pp. 68–70; Robert Dodd Draft Registration; *New York Times*, November 20, 1918; *New York American*, November 20, 1918.

    10. Peterson, "Lost Battalion," pp. 8–9.

    11. McCollum, *History and Rhymes*, pp. 70–74.

    12. Manson, "Through Hell," p. 411; Johnson and Pratt, *Lost Battalion*, p. 219.

    13. *Lima (Ohio) News*, October 17, 1937.

    14. Stromee Diary; *Traverse City (Mich) Record Eagle*, August 28, 1947; Holderman, "Operations," p. 33.

    15. Stromee Diary; 308th Infantry, Supplementary Report, Drum MS; Miles, *308th Infantry*, p. 166.

    16. York, *Mud and Stars*, p. 213.

    17. Holderman quotes: Revnes Court Martial, pp. 124, 135; Peterson, *Lost Battalion*, "Wm. F. Johnson"; Johnson and Pratt, *Lost Battalion*, pp. 147–48; Speich quote: Sweeney, *Buffalo in the War*, p. 248.

    18. Peterson, *Lost Battalion*, "Emil A. Peterson;" Peterson, "Lost Battalion," p. 9; Johnson and Pratt, *Lost Battalion*, pp. 150–52.

    19. McCollum, *History and Rhymes*, pp. 75–82, Hollingshead quote on p. 76; *New York Sun*, April 2, 1919; Prinz to Hollingshead, May 19, 1939, Baldwin MS.

    20. Revnes Court Martial, pp. 81–83, 116, 125, Hollingshead quote on p. 82; Miles, *308th Infantry*, p. 166; McCollum, *History and Rhymes*, p. 82; Johnson and Pratt, *Lost Battalion*, pp. 244–46, Whittlesey quote on p. 246; *Lost Battalion Survivors, 1957*, p. 6.

    21. Revnes Court Martial, p. 81, 125; Miles, *308th Infantry*, p. 167. The letter is reproduced at Miles, *308th Infantry*, facing p. 61.

    22. Peterson, *Lost Battalion*, "Fred Evermann"; *Sandusky (Ohio) Register*, April 12, 1919; Miles, *308th Infantry*, p. 168; Revnes Court Martial, pp. 126, 127; Holderman, "Operations," p. 40; Maguie, "Private Krotoshinsky," p. 327; Johnson and Pratt, *Lost Battalion*, p. 247; Johnson, *Without Censor*, p. 232.

    23. York, *Mud and Stars*, p. 213.

    24. Miles, *308th Infantry*, pp. 167–68 (Whittlesey quote), 171; McKeogh, "Whittlesey," p. 113; Johnson and Pratt, *Lost Battalion*, p. 305; Holderman, "Operations," p. 39; Johnson, *Without Censor*, p. 229; Tuite quote: *New York American*, October 13, 1918.

    25. Miles, *308th Infantry*, p. 168; Peterson, *Lost Battalion*, "Arnold Morem"; *New York Times*, May 4, 1919, sec. 9; *Brooklyn in the War*, p. 40; adjutant and Averill quotes: Nettleton, *Yale in the War*, pp. 146–47.

    26. Holderman, "Operations," p. 40; Peterson, *Lost Battalion*, "Boys From Butte, Montana"; Nell, *Lost Battalion*, p. 97; Miles, *308th Infantry*, p. 322.

    27. *New York Times*, November 21, 1918; Miles, *308th Infantry*, pp. 295, 318, 320 330, 332.

    28. Peterson, *Lost Battalion*, "Boys From Butte, Montana," "Ludvig Blomseth"; Holderman, "Operations," p. 40; Revnes Court Martial, pp. 128–29; Johnson and Pratt, *Lost Battalion*, pp. 206–7, 248.

    29. *Lima (Ohio) News*, October 17, 1937.

30. Miles, *308th Infantry*, pp. 168–69; 308th Infantry, Supplementary Report, Drum MS; Holderman, "Operations," p. 41; Nell, *Lost Battalion*, p. 97.

31. Revnes Court Martial, p. 239.

32. Rainsford, *Upton to the Meuse*, pp. 206–7; 77th Division, *Summary of Operations*, pp. 57–59.

33. Johnson and Pratt, *Lost Battalion*, p. 253.

34. Ibid., pp. 251–52, 255; Maguie, "Private Krotoshinsky," p. 338.

35. *Jamestown (N. Y.) Evening Journal*, April 7, 1931; citation quoted in Miles, *308th Infantry*, pp. 285, 292.

36. Revnes Court Martial, p. 83; Whittlesey quote: Miles, *308th Infantry*, p. 243; McMurtry quote: *New York American*, October 13, 1918; Statement of Thomas G. Pool, April 23, 1929, ABMC Files.

37. Miles, *308th Infantry*, p. 169.

38. Revnes Court Martial, p. 104.

39. Ibid., p. 83; Nell, *Lost Battalion*, p. 98; Manson, "Through Hell," p. 411; Miles, *308th Infantry*, p. 243.

40. York, *Mud and Stars*, p. 73.

41. Revnes Court Martial, p. 83.

CHAPTER 12: LIVING LEGENDS

1. Holderman, "Operations," p. 43; Miles, *308th Infantry*, p. 171; "My God!" *Americans Defending Democracy*, pp. 333–36.

2. Messages Sent and Received, Headquarters, 77th Division, 14h45, October 8, 1918; Alexander, *Memories*, p. 229; Tillman quote: *Americans Defending Democracy*, pp. 336–37.

3. Peterson, *Lost Battalion*, "Corp. Olof Nelson"; *Lima (Ohio) News*, October 17, 1931; *Tri–City (Pasco, Kennewick, and Richland, Wash.) Herald*, October 7, 1968; Stromee Diary; Alexander, *Memories*, pp. 229–30; Manson, "Through Hell," p. 411.

4. Johnson and Pratt, *Lost Battalion*, pp. 263–64; Alexander, *Memories*, pp. 229–30.

5. *New York Times*, November 10, 1929, sec. 3.

6. Messages Sent and Received, Headquarters, 77th Division, no time stated, October 8, 1918; 10h45, October 8, 1918; 18h05, October 8, 1918, Drum MS; Holderman, "Operations," p. 44; Miles, *308th Infantry*, p. 270.

7. Other writers have stated that Whittlesey's command had 194 effectives, excluding Whittlesey and McMurtry, after being relieved. This total obviously refers only to the two battalions of the 308th Infantry and does not include Holderman's company or the remaining machine gunners. Griffin quote: Friedel, *Over There*, pp. 174–75; *Americans Defending Democracy*, p. 333; 308th Infantry, Supplementary Report, Drum MS; Miles, *308th Infantry*, p. 254; Alexander, *Memories*, p. 211.

8. Miles, *308th Infantry*, p. 345; Davis, *307th Ambulance*, pp. 142–44.

9. Davis, *307th Ambulance*, p. 148; Conklin, *First Aid*, p. 49.

10. Gordon, "Sidney Smith," p. 33.

11. Davis, *307th Ambulance*, p. 148; *Lima (Ohio) News*, October 17, 1937; Conklin, *First Aid*, p. 49; Peterson, *Lost Battalion*, "Joseph Giefer"; 77th Division, 302nd Sanitary Train, Reports, 307th and 308th Ambulance Companies, October 7–8, 1918, Triage, 308th Field Hospital, October 8, 1918.

12. Peterson, *Lost Battalion*, "John A. McNearney," "Clyde Hintz"; *Nevada State Journal*, February 6, 1919; 77th Division, Operations, Messages Received, October 9, 1918; "showing the location": *New York Tribune*, May 2, 1918; 77th Division, 302nd Sanitary Train, Division Sanitary Inspector Report, October 11, 1918; *Waukesha (Wis.) Freeman*, September 11, 1919.

13. Macgill, *Soldier Songs*, pp. 57–58.

14. Dickson, *War Slang*, p. 30; *Sandusky (Ohio) Register*, April 12, 1919; Whittlesey quote: Johnson, *Without Censor*, pp. 235–36; McKeogh, "Whittlesey," p. 112; Nell, *Lost Battalion*, pp. 98–99.

15. Runyon quotes: *New York American*, October 10 and 13, 1918; *Traverse City (Mich.) Record Eagle*, August 28, 1947.

16. Revnes Court Martial, p. 83; Johnson, *Without Censor*, p. 233; Miles, *308th Infantry*, p. 170; Morem quote: *Post-Bulletin (Rochester, Minn.)*, August 23, 1972; Tjentland, "Martin O. Lokken."

17. York, *Mud and Stars*, p. 175.

18. *Jamestown (N. Y.) Evening Journal*, April 7, 1931.

19. *New York American*, October 10, 1918; Peterson, *Lost Battalion*, "Otto Novotny," "John A. McNearney"; Tjentland, "Martin O. Lokken"; John, "Lost Battalion," TS.

20. Manson, "Through Hell," p. 411; Larney quote: *Lima (Ohio) News*, October 17, 1937; Hardon, *43bis*, pp. 313–14, 317–18.

21. Irving Klein Questionnaire, American Jewish Historical Society; *Lost Battalion Survivors, 1955*, p. 2.

22. *New York Times*, May 4, 1919, sec. 9; September 24, 1951.

23. Peat, *Legion Airs*, p. 107.

24. *Reno Evening Gazette*, February 14, 1919; *Nevada State Journal*, February 6, 1919.

25. Maguie, "Private Korotshinsky," p. 327; Hardon, *43bis*, p. 318; Rainsford, *Upton to the Meuse*, p. 218.

26. The myth of Cher Ami began with Rose Wilder Lane's "A Bit of Gray in a Blue Sky," which appeared in the *Ladies' Home Journal* in August 1919. This is a fictionalized account, loosely based on the Lost Battalion episode. Lane concludes her account by mentioning that Cher Ami was still carried around in a cage adorned with a Distinguished Service Cross. Actually, the pigeon was dead by that time and, despite popular legend, there is no concrete evidence that a DSC was actually awarded to the bird. The last accurate published account of Cher Ami's wound appeared in a nationally syndicated newspaper strip by the *Book of Knowledge* in 1929. *New York Times*, October 10, 1918; May 25, 1919, sec. 7; January 22, 1928, sec. 9; "Major Whittlesey's answer": Woollcott, *Command is Forward*, p. 124;

Lane, "Bit of Gray," pp. 33, 98; *Lancaster (Ohio) Daily Gazette*, February 21, 1929; February 22, 1929.

27. Miles, *308th Infantry*, p. 244; John, "Lost Battalion," TS.

28. York, *Mud and Stars*, p. 209.

29. Miles, *308th Infantry*, pp. 173–75; Hussey, *Company E*, p. 60; Wilhelm quote: Sweeney, *Buffalo in the War*, p. 247; "taking my life in my hands": *Americans Defending Democracy*, p. 335.

30. Miles, *308th Infantry*, pp. 174–75; "It was a command": *New York Sun*, November 22, 1918.

31. *New York Sun*, November 22, 1918.

32. McCollum, *History and Rhymes*, p. 5.

33. *New York Sun*, December 6, 1918; *New York Times*, December 6, 1918; December 25, 1918.

34. *New York Sun*, December 16, 1918; Johnson and Pratt, *Lost Battalion*, pp. 178–80; Whittlesey, "Military Preparedness," p. 94.

35. Miles, *308th Infantry*, pp. 175–76, 192–94; Hussey, *Company E*, p. 60; Revnes Court Martial, p. 179; John, "Lost Battalion," TS; Nell, *Lost Battalion*, pp. 106, 110, 116–17.

36. Miles, *308th Infantry*, pp. 192–95, 197, 199–200, 204; Hussey, *Company E*, pp. 69–70; "reaction to news" and "picking up butts" quotes: Field, *Battery Book*, p. 135.

37. Hussey, *Company E*, p. 114.

38. Miles, *308th Infantry*, pp. 213–15.

39. Ibid., p. 215.

40. Ibid., pp. 217–18; "first time that": Hussey, *Company E*, p. 77.

41. Johnson and Pratt, *Lost Battalion*, pp. 264–65; General Court Martial Orders No. 112, AEF, February 26, 1919.

42. Revnes Court Martial, p. 119; *New York Sun*, November 15, 1918; Holderman recommendation: McCollum, *History and Rhymes*, pp. 39–41.

43. Fraser, *Soldier and Sailor Words*, p. 70.

44. Miles, *308th Infantry*, pp. 283–332; *77th Division*, pp. 193–97; *New York Times*, April 20, 1919, sec. 1; Doty, *Historic Annals*, 1: 304; Liner, "Yom Kippur," p. 251.

45. Hussey, *Company E*, p. 81; Cheseldine, *Ohio in the Rainbow*, p. 316.

46. Miles, *308th Infantry*, pp. 224–25; Smith, *305th Machine Gun Battalion*, pp. 90–91.

47. Field, *Battery Book*, pp. 140, 141, 144.

48. Miles, *308th Infantry*, p. 226.

49. Ibid., p. 227; Hussey, *Company E*, p. 112; McCollum, *Our Sons*, p. 202.

50. Miles, *308th Infantry*, p. 222; McCollum, *Our Sons*, pp. 204–5; Howard, *304th Field Artillery*, p. 243; Field, *Battery Book*, p. 158.

51. Niles, *Songs Mother Never Taught*, p. 38.

52. McCollum, *History and Rhymes*, p. 53; *New York Times*, May 5, 1919 (Alexander quote), December 18, 1921 (Pershing quote), September 25, 1932 (McMurtry quote); *Lima (Ohio) News*, April 10, 1938.

53. *New York Tribune*, May 2, 1918.

54. Matthews, *Our Soldiers Speak*, p. 357; Halligan quote: *New York Sun*, April 30, 1919; *New York Times*, April 27, 1919, sec. 3.

55. *New York Times*, April 27, 1919, sec. 3.

56. Levenger, "Challenge," p. 136

57. *New York Call*, April 26, 1919; Hussey, *Company E*, pp. 123–24; "'New York's Own,' Parades" p. 690; Field, *Battery Book*, p. 162; Howard, *304th Field Artillery*, p. 244.

58. "'New York's Own' Parades," p. 690; Field, *Battery Book*, p. 164; Hussey, *Company E*, p. 127; McCollum, *Our Sons*, p. 207.

59. Shookhoff, *Machine Gun Company*, p. 98.

60. Smith, *305th Machine Gun Battalion*, p. 91; *Hickoxy's Army*, p. 46.

EPILOGUE

1. *New York Times*, June 20, June 24, July 31, 1919, and November 29, 1921.

2. *New York Times*, July 3 and September 8, 1919; *Gastonia (N. C.) Daily Gazette*, April 2, 1928; *Ironwood (Mich.) Daily Globe*, August 6, 1928.

3. *New York Times*, July 12, 13, 15, 18, 20, and November 30, 1921.

4. McCollum, *History and Rhymes*, pp. 7–8, Averill quote on p. 8; *New York Times*, August 11, 1921; November 30, 1921.

5. Dewey, "Unknown Soldier," pp. 3–9; *New York Times*, October 25, 1921; November 29, 1921; August 8, 1942.

6. *Stars and Stripes*, June 7, 1918.

7. *New York Times*, November 29 and 30, 1921; December 1, 1921.

8. Ibid., November 29, 1921; Averill quote: McCollum, *History and Rhymes*, pp. 7–8.

9. *New York Times*, December 4, 1921.

10. Elwood, "Argonne Cemetery," p. 507; *New York Times Magazine*, May 11, 1930.

11. "Killed in France," *Trench and Camp*, September 2, 1918.

12. Wister, *Neighbors Henceforth*, p. 417.

13. Foreman, *World War Service*, 1:636–37; A. D. Hughes to Sarah E. Halligan, March 18, 1932, William C. Halligan Burial File.

14. Peterson, "Lars Olson"; *The Helena (Montana) Independent*, May 22, 1941; Gordon, "Sidney Smith," p. 34; Boyd Leuenberger to author, February 17, 2004.

15. *Charleston Daily Mail*, November 20, 1930 and April 21, 1931; John, "Lost Battalion," TS.

16. York, *Mud and Stars*, p. 169.

17. *Lost Battalion Survivors, Passing in Review, 1955*, pp. 2, 3; *Lost Battalion Survivors, 1955*, p. 3; *Lost Battalion Survivors, 1957*, p. 6; Johnson and Pratt, *Lost Battalion*, p. 284.

18. Johnson, "The Lost Battalion," pp. 54–57, 80–86.

19. Carl J. Peterson, *Lost Battalion Survivors*.

20. *Lost Battalion Survivors, 1955*, p. 1, and *Lost Battalion Survivors, 1958*, p. 5, reunion rosters in Baldwin MS; *New York Times*, September 23 and 25, 1938, September 27, 1954, September 26, 1955.

21. *Lost Battalion Survivors, 1958*, pp. 7, 8, Baldwin MS; *New York Times*, February 2, 1940 and September 27, 1954.

22. *Lost Battalion Survivors, 1957*, p. 4, Baldwin MS.

23. *Lost Battalion Survivors, Passing in Review, 1955*, pp. 2, 3; *Lost Battalion Survivors, 1955*, pp. 2, 3; *Lost Battalion Survivors, 1959*, pp. 2, 4, 5. All in Baldwin MS.

24. John, "Lost Battalion," TS.

25. Walter J. Baldwin, "I Wonder," Baldwin MS.

26. *Lost Battalion Survivors, 1958*, p. 10, and *Lost Battalion Survivors, 1957*, p. 7, Baldwin MS; Peterson, *Lost Battalion*, "Arnold Morem"; *New York Times*, February 2, 1940.

BIBLIOGRAPHY

BOOKS

Adams, John W. and Lee McCollum. *"Our Company"*. Seattle: Lumberman Printing Co., 1919.

[Adler, Julius O.] *History of the Seventy-Seventh Division*. New York: 77th Division Association, 1919.

Alexander, Robert. *Memories of the World War, 1917–1918*. New York: Macmillan and Co., 1931.

Americans Defending Democracy. New York: World's War Stories, 1919.

An Honor Roll Containing a Pictorial Record of the Loyal and Patriotic Men from Whitman County, Washington, U. S. A., Who Served in the World War 1917–1918–1919. Pullman, Wash: L. E. Wenham, 1920.

Batchelder, Roger. *Camp Upton*. Boston: Small, Maynard & Co., 1918.

Berry, Henry. *Make the Kaiser Dance*. Garden City, N.Y.: Doubleday and Co., 1978.

Blowers, George E. *Roundtrip, Ledyard to France with the 308th Infantry*. 1972.

Blumenstein, Christian. *Whiz bang!*. Buffalo: Christian Blumenstein, 1927.

Braim, Paul F. *The Test of Battle*. Shippensburg, Pa.: White Mane Books, 1998.

Brooklyn and Long Island in the War. Brooklyn: Brooklyn Daily Eagle, 1918.

Brophy, John, and Eric Partridge. *The Long Trail*. Freeport, N.Y.: Books for Libraries Press, 1972.

Cheseldine, R. M. Ohio in the Rainbow. Columbus: F. J. Heer Printing Co., 1924.

Coffman, Edward M. *The War to End All Wars*. New York: Oxford University Press, 1968.

Columbia County in the World War. Albany: J. B. Lyon Co., 1924.

Conklin, William D. *First Aid on Four Fronts in World War I*. Danville, N.Y.: 1968.

Cothren, Marion B. *Cher Ami, The Story of a Carrier Pigeon*. Boston: Little, Brown and Co., 1934.

Crane, Ellery Bicknell. *History of Worcester County Massachusetts*. 3 vols. New York: Lewis Historical Publishing, 1924.

[Crawford, Gilbert H., Thomas H. Ellett, and John J. Hyland]. *The 302nd Engineers: A History*. 1919.

Crump, Irving. *Conscript 2989*. New York: Dodd, Mead and Co., 1918.

Dakota County in the World War. Red Wing, Minn.: 1919.

Davis, Delbert. *307 at Home and in France*. Garden City, N.Y.: Country Life Press, 1919.

Demaree, Joseph P. *History of Company A (308th Infantry) of the Lost Battalion*. New York: George U. Harvey, 1920.

Dickson, Paul. *War Slang*. New York: Pocket Books, 1994.

Doty, William J. *The Historic Annals of Southwestern New York*. 3 vols. New York: Lewis Historical Publishing, 1940.

Downs, John P., and Fenwick Y. Hedley, eds. *History of Chautauqua County New York and Its People*. 3 vols. Boston: American Historical Society, 1921.

Dukehart, Morton M. *My Heritage*. Baltimore: 1947.

Eisenhower, John S. D. *Yanks: The Epic Story of the American Army in World War I*. New York: Free Press, 2001.

Field, Francis L., and Guy V. Richards. *The Battery Book, A History of Battery "A" 306 F. A.* New York: DeVinne Press, 1921.

For God and Country. Sioux City, Iowa: Edward H. Monahan Post 64, American Legion, 1923.

Foreman, Edward R., ed. *World War Service Record of Rochester and Monroe County, New York*. 2 vols. Rochester: City of Rochester, 1924.

Fraser, Edward, and John Gibbons. *Soldier and Sailor Words and Phrases*. London: G. Routledge and Sons, 1925.

Friedel, Frank. *Over There*. Philadelphia: Temple University Press, 1990.

Fussell, Paul. *The Great War and Modern Memory*. New York: Oxford University Press, 1975.

Gibbons, Herbert A. *Songs from the Trenches*. New York: Harper and Brothers, 1918.

Glass, Joseph, Henry L. Miller, and Osmund O'Brien. *The Story of Battery D, 304th Field Artillery, September 1917 to May 1919*. New York: Commanday-Roth Co., 1919.

Harbord, James G. *The American Army in France, 1917–1919*. Boston: Little, Brown and Co., 1936.

Hardon, Anne F. *43bis War Letters of an American V. A. D.*. New York: 1927.

Haulsee, W. M., F. G. Howe, and A. C. Doyle. *Soldiers of the Great War.* 3 vols. Washington: Soldiers Record Publishing Co., 1920.

Herschell, William. *The Kid Has Gone to the Colors and Other Verse.* Indianapolis: Bobbs-Merrill Co., 1917.

Hickoxy's Army; Being a Sort of History of Headquarters Company, 306th Field Artillery, 77th Division, A. E. F. New York: J. J. Little & Ives, 1920.

History of Company D, 308th U.S. Infantry. New York: 1919.

History of the Fortieth (Sunshine) Division. Los Angeles: C. S. Hutson & Co., 1920.

History of the 305th Field Artillery. Garden City, N.Y.: Country Life Press, 1919.

History of the 306th Field Artillery. New York: Knickerbocker Press, 1920.

History of the 306th Infantry. New York: 306th Infantry Association, 1935.

History of 308th Ambulance Company 302d Sanitary Train 77th Division. New York: 1919.

Holbrook, Franklin F. *St. Paul and Ramsey County in the War of 1917–1918.* St. Paul: Ramsey County War Records Commission, 1929.

Honor Rolls Containing a Pictorial Record of the Gallant and Courageous Men from Cascade County, Montana, U. S. A., Who Served in the Great War 1917–1918–1919. Great Falls, Mont.: War Book Publishing, 1919.

Howard, James M. *The Autobiography of a Regiment; A History of the 304th Field Artillery in the World War.* New York: 1920.

Hunt, Frazier. *Blown In by the Draft.* Garden City, N.Y.: Doubleday, Page & Co., 1918.

Hussey, Alexander T., and Raymond M. Flynn. *The History of Company E, 308th Infantry (1917–1919).* New York: G. P. Putnam's Sons, 1919.

In the Service; The Great World War Honor Roll, Southwest Washington. Centralia, Wash.: F. H. Cole Printing.

In the World War, Fillmore County, Minnesota. St. Paul: Ola M. Levang, 1919.

In the World War, 1917–1918–1919. Ipswich, S.D.: Ipswich Tribune, 1919.

Jantzen, Steven. *Hooray for Peace, Hurrah for War.* New York: Alfred A. Knopf, 1972.

Johnson, Thomas M. *Without Censor.* Indianapolis: Bobbs-Merrill Co., 1928.

———, and Fletcher Pratt. *The Lost Battalion.* Indianapolis: Bobbs-Merrill Co., 1938. Reprint, Lincoln: University of Nebraska Press, 2000.

McCollum, Lee. *History and Rhymes of the Lost Battalion.* Columbus, Ohio: 1928.

———. *Our Sons at War.* Chicago: Bucklee Publishing Co., 1940.

McKeogh, Arthur. *Over the 77th's War Ground.* New York: 1929.

———. *The Victorious 77th Division (New York's Own) in the Argonne Fight.* New York: John H. Eggers Co., 1919.

Macgill, Patrick. *Soldier Songs.* London: Herbert Jenkins Ltd., 1917.

Mason, William H. *Snohomish County in the War.* Everett, Wash.: 1920.

Matthews, William, and Dixon Wecter. *Our Soldiers Speak 1775–1918.* Boston: Little, Brown and Co., 1943.

Mead, Gary. *The Doughboys: America and the First World War.* New York: Overlook Press, 2000.

Merrill, James M., ed. *Uncommon Valor.* Chicago: Rand McNally, 1964.

Miles, L. Wardlaw. *History of the 308th Infantry 1917–1919.* New York: G. P. Putnam's Sons, 1927.

Milham, Charles G. *"Atta Boy!": The Story of New York's 77th Division, U.S.A.* Brooklyn: Brooklyn Daily Eagle, 1919.

Minder, Charles F. *This Man's War.* New York: Pevensey Press, 1931.

Morse, Daniel P. *The History of the 50th Aero Squadron.* New York: Blanchard Press, 1920.

National Society of the Colonial Dames of America. *American War Songs.* Philadelphia: Longwood Press, 1925.

Nell, John W. *The Lost Battalion, A Private's Story.* San Antonio: Historical Publishing Network, 2001.

Nettleton, George H. *Yale in the World War.* 2 vols. New Haven: Yale University Press, 1925.

Niles, John J., Douglas S. Moore, and A. A. Wallgren. *The Songs My Mother Never Taught Me.* New York: Gold Label Books.

The Official Roster of Ohio Soldiers, Sailors and Marines in the World War 1917–1918. 23 vols. Columbus: F. J. Heer Printing Co., 1926.

Ottosen, P. H. *Trench Artillery A. E. F..* Boston: Lothrop, Lee and Shepard, 1931.

Palmer, Frederick. *Our Greatest Battle (The Meuse-Argonne).* New York: Dodd, Mead and Co., 1919.

———. *With My Own Eyes.* Indianapolis: Bobbs-Merrill Co., 1933.

Peat, Frank E., and Lee O. Smith. *Legion Airs: Songs of the Armed Forces.* New York: Leo Feist, 1949.

Pershing, John J. *My Experiences in the World War.* 2 vols. New York: Frederick A. Stokes Co., 1931.

Peterson, Carl J. *Lost Battalion Survivors from Minnesota and the Northwest.* Hayfield, Minn.: 1939.

Putnam, Eben, ed. *The Gold Star Record of Massachusetts.* 2 vols. Boston: Commonwealth of Massachusetts, 1929.

Rainsford, W. Kerr. *From Upton to the Meuse.* New York: D. Appleton, 1920.

Ranlett, Louis F. *Let's Go! The Story of A. S. No. 2448602.* Boston: Houghton, Mifflin and Co., 1927.

Rookie Rhymes. New York: Harper and Brothers, 1917.

Roster of the Men and Women Who Served in the Army or Naval Service (Including the Marine Corps) of the United States or Its Allies From the State of North Dakota in the World War, 1917–1918. 4 vols. Bismarck, N.D.: Bismarck Tribune Co., 1931.

St. Lawrence University in the World War 1917–1918. Canton, N.Y.: St. Lawrence University, 1931.

Schweinickle, O.U. *The Book of a Thousand Laughs.* Np.

Shookhoff, Samuel. *The Story of the Machine Gun Company of the 307th Infantry, 77th Division, A.E F.* New York: S. Shookhoff, 1920.

Shore, Chester K. *Montana in the Wars*. Miles City, Mont.: Star Printing Co.,
  1975.
Smith, Henry W. *A Story of the 305th Machine Gun Battalion, 77th
  Division, AEF*. New York: Modern Composing Room, 1941.
Stallings, Laurence. *The Doughboys*. New York: Harper & Row, 1963.
Sterba, Christopher M. *Good Americans*. New York: Oxford University
  Press, 2003.
Stevenson, Burton E. *Poems of American History*. Freeport, N.Y.: Books for
  Libraries Press, 1970.
Sullivan, James, ed. *History of New York State*. 6 vols. New York: Lewis
  Historical Publishing, 1927.
Sullivan, Maurice J., ed. *Nevada's Golden Stars*. Reno: A. Carlisle and Co.,
  1924.
Survivors of the Lost Battalion as of April 12, 1949. 1949.
Sweeney, Daniel J. *History of Buffalo and Erie County 1914–1919*. Buffalo:
  Committee of One Hundred, 1919.
Thomas, Shipley. *The History of the A. E. F.*. New York: George H. Doran
  Co., 1920.
Through the War with Company D 307th Infantry 77th Division. New York:
  1919.
Tiebout, Frank B. *A History of the 305th Infantry*. New York: 305th Infantry
  Auxiliary, 1919).
Van Every, Dale. *The A. E. F. in Battle*. New York: D. Appleton and Co., 1928.
Vogel, Frederick G. *World War I Songs: A History and Dictionary of Popular
  American Patriotic Tunes, with over 300 Complete Lyrics*. Jefferson,
  N.C.: McFarland Co., 1995.
War Records of the Knickerbocker Club 1914–1918. New York:
  Knickerbocker Club, 1922.
Williams College in the World War. New York: The President and Trustees
  of Williams College, 1926.
Wister, Owen. *Neighbors Henceforth*. New York: Macmillan Co., 1922.
Woollcott, Alexander. *The Command Is Forward*. New York: Century Co.,
  1919.
York, Dorothea. *Mud and Stars: An Anthology of World War Songs and Poetry*.
  New York: Henry Holt and Co., 1931.

MANUSCRIPTS

Baldwin, Thomas. Letters and Reunion Newsletters.
Edwards, Marvin. Documents and Newspaper Clippings Relating to Irving
  Sirota.
Gordon, Robert W. "Inferno" Collection. Archive of Folk Culture, American
  Folklife Center, Library of Congress.
John, Ralph. "I Was One of the Lost Battalion." Typescript in the Thomas
  Baldwin Collection.
McElroy, Joseph. Letters. Author's collection.

Missouri, Office of the Adjutant General. World War I Service Cards.

Peterson, Emil. "Lost Battalion." Typescript in Ovin A. Peterson Collection.

Stacey, Cromwell. "My Experience in the Argonne Forest in Command of the 308th Infantry of the 77th Division." ebay 914309132.

Stromee, Leo A. Diary. ebay 1145110502.

U.S., National Archives, Record Group 92. Records of the Office of the Quartermaster General, Graves Registration Service Cards and Card Register of Confirmed Burials of American Soldiers.

———. Record Group 117. American Battle Monuments File, Nelson M. Holderman, "Operations of the Force Known as 'The Lost Battalion,' From October 2nd to October 7th, 1918, Northeast of Binarville, In the Forest of Argonne, France." Lost Battalion Correspondence.

———. Record Group 120. Records of the American Expeditionary Forces. (World War I), 77th Division, 302nd Sanitary Train, 307th Infantry, 308th Infantry, 306th Machine Gun Battalion, and 53rd Pioneer Infantry.

———. Record Group 120. Records of the American Expeditionary Forces. (World War I), Records of the Judge Advocate General, Court Martial of Lieutenant Maurice S. Revnes.

———. Records of the World War I Branch. (Thomas Files), 1918–1946, Historical Section, Army War College. "The Operation of the So-Called 'Lost Battalion,' Oct. 2nd to Oct. 8th, 1918."

———. World War I Selective Service Draft Registration Cards, 1917–1918, Microfilm Publication M1509.

U.S., United States Army Military History Institute. Lost Battalion of 308th Infantry Regiment, Documents File, October, 1918, "Personal File of Major H. A. Drum."

———. Arthur E. Dewey, "Selection of the Unknown Soldier."

Whittlesey, Charles W. Manuscript Collection, Williams College Archives.

UNITED STATES PUBLICATIONS

American Battle Monuments Commission. *77th Division, Summary of Operations in the World War.* (Washington: Government Printing Office, 1944).

General Headquarters, AEF. *Combat Instructions* [September 5, 1918]. (1918).

———. *Notes of Recent Operations No. 3.* (1918).

Historical Section, General Staff. *A Survey of German Tactics 1918.* (1918).

List of Members of the A. E. F. Reported as Missing in Action to the War Department, (1919).

List of Official U. S. Photographs Illustrative of the Activities of the Seventy-seventh Division. (Washington: Government Printing Office, 1919).

List of U.S. Official Photographs Illustrative of Activities in the Argonne Offensive. (Washington: Government Printing Office, 1919).

Moore, William E., and James C. Russell. *U. S. Official Pictures of the World War Showing America's Participation.* 4 vols. (Washington: Government Printing Office, 1921).

Pilgrimage For the Mothers and Widows of Soldiers, Sailors, and Marines of the American Forces Now Interred in the Cemeteries of France. (Washington: Government Printing Office, 1930).

Songs of the Soldiers and Sailors U. S. (Washington: Government Printing Office, 1917).

ARTICLES

"A Yoder and the 'Lost Battalion.'" *Yoder Newsletter* no. 41 (April 2003): 1, 4–6.

Bellows, Henry A. "A Congressional Medal of the Argonne," *Bellman* 26 (May 3, 1919): 487–89.

Boyer, D. Royce. "The World War I Army Bandsman: A Diary Account by Philip James." *American Music*, 14, no. 2 (Summer 1996): 185–204.

Byers, Frances F. "Camp Upton—The Melting Pot," *World Outlook* 4 (April 1918): 15.

Dwyer, Norval. "Camp Upton Story." *Long Island Forum* 33 (February 1970): 31–34; (March 1970): 54–57.

Eager, Sherman W. "The Lost Battalion." *Scabbard and Blade Journal* 20, no. 4 (April 1936): 2–4.

Elwood, P. H., Jr. "The Argonne Cemetery of the A. E. F. at Romagne-Sous-Moutfaucon, France." *Architectural Record* 47 (June 1920): 507–11.

Fortescue, Granville. "Training the New Armies of Liberty." *National Geographic Magazine* 32, no. 5 (November 1917): 421–38.

Fuller, Hurley E. "'Lost Battalion' of the 77th Division." *Infantry Journal* 28, no. 6 (June 1926): 597–608.

Gordon, Dennis. "Sidney Smith of the Lost Battalion." *Montana Prospector Magazine* (Spring 1981): 28–35.

Johnson, Thomas M. "The Biggest Battle Americans Ever Fought." *American Magazine* (November 1927): 46–50, 195–206.

———. "The Lost Battalion." *American Magazine* (November 1929): 54–57, 80–86.

Johnson, Willis F. "Students at Camp Upton." *North American Review* 211 (January 1920): 44–50.

Lane, Rose W. "A Bit of Gray in a Blue Sky." *Ladies' Home Journal* 36, no. 8 (August 1919): 33, 98.

Levenger, Lee J. "The Challenge of the Returning Soldier." *American Hebrew and Jewish Messenger* 105, no. 6 (June 20, 1919): 136, 149

Lewis, Edwin N. "In the Argonne's Mist and Mystery." *American Legion Weekly* 1, no. 13 (September 26, 1919): 7–9, 29–34.

Liner, Irving. "Five Days Yom Kippur in the Argonne." *American Hebrew and Jewish Messenger* 104, no. 9 (January 10, 1919): 251.

McCarthy, Joe. "The Lost Battalion." *American Heritage* 28, no. 6 (October 1977): 86–95.

McKeogh, Arthur. "Runner Quinn." *Saturday Evening Post* (August 16, 1919): 154.

———. "The Lost Battalion." *Collier's* 62, no. 10 (November 16, 1918): 5–6, 18–26.

———. "Whittlesey's Other Answer." *Everybody's Magazine* 40 (April 1919): 64, 111–113.

Maddox, Robert. "Ordeal of the 'Lost Battalion." *American History Illustrated* 10, no. 8 (December 1975): 22–33.

Maguie, Meyer. "Private Krotoshinsky's Own Story." *American Hebrew and Jewish Messenger* 105, no. 15 (August 22, 1919): 327, 338.

Manson, Robert. "Through Hell With the 'Lost Battalion.'" *American Hebrew and Jewish Messenger* 104, no. 17 (March 7, 1919): 400, 411.

"'The Melting–Pot Division' That Pierced the Argonne Forest." *Literary Digest* 61 (May 24, 1919): 85–90.

"Miles-Breckenridge Memorial Issue." *The 308th Infantry Rumor* (December 1948).

"'New York's Own' Parades." *American Hebrew and Jewish Messenger* 104, no. 26 (May 9, 1919): 690.

Richardson, James M. "The Rescue of the Lost Battalion." *Popular Aviation–Aeronautics* (May 1931): 8–10, 62–63.

Rindge, Fred H. "Uncle Sam's Adopted Nephews." *Harper's Magazine* 137 (July 1918): 281–89.

Ruffin, Steven A. "They Found the 'Lost Battalion.'" *Air Power History* 36 (Fall 1989): 14–19.

Showalter, William J. "America's New Soldier Cities." *National Geographic Magazine* 32, no. 5 (November 1917): 439–76.

Swindler, Henry O. "The So-Called Lost Battalion." *American Mercury* 15 no. 59 (November 1928): 257–65.

Tjentland, Lowell. "Remembering Martin O. Lokken: The Lost Battalion, WWI." *Cottonwood County Historical Society Newsletter* (Winter 2002).

Tryon, Warren S. "The Draft in World War I." *Current History* 54, no. 322 (June 1968): 339–44, 367–68.

Whittlesey, Charles W. "Military Preparedness," *New Republic* 22 (March 17, 1920): 94.

NEWSPAPERS

Brooklyn Daily Eagle
Charleston (W. Va.) Daily Mail
Jamestown (N. Y.) Evening Journal
Lima (Ohio) News
Nevada State Journal
New York American
New York Call
New York Sun
New York Times
The New York World
Post-Bulletin (Rochester, Minn.)

Reno Evening Gazette
Sandusky (Ohio) Register
Sentinel-Courier (Cooperstown, N. D.)
Stars and Stripes
Stevens Point (Wis.) Daily Journal
Traverse City (Mich.) Record Eagle
Tri-City (Pasco, Kennewick, and Richland, Washington) Herald
Waukesha (Wis.) Freeman

WEBSITES

http://sites.hsprofessional.com/johnrcotter/lost_battalion.html
http://www.abmc.gov
http://www.interment.net
http://www.lihistory.com
http://www.longwood.k12.ny.us/history/index.html
http://www.worldwar1.com/tgws/

INDEX